Oxford Studies in the
History of Art and Architecture

GENERAL EDITORS
Francis Haskell   Charles Mitchell
John Shearman

Virginia Spate

Orphism

The evolution of non-figurative
painting in Paris 1910–1914

Clarendon Press · Oxford · 1979

Oxford University Press, Walton Street, Oxford OX2 6DP

OXFORD   LONDON   GLASGOW   NEW YORK
TORONTO   MELBOURNE   WELLINGTON   CAPE TOWN
NAIROBI   DAR ES SALAAM   KUALA LUMPUR
SINGAPORE   JAKARTA   HONG KONG   TOKYO   DELHI
BOMBAY   CALCUTTA   MADRAS   KARACHI

Published in the United States by
Oxford University Press, New York.

British Library Cataloguing in Publication Data

Spate, Virginia
Orphism.—(Oxford studies in the history of art and architecture).
1. Orphism (Art)
I. Title   II. Series
759.06   ND548   77-30477
ISBN 0-19-817197-8

Printed and bound in Great Britain by
William Clowes (Beccles) Limited, Beccles and London

To my parents
who showed me the joy and meaning of sight

Acknowledgements

This book began life as a doctoral thesis for Bryn Mawr College. I am profoundly grateful for the support given me by the College, in particular, for its award of the Fanny Workman Bullock Fellowship which enabled me to pursue my research in Paris. I would also like to thank the Samuel H. Kress Foundation for giving me a grant which helped me to continue my research in Paris in 1967. I am pleased to be able to acknowledge a generous grant towards the cost of reproductions from the British Academy.

My supervisors at Bryn Mawr College were Mr. James Fowle—who taught me a great deal about looking at painting—and Professor Charles Mitchell. It was Professor Mitchell's idea that I should study Orphism and I can say, without reservation, that my work would not have been completed without his constant encouragement and enthusiasm.

I must express my gratitude to Sonia Delaunay for her generous help in providing information and photographic material and for her ability to make the past live in the present.

I am deeply grateful to those collectors who showed me their works and allowed me to reproduce them: to Mr. and Mrs. A. M. Burden; Monsieur Louis Carré; Madame Simone Collinet; Mr. and Mrs. Ralph Colin; Mr. Eric Estorick; Herr Wilhelm Hack; Mr. Joseph H. Hazen; Dr. Riccardo Jucker; Mrs. Barnett Malbin: Mme M. Mladek; Mr. J. V. Mladek; Dr. Gianni Mattioli; Mme Olga Picabia; Mr. and Mrs. Neil Reisner; Mr. Nelson A. Rockefeller; Mr. and Mrs. Herbert and Nanette Rothschild; Signor Arturo Schwarz; Mr. and Mrs. Burton G. Tremaine; Mr. Richard Weil. I would like to thank Mme Andrée Martinel-Kupka for her permission to quote from an early manuscript by Kupka which was kindly shown to me by Margit Rowell of The Solomon R. Guggenheim Museum.

I owe much to the staffs of museums and libraries, above all, the Museum of Modern Art, New York, the Philadelphia Museum of Art, the Solomon R. Guggenheim Museum, the Musée National d'Art Moderne, the Bibliothèque Nationale, the Bibliothèque Jacques Doucet, the New York Public Library, the British Library.

Acknowledgements

In particular, I would like to acknowledge the help of the staff of the Národní Galerie, Prague, for its courteous and generous assistance in showing me the works of Frank Kupka and in providing me with photographic material.

I have pleasure in being able to thank my colleagues for their generosity and patience; I can name only a few: Professor William Camfield, whose thesis on Picabia was of great importance to me; Dr. Christopher Green, who offered invaluable suggestions on how to discipline my thesis into a book and with whom I had endless— and enjoyable—discussions about specific aspects of Léger's work; to Dr. John Golding, whose book on Cubism was an inspiration and who read my typescript in its final stages and gave me the encouragement I needed to get it done; to Mrs. Angelica Rudenstine, Resident Curator of the Solomon R. Guggenheim Museum, whose enthusiasm is always infectious and who inspired me to emulate her dedicated attention to detail. But as I name these few, a crowd of other faces comes into my mind; piles of letters from people I never met bear witness to the help which I received from so many that I cannot name them, but who may be sure that I thank them in my heart.

Finally, I owe a less tangible but no less deeply felt debt to my friends who, over the years, encouraged my work, discussed ideas, and shared the paintings with me.

Cambridge, June 1975   VIRGINIA SPATE

Contents

List of illustrations

All paintings are executed in oil on canvas unless otherwise stated. Graphic works are executed on paper unless otherwise stated. All measurements are in centimetres, and height precedes width.

Apart from those supplied by the collectors and museums listed, photographs and/or permission to reproduce them were obtained from the following:

Madame Sonia Delaunay: 18, 20–2, 30–1, 116, 120–1, 126, 137, 141, 150–1, 153–5, 158–9, 160–2.

Réunion des Musées nationaux, Paris: 6, 10, 13–14, 19, 27, 29, 49–50, 59–60, 80, 90–6, 100, 103–5, 107, 112–14, 130, 133–4, 136, 149, 155, 163, 165, 171, 174, 176, 190, 193, 213, 247.

Archives photographiques, Paris: 13, 175, 182, 193.

The Witt Library, London: 123, 178, 181, 209, 223.

Galerie Louise Leiris, Paris: 146, 177, 195.

Additional photographic credits:

N. Mandel, Paris: 216; Robert David, Paris, 18; Jacqueline Hyde, Paris: 220; Étienne Hubert, Paris: 116, 152.

1 Francis Picabia, *La Source*, 1912 (249 × 250).

Introduction

*Historically, there really was a change of
understanding, thus of technique, of modes of seeing...*

Delaunay, 1939–40[1]

Orphism is one of the most elusive movements in the history of twentieth-century painting. The name was given by a poet to a rather mixed group of painters, none of whom was particularly happy about it: the poet was Apollinaire; the occasion, a lecture at the Salon de la Section d'Or in Paris in October 1912; and the artists were Robert Delaunay, Fernand Léger, Francis Picabia, and Marcel Duchamp, all of whom, Apollinaire claimed, were moving towards 'pure painting'. Apollinaire may also have included František (or Frank) Kupka, a Czech living in Paris who had already painted works of an unprecedented purity, but, if he did name Kupka in his lecture, he did not mention him when he published his definition of 'Orphic Cubism' in his book, *Les Peintres cubistes* in 1913.[2] Apollinaire first defined Orphism as a branch of Cubism, but soon recognized that it was something different and expanded its scope by equating it with 'Simultanism' and by including members of the Blaue Reiter and Futurist groups.[3] However, Kupka is said to have immediately rejected Apollinaire's classification; Duchamp said that he joined the 'movement' because it amused him to do so, but within a month, he had decided to give up painting; Léger seems to have been uninterested and probably could not imagine that a word like Orphism, with its mystical connotations, could have anything to do with his robust and straightforward art. Thus only Picabia and Delaunay accepted the designation, and Delaunay tried to limit it to his own kind of painting. Later he claimed that Apollinaire's invention of the term was simply an art-political manœuvre designed to present the avant-garde as a united front, and there is some truth in this assertion.[4] In the second half of 1912, these artists were painting works which were very different in both form and content, and, although they often met, they shared no artistic programme. All these factors led Apollinaire to remark somewhat defensively that many painters had been surprised to have been included in this tendency, and, by 1916, to admit that his classification 'laid no claim to be definitive as to the artists themselves'.[5]

For these reasons, Orphism has never been taken seriously. Nevertheless Apollinaire had perceived the first stirrings of something that was very real—an art which would dispense with recognizable subject-matter and would rely on form and colour alone to communicate meaning. Moreover, not only did he foretell the coming of 'pure painting', but he singled out those who by mid-1912 had arrived at near-abstraction through a process of intensive formal experimentation, and did not bother with those who were creating decorative abstraction.[6] It is thus reasonable to use his term on the principle of not throwing out a lively baby with a considerable amount of Apollinairean bathwater.

It may seem hazardous to base a study on such unstable definitions and classifications, and yet to do so enables one to get to the heart of the specific historical situation, by locating oneself in a particular context in Paris in the few months that were to elapse between the first flowering of the new art and its collapse at the outbreak of war. One is thus better able to understand the nature of the experiences which the artists were trying to embody.

The first historians of abstract art assumed a more or less unbroken and inevitable progress towards it; recent historians have been more critical and have devoted much of their time to proving that the early phases of abstract art were not as abstract as they seemed. Both approaches rest on the assumption that there existed an ideal of a pure abstract art, but the development of the Orphists shows that the early evolution of abstract art was an empirical, not a theoretical, process and that it was realized *through the process of painting*. They glimpsed the functions of a non-representational art but they did not pursue any heroic upward path, and, although they realized some authoritative examples of the new art, they did not always pursue their discoveries with any consistency. However, their very inconsistencies reveal the difficulties of the struggle towards an unknown art, and add to our understanding of the work of artists in which idea was more fully identified with form.

Pure painting did not necessarily mean non-representational painting: it signified painting which had its own internally coherent structure independent of naturalistic structural devices. It allowed for great variety of expression, and this is precisely what is found in Orphist painting which ranges from the powerful physicality of Léger's works to the curious immateriality of Picabia's. The variety of expression corresponds to a variety of approaches: Delaunay and Léger were concerned with the expression and signification of sensation; Kupka wished to express mystic consciousness, while

Duchamp and Picabia sought to embody psychological experience. However, despite differences of expression, by the autumn of 1912 their art had reached equivalent levels of purity: they retained recognizable subjects but these were being absorbed by increasingly abstract structures. Kupka had reached this stage about a year earlier and he also preceded the other painters in the development of fully non-naturalistic structures which he realized in late 1911 or early 1912 (see *Les Disques de Newton*, Pl. 81), while Picabia, Delaunay, and Léger did so only in early 1913. In these new structures, the painters stopped using forms which are darker or more concentrated at the base of the painting and which are used in naturalistic painting to create the ground-plane on which perspective space is constructed. The new structures were composed of evenly weighted forms moving freely in non-gravitational space. They are able to impose their own scale, because they are no longer dependent on the human measure (Léger retained the figure in some works, but undermined its physical reality), and can thus draw the spectator into their unique concentrated physical existence, for they are, in Apollinaire's phrase, 'new worlds with their own physical laws'.

The basic premise of this study is that these structural changes embody changes in meaning or consciousness. I have therefore made a close examination of individual paintings and the way in which one sees them.

The Orphists conceived of their art as an expression of 'modern consciousness' and were influenced by contemporary science, technology, literature, and philosophy as well as by the actual experience of living in the contemporary world. Their awareness of this world was of such complexity that it could not be embodied in structures which show only finite things in one place at one moment in time. They wanted to express what was called 'Simultanism', the mind's grasp of the simultaneous existence of an infinitude of interrelated states of being. Each painter went through a phase in which he tried to express this form of consciousness by means of specific images. However, the actual process of trying to grasp such experience through painting seems to have made them aware of the inwardness of the experience and to have led them to believe that it was form, not specific image, which could embody the experience they sought, since specific images tied them to the world of verbal concepts and they wished to transcend verbal consciousness. Their belief in these new modes of consciousness was often confirmed by what they knew of mystic and the occult (as the designation Orphism suggests), but their interest in such things does not mean that they sought to escape the modern world; rather that they welcomed any mode of penetrating its reality. Conscious modernism does not, therefore, explain the new art. To understand it, one has to understand something of the artists' creative processes and to understand the significance of the fact that their abstract structures were prefigured in their earliest works and pre-dated their specific modernist images. The origins of these images lay deep in the artists' subconscious, but once they became conscious of them, they clarified and intensified them and defended them as communicating essential truths.

Similar movements towards non-representational art were taking place in many other parts of Europe. Although they cannot be tied to any specific social situation or psychological type, they must be seen in the context of a wider social situation in which the artist was becoming increasingly isolated, due to the decline in the functions of public art and to his own sense that naturalistic art—that preferred by the public—was inadequate to deal with the vastness and complexity of the modern world. The artist then tended to turn inwards and to become concerned with the nature of his own consciousness. This had, of course, been true of late nineteenth-century artists, in particular of the Symbolists, but the Orphists differed from the latter in their optimism, in their openness to the modern world, and in their belief that their concern with inner consciousness, with non-verbal and non-conceptual experience, could have a relevance that went beyond their immediate circle of admirers.

The Orphists' range of expression and ideas was equalled by the range of their social origins. Kupka had the most unusual background.[7] He came from a modest Czech provincial family, and studied in Prague and Vienna where he was deeply influenced by the *fin de siècle* retreat from contemporary life. He came to Paris in 1895 and lived for over ten years in the peculiar make-believe world of Montmartre. Like many late nineteenth- and early twentieth-century artists, he was both an anarchist and a mystic, and there is probably some connection between the inwardness of his art and his desire for a society based on internal truth rather than external law. Both Picabia and Delaunay were from the *haute bourgeoisie*, although each passed an abnormally lonely childhood which distanced him from this background.[8] Picabia's early work was essentially painted for this kind of society, but after some years he rejected it. He said that a 'personal anguish' always drove him to explore the unknown,[9] and the content of his art was profoundly subjective. This is true also of Duchamp who came from a cultured provincial bourgeois family, yet who was as anarchistic as Kupka, while Léger was born into a family of Norman peasant farmers with whom he kept in close touch. He and Delaunay were less inward-looking than the other three. Probably under the influence of his wife, Sonia, Delaunay came to insist that the principles of his art were applicable to all the arts of design, and thus gave it a public function; one senses too that Léger was not satisfied with a private art, since he renounced it as soon as he had contact with another life during the war. However, both saw the function of their art as providing an alternative to habitual modes of seeing in order to communicate the essential in modern life. In short, all the Orphic painters believed that it was through exploring their own consciousness in the act of painting that they could approach the modes of consciousness that were meaningful for others.

One of the most significant aspects of Orphism was its expression of non-conceptual experience. Early abstract art ranged from Symbolist abstraction, based on the assumption that the pictorial forms 'stood for' a more or less definable idea or emotion, to a kind of abstraction inspired by a belief that the painting was not a sign for something other than itself and that it somehow contained all emotion and meaning in itself. A completely non-symbolic form cannot exist (for a created form always embodies or evokes some emotion or some state of being which is separate from it); however, the idea that painting could dispense with symbols for *known* emotions, states of mind, or ideas caused an extraordinary liberation of form and created consciousness of states of being which escape words. Symbolist and non-conceptual abstraction generally rested on different kinds of structure. The former tended towards abstract illusionism—that is, towards structures which are based on naturalistic relationships, but which do not represent the appearance of nature (see Pl. II). The other depended on self-contained structures which might evoke aspects of the external world, but which were not based on its structure (see Pl. VII). Abstract illusionism tends to turn the attention from the painting itself to speculation about its source, but when the artist was liberated from naturalistic relationships, he was able to develop forms in such a way that they focus attention on themselves, demanding from the spectator a still, silent concentration (see Pl. III).

The Orphists found the consciousness they sought in the process of painting—either in the process of improvising directly on the canvas, or in the process of developing a theme from one canvas to another. In this process, they surrendered intellectual, conceptual consciousness in a self-forgetting yet intensely aware absorption in the way in which inchoate material forms a structure. However, they also exhibited their paintings, and thus implied that their experience was relevant for others. The observer can, in fact, absorb himself in the development of the structure, in the pure, concentrated world of the painting, and can thus attain consciousness analogous to the artist's.

The Orphists thus grasped the *raison d'être* of non-representational art: that of giving the artist, and, in a different way, the observer, an awareness of the functioning of his own consciousness. This art rests on the assumption that the act of seeing, in so far as it creates consciousness, is in itself significant (such consciousness does, of course, function on many different levels: in the case of Orphism, it ranges from consciousness of pure sensation to consciousness of man's psychic depths). It is anti-intellectual and anti-humanist in the sense that it does not concern itself with the examination of human thought or conduct. Apollinaire recognized this, and wrote in 1913 of a new art 'which is not simply the prideful expression of the human species'.[10] Yet, in a deeper sense, Orphism was concerned with the human meaning of the act of creation and it can tell us much about the nature and function of art in our society.

Section I **The background to Orphist painting**

2 Frank Kupka, *La Création*, 1911–20 (115 × 125).

Chapter 1 The history of Orphism, 1910–14

Je suis ivre d'avoir bu tout l'univers
Sur le quai d'où je voyais l'onde couler et dormir les bélandres
Ecoutez-moi je suis le gosier de Paris
Et je boirai encore s'il me plaît l'univers

Apollinaire[1]

The young painters and writers of Paris were conscious of their city as the very embodiment of Simultanism. They experienced it as the context—or rather the condition—of their perpetual transformation of the past; their ceaseless creation of new forms, new ideas, new states of consciousness. The city still retained traces of its medieval form, fragmented but not effaced by the great replanning of the nineteenth century, and was now being charged by new energies— by the increasing speed and voracity of transport, by electricity, by the wireless. The trains which linked Paris with the rest of Europe were breaking down its old self-sufficiency, just as it was released from its earthly dimension by the invention of the aeroplane and by the erection of the Eiffel Tower whose wireless station was felt to communicate not only with the rest of the world but with the entire universe.[2]

At the same time Paris was small enough to allow the individual artist or writer to participate creatively in the interchange of ideas on a personal level. This communication was enriched by contacts with his European colleagues who visited, exhibited, and published in Paris and who demanded visits, exhibitions, and publications in return. The Parisian context seems to have favoured the growth of a multitude of small groups of artists and writers which formed, absorbed, divided, and re-formed. They were never exclusive and were linked by innumerable personal ties and, although they were often locked in bitter controversy, they tended to share fundamental ideas about the 'new reality'.[3] They lived on the fringes of European society, yet believed that they could transform the consciousness of that society.

Orphism must be seen in this context. It was not a firm,

ideologically consistent movement, but a temporary coincidence of tendencies which were different in character but which were moving towards the non-figurative. The individual Orphists were as close to other groups as they were to one another, and they differed from the others only in the intensity of their exploration of 'pure painting'.

A few examples can give a sense of the constant opportunities for exchange of ideas between individuals and groups: the poets and critics, Apollinaire, Max Jacob, André Salmon, René Arcos, and Jules Romains could meet Picasso, Braque, Delaunay, and Léger at the *soirées* which Rousseau held before his death in 1910;[4] Braque and Picasso used to walk from Montmartre to the meetings of poets and painters at the Closerie des Lilas café in Montparnasse; Apollinaire would lead his friends all over Paris in a never-ending enchantment of words; the Cubists who (unlike Braque and Picasso) exhibited at the Salons held regular meetings on the Left Bank, at Courbevoie, or Puteaux; the younger poets read their works at the Salons. Each of the most important journals associated with the new movements in art—the *Soirées de Paris*, *Montjoie!*, and *Poème et drame*—organized regular functions. The multitude of 'little' magazines were particularly useful in effecting the cross-fertilization of ideas. They were frequently the mouthpiece of one man and his immediate friends, and have a peculiarly intimate character so that they can be read today as records of conversations long past in which one can observe ideas in the making and see the way in which philosophy and technology entered the world of artists and writers. The *Soirées de Paris* (February 1912 to August 1914) was largely edited by Apollinaire and reflected his many-sided character in articles which were trivial or profound, ephemeral or enduring. It sought to register what he called 'la vie ambiante' with all its complexities and contradictions. Its contributors were generally Apollinaire's earliest friends—Salmon, Jacob, Billy—the 'fantaisistes'. Its receptions were attended by Braque, Picasso, Duchamp, Léger, the Delaunays, and the Picabias. *Montjoie!* (February 1913 to June 1914) was edited by Riciotto Canudo and came to be regarded as the organ of Orphism in its fashionable and decorative aspects. Delaunay described it as the 'rendezvous of avant-gardisme', and at its meetings the world of fashion met with the fashionable avant-garde for it assimilated all modern tendencies in one monstrous 'ism': 'Cerebrism'.[5] Its gatherings included the poets and critics of the different schools, Apollinaire, Barzun, Mercereau, Allard, Cendrars; the composers, Stravinsky and Satie; the artists, Delaunay, Léger, Chagall, Villon, Duchamp-Villon, Morgan Russell, Gleizes, Larionov, and Goncharova. Henri-Martin Barzun's *Poème et drame* (December 1912 to March 1914) was primarily a mouthpiece for his relentless championing of what he regarded as his own movements:

'Dramatism' and 'Simultanism'. It was also the organ of those artists and writers who had had connections with the communal experiment of the Abbaye de Creteil—Romains, Mercereau, Gleizes, and Barzun himself. In late 1912 they formed a new group, the Artistes de Passy which organized monthly dinner-lectures which were attended by most of the young French poets, and by Gleizes, Metzinger, Villon, Duchamp-Villon, Duchamp, Picabia, Léger, and Delaunay.[6]

Apollinaire is found in the guest-list of every event—the receptions and musical evenings organized by the *Soirées de Paris*; the dinner-lectures of the Artistes de Passy; the exhibitions, poetry-readings, music, and dance-recitals in the *Montjoie!* attic.

Then there were the links across Europe: Severini lived in Paris and was the liaison with the Italian Futurists; Marinetti and his painter friends burst in with manifestos, exhibitions, lectures, and debates; Kandinsky exhibited in the Indépendants, corresponded with Delaunay, and sent him his books and his friends—Klee, Marc, and Macke; Mondrian, De Chirico, Chagall, Brancusi, Archipenko, Larionov, Goncharova, and hundreds of other artists were lured to Paris.

These are no more than fragments of the reality inspiring Apollinaire's poem 'Liens' of 1913:

> *Cordes faites de cris*
> *Sons de cloches à travers l'Europe*
> .   .   .
> *Rails qui ligotez les nations*
> *Nous ne sommes que deux ou trois hommes*
> *Libres de tous liens*
> *Donnons-nous la main*[7]

The background to all these experiments of the pre-war years was formed by the continuing presence of late nineteenth-century art and theory. The great retrospective of Cézanne's painting in 1907 (accompanied by important articles by Denis and Bernard, and by the publication of some of his letters[8]) was the single most important event, but the living survivors of the nineteenth century also played an important role. Monet, Rodin, and Renoir were the greatest of these, but the Symbolists and Neo-Impressionists—who exhibited throughout this period—had a more direct influence on the tendency towards non-figurative art. Symbolist theory was perhaps even more important and Maurice Denis, in particular, wrote a series of illuminating articles on the difference between imitative and 'representational' painting which seem to have influenced his younger contemporaries.[9]

The young poets who were associated with the Cubists and Orphists were steeped in Symbolist poetry and met regularly at the

Closerie des Lilas, the café of the Neo-Symbolists. With the exception of Léger, the Orphist painters were profoundly influenced by Symbolist poetry, above all, by that of Mallarmé. Symbolism made the younger generation aware of the subtle inner workings of the mind and of the necessity of mental activity in creation. It had the most obvious influence on the painters who had trained in the 1890s—Kupka, Picabia, and, outside Paris, Kandinsky and Mondrian)—and who were inclined towards the mystic, insisting on the inner subjective meaning of their art. Their paintings tended to be less material than those of Delaunay and Léger who believed more strongly in the significance of perceptual experience. Kupka, Picabia, and Kandinsky were deeply influenced by the Symbolists' analogy between music and a new pure painting which would act 'on the soul' without the intermediary of recognizable subject-matter.[10] The analogy was dependent on the 'theory of correspondences'. This was, in fact, less a theory than a series of speculations on the relation between sensation and inner life, the material and the spiritual, in which a number of writers, philosophers, and artists accounted for the way that sensation can arouse feelings of great intensity and profundity by suggesting that such sensations were intimations of an invisible, spiritual order of being. From this they came to believe that form, line, and colour can themselves evoke subjective states and suggest levels of spiritual being; thus Kupka and Picabia, like the Futurists and the artists of the Blaue Reiter, passed through a phase of using abstract pictorial elements to embody what Kupka called 'soul impressions'.[11] This rather literal symbolism—in which emotions are translated into the language of line and colour—was an important phase in the development towards the non-representational painting which arouses forms of consciousness which cannot be decoded into another language. This development—illustrated by the transition from Kupka's *Nocturne* to his *Plans verticaux* (Pls. 101 and III)—was foretold by Kandinsky in *Ueber das Geistige in der Kunst*: 'Cruder emotions, like fear, joy and grief...will no longer attract the artist...his work will give...emotions subtle beyond words.'[12]

Symbolist theory also exerted a profound influence through its insistence on the artist's need to *transform* his material into the unique world of painting. The influence of this concept can be seen particularly clearly in the representation of light—a quality that was central to Orphism. Light embodied essential aspects of 'la vie moderne'. Painters and poets were imaginatively affected by the hypothesis that the smallest particle of matter, the atom, is animated by electrical impulses, and their imagination was further stirred by the electric lights which were being installed in the streets of Paris and by the electrical transmission of radio waves into space.[13] Scientific discovery thus led artists to realize that 'movement and light destroy the materiality of bodies', and to represent this process in works like Kupka's *Femme cueillant des fleurs*, Delaunay's *Tour Eiffel*, Boccioni's *La Strada entra nella casa* (Pls. 92, 4, and 3).[14] These scientific discoveries gave new resonance to the ancient image of light as a metaphor for the assimilation of the individual in the universal or for man's power to create meaningful order from chaos.

From the time of Impressionism, painters had been preoccupied with the representation of light. In 1906, Denis wrote an article called 'Le Soleil' in which he described the sun as 'the god of modern painting' and, indeed, the fascination by what the Futurists called 'radiant visions of light' was shared by nearly all the painters who were to develop forms of non-figurative art, all of whom passed through an Impressionist or a Neo-Impressionist phase.[15]

Both Léger and Delaunay emphasized the significance of Impressionism for the genesis of modern art.[16] Although Monet was painting and exhibiting increasingly radical works which clearly influenced Delaunay, Neo-Impressionism was more important in

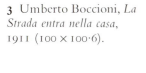

3 Umberto Boccioni, *La Strada entra nella casa*, 1911 (100 × 100·6).

4 Robert Delaunay, *La Tour Eiffel*, 1911 (195·5 × 129).

helping painters evolve non-naturalistic structures. There was a resurgence of interest in Neo-Impressionism in 1911. In 1912, Apollinaire—who had cheered 'the rout of Impressionism' two years earlier—declared that the *rapprochement* between Delaunay and the Neo-Impressionists was the 'great event' of the Salon des Indépendants. The new interest in Neo-Impressionism was partly fired by the Cross retrospective at the Indépendants of 1911 and by the republication of Signac's book *D'Eugène Delacroix au néo-impressionisme*, but more basically, it was caused by the painters' desire to find a more constructive way of representing light than that offered by the Impressionists.[17] The Neo-Impressionists had enlarged the tiny dots which they had used in the 1880s and 1890s into large rectangular strokes of thick paint which do not blend in the eye. They did so because they found that if they were to realize the intense sensations caused by light, they had to emphasize abstract pictorial qualities at the expense of imitative ones. Cézanne had come to the same conclusions. Denis quoted him as saying: 'I was happy when I discovered that the sun, for example, cannot be reproduced, but that it is necessary to represent it by another element ... by colour.'[18] This realization was central to Symbolist theory, and was the main theme of Denis's articles.

The paintings of Cézanne and the Neo-Impressionists, together with the theories of the Symbolists, were essential to the development of Fauvism, which influenced all the Orphists either directly or indirectly through its emphasis on the abstract constructive power of colour. In his 'Notes d'un peintre' of 1908, Matisse too emphasized that one cannot imitate nature, and that in order to express the essential in nature one has to depart from its superficial appearance and emphasize the abstract pictorial construction.[19] He used the reactions between pure non-naturalistic colours to express sensations of space, of volume in space, and of light radiating in space, and he thus created the first radical break with illusionistic pictorial structures. His influence was profound, and was not superseded but merely made less obvious by the general tendency towards a more austere geometrical art which succeeded the Cézanne retrospective in 1907.

Cubism was also decisive in the development of Orphism—the closeness of the relationship between them was suggested by Apollinaire who defined 'Orphic Cubism' as one of the two most important tendencies *within* the Cubist movement, before he went on to recognize that it had developed into something different from Cubism.

Cubism showed the future Orphists how they could break solid objects into small planes which could express the dynamic action of light and the dynamic interaction of space and matter. It gave them a means of associating objects which did not exist together in reality, but which were brought together by the dynamic processes of the mind. The Cubists thus enabled the Orphists to go beyond the objective world to which they themselves remained firmly attached, and in fact (with the exception of Kupka) none of them entered the transitional style which led towards non-figurative art until they had had some contact with Cubist painting.

Delaunay and Léger had met by 1907, but it is not certain when they first saw Cubist or proto-Cubist paintings by Braque and Picasso. Léger said that without Apollinaire and Jacob he would not have known 'what was going on in Montmartre. They told me to go to Kahnweiler's gallery and there I and good old Delaunay saw what the Cubists were doing... Delaunay was surprised at their grey

5 Georges Braque, *Le Portugais*, 1911 (116 × 81·3).

canvases, and cried out "But these chaps paint with spiders' webs".'[20] There is no record as to when Delaunay and Léger met Apollinaire and Jacob, but since they were all regular visitors to Rousseau's receptions they could have met well before 1910. Delaunay knew Rousseau before he went on a year's military service from the autumn of 1907. His remark on 'spiders' webs' would have been appropriate to the kind of paintings which Braque exhibited in Kahnweiler's in November 1908 and which Delaunay saw. He had other possible contacts with Braque and Picasso; by 1905 he was a close friend of Jean Metzinger who lived in Montmartre (as did Delaunay in 1907), only a few streets from Picasso and who was known to Apollinaire—at least as a poet—by 1908; in 1907 Delaunay painted a portrait of Wilhelm Uhde, the friend and patron of Rousseau, and one of the first dealers to exhibit the Cubist works of Braque and Picasso. Uhde owned a large collection of Cubist paintings and was frequently visited by Braque, Derain, and Picasso;[21] Delaunay met his future wife, Sonia Terk, in Uhde's apartment; she married Uhde in 1909, but divorced him to marry Delaunay in 1910. There were thus many opportunities for Léger and Delaunay to see Braque's and Picasso's proto-Cubist and early Cubist paintings of 1909–10: Delaunay's *Autoportrait* (1909) and Léger's *Le Pont* (1909–10) (Pls. 6 and 179) suggest that they had seen such works, for they are not simply Cézannesque geometrizations of the natural world, as are the contemporary works of Gleizes and Le Fauconnier, but are formally dense and complex in ways that suggest knowledge of Cubist painting.

Sometime in 1910, Delaunay and Léger came into contact with Gleizes and Le Fauconnier (Delaunay and Metzinger were introduced to Gleizes by the socialist critic and poet, Alexandre Mercereau). Gleizes and Le Fauconnier were developing a form of Cubism which was naturalistic, in the sense that the structure was based on naturalistic conventions of suggesting the forces of gravity and of indicating the position of objects in space—even if these conventions were distorted. They were influenced by Cézanne and, by late 1910, by Braque and Picasso. Gleizes stated that they 'discovered each other seriously' at the time of the Salon d'Automne and that, having recognized what they had in common, they also felt 'the necessity' of forming a group, of visiting each other, and of exchanging ideas. I shall call this group of Cubists the 'Salon Cubists', since unlike Braque and Picasso they exhibited in the annual Salons and sought a public role for their art.[22] Le Fauconnier began weekly meetings in his studio in the rue Visconti (off the rue des Grands-Augustins, where the Delaunays lived after their marriage) which were attended by the Delaunays, Léger, Gleizes, Metzinger, Rousseau (the meetings must therefore have begun before his death in September), and Jules Romains, the Unanimist poet.[23] Gleizes had been a member of the Abbaye de Creteil (1906–8), an experiment in communal living by a group of writers and artists which included Henri-Martin Barzun and René Arcos (whom Apollinaire described in 1908 as 'a cosmogonic who perceives the movement of the spheres and who floats in ecstasy among the nebulae').[24]

The Salon Cubists exhibited together in the famous Salle 11 at the Salon des Indépendants of 1911. Gleizes, Metzinger, Le Fauconnier, Léger, Delaunay, and several other painters who showed work in this room were promptly named 'Cubists'. Apollinaire was at first sceptical of their right to this title (which, he believed, belonged solely to Picasso), but in June he recognized them as a group and allowed them the name. Although Delaunay and Léger were members of this group, one has the impression that they stood out from it by virtue of both their originality and their temperaments. Severini described how they seemed different from the others in being like boxers or racing-drivers.[25]

Since the meetings in Le Fauconnier's studio on the Left Bank and Gleizes' studio at Courbevoie included the writers of the Abbaye or others influenced by them like Jules Romains and the poet-critics,

6 Robert Delaunay, *Autoportrait*, 1911 (73 × 60).

Roger Allard and Alexandre Mercereau, one would be justified in supposing that the discussions would have centred on the nature of modern life and on the means of expressing it: above all, on the expression of dynamism and simultaneity. Certainly these ideas soon appeared in comments on Cubism published by members of the group.

The Bergsonian emphasis on constant change and the processes of time had entered French art-criticism in 1908 with Apollinaire's article, 'Les trois vertus plastiques'.[26] This, however, was a poetic evocation of the mutability of nature and the necessity of responding to it, rather than a response to the actual qualities of contemporary painting. Such a response came first from a painter, Metzinger, in his perceptive 'Note sur la peinture' published in November 1910, when he noted that in Braque's painting 'the whole image radiates in time; the picture is no longer a dead portion of space'.[27] Metzinger had real insight into the nature of the contemporary painting of Braque and Picasso which does, indeed, demand that one experiences it in time. The two painters were now constructing their paintings with a linear scaffolding, partly derived from the object, partly invented, on which they improvised patches of dark and light paint which suggest shadow and illumination but which never solidify into the shadow and illumination of specific objects (see Pl. 5). They piled up these planes so that they sometimes assume the form of objects, but as soon as such an object seemed to be emerging as a separate entity, they broke it back into the fluctuating relief. The eye is thus made to search for a means of resolving the visual clues into the stable objects, yet, such is the ambiguity of the structure, that solids ceaselessly translate into space; depression into projection; object into an infinity of shifting planes. After the autumn of 1910, all the critics emphasized the dynamism of both Montmartre Cubism and Salon Cubism. For example, Allard claimed that Metzinger's *Nu* (Pl. 7) shown in the Salon d'Automne contained 'the essential elements of a synthetic experience taking place in time'.[28] Metzinger created this experience by fusing the planes of the figure with the planes which surround it, so that one becomes absorbed in the way the figure melts into the fluctuating planes and then reasserts itself because of the specificity of its details. Curiously, this was perhaps Metzinger's most radical painting, and in succeeding works (Pl. 8) he tended to re-emphasize contours and naturalistic details so that one is able to isolate the figure in space and to transfix it in time—as one cannot do with Braque's and Picasso's figure-paintings of 1911 since they did not abstract their forms directly from the model. However, despite their relative lack of success, it is clear that the Salon Cubists intended to develop structures which would be apprehended in time.

It is also probable that the Salon Cubists discussed the representation of simultaneous experience, as this was one of the major preoccupations of their poet friends. The desire to express simultaneity was one of the most important influences on the evolution of art in this period and on the evolution of non-figurative art in particular.[29] Basically, it was an attempt to embody a *change of consciousness* in response to a feeling that sequential modes of thought and expression were inadequate to realize the fullness and complexity of life and, even less, the fullness and complexity of modern urban life. Instead of focusing on a single thing or a simple group of things, instead of following a single thread of feeling, instead of concentrating on a single clear emotion, the Simultanists tried to represent the interrelatedness of all things, mental events, and feelings which might be widely separated in time and space but which were brought together by the mind. They sought to express their sense of the unity of all being and of the way in which individual separateness breaks down and is fused with the whole. The roots of these aspirations lay in Romanticism, but they were given new life by their awareness of the changing conditions of modern life.

The concept of Simultanism was deeply influenced by Bergson whose philosophy was very popular and very accessible: his lectures at the Collège de France were open to every one, there were many articles on him in both avant-garde and traditionalist journals, and his philosophy was studied by the artists at Puteaux.[30] It is clear that his vivid suggestive images and his anti-conceptual bias appealed to

7 (*left*) Jean Metzinger, *Nu*, 1911.
8 (*right*) Jean Metzinger, *Le Goûter*, 1911 (75 × 69.5).

creative artists and writers. His influence was so great that Romain Rolland could write of: '...this almost unanimous agreement, this joyous enthusiasm of young intellectuals [for Bergson's philosophy]. He who would one day wish to understand our epoch, will find part of its deepest soul... reflected in the prestigious mirror of this poetic system of thought.'[31] Bergson tried to define the very nature of consciousness; he turned his attention *inwards* so that he could seek awareness of the 'self that endures'. He believed that all is simultaneously present to this consciousness and that it is perpetually mobile, ceaselessly transforming its past into its present through memory, so that its present is composed of an infinite number of interpenetrating tenuous states of being.[32] These states are indivisible since the mind itself never ceases to move and to transform specific states of being into the flux of the whole. Bergson maintained that analytical reasoning or conceptual knowledge destroy one's sense of this inner consciousness, since they split the 'fluid continuity of the real' into separate states which are thus deprived of their unique inner life.[33] He devoted much of his writing to a search for images that could convey the nature of this consciousness; but it was an impossible task, for his exposition involved his reader in the 'spatialized' time of the written text, and each image he used crystallized the mind's flow at a fixed point. It was perhaps only non-representational art which could awaken the form of consciousness which he tried to express in words.

The poets connected with the Abbaye were probably the first group to be consciously preoccupied with the expression of simultaneity. In works like Romains's *La Vie unanime* and Barzun's *La Terrestre tragédie* (both published by the Abbaye in 1907), they sought to embody the relationship of the individual to the collective and to the universal: the way the single 'I' is absorbed in the rhythms of the city or the vast energies of the universe. They wished to express the essence of modern life—the life of the crowd, of the city; the speed of new forms of transport; the marvels of modern science; the new consciousness of the processes of time. Marinetti was a frequent visitor to the Abbaye, and his Futurism was clearly influenced by these ideas.[34] Such concepts had little immediate influence on painting simply because painters did not have the means to effect the necessary synthesis of such complex materials until they had come into contact with Cubism itself.

Thus when Gleizes, Metzinger, Le Fauconnier, Léger, and Delaunay first tried to express Simultanist experience in 1910–11, they did so by juxtaposing separate objects or separate viewpoints of objects so that these might cumulatively give expression to complex experience, and until the second half of 1912, most self-consciously Simultanist paintings were based on this enumerative principle. The poetry of the Abbaye was similar—for example, in *La Terrestre tragédie*, Barzun monotonously *listed* a sequence of images, so that even if he was trying to represent the simultaneous awareness of things widely separate in space and in time, the *structure* of his poem was in no way simultaneous.[35] Nor does the pictorial use of the multiple viewpoint in fact communicate a sense of the simultaneous existence of different aspects of an object, but only the artist's successive analysis of them, for each viewpoint is simply a single point of recognition which, in Bergsonian terms, fragments one's experience of the wholeness of the image into a sequence of separate observations and destroys one's sense of the unity of time and space. Some painters seem to have realized this, and later in 1911 Léger and Delaunay sought more abstract ways of embodying simultaneous experience (see Delaunay's *Fenêtre sur la ville. nᵒ 3* and Léger's *La Noce* (Pls. 132 and 190).

The French painters' rather literal expression of movement and simultaneity between 1910 and mid-1912 may have been influenced by the Futurists' ideas on using a cinematic technique for representing such things, for there is little evidence that the French experimented in this way before the Futurists had published their ideas on the expression of modern life in 1910.[36]

Futurism entered the French art-scene with the publication of the 'Manifeste des peintres futuristes' ('La pittura futurista. Manifesto tecnico') in the French newspaper, *Comoedia*, on 18 May 1910.[37] The manifesto was illustrated with puerile caricatures by André Warnod, a critic and illustrator on the fringes of the Montmartre group, which included sketches of the multi-legged horse (which illustrated the representation of movement through multiplication of the image); the house which occupied the orb of the sun (the perceptual telescoping of space); the gulf to the centre of the earth (the power of energy to break down stabilized concepts of form); the horse on a person's cheek (the movement of perception which rearranges natural reality); figures swallowed by the sun (the belief that light destroys the materiality of bodies); the 'suffering' light-bulb (the realization that man is no longer the 'centre of universal life'). Nearly all of these were themes which were to concern the French painters— they may have been repeated in Marinetti's lecture in Paris in March 1911.

The Futurists' suggestion that movement could be represented by means of its successive phases may have influenced French painters, since Léger, Duchamp, and Kupka all attempted to represent movement in this way in works of 1910–11 (see Léger's *Essai pour trois portraits*, Duchamp's *Portrait*, and Kupka's *Femme cueillant des fleurs*, Pls. 183, 9 and 91). However, Kupka had experimented with such ideas before 1910 (see his *Cavaliers*, Pl. 90) and, as Duchamp

I Robert Delaunay, *Les Fenêtres simultanées*, 1912 (oval, 57 × 123).

II Frank Kupka, *Amorpha, Fugue en deux couleurs,* 1912 (211 × 220).

pointed out, there were alternative sources in 'chrono-photographs ... and ... the motion picture with its cinematic techniques'.[38] At the same time, it is possible that the Futurists gave an impetus to the use of such technological devices in an artistic context, for it was apparently only after publication of the manifesto that Kupka moved from a slight graphic experiment to an imaginative use of the idea in the *Femme cueillant des fleurs* series, or that Delaunay began to use transparent planes to suggest the dynamic cinematic movement of sight as it sweeps through space (Pl. 4).[39]

It would thus seem that the Futurists' *written* ideas stimulated the imagination of the French painters before they themselves could realize them, and that it was only when they had seen French painting that they were able to do so.

This process can be seen clearly in the artistic transformation of the scientific and technological discoveries which were creating a new awareness of the physical world. To illustrate the general accessibility of such discoveries, I quote from the science-notes of the *Mercure de France* to which Apollinaire contributed gossipy articles and which was probably read by his friends. The science correspondent wrote in September 1911: 'Everyone knows that white light decomposed by the prism forms a spectrum which, for our eye, extends from red to violet; but beyond this the spectrum continues by invisible rays which are revealed by their action on the photographic plate.'[40] He defined these radiations as 'waves in the ether'. Such facts had been *known* to artists since Impressionism, but the mode of *conceiving* the objective world is new and finds an echo in contemporary art. The Futurists described how the movements of a figure are prolonged 'like waves in space', and, at much the same time, Kupka represented the successive phases of movement like transparent ripples in space, while Delaunay embodied the passage of the eye through space in a similar way (Pl. 4). This kind of awareness had appeared earlier in poetry. For example, in 1907, Romains described how the movements of a boat on a river were prolonged into space:

> Son mouvement paraît
> Etre, d'en bas, tendu
> Jusqu'à l'air de la ville...[41]

Again, however, these things do not seem to have appeared in French painting in any consistent way until formulated by the Futurists.

Picabia, Duchamp, and Kupka do not seem to have come into contact with Gleizes, Metzinger, Léger, and Delaunay until mid-1911. Picabia and Duchamp met in late 1910 or early 1911.[42] They had both participated in an exhibition organized by the Société normande de peinture moderne in Rouen in late 1909. This association of Post-Impressionists and Fauves was based in Rouen,

9 Marcel Duchamp, *Portrait (Dulcinée)*, 1911 (146 × 114).

but had a number of Parisian members including the Duchamp brothers and Picabia. It organized a series of exhibitions including the Exposition d'art contemporain in Paris in November 1911 which included Léger, Picabia, Gleizes, Metzinger, the Villon brothers, Archipenko, and a number of Fauves and Post-Impressionists. It gave its participants the idea of holding an exhibition of avant-garde art which was realized in the Salon de la Section d'Or a year later. Picabia met Apollinaire at the Salon des Indépendants of 1911, and shortly afterwards introduced him to Duchamp at his own home in the seventh *arrondissement*, but he does not seem to have become really friendly with him until the summer of 1912 when he took him on a car-trip to England.

Duchamp-Villon was on the hanging committee of the Salon d'Automne and hung the work of Gleizes, Metzinger, Léger, and the Villons together in Salle 8. (Delaunay did not submit works to this Salon after one of his paintings had been refused in 1907.) Kupka and Picabia were together in Salle 7, 'the room of the frenzied colourists'.[43] Although there was little in common between the brilliantly coloured works of Kupka and Picabia (Pls. 102 and 218), the dense sober works of Léger, Gleizes, and Metzinger (Pls. 183 and 8) and the luminous immaterial 'cubism' of Villon and Duchamp (Pl. 9), these painters began to meet regularly at the Villon's establishment at Puteaux.[44] It was at Puteaux that the artists whom Apollinaire described as 'Orphic Cubists' came together (he, of course, was a regular visitor), and it was there that the ideas which led them towards pure painting were discussed. Kupka lived next door to the Villons, shared their garden and came to their meetings. Little is known about Delaunay's relation to the Puteaux group for there is no evidence that he attended its meetings, but, since his closest friends did, it is reasonable to assume that he did too. However, he found it difficult to sustain friendships with artists who did not accept him as a master, and the irreverence of Picabia and Duchamp at Puteaux would have been less congenial to him than the more sober meetings at the rue Visconti and Courbevoie. He preferred one-man exhibitions to their mixed exhibitions, and in 1912 he publicly asserted his independence of the group.[45]

Villon claimed that when he and his brothers met the 'Salle 45' Cubists in mid-1911, they knew little about Cubism and 'had never frequented either Braque or Picasso'.[46] However, by late 1911—possibly earlier—Duchamp had been introduced to them by his friend, the mysterious 'amateur mathematician', Maurice Princet.[47] Moreover, it is unlikely that he could have painted works like the *Portrait* (*Dulcinée*) without some knowledge of Cubism, which must have enabled him to break down the self-contained forms of his earlier works into interpenetrating transparent planes and to use the resulting ambiguity to express mental experience in *Yvonne et Magdeleine déchiquetées* (Pl. 219) and *Portrait (Dulcinée)*.

Duchamp's paintings formed part of a revival of subjectivism which occurred in the second half of 1911, after it seemed to have been banished from avant-garde art by the Fauves' emphasis on sensation and the Cubists' emphasis on structure. A number of painters at this time became interested in expressing the processes of memory and associative thought, and were probably influenced by Bergson's examination of inner consciousness and the dynamic processes of memory. Once again Kupka seems to have led the way in his *Touches de piano/Lac* (Pl. 97) which he probably painted in 1909

10 Marc Chagall, *À la Russie, aux ânes et aux autres*, 1911 (156 × 122).

11 Gino Severini, *Souvenirs d'un voyage*, 1911.

(though it is difficult to date any but a few of his pictures accurately). Chagall also contributed to this tendency with works like *A la Russie, aux ânes et aux autres* (Pl. 10) which was perhaps shown in the Salon des Indépendants in 1912;[48] Severini did so too, with his *Souvenirs d'un voyage* (Pl. 11), a jumble of images ranging from Sacré-Cœur in Montmartre to the well of his native village in Italy, suggesting not merely the simple memories of a voyage, but a voyage in memory into childhood and the experiences which had formed his present consciousness. Apollinaire explored similar forms of consciousness in poems like the dense and mysterious 'Cortège' first published in November 1912 but written earlier.[49]

It is also possible that psychic experience was discussed at Puteaux and Courbevoie. Alexandre Mercereau, the writer and organizer of several international Cubist exhibitions, Jaques Nayral, the poet and critic who was brother-in-law to Gleizes (who exhibited a portrait of him at the Salon d'Automne of 1911), and Eugène Figuière, the publisher (who issued Gleizes' and Metzinger's *Du Cubisme* and Apollinaire's *Les Peintres cubistes*), were all interested in psychic research. Mercereau was secretary and Figuière and Nayral were founder-members of the Société internationale des recherches psychiques in mid-1911,[50] while Mercereau contributed to *La Vie mystérieuse*, a spiritualist journal published by Figuière. Kupka was also interested in spiritualism and had himself been a medium in Vienna, and it is possible that paintings like *Plans par couleurs* (Pl. 103)

were inspired by spiritist belief in the 'aura', the spiritual light which
emanates from the body. Such beliefs were given a pseudo-scientific
justification by the new discoveries about the structure of matter, and
were also reconcilable with Unanimist ideas about the almost
palpable substance which fused the individual with the group or
united him to the larger rhythms of the city or of nature. Kandinsky's
art shows how spiritist ideas influenced the evolution of non-
figurative art; they may also have influenced Picabia's and Kupka's
development of such an art in 1912–13.

Picabia and Kupka had scarcely been touched by Cubism in
1911—Kupka, in fact, was never deeply influenced by it. Picabia was
still painting Synthetist abstractions from nature, although he had
been speculating on the possibility of creating an art similar to music
since 1908. It was only after acquiring an understanding of Cubism
that he was able to realize his ideas. However, he probably
introduced the subject of pure painting and musicalist painting into
the discussions at Puteaux.

Kupka could also have contributed to the discussion of such ideas,
and, unlike Picabia, he was well on his way to realizing them in
works like the *Nocturne* of *c.* 1910–11 and *Les Disques de Newton* (Pls.
101 and 81). Villon stated that his work was 'already rather abstract'
in 1911, while Duchamp wrote: 'Almost fifty years ago, Kupka gave
a memorable reception on New Year's day in his studio in the rue
Caulaincourt [before he moved to Puteaux in 1906]. Shortly
afterwards, he began to *see* abstract.'[51] Duchamp added that
Apollinaire called this kind of painting Orphic. This makes it clear
that Kupka was on friendly terms with the Villon brothers from an
early date and that his abstract painting had soon been seen as
remarkable.

Contacts with the Futurists became more direct in late 1911. The
Futurists planned to have an exhibition in Paris in December and,
probably as advance publicity, Marinetti's book *Le Futurisme* (which
included the 'Technical Manifesto' of 1910) was published in the
autumn. Marinetti also gave a lecture on Futurism in October.
However, Severini had visited Italy in the summer, where he had
persuaded his friends that they were not ready to exhibit in Paris and
that they should first see some avant-garde painting. Accordingly,
Boccioni, Carrà, and Russolo came to Paris to see the Salon
d'Automne and Severini also took them to visit some artists,
including Picasso and Braque, but it is not certain whether they met
any of the Salon Cubists. Boccioni stated that he did not meet Léger
until after the Indépendants of 1912.[52] However, he did meet
Apollinaire, who wrote a condescending note about Boccioni's ideas
on expressing 'states of mind' in his 'Vie anecdotique' in the *Mercure
de France* of 16 November. It is possible that there was more serious

discussion of this fundamental matter, and that it added something to the subjectivist tendency I have already mentioned.

Another important contact—that between Delaunay and the Blaue Reiter group—was established in late 1911. Elizabeth Epstein, a painter and friend of Kandinsky, had noted Delaunay's work at the Salon des Indépendants of 1911. She sent photographs of Delaunay's paintings to Kandinsky, who responded with photographs of his own work and an invitation to show in the first Blaue Reiter exhibition in December 1911. They wrote to one another and reached what Delaunay took to be a coincidence of views in early 1912.[53] Delaunay received further encouragement from the German painters when he later felt isolated in Paris and misunderstood by his French friends.

Kandinsky's book, *Ueber das Geistige in der Kunst* was published in January 1912, and he sent a copy to Delaunay who asked Elizabeth Epstein to translate it for him.[54] Kupka, Apollinaire, and Gabrielle Buffet, Picabia's wife, could all read German: thus Kandinsky's ideas were accessible to the French. There are in fact strong similarities between the ideas of Kandinsky, Kupka, and Picabia, although many could have derived from common sources rather than direct contacts between them.

1912 was the decisive year in the development of Orphism—and, indeed, of non-figurative art in general.

The journal, the *Soirées de Paris*, was founded in February 1912. It was the medium for Apollinaire's most important articles on the new art, some of which were incorporated in his book, *Les Peintres cubistes: Méditations esthétiques*, which he wrote between May and late August and published in April 1913. The book also contained chapters on individual artists written in close consultation with them.

The first significant event of the year was the Futurist exhibition which opened on 7 February with much publicity. Between the time of the Futurist visit in October 1911 and the Salon des Indépendants in March 1912, Delaunay, Léger, and Duchamp each produced at least one painting that was almost an illustration of certain aspects of the Futurist programme, although also containing elements which implicitly criticized other aspects. It seems as if the French learned much from these experiments, for almost immediately afterwards they moved towards a more abstract, pictorial expression of the same ideas. This pattern was typical of the period, since the French and Italians were simultaneously attracted and repelled by one another's ideas and paintings.[55]

The Futurists seem to have made the French painters much more aware of the problems of expressing dynamism and Simultanism. Of course, these problems were not new to the French avant-garde,

but the Futurists put them with such force that they were seen in a
new light. It is suggestive that the French critics—who were very
close to the artists—interpreted much of the Futurist programme as
novel, and although they were unimpressed by the Futurists'
paintings, they were interested in their ideas. Apollinaire, for
example, was critical of their anecdotal subject-matter, but noted
that the titles of the Futurists' works suggested the possibility of
synthesizing a number of complex themes in order to express
simultaneous experience, rather than limiting themselves to the
complexities of a single theme which was, indeed, characteristic of
French painting until the second half of 1911.[56] Until that time,
French painters tended to restrict themselves to relatively simple
subjects—still-life, landscape, isolated figures, or small groups of
figures—and limited their expression of simultaneity to the presentation of separate viewpoints. In June 1911 Apollinaire claimed
that the Salon Cubists were ready to confront 'vast subjects' which
suggests that they were becoming more ambitious, even if they had
not yet found the means of realizing complex synthetic experience.[57]
It was, in fact, only later in the year that they began to interweave
separate *themes*—as Léger did in *La Noce* (Pl. 190) and Gleizes did in
his *Baigneuses* (Musée d'Art Moderne de la Ville de Paris)—whereas
the Futurists had pursued such complex themes as early as 1910 when
Boccioni began his *Città che Sale* (Museum of Modern Art, New
York) with its vast vistas and dynamic interpenetration of separate
images. Léger's painting is closely related to Severini's huge *Danse du
Pan-pan à Monico* (Pl. 12) which he began in 1910; since Severini was
a regular visitor to the meetings of poets and painters at the Closerie
des Lilas, and knew the Salon Cubists by the autumn of 1911 at the
latest, he may have communicated information about the Futurists'
paintings and ideas to the French.[58]

Carrà said in 1913 that, at the time of the Paris exhibition, the
Futurists were the first to talk about 'our concept of simultaneity',
while the French were still preoccupied with 'pure aesthetics'.[59] He
exaggerated only slightly—as is suggested by the fact that
Apollinaire's reaction to the exhibition was to emphasize the purity
of French painting.[60] Moreover, only three days before the
exhibition opened he published an important article in the *Soirées de
Paris*, 'Du Sujet dans la peinture moderne', in which he maintained
that modern painting was moving towards greater purity and
abstraction; yet at the same time, the Futurists' insistence on the
dynamic Simultanist expression of modern subjects attracted him, as
it attracted the French painters.

The Futurists' catalogue contained the most explicit statement that
had yet appeared about the necessity of expressing Simultanist
experience in painting. However, the examples they cited and the

12 Gino Severini, *La Danse du Pan—Pan à Monico*, 1911–12.

works they exhibited made it clear that they conceived Simultanism in enumerative terms. Delaunay's *Ville de Paris* and Léger's *Le Fumeur* (Pls 136 and 192) seem to have been influenced by this conception. Both paintings represent the city which—as an entity composed of an infinite variety of forms, movements, feelings, and experiences—was a favourite image for the poetic expression of simultaneity and the dynamism of modern life; it was so used by Verhaeren, by Marinetti, Cendrars, and Apollinaire and, most influentially, by Romains in his books, *La Vie unanime* and *Les Puissances de Paris* (1911).[61] In his poem 'Dimanche' from *La Vie unanime*, Romains evoked the whole life of a city, weaving all aspects of human existence into its great totality. He described how the city:

> *...voudrait se dilater sans se dissoudre*
> *Mêler à ses maisons de l'espace et du vent*
> *Faire couler le ciel dans les rues élargies*
> *Rester une et devenir illimitée*[62]

Delaunay's *Tour Eiffel* and Léger's *Fumées sur les toits* series (1909–12 and 1911–12 respectively, Pls. 4 and 186) were clearly related to this kind of vision, but *La Ville de Paris* and *Le Fumeur* embodied more

13 Fernand Léger, *Le Passage à niveau*, 1912 (92 × 77).

complex Simultanist subjects. After painting them both artists moved back to simple subjects—Delaunay to begin his *Fenêtres*, and Léger the figure and landscape studies (Pl. 13) which would lead to his near abstract *Contrastes de formes*. This was, I believe, because they had learned from their Futuristic experiments that it was *structure* rather than subject which embodies Simultanist experience. This realization was central to the development of Orphism.

The Futurists also made the French reconsider the representation of movement. Of course, as Duchamp pointed out, 'the whole idea of movement, of speed was in the air',[63] and the French did not need the Italians to tell them so. Nevertheless, they do seem to have been influenced by the Futurists' proposals for expressing movement by splitting it into its separate phases, although they stopped depicting movement in this way after early 1912, when they began to embody it by creating more abstract structures which keep the eye in constant movement (see Kupka's *Étude pour Amorpha, Chromatique chaude* (1911–12), Delaunay's *Fenêtres* (1912), Léger's *Femme en bleu* (1912), Duchamp's *Le Roi et la reine entourés de nus vites* (1912): (Pls. 14, I, 195, and 236). Picabia became interested in the representation of movement later than the others, but soon reached an equivalent degree of abstraction. He painted *Paris* (Pl. 221) shortly after the

Futurist exhibition of 1912, probably in response to the Futurists' emphasis on urban dynamism, while the *Danses à la source I* (Pl. 224), which he painted in the early summer, was probably influenced by Futurist colour dynamism. He represented movement figuratively in both works, but in the *Danses à la source II* (Pl. 235), painted later in the summer or in the autumn, Picabia discovered how to represent movement abstractly.[64]

The French painters could well have been applying a lesson learned from Symbolist theory—that one cannot imitate such qualities as light or movement, but that one can find equivalents for them in the abstract structural properties of paint. They were also influenced by Bergson's insistence on the indivisible continuity of experience. Moreover, the actual sight of Futurist painting—after so much theory—made them recognize that the Futurists confused the 'simultaneous' with the 'successive', as was pointed out by Delaunay, by the critic Cartault in his review of the exhibition, and later by Jacques Villon.[65]

Thus, once again, the Futurists' challenge seems to have made the future Orphists reconsider their means of expression and strengthen the abstract structure of their paintings. Indeed, it was in the months immediately succeeding the Futurist exhibition that the Orphists made a decisive move towards non-figurative painting.

14 Frank Kupka, *Étude pour Amorpha, Chromatique chaude*, 1911–12 (85 × 128).

In his article, 'Du sujet dans la peinture moderne', Apollinaire referred to the appearance of a new, pure painting which had analogies with music. Such ideas were undoubtedly being discussed at Puteaux, since both Kupka and Picabia were interested in the relationship between the two arts. There is an echo of these discussions in Gleizes' and Metzinger's *Du Cubisme*: 'The painting should imitate nothing and should nakedly present its reason for existing ... Nevertheless, we must admit that reminiscences of natural forms should not be absolutely banished—at least, not yet. An art cannot be raised to the level of a pure effusion all at once.'[66] Apollinaire also discussed these ideas with Delaunay, who found confirmation of them in Kandinsky's work; they may both have been influenced by Kandinsky's ideas on the relationship between painting and music as expressed in his book *Ueber das Geistige in der Kunst* and embodied in the paintings which he exhibited in the Indépendants in 1911 and 1912 (Pl. 15). Delaunay regarded them favourably, but Apollinaire who noted his presence for the first time, was less enthusiastic, writing: 'Kandinsky pushes Matisse's theory of obedience to instinct to extremes and he obeys it further only at his peril'. However, by February 1913 he had enrolled him among the Orphists, and by March was praising him as 'an artist whose art seems to me as serious as it is significant'.[67] In the meantime, a number of Parisian artists had moved towards Kandinsky's extreme position. The sight of his works in French exhibitions must have been an encouragement to those interested in pure painting, even if his style was too personal to have had a direct influence on them.

15 Wassily Kandinsky, *Improvisation 23*, 1911 (110·5 × 110·5).

The idea of the relationship between painting and music had an important, although not perhaps an essential, role to play in the development of Orphism. Kupka and Picabia were inspired by the purity of music, and adapted musical processes of improvisation and musical structures to painting. Kupka was the first artist to follow the idea into pure non-figurative art as in *Amorpha, Fugue en deux couleurs* (Pl. II). He was inspired by beliefs similar to those which were influencing Kandinsky—in particular, the belief in the dissolution of matter into pure spiritual energy in which vibrations of sound or colour can create corresponding vibrations in the soul.[68] While Kupka was painting his first major musicalist works, Picabia was also developing his ideas on the relationship between the two arts. The *Danses à la source II* was the first work in which he tried to free pictorial from objective form so that he could use it 'musically', but since the work was still abstracted from a specific scene, its vestigial naturalistic structure prevented the really free deployment of form, and in this sense the work was closer to Synthetist musicalism than to Orphism. When Picabia painted his first truly abstract paintings in early 1913, he also wrote about them in musicalist terms which suggest that he may have been influenced by spiritualist ideas similar to those which had inspired Kupka and Kandinsky.

Although neither Delaunay, Léger, nor Duchamp was directly inspired by music, it is probable that the discussions on the relationship between the two arts made them aware of the unique qualities of their own, and to emphasize that it communicates its meaning 'simultaneously', not 'successively' as music does. Delaunay certainly thought in this way, and the musical analogy encouraged his development of pure, concentrated pictorial structures. He was probably painting his first *Fenêtres* when Paul Klee visited him in April; when he exhibited two of them (Pls. 141 and I) in the Moderner Bund in Zurich in June, Klee commented that Delaunay had created: 'the model of the autonomous painting, living without a natural motif, with an entirely abstract plastic existence'.[69] Klee seems to have been the only person to have written specifically about the *Fenêtres* in this period, but this was partly due to the fact that Delaunay did not exhibit his abstract or near-abstract works in France. During the summer Delaunay wrote two articles, 'La Lumière' which he sent to Klee who translated it for *Der Sturm*, and 'Réalité, Peinture pure' which was edited by Apollinaire for the December issue of the *Soirées de Paris*.[70] They provide the theoretical basis for Delaunay's abstraction, and it was largely from them that Apollinaire derived his ideas on Orphism and on pictorial Simultanism.

Between late spring and autumn, Duchamp, Picabia, and Léger were also moving towards abstract art. Duchamp painted a series of

strange works on sexual themes (*Le Roi et la reine entourés de nus vites,
Le Passage de la vierge à la mariée,* and *La Mariée,* Pls. 236, 239, and
16). These are essentially non-figurative works which play on figural
associations to express ambiguous subjective experience. It may be
significant that some of Kupka's works also had a disguised erotic
content, while Picabia developed similar themes in 1913–14 (Pls. 73
and 251). Picabia's first *Danses à la source* (Pl. 224) was a Synthetist
simplification of a specific scene, but in the second version, painted
later in the summer or autumn (Pl. 235), he fragmented the figures
and their surroundings into minute forms which create an effect of
kaleidoscopic movement which counters any figurative interpretation. At the same time, Léger was working on his *Femme en bleu* (Pl.
195) in which the figure is swallowed up in the clash of shape and
colour. He was also beginning to work on what were to become his
Contrastes de formes series in which he sought to express pure
dynamism.

All of these developments must have convinced Apollinaire of the
reality of the tendency towards 'pure painting' about which he had
written at the beginning of the year.

During 1912 the Puteaux artists were planning an exhibition of
avant-garde painting which they were to call the Salon de la Section
d'Or. It was partly financed by Picabia, and there was some criticism
of his attempts to direct it.[71] It was intended to encompass all
contemporary tendencies so that the title could not really mean
anything very specific—in fact, only Gris seems to have used the
golden section—which was, according to Duchamp, more 'in the air
than on the canvas'.[72] Some of the Puteaux group were concerned
about the relationship between modern art and tradition and—
perhaps in response to the Futurists' challenge—they sought
continuity with the French classical tradition and its values of order,
rationality, and clarity: the title, the Section d'Or, might have been
intended to have such a connotation.[73]

The title also had a less rational side. A number of participants in
the Puteaux discussions believed that the artist should penetrate
beyond the world of appearances to discover the non-visible forces
and relationships which underlay it. They did not develop any
coherent aesthetic theory, but they drew on tradition, science, the
antique, or the occult if such sources confirmed their own intuitions
about the nature of experience. Thus, although several members of
the Puteaux group were interested in and had read Leonardo's *Traité
de la peinture* (translated by Péladan in 1910), they were not interested
in his mathematical demonstration of ideal systems of proportion,
but were fascinated by him as one who penetrated behind the façade
of nature to discover how it functioned.[74]

It was in a lecture at the Section d'Or exhibition on the afternoon of 11 October 1912 that Apollinaire defined 'Orphic Cubism'. The scene has been described by Nicolas Beauduin, the 'Dynamist' poet who was there among 'all the habitués of those circles where the golden section and, above all, that indefinable "fourth dimension" were discussed', when Apollinaire 'who sported a magnificent three-piece suit (genre smoking), a stiff collar and a bow-tie, presented the canvases'.[75] In the lecture Apollinaire categorized the various tendencies which he saw developing in Cubism. He divided it into two major tendencies: Scientific Cubism (the creation, above all, of Picasso) and Orphic Cubism; and two minor tendencies—Physical Cubism and Instinctive Cubism—which do not seem to have much meaning but which did enable Apollinaire to enrol practically every important artist under the banner of Cubism. Apollinaire defined Orphic Cubism as: 'the art of painting new structures with elements which have not been borrowed from visual reality, but have been entirely created by the artist...' Delaunay, he said, was 'inventing' this art, and Léger, Duchamp, and Picabia were 'struggling' towards it.[76]

Beauduin wrote very specifically about Kupka's paintings: 'I can still see those three canvases illuminating the purple silk of the panel and detaching themselves from it through the purity of their abstraction.' He claimed that it was in front of these paintings that Apollinaire paused to deliver his sibylline definition and stress the relationship between the new painting and music. However, Apollinaire did not mention either Kupka or music when he inserted his definition in the proofs of *Les Peintres cubistes* in October, and since Kupka's works were not listed in the catalogue of the Section d'Or, there has been some doubt as to whether he did exhibit.[77] Beauduin maintained that it was upon Apollinaire's insistence that Kupka was invited to exhibit, but that his works arrived too late to be included in the catalogue. If his account is true—and it is unlikely that he invented it—it suggests that Apollinaire had been struck by the two *Amorpha* paintings (Pls II and 82) exhibited at the Salon d'Automne which opened a week earlier than the Section d'Or. This suggestion is strengthened by Kupka's comment that Apollinaire's use of the musicalist term Orphism for the new painting was an obvious one because his paintings were rhythmic and had musical titles.[78] However, Apollinaire did not comment on them in his very summary review of the Salon, although they made a strong if not favourable impression on the other critics, one of whom described them as 'geometrically bizarre, monstrously huge figures',[79] and, indeed, the sheer scale of these first abstract paintings must have been stunning. Kupka's mysterious art does relate more closely to Apollinaire's dense and obscure words than do the relatively straightforward works of Delaunay, Léger, and Picabia, but, again according to Beauduin, Kupka dissociated himself from Apollinaire's classification immediately after the lecture. His name was therefore excluded from the published definition, and in fact never appeared in any of Apollinaire's voluminous writing on art. Apollinaire corrected the proofs of *Les Peintres cubistes* while he was staying with the Delaunays for three months at the end of 1912, waiting to move into his flat nearby in the Boulevard Saint-Germain. Delaunay had refused to exhibit in the Section d'Or and had written a letter to *Gil Blas* on 25 October dissociating himself from the Cubists. However, he did influence *Les Peintres cubistes*, as can be seen in the changes to the proofs which express reservations about the 'purity' of the works of Duchamp and Picabia.[80]

The painters whom Apollinaire named as Orphists were impelled towards the non-figurative for very different reasons: Duchamp and Picabia wished to express inner subjective experience, while Delaunay and Léger were more interested in embodying sensation. Apollinaire's definition could, therefore, be only the loosest of categories. Unfortunately he chose to define it narrowly and in terms strongly influenced by Delaunay, and this caused his rather desperate juggling as to the identity of the Orphic Cubists. He named Léger, Picabia, and Duchamp as Orphic Cubists and discussed them at length in the 'meditations' on Cubism, but reserved Delaunay and Kupka for a volume of meditations on Orphism which was never written;[81] in a contemporary article, he linked Picabia, Duchamp, and Delaunay as breaking with the 'conceptualist formula', but does not mention Léger.[82] He wrote in the same article: 'This will be pure painting', clearly thus still conceiving the new art as a thing of the future, and indeed none of his Orphic Cubists had painted a pure non-figurative work. Only Kupka had done that.

Immediately after Apollinaire's lecture at the Section d'Or, he, Picabia, and Duchamp drove to the Jura for a visit.[83] It was then that Duchamp began to elaborate those intellectual games which were to lead to his *Mariée mise à nu par ses célibataires, même* (1915–23). Thus, while he had contributed to the development of Picabia's Orphism, by showing how subjective experience could be evoked by evocative but non-specific forms, he could not participate in the further development of Orphism, since it was moving towards the expression of non-conceptual experience by means of the pictorial medium alone, while he himself was turning to the intellectual examination and undermining of the habitual preconceptions which determine how we run our lives.

The poet, Blaise Cendrars, entered on the scene in the second half of 1912, from when he played an important part in the development of the expression of modern life. A great traveller, he had actually lived the Simultanist experiences about which he wrote, for he had

III Frank Kupka, *Plans verticaux III*, 1912–13 (200 × 118).

IV Robert Delaunay, *Soleil, Lune. Simultané 2*, 1913 (133 cm diam.).

crossed Europe and Russia as far as China in trains which moved so fast as to transform landscape into a tumbled kaleidoscope of images; through spaces so vast that time moved slowly, and the young man was able to pursue the continuity of his own memories as they flowed through the scenes which moved in front of him. He had lived in New York, most modern of cities, and had even helped construct one of the first aeroplanes.

He returned to Paris in the early summer of 1912 and immediately visited Apollinaire with a copy of his poem 'Pâques à New York', whose strange intermixture of old and modern images probably influenced Apollinaire's 'Zone' which was being written during the summer. Sonia Delaunay wrote: 'The poem "Pâques" which Cendrars brought to us the day after we met him at Apollinaire's overwhelmed us, and from that time until the war it became a part of our lives.'[84] Cendrars must have met Léger at this time, since Léger now lived close to the Delaunays in the rue de l'Ancienne Comédie. Léger shared Cendrars's interest in modern life and they became very friendly—they used to meet every day after work in a nearby café, 'Aux Cinq Coins', about which Cendrars wrote a poem.[85]

By December 1912 Delaunay had persuaded Apollinaire that his Orphism was different from Cubism,[86] although Apollinaire did not consistently maintain the distinction. They visited Berlin together for the opening of Delaunay's exhibition in Der Sturm gallery in late January, where Apollinaire gave a lecture linking Orphism to Barzun's literary movement, 'Dramatism' (to which he was giving temporary allegiance) and to recent German painting—in particular, to the painting of Kandinsky, Marc, and Macke which they may have seen in Der Sturm gallery.[87] As Delaunay turned away from his French friends, he came closer to the painters of the Blaue Reiter, and a letter he wrote to Marc suggests how important these new contacts were in giving him 'that beautiful assurance, that fine impulse towards the true painting... that ardour for life, light, colour, these are the simultaneous impressions which I have kept and which give me confidence.'[88] It was probably not coincidental that he made his public break with Cubism a little over a month after he had been visited by Marc and Macke in September 1912.

The Salon des Indépendants of 1913 gave Apollinaire the opportunity to declare the coming of the art he had foretold: 'du Cubisme sort un nouveau cubisme', he cried, 'le règne d'Orphée commence', and he expanded the scope of Orphism by referring to it as, 'Orphism, pure painting, simultaneity'.[89] The increase in colourist non-figurative painting justified his assertion of a new art-form and his ideas were accepted by other critics, for, unlike Cubism, Orphism met with no great hostility, and the only note of disapproval was Vauxcelles's remark that Cubism was now

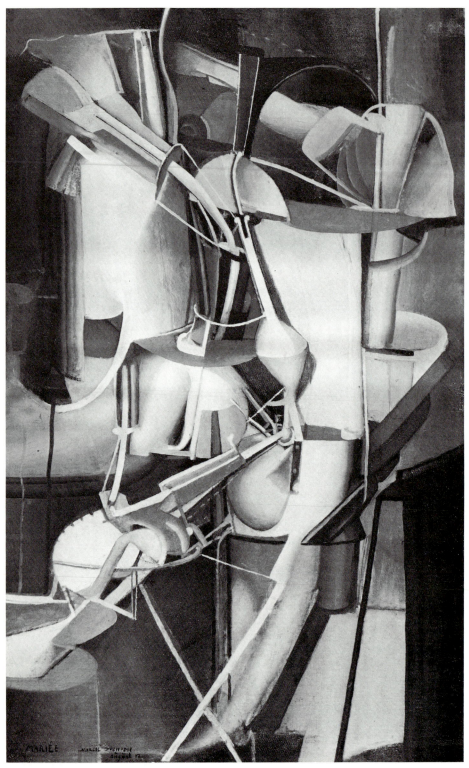

16 Marcel Duchamp, *La Mariée*, 1912 (89·5 × 55).

surpassed by 'a new folly, this time mystical'.[90] Warnod's comments were more typical: 'Cubism and Orphism come from the same family. While Cubism is concerned with drawing in its entirety, Orphism is a research into 'pure' painting ... into painting considered only as such. In comparison with Cubist paintings ... Orphic paintings will be dazzling in colour, one will study in them the radiation of light through planes ...'[91] Apollinaire stated that:

This tendency is not a sudden invention; it is the slow and logical evolution of Impressionism, Divisionism, of the school of the Fauves and of Cubism. The word alone is new; many painters have been surprised to be included in this tendency and it is interesting to note that very different painters converge in their researches and tend, independently of one another, towards the same expression.[92]

This time Apollinaire included Delaunay, Léger, Gleizes, Metzinger, Picabia, and Bruce (a follower of Delaunay) in the Orphist group, but once again he used the vocabulary appropriate to Delaunay's *non-figurative* works to describe works which were, on the whole, merely brightly coloured Cubistic paintings, and he elevated to a general law Delaunay's comments on the pure painting of a world without objects.[93] This was the more inappropriate since Delaunay himself had not followed the principles he had set down in his 1912 essays, and had sent in a figurative Salon 'machine' with a modernist programme, the *Équipe de Cardiff F.C.* (Pl. 151). Hedging his bets, Apollinaire also greeted the return of the subject, whose passing he had no less enthusiastically celebrated a year earlier. He ignored the fact that the subject in Léger's work, the *Nu dans un atelier* (Pl. 196), had 'little or no significance' (to quote from his essay 'Du Sujet dans la peinture moderne'); he made no mention of the most important non-figurative work in the Salon, Kupka's extraordinary *Plans verticaux* (Pl. III); and he stated that Picabia's *Procession* (probably the abstract one later exhibited in the Herbstsalon) (Pl. 238), was 'too unconscious to confine to Orphic Cubism'.[94]

Whatever the inconsistencies of Apollinaire's attempts at definition, he was the first critic to note the very real movement towards non-figurative painting and to do so only a short time after Kupka had evolved non-referential, non-gravitational structures in about 1911, at the same time that Delaunay, Léger, and Picabia developed similar structures in late 1912 and 1913.

The impetus which had taken Kupka so far and so fast seems to have slackened suddenly; after early 1913 he did not produce any works of the startling originality and purity of the *Amorpha, Fugue en deux couleurs* or the *Plans verticaux*. It was at this time that Delaunay began painting his *Soleil, Lune. Simultané* series (Pls. IV, 160–4, and 166); that Picabia painted his first real non-figurative works which were inspired by memories of personal encounters rather than specific scenes (see *Udnie, jeune fille américaine*, Pl. VII); and that Léger painted his *Femme dans un fauteuil* (Pl. V) in which the subject was no more than a pretext for the expression of the dynamism of modern life. Léger explained the nature of his works in two lectures in early 1913 and 1914, 'Les Origines de la peinture et sa valeur représentative' and 'Les Réalisations picturales actuelles', in which he insisted that the realism of a work was absolutely independent of its imitative qualities.[95]

He shared many ideas with the Futurists[96] and claimed that Futurism proved the universality of the new movement, and, indeed, a number of the Futurists and of the Blaue Reiter group moved towards non-gravitational painting at the same time as the Orphists. Severini, Balla, Boccioni, and Russolo all moved from the diagrammatic depiction of the movement of specific objects or figures to the representation of pure energy by means of colour ceaselessly moving in measureless space (Pls. 17 and 15). The same universality can be observed in contemporary literary movements.

17 Giacomo Balla, *Mercurio passa davanti al sole visto col cannochiale*, 1914. Tempera on paper (120 × 100).

In 1913, the critic Jean-Desthieux wrote:

All these words—Paroxysm, Dramatism, Unanimism, Futurism, Visionarism, Impulsionism, etc., affirm one tendency...

Originating from the purest Symbolism, contemporary innovatory poetry is clearly evolving towards an art which expresses our epoch of intense action more completely and synthetically... [and] which is more expressive of the new beauty... All seek to attain the universal and the cosmic. All seek to come out from themselves, to transcend themselves and to attain consciousness and understanding of the 'great world harmony'.[97]

Poets, philosophers, and scientists were employing images similar to those of the painters: the scientists conceived the universe—from the smallest particle of matter to the structure of planetary systems—in these terms, while writers and philosophers used such metaphors for the structure of the human consciousness and its relation to the external world. The science correspondent of the *Mercure de France* of June 1913 described the atom as a 'sort of planetary system with a great central nucleus like a sun, charged with positive electricity [and] surrounded by a swarm of innumerable tiny planets', and defined matter as 'a turbulent movement of the ether'.[98] Bergson used similar images in attempting to describe the relationship between the individual intellect and the whole. He believed that the intellect was detached from 'the fluid continuity of the real', but that there was no sharp division between them because it was like 'a solid nucleus formed by means of condensation' which 'does not differ radically from the fluid surrounding it' and can thus be reabsorbed in it.[99] The circular expansion of light was used by poets to suggest the expansion of consciousness from the single self to embrace and to become one with all life. Romains used the image in this way:

> Des effluves en cercle émanant de mon corps;
> Ils se détachent doucement; je les regarde
> Chaque seconde s'éloigner et s'élargir
>
> Des rayons vigoureux projettent les parcelles
> De mon âme dissociée.
> Les forces qui faisaient l'unité de moi-même
> Se délivrent et volent aux masses inertes
> Pour que les forces qui dormaient soient réveillées[100]

Barzun employed similar images in his attempt at a modern epic, 'L'Hymne des forces' (1911–12). In one place he described how, from the turbulent movement of matter:

> Je résulte: soleil au centre nébulaire, amas stellaire, ion d'éther
> Je franchi l'infini d'un seul jet de lumière...[101]

Cendrars too employed circular images of light to suggest Simultanist consciousness, but unlike Barzun, he used a genuinely modern construction based on sharp contrasts of images which were linked neither by logic nor by narrative sequences:

> *Il pleut les globes électriques*
> *Montrouge Gare de l'Est Métro Nord-Sud bateaux-mouches monde*
> *Tout est halo*
> *Profondeur...*[102]

Delaunay used the words 'halo', 'halos' when speaking of his desire for union with others and insisted that *profondeur* (the word Bergson used to indicate the interpenetration of mental states in the depths of consciousness) was the essential quality of Simultanist art.[103] The theme of the circular radiation of light was, of course, central to both his figurative and non-figurative paintings, as it was for Kupka, Balla, and Severini.

Images of the circular expansion of light often had very specific modernist sources—thus the new electric light inspired the Delaunays (see Sonia Delaunay's *Étude pour Prismes électriques*, Pl. 18) and Jules Romains (see his 'Le Présent vibre' in *La Vie unanime*). It is

18 Sonia Delaunay, *Étude pour Prismes électriques*, 1913. Pastel crayon (30 × 20).

also possible that the eclipse of the sun which occurred in April 1912 and was visible in the Paris region profoundly affected the imagination of contemporary artists. A newspaper account of its expected appearance neatly relates the image of the sun to that of the Eiffel Tower: it refers to the rainbow effects 'vaguely recalling halos' emitted by the sun when it is almost obscured by the moon, and of how radio waves activated by the station on the Eiffel Tower would co-ordinate the time of the phenomenon around the world.[104] Modes of transport show how contemporary life affected the perception and imagination of artists, for the speed of transport could give the individual the sensation that his personal consciousness was being absorbed into the energies which pervade the universe. For example, the driver of a car in Mirbeau's novel, *La 628-E8* (1908), describes how he was exalted by the speed of cars, aeroplanes, and boats, and how

each turn of the wheel, each beat of the propellor, each pulse of the sail…multiplies to infinity the circles of air or water which are concentric to my gaze…and their dizzy addition creates my sense of moving space.… Then I gradually become conscious that I am myself part of this space…I feel that I am a particle of this motor-force which makes all the organs, the springs, and wheels of this inconceivable factory, the universe, beat, expand, contract, and turn.[105]

This kind of experience clearly inspired the Futurists and Delaunay—see the *Stati d'animo: Quelli che vanno* or the *Hommage à Blériot* (Pls. 139 and 172). Romains, too, expressed the sensations aroused by modern transport in *La Vie unanime*:

> La roue de l'omnibus qui fait des étincelles
> Et la roue du soleil qu'embourbent les nuages
> Donnent un rythme à ma pensée impersonelle
> Je suis un tournoiement majestueux d'images[106]

He suggests that the intensity of his physical sensations precludes the intellectual ordering of experience, for the images beat in on his consciousness without his being able to sort them into specific personal meaning. Léger spoke of the same kind of experience in his lecture of 1914, 'Les Réalisations picturales actuelles':

When one crosses a landscape in a car or a train, the landscape loses in descriptive value, but gains in synthetic value… Modern man registers a hundred times more impressions than an eighteenth-century artist … All this has influenced the condensation, variety and fragmentation of forms of the modern painting.[107]

All the Orphists had become aware—through literature, philosophy, and their own experience—of the ways in which science and the machine were changing consciousness, yet their reactions to such changes were various, ranging from Kupka's mysticism to Léger's straightforward modernism. Nevertheless, Kupka's mysticism was as much a response to certain aspects of twentieth-century experience as was Léger's modernism, and Léger's desire to replace conceptual consciousness of the world of objects with a new consciousness of pure dynamism contains something of the experience which Kupka sought. Their representations of movement, of simultaneity, or of the structure of matter were not simply illustrations of scientific interpretations of the external world, for they actually embodied a new awareness of the individual's relationship to the external world.[108]

The dominant tendency of avant-garde art in the Salon d'Automne of 1913 was towards abstraction. In his review of the Salon, Apollinaire commented on the influence of 'Cubism, Orphism, simultaneous contrasts', but clearly did not have anything constructive to say about the most important Orphist works in the Salon, Kupka's *Localisations des mobiles graphiques* Pl. 111) and Picabia's *Udnie* and *Edtaonisl* (Pls. VII and VIII).[109] Neither Delaunay, Duchamp, nor Léger exhibited—Delaunay would not exhibit at this Salon, Duchamp was no longer painting, and Léger had recently signed a contract with Kahnweiler and only exhibited with him; Apollinaire must therefore have been referring to the increase in brightly coloured painting of a lyrical or abstract kind.

Apollinaire called the Herbstsalon organized in Berlin by *Der Sturm* in September 1913 'the first Salon of Orphism'. Its claim to the title was real, as it included important works by Léger and Picabia, and a group of works which practically amounted to an independent exhibition by the Delaunays (it contained his *Soleil, Lune. Simultané* paintings—with titles like *Contraste simultané mouvement de couleur profondeur prisme lune 2*—and her Simultanist objects, such as a cushion called *Voir mouvement couleurs profondeur*).[110] The Futurists and Kandinsky—whom Apollinaire had dubbed 'an instinctive Orphist'—also exhibited.

Orphism was at its height from the spring of 1913 to that of 1914. Its maturity was marked by a series of vibrant works, with richly coloured, ceaselessly mobile, complex structures ranging from Kupka's paintings of the evolution of matter and Picabia's haunting subjective works, to those paintings in which Delaunay and Léger asserted the joy and significance of perceptual experience (Pls. 73, VII, IV, and VI).

Orphism was also becoming more diffuse, and in doing so it tended to become weaker, thus being already in decline before the war destroyed it. Its exponents seem to have glimpsed the function of non-figurative art; they painted some magistral examples of it, but did not sustain their promise. There were many reasons for this. The

V Fernand Léger, *La Femme dans un fauteuil*, 1913 (130 × 97).

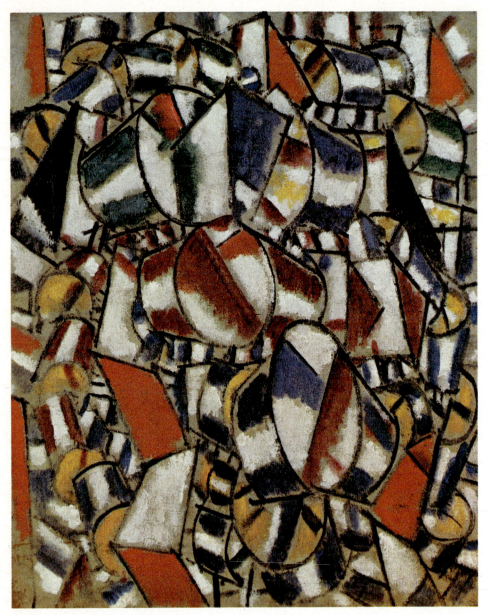

VI Fernand Léger, *Contrastes de formes*, 1913 (100 × 81).

VII Francis Picabia, *Udnie, jeune fille américaine (danse)*, 1913 (300 × 300).

VIII Francis Picabia, *Edtaonisl (ecclésiastique)*, 1913 (302 × 300).

first, and perhaps the most basic, was the constant fear of war which seemed, according to the daily press, increasingly likely to break out at any time. The Orphists did not share the Futurists' belief in the value of war and so their art, which was founded on a faith in 'la vie moderne', was inevitably undermined. Secondly, Orphism had a tendency to the decorative, and as such it was eagerly assimilated by the avant-garde of fashion, ever eager for the new if not the profound. Thirdly, the Orphist painters were always attracted by the explicit modernism of the writers and seemed to find it hard to continue to develop their abstract pictorial structures. Finally, it was affected by the new emphasis on fantasy—the revival of symbolism and the iconoclasm of nascent Dadaism—all of which were probably intensified by the external menace.

At this stage in the development of Orphism, it is both possible and necessary to make a distinction between constructive Orphism and decorative Orphism, and between Orphism in painting and Orphism applied to the world of design. This distinction is necessary because each of these categories demands a different kind of attention and awakens different forms of consciousness. Pictorial Orphism requires that one's attention should be strongly concentrated on the individual work; this form of attention is different from that paid to the objects which surround one in everyday use. The structure of constructive Orphism is more dense, concentrated, and ambiguous than its decorative counterpart and thus more fully absorbs the spectator in its own being. Confusion between these different experiences did, I think, contribute to the weakening of constructive Orphism.

Delaunay was, in Gertrude Stein's words, 'inordinately ambitious',[111] and he was determined to make his intuitive, empirical, and very personal style into a universal one. Thus he wrote in 1912, 'The means of expression should not be individual, on the contrary they should be at the service of any inspiration towards beauty.'[112] He seems to have been uneasy with those who did not recognize his primacy, and surrounded himself with a group of disciples who took up the most obvious aspects of his Orphism—its bright colour and fluid structure. These disciples first appeared in the Salon des Indépendants of 1913 and became more numerous and more obvious in each succeeding Salon. They included the Americans, Patrick Henry Bruce and Arthur B. Frost, and the Armenian, Georges Yacouloff, who spent the summer of 1913 with the Delaunays at Louveciennes. Chagall and Archipenko also visited them, but their art was already formed and they maintained their personal modes of expression. Sonia Delaunay, too, adopted her husband's ideas on colour construction. She had earlier painted Fauve works of some power (Pl. 19), but does not seem to have painted between the time

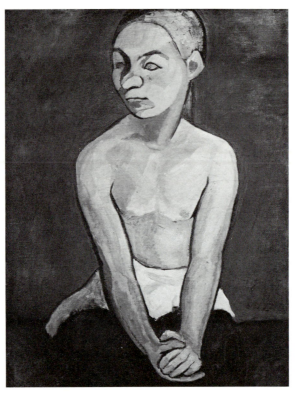

19 Sonia Delaunay, *La Jeune Finlandaise*, 1908 (80 × 64).

of her marriage to Robert in early 1910, and early 1913 (some paintings are dated 1912, but for stylistic reasons it is more likely that they were painted in 1913—see Pl. 163). Instead she began to make decorative objects (such as a coverlet for their baby son, born in 1911, bookbindings, posters, furnishings, and clothes: Pls. 20–1, 30–2, 149–150, and 153–5). She did a number of drawings of figures absorbed in the dynamic radiation of electric light in early 1913 (Pl. 18), and in the same year she painted her first major Orphist works, evocations of the rhythms of dance and light at the Bal Bullier, a popular dance-hall in the Boulevard Saint-Michel (Pls. 22 and 157). Like Picabia's paintings of the dance, these may have been influenced by Severini's paintings of this theme. Sonia Delaunay later said: 'Every Thursday we used to meet our painter or poet friends [Chagall, Bruce, Cendrars, Apollinaire, Cravan] at the Bal Bullier, among the students and midinettes. The fox-trot, the tango had just appeared there. The continuous, undulating rhythm of the tango caused my colours to "move". I painted the Bal Bullier and, later, the Electric Prisms.'[113] She exhibited her *Prismes éléctriques mouvement couleur 'Simultané'* at the Indépendants of 1914 with Robert Delaunay's *Disques solaires, Forme, 'Simultané'. Au grand constructeur Blériot* (Pls. 171–2), Bruce's *Mouvement, Couleurs, Espace 'Simultané'*, and Frost's *Soleils 'Simultanés'* (Pl. 23). They thus clearly affirmed their identity

20 Sonia Delaunay, cover for Blaise Cendrars's 'Les Pâques', 1 Jan. 1913. Papier collé (25 × 15).

21 Sonia Delaunay, design for a poster, 1913–14. Papier collé (66 × 81·5).

22 Sonia Delaunay, *Le Bal Bullier*, 1913 (97 × 130).

as a group, which was given extra emphasis since their paintings were hung with those of Picabia and the 'Synchromists'.

Bruce and Frost were typical of the many painters who embraced the decorative aspects of Orphism (Pls. 23–5), moving painlessly from decorative Post-Impressionism, through decorative Fauvism to decorative abstraction, and forming a broad current of taste. Their works represent the transmissible, predictable side of Delaunay's 'métier simultané', and they lack the essential constructive ambiguity of Delaunay's painting which derived from his Cézannist-Cubist inheritance.

Salmon wrote in his review of the 1914 Salon: 'Orphism or simultanism seem to me perilous for the future of miraculously regained form. One must return neither to Fauvism nor to Impressionism.'[114] He excepted Delaunay 'and his group' from his criticism, but he must have been referring to the great increase in colourist painting by such painters as Valensi, Survage, and the Synchromists.

The Synchromists Morgan Russell and Stanton MacDonald-Wright exhibited together in the Bernheim-jeune gallery in October–November 1913. This was, curiously, the single most important exhibition containing non-figurative art in Paris before the war, for Delaunay exhibited his non-figurative works only in Germany. The Futurists had exhibited in this gallery in 1912, and the Synchromists followed them in publishing a catalogue with a joint preface and two individual statements, but they did not attract anything like the interest that the Futurists had created for themselves.[115] They insisted that their work was different from that of the Orphists, saying that to confuse it with the latter (as a critic had done at the Indépendants) 'was to mistake a tiger for a zebra with the pretext that both have striped skins'. It is difficult to believe that their work was independent of Orphism, since it is particularly close to the circular forms of Kupka and Delaunay (Pls. 25 and 26), whose ideas they shared on the equivalence between paint-colour and natural light, as well as consequent belief that abstract colour relationships were sufficient subject for a painter. However, they claimed that the Orphists retained 'naturalistic analogies' (like an Impressionistic colour perspective) and an 'illustrative subject'. This suggests that when they wrote their essays and painted their first non-figurative works in the summer of 1913, they had not seen Delaunay's *Soleil*,

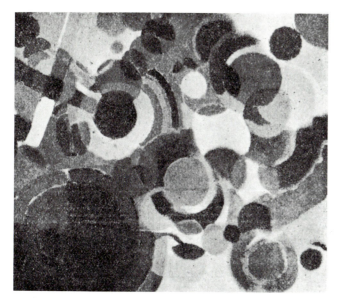

23 Arthur B. Frost, *Soleils simultanés*, 1913–14.

24 Patrick Henry Bruce, *Composition*, 1913.

Lune. Simultané series or even his *Fenêtres* (which were not exhibited in Paris) or that they knew of them only through the works of their fellow American, Bruce, who was deeply influenced by Delaunay and had worked in the Matisse atelier at the same time as Russell.[116] They had probably seen Kupka's work, for Wright's abstract impressionist paintings have strong similarities to the immateriality and luminosity of the *Amorpha, Chromatique chaude.* Russell's works were closer to Delaunay's colour-constructions, but although they were more abrupt and violent in execution, they lacked the densely worked physical ambiguity of Delaunay's paintings. Like Wright, Russell gave a straightforward representation of form in space, whereas Delaunay constantly transformed one into the other. The difference may partly be explained by Russell's lack of interest in Simultanism. Thus he wrote: 'We have conceived light as interconnected chromatic undulations... These "colour rhythms" introduce the notion of time... into painting: they give the illusion that the painting develops in time like music, while, strictly speaking, traditional painting develops in space so that the spectator can simultaneously embrace all its elements in one glance.' Russell maintained that he was not concerned with 'mystical painting' and yet he clearly considered the possibility of adapting musical time to painting; this may be one reason why Synchromist paintings lacked the density of the non-figurative works of Delaunay, Picabia, and Léger, even though they did conform to the general tendency

25 (*left*) Morgan Russell, *Synchromy No. 2. To Light* (or *Synchromie en bleu vidacé*), c. 1913 (33 × 24·5). **26** (*right*) Stanton MacDonald Wright, *Still-Life Synchromy*, 1913 (50·8 × 50·8).

towards paintings with circling, non-gravitational structures.

The analogy between music and painting became more popular as Orphism became more diffuse. Kupka's *Solo d'un trait brun* (Pl. 89) in the Indépendants of 1913 was perhaps the most important direct application of the analogy which was taken up much more subtly in Picabia's musicalist *Udnie* and *Edtaonisl* and more directly in the works of Valensi, Survage, and Rossiné. Valensi gave a lecture on the analogy between the two arts in late 1913. Extracts from his talk were published in *Montjoie!* and show the Symbolist origin of such ideas very clearly: 'Then why not conceive of "pure painting"? Just as the musician has his notes, why not suppose that colour, by its intrinsic force, could express the thought of the painter?'[117] His ideas were close to those of Picabia and Kupka, but his expression of them was laboured and arbitrary. In the Section d'Or exhibition, he showed paintings in which he had tried to synthesize subjective impressions of cities in a Simultanist manner (Pl. 27), but although he then began to employ colour-rhythms derived from Delaunay's paintings, his structures remained essentially naturalistic. Survage was also interested in the analogy between painting and music; as he explained in a lecture in 1914, he planned to exploit the relationship cinematically, and he exhibited a project for this in a sequence of paintings representing the growth of coloured forms in the Indépendants of 1914 (Pl. 28).[118] Rossiné was also interested in the analogy and in 1914 began to develop a colour-clavier. He had painted a completely abstract painting apparently as early as 1910 (Pl. 29), but did not pursue his discovery. The painting has certain similarities to Picabia's abstract works and could have influenced them.[119]

Survage and Rossiné were Russian (Rossiné's original name was Baranoff), as was Sonia Delaunay who naturally created a Russian circle which included Chagall and Archipenko; Yacouloff was Armenian, and Valensi was born in Algiers, while Wright, Russell, Bruce, and Frost were Americans. It is, in fact, remarkable that so many of the artists responsible for the diffusion of decorative Orphism were not French. This was probably not coincidental, and may be explained by the fact that they came from artistic traditions which had not passed through the great formal revolution which had taken place in French art between about 1880 and 1912. It was also true of Kupka, Balla, Severini, and Kandinsky, who all played an extremely important role in the evolution of non-figurative art but whose work often lacks the formal density of the best paintings by Léger, Delaunay, Picabia, and Duchamp.

Apollinaire noted 'signs of lassitude' in the Salon des Indépendants of 1914. He attributed this situation to the very success of the hitherto 'anti-academic' Salon which attracted painters who

27 Henri Valensi, *Rythme de la Sainte-Moscou*, 1912 (89 × 116).

28 Léopold Survage, *Rythme coloré* (study for a film-sequence), 1913. Water-colour (33 × 31).

29 Vladimir Rossiné (also known as Vladimir Baranoff-Rossiné), *Composition abstrait*, 1910 (149 × 101).

would previously have wished to exhibit in the official Salons. This, he said, 'disagreeably changes—in a fashionable direction—the spirit of the Société des Indépendants'. He declared that there were too many tendencies to categorize them in any useful way, but he noted that Picabia's Orphist art was growing in stature, and described Delaunay's *Hommage à Blériot* as 'labyrinths of whirling Futurism'.[120]

During the last years before the war, exhibitions and press comment multiplied; the Futurists added an element of competitive publicity which so affected the art-world that Salmon was led to criticize 'the deplorable intrusion of politics into art'.[121] He was not referring to political controversy, but to artistic and literary quarrels about precedence in certain discoveries and about possession of the 'true way'. Again, it is likely that the increase in the number and bitterness of quarrels was due to the general mood of unease created by the ever-present threat of war.

Delaunay's insistence on his primacy contributed to this situation.

He engaged in a number of activities designed to promote what he believed to be the one true way in art; he wrote articles, promoted lectures in Germany and Russia, sent letters to the press on questions of artistic precedence, and surrounded himself with disciples. When he did exhibit in France after early 1912, he showed only great Salon 'machines' on Simultanist subjects, and reserved his experimental works for one-man exhibitions (as was, virtually, that at the Herbstsalon) which were like personal manifestations with a clear central theme—given, for example, to his 1913 exhibition in Berlin by the beautiful blue and gold catalogue prefaced by Apollinaire's 'Fenêtres', and to the Herbstsalon show by the resonant poetic titles. He claimed that he and his friends had discovered:

the new representative and simultaneous *métier*: painting, sculpture, furniture, architecture, books, posters, dresses, etc. etc. . . .

We are finding the new technique which must serve a new aesthetic, that is, one which is representative and not descriptive, like simultaneous contrasts, complementaries, and dissonances. Constructive colour is the [fundamental] technique in all the new manifestations of Modern Art.[122]

The Delaunays seem to have been the first twentieth-century painters to attempt to apply a pictorial discovery to all forms of expression (although they may have been influenced by the Puteaux Cubists' scheme to relate the new painting to architecture in the 'Maison cubiste' in the Salon d'Automne of 1912). It is probable that it was Sonia Delaunay, an able and ambitious woman, who conceived the idea, for it was she who first put it into practice as a natural continuation of the handicrafts which had occupied her in the years during which she was not painting.[123] Her activities first had public impact in the autumn of 1913, although she had made 'simultaneous' spectacles for Apollinaire, as well as 'simultaneous' curtains and cushions for his apartment into which he moved in late 1912, and also bound books by Mallarmé, Rimbaud, Laforgue, and Cendrars. Her work on books culminated in her revolutionary design for Cendrars's 'La Prose du Transsibérien et de la petite Jehanne de France', which was published in October 1913 as 'the first simultanist representation in book form'—a claim which provoked violent controversy but which the boldly innovative format and typography fully justified (Pls. 154–5). The poem was shown in the Herbstsalon with her other Simultanist objects, alongside Delaunay's Simultanist paintings and his one ill-advised Simultanist sculpture (Pl. 169), and was at the same time launched on the Parisian art-world.[124] More or less simultaneously the Delaunays created a stir by appearing at the Bal Bullier and the Salon d'Automne in Simultanist clothes designed by Sonia (Robert, for example, wore 'a violet jacket and a blood-red overcoat').[125] Cendrars said that the Futurists telephoned Milan with details of the clothes the Delaunays wore to the Bal Bullier, adding that in this way: 'their actions...gestures and...harlequin clothes were known and aped in the whole world by an avant-garde which wished to keep in touch with the latest Parisian fashions.'[126] The Simultanist clothes were composed of materials of contrasting texture and colour (Pls. 30–2). Unlike most contemporary fashion with its muted colours and soft materials emphasizing the lines of the body, the bold designs and brilliant colours seem actually to conflict with the body, and Delaunay himself said that the contrasts of colours either 'exalted or fragmented the human form'.[127] Cendrars brilliantly evoked this effect in his poem 'Sur la robe elle a un corps' (1914):

> *Tout ce qui fuit, saille, avance dans la profondeur*
> *Les étoiles creusent le ciel*
> *Les couleurs déshabillent*
> . . .
>
> *Ventre*
> *Disque*
> *Soleil*
> *Les cris perpendiculaires des couleurs tombent sur les cuisses*
> . . .
>
> *Il y a dans la traîne la bête tous les yeux toutes les fanfares*
>   *tous les habitués du bal Bullier*[128]

30 Sonia Delaunay, Simultanist dress, 1913–14. Mixed fabric.

Sonia Delaunay's efforts accorded with an increasing interest in the decorative arts, which received further impetus by the designs for the Russian ballets which were particularly impressive in giving a sense of overwhelming, all-encompassing colour. A number of those associated with the ballets were welcomed into avant-garde circles. Thus Larionov and Goncharova (who came to Paris as designers for the ballet and held an exhibition which included their Rayonnist works in June 1914), as well as Stravinsky, appeared frequently at the functions held by *Montjoie*! Stravinsky's *Sacré du printemps* (first performed in May 1913) became a rallying-point for the avant-garde who saw it as a confirmation of the universality of the new art, appearing in all European countries and in all manifestations of cultural life—literary, musical, and visual.[129] This artistic synthesis can be seen particularly clearly in a special number of *Montjoie*! which was devoted to the art of the Russian ballets and to contemporary decorative arts. Canudo contributed a manifesto, 'Notre esthétique: A propos du 'Rossignol' de Strawinsky', in which he attempted to describe the factors common to various avant-garde movements. There were also articles on contemporary architecture, fashion, posters, street-design, and book-binding, stressing the necessity for a renewal of the decorative arts under the slogan 'L'art

31 (*left*) Sonia Delaunay,
Simultanist clothes and
objects, 1913–14.
32 (*right*) Sonia Delaunay,
Simultanist clothes and
objects, 1913–14. The
paintings are by Robert
Delaunay.

moderne doit correspondre aux mœurs modernes'. A number of
Sonia Delaunay's works were illustrated in these articles.[130]

There was a strong fashionable side to these activities. Salons and
exhibitions were events in the social calendar and could be described
in terms like the following: 'Crush. Dust. Perfumes. There are Slavs,
Scandinavians, people from Munich, and even some Parisiennes who
are not sworn into the little sects of the Left Bank. Not much in the
way of fashion.'[131] Of course, this social side had long been
characteristic of exhibition art, but there was something new in the
rapidity with which the public now absorbed its biannual artistic
shocks and came back with a demand for more. Its capacity to absorb
everything, and to reduce all art to a fashionable event, probably
strengthened the provocative attitude of certain artists. There had
been a consistent Dadaist tendency in Paris since the time of Jarry, but
the attack on bourgeois convention and rationality became stronger
in the last year before the war. Duchamp, Picabia, and Apollinaire
followed Jarry in turning the rational inside out, showing it to be
absurd and sanctioned only by habit. Duchamp abandoned painting,
and in 1913 produced his first 'ready-made', the bicycle wheel, and at
the same time began work on his monument to nonsense, the *Mariée
mise à nu par ses célibataires, même*; Apollinaire wrote of 'that most
modern of stimuli, surprise'; and Cravan distributed a review of the
1914 Indépendants which for brutal, unsolicited, vigorous scurrility
equalled anything produced by Dada.[132]

At the same time artists turned increasingly to the expression of
dream, memory, and mental processes (also reflected in the renewed
interest in Redon).[133] Although this tendency had not been
interrupted since the time of the Symbolists, it had for a while ceased
to occupy avant-garde art; it began to do so again in 1911 (as I have
shown in the case of Duchamp and others), and became increasingly
strong in 1913–14. Now Apollinaire—who had defended 'pure
painting'—wrote enthusiastically about Chagall and Chirico.

These two tendencies, marked by the desire both to destroy habitual modes of thought and to express the artist's inner world, had been influential in the evolution of non-figurative art because it too sought to express new forms of consciousness. However, the tendencies became progressively stronger as war approached, and, as they did so, they tended to divert painters from that intensive exploration of form which was the very essence of Orphism.

The war destroyed French non-figurative art, even though it killed none of its exponents. Duchamp and Picabia went to New York where they turned decisively to Dada, and neither of them ever returned to abstract art; Léger's experiences at the front convinced him that he should give up pure painting and devote himself to the expression of modern life in figurative terms; Delaunay was declared physically unfit for service, and went to Portugal where he painted a series of brilliantly coloured figure-pieces and still-lifes. After the war he continued to work in a figurative style, often producing crude repetitions of his pre-war themes, and returned to non-figurative art only in the late 1920s when he began his series of huge, interlocked, endlessly turning disks. After his death in 1941 his widow, Sonia Delaunay, continued to develop the art whose principles they had discovered together. Kupka was the only Orphist to continue the exploration of non-figurative art throughout the 1920s and, by the end of the decade, he had at last attained a personal style of great purity and beauty.

During the war the centres of development of non-figurative art moved from Paris and Munich to Holland, Russia, and Switzerland. Yet the new developments were led by artists who had either been in Paris before the war or who, by means of journals, personal contacts, and travelling exhibitions, had known what was happening there in those immensely fruitful years.

Chapter 2 Apollinaire's Orphism

Orpheus and Orphism in Apollinaire's poetry

Picasso described this as a period when 'peintres et poètes s'influençaient tour à tour';[1] the Cubist and Orphist painters were, in fact, more closely involved with poets than with other painters and were deeply interested in nineteenth-century poetry, particularly that of Mallarmé, Rimbaud, Baudelaire, and Laforgue. Delaunay, Duchamp, Kupka, and Picabia were influenced by Mallarmé; Duchamp was inspired by Laforgue, Kupka by Baudelaire, and only Léger steered clear of the poets and preferred to 'pick everything up in the street'. Apollinaire was probably more important to his friends as a poet, as a creator in his own right, than as a writer on art, and similarly, his most important contribution to our understanding of the art of his time is his poetry, not his criticism. Apollinaire's writings on art have been much criticized, not only by other critics and historians, but by the artists about whom he wrote: there is scarcely one who did not later complain that Apollinaire knew nothing about the visual arts. Their criticism is not surprising, for Apollinaire was deliberately obscure in his pronouncements on art, believing that the critic should awaken a sense of the mystery and the triumph of creation, not that he should explain it.

Apollinaire's friendship always quickened the development of an artist. He was extraordinarily receptive to the ideas of others, often seeming to become aware of them before they were fully formed, so that he was able to help bring them to consciousness; but he was content to be present at the birth of an idea and rarely followed its growth to maturity. He was fickle—to the individual artist though not to the new art—and once he had removed the potent charm of his attention, he left many an artist wondering just what the substance of his ideas was. Also, although artists were glad to have a champion, they were frequently embarrassed by the terms he used to characterize their art, and enraged when he incorporated them, willy-nilly, in some new grouping of the avant-garde—a grouping that was, as often as not, strategic rather than aesthetic.

Yet, if Apollinaire *was* ignorant about the visual arts, the list of

artists whom he was the first to appreciate is astonishing for it ranges
from the earliest Cubists to the first abstract painters and the
immediate predecessors of the Surrealists. No other critic rivalled his
perspicacity. Apollinaire also supported many artists who have since
disappeared from history, for he was determined not to discourage
any young artist and believed that it was necessary that 'mediocre
things should appear at the same time as the sublime' if the new
movement in art was to affirm itself.[2] Thus Delaunay—who had
suffered from Apollinaire's fickleness—could still write: 'It needed
an Apollinaire to disclose the first steps, the first cells of this new art;
in a brilliant way he made the fundamental definitions [which
distinguish] between traditional painting and that which was
evolving, definitions which still retain *their full value*.'[3]

Apollinaire wrote his first serious art-criticism in 1908 when he
was particularly close to Picasso. He was also writing a group of
visionary poems (including 'Le Brasier', 'Cortège', and 'Les
Fiançailles'[4]) in which he tried to express the emotional meaning of
creation by exploring the relationship between the personal self and
its transcendence in the creation of something that is *other* than the
self. Apollinaire made his first —and almost his only—clear reference
to Orpheus in the same year, at a lecture on the new poets at the Salon
des Indépendants. He probably felt that he had at long last discovered
his individual poetic form, and the lecture was an assertion of his
identification with the young avant-garde: 'Nouveaux Amphions,
nouveaux Orphées!' he cried: 'the young poets about whom I have
been speaking will soon compel admiration and will make the very
stones and wild animals responsive to their strains'.[5]

The language of Apollinaire's early art-criticism is the language of
the visionary poems. He employed it again in 1912, at the same time
that he began to use the term 'Orphism' to distinguish a group of
painters who were creating 'new universes' independent of the
natural one. Delaunay later comments: 'When Apollinaire saw that
an art of colour was being born, he identified it with poetical (and
musical and plastic) developments as the fancy took him. However,
as a poet, he did not perhaps see the very constructive aspects of the
new art.'[6] Apollinaire's Orphism was literary in origin, and it is
therefore necessary to examine it more closely in order to understand
the particular character of both written and pictorial Orphism.

Apollinaire was deeply influenced by the nineteenth-century poets
who saw Orpheus as the ideal embodiment of the poet whose song
had the power of illumination, that is, of giving meaning to the
mystery of life.[7] Orpheus himself rarely appears directly in
Apollinaire's poetry—he is there by inference, or by the association
or resonance of an image: as the poet who sought to repair the loss of
a loved one through song; as the poet torn apart by savage women

but whose song survives death; as the poet whose song tames wild
animals and makes sense of the whole disordered world through
form; as the poet of light whose words are revelations of the mystery
of being and of creation.[8] These ideas are associated with many other
mythological figures, but Apollinaire did not find it necessary to be
explicit, for he was not interested in ancient myth or esoteric doctrine
as such, and made use of them only when they struck some chord in
his own inner consciousness.

Apollinaire was haunted by the way in which time threatens the
inner self by fragmenting the living continuity of consciousness into
a series of externalized images of a dead past, and he found that he
could regain a sense of the integrity of the inner self through the act of
creation which enabled him to transform his past into his present
consciousness. This is the personal signification in his lines:

> *En moi-même je vois tout le passé grandir*
>
> .   .   .
>
> *Rien n'est mort que ce qui n'existe pas encore*
> *Près du passé luisant demain est incolore*
> *Il est informe aussi près de ce qui parfait*
> *Présente tout ensemble et l'effort et l'effet*[9]

Apollinaire's experience of the inner significance of the creative act
led him to assert that the poet has power over 'the words which make
and unmake the universe',[10] and that he is like a god who can create a
'new universe' in which he is free from the threat of time. This was
the reason for his claim that 'artists are . . . men who strive to become
inhuman'.[11] He found a sense of wholeness and meaning in the
writing of a poem, and expressed this sense by the image of light as
the all-embracing consciousness of the poet able to triumph over
time and space and to create the uniquely concentrated, uniquely
expansive poetic world which embodies his sense of the wholeness of
the inner self.

Apollinaire's visionary poems are epics of the struggle to create
inner meaning, and he seems to have been speaking of his own
struggles when he wrote in *Les Peintres cubistes: Méditations
esthétiques:*

Other poets, other artists . . . go towards nature and, having no immediate
relationship with her, they have to draw everything from themselves . . . and nothing is expressed unless they themselves have stammered
it, stammered it so often that through repeated efforts, repeated trials, they
sometimes succeed . . . in saying what they wish.[12]

However, he had perpetually to renew the experience of attaining
meaning, and the visionary poems contain great plunges of mood,
from exaltation in the poet's power of creating wholeness, to despair

at the betrayal which time brings. Apollinaire interweaves the humble, despairing ironic 'I' who wanders the streets of Paris and pieces together his past, with grandiose visions of a limitless universe filled with the soaring lights of sun and stars.

The past which Apollinaire sought to restore to himself lies in the very depths of consciousness, and he expressed something of the mystery of these depths by using language of dense but resonant obscurity, making it yet more impenetrable by cutting out explanatory transitions between both individual words and more extended images. Thus, to use Baudelaire's words, 'he expresses that which is obscure and only partially revealed with an *absolutely necessary obscurity*'.[13] His images can never be given a simple, clear meaning, for they are dense and many-faceted and arouse multiple fluctuating associations. This is particularly true of his images of light and shadow, which he imbued with the obsessive inconstancy and ambiguity of images experienced in dream.[14] He used light as a metaphor for his attainment of poetic wholeness and dedication to his consuming vocation, and the metaphor probably represents a lived experience since light is naturally associated with the giving of life and shadow with mortality. However, Apollinaire gave such images greater resonance and density, by associating them with ancient metaphors revived by nineteenth-century poets to express the primordial unity of all matter and the aspiration of the soul to be reunited with light, the divine source of all being.

Apollinaire used images of light or flame when evoking the process by which the dead past is transformed into new consciousness:

> *J'ai jeté dans le noble feu*
> *Que je transporte et que j'adore*
> *De vives mains et même feu*
> *Ce Passé ces têtes de morts*
> *Flamme je fais ce que tu veux*[15]

'Le Brasier' and 'Les Fiançailles' are ardent with light and flame which strangely consume the vivid images drawn from the life of everyday Paris, from memory, and from the writings of the past. The poet transforms all into his 'new universe': 'Tous les mots que j'avais à dire se sont changés en étoiles'; 'Les fleurs à mes yeux redeviennent des flammes'; 'Et les roses de l'électricité s'ouvrent encore / Dans le jardin de ma mémoire'.

Shadow also enters the poem:

> *Et je souris des êtres que je n'ai pas créés*
> *Mais si le temps venait où l'ombre enfin solide*
> *Se multipliait en réalisant la diversité formelle de mon amour*
> *J'admirerais mon ouvrage*[16]

Apollinaire associated shadow with human consciousness and with the material embodiment of the ecstatic vision. He expressed this more clearly in a contemporary article on Braque: 'He no longer owes anything to the things which surround him. His mind has deliberately challenged the shadows of reality so that he creates pictorially a universal rebirth in and from himself.... If he relies on human methods, on material means, it is to ensure that his lyricism shall have substance.'[17]

Apollinaire inherited the conception of poetry as an exploration of the mystery of the universe from the nineteenth-century predecessors, Hugo, Gerard de Nerval, Baudelaire, Rimbaud, and Mallarmé. Like them, he explored the occult, astrology, magic, and the kabbala; he probably read the works of the illuminists, the hermetic philosophers, and the alchemists, as well as the works of *fin de siècle* writers who attempted to revive the ancient mysteries. In short, he was interested in those who suggested that, beyond the visible material world, there is a more profound spiritual world to which the soul aspires and which is revealed only to and by the initiate.[18] There is, however, an essential difference between Apollinaire and most of his nineteenth-century predecessors who sought to enunciate a doctrine and to reveal the inner spiritual meaning of ancient myth and religion. Apollinaire was not interested in doctrine, and while many of his predecessors believed in the existence of a spiritual realm which was independent of them (even while they aspired to union with it), he himself was concerned only with inner experience. His heterogeneous knowledge was at the service of a task which he described in his article on Matisse in 1907 as 'this perilous voyage in search of your own personality. It proceeds from science to conscience and leads to a complete forgetfulness of all that is not in your self'.[19] Thus he used words less to transmit ideas than to give shape to a certain consciousness, and, since he found the creative act to be of such mysterious centrality, he could express its significance only in language that has the resonance of centuries of belief and which yet remains mysterious.

Apollinaire's transformation of past dogma into personal expression can be seen particularly clearly in his treatment of the figure of Orpheus. In 1907 he wrote 'Le Bestiaire ou marchande de quatre saisons', a collection of playful quatrains which he published in 1910 as the 'Cortège d'Orphée', after revision which made it characteristically more mysterious. He substituted Orpheus for the *marchande* and gave him the following lines:

> *Admirez le pouvoir insigne*
> *Et la noblesse de la ligne:*
> *Elle est la voix que la lumière fit entendre*
> *Et dont parle Hermès Trismégiste en son Pimandre.*

Apollinaire gave an explanatory note: '"Soon", one reads in the *Pimandre*, "shadows fell... and from them came an inarticulate cry which sounded like the voice of light". Is not the "voice of light" drawing, or rather, line? And when light is fully expressed all becomes coloured'...[20] Although this grandiloquent language sits uneasily with the Dufy woodcuts which illustrated the volume, it is a prophetic expression of what Apollinaire was to find meaningful in Orphist painting. Apollinaire took his quotation from Pimandre's revelation of the creation, according to which light was 'the primordial form' from which derive the manifold forms of the material world created from the interaction between shadow and the 'voice of light', for the 'voice of light' is embodied in the Word through which truth may be revealed to man.[21]

Apollinaire had probably read Ballanche's *Orphée* (1827–29), since Ballanche also linked Orpheus and Pimandre in Orpheus' account of his vocation:

Is there not a voice in all things?... Are not the objects of nature emblems whose explanation man seeks after having lost it? And must not this explanation be found in speech?... One day... I seemed to see a great light which enveloped the immensity of nature... I had a real but obscure and indefinable sense of the essence and unity of all that exists. I then heard a sound, but a mental sound, and it seemed to be the voice of light. I questioned myself and the voice replied within me.[22]

Ballanche was expressing an idea that was central to the mystic poetry of the nineteenth century: that of the double signification of language. Language, it was believed, had originally had the function of revealing the meaning of existence, but had gradually lost this profound function through being used only for the commonplaces of everyday communication. The mystic poets felt that it was their task to restore the original function of language; thus Mallarmé wrote: 'Poetry is the expression of the mysterious consciousness of certain aspects of existence by human language restored to its essential rhythms; it thus endows our stay with authenticity...'[23] Mallarmé wrote a letter to Verlaine in 1885 about his dream of writing '*the Book* [containing]... the Orphic explanation of the Universe...'[24] Although the letter was not published, Valéry wrote a sonnet on the miraculous creative powers of Orpheus in the 1890s, and at about the same time also an unpublished note called 'Orphisme' in which he invoked 'the explanation of the world by poetry... The poet recreates the world ... by means of unique, eternal, and diverse rhythms'.[25] It is thus possible that some hint of Mallarmé's 'Orphic explanation of the Universe' had filtered through to Apollinaire.

In the nineteenth century the belief in the word as revelation tended to rest on a faith in a spiritual reality behind the material world, but in the early twentieth century there was a widespread change from the search for meaning in doctrines which posited a spiritual reality independent of the individual, to a search for meaning within individual consciousness. Although Apollinaire's language was deeply influenced by the language of the believers, he turned increasingly to the exploration of his inner consciousness, and although he shared the belief in the magical power of the word, there is no evidence that he possessed any spiritual faith in the true sense. Thus he simply used the 'revelations' of Hermes Trismegistus or Orpheus to give depth to his personal experience of the power of words to create form from the formless, meaning from chaos, and (metaphorically) light from darkness. He was not given to questioning the world of the senses, so when he spoke of the unity of the self with the whole, he was evoking a form of consciousness, not enunciating an article of faith. This is true even when he spoke in terms which recall the mystics, as in his assertion of 1918: 'man is man and all that is in nature is in man. I firmly believe that he is a microcosm; moreover, is not every particle of the universe—including the immaterial ether—a microcosm?'[26] In his lecture, 'L'Esprit nouveau', he described how the poet can draw the reader 'into the universes which palpitate ineffably above our heads, into those nearer and yet further away from us which gravitate about the same point of infinity as that which we bear within ourselves.'[27] He was evoking the way that the poet's consciousness can expand to embrace the whole universe—which ranges from the light of the sun to the streets of Paris and from the mythical past to his own individual past—and the way that it can simultaneously concentrate those experiences in itself. He explained elsewhere how he tried to arouse this consciousness: 'You know that my method … is to observe that which comes before my senses in order to deduce from it that which lies beyond my immediate senses. I believe that a small thing—of whatever kind—gives the image of greater and still greater or even smaller things as far as infinity.'[28] Jules Romains expressed similar ideas in a more literal way, which also illustrates the change from interest in the spiritual 'other' to a concern with the mind's processes. For example, in *La Vie unanime*, he evoked the 'radiation' of the mind by listing the images it absorbed in its centrifugal movement, but he also stressed that 'nothing ceases to be internal', and thus suggested that the experience of totality is a mental one.[29]

Apollinaire's poetry, then, represents an aspiration to overcome temporality through the act of creation, an act which depended on an equally strong sense of the reality of the world which is subject to time. His poems rise and fall between the ecstasies of 'les hauteurs où pense la lumière' and the simple pleasures of everyday life:

> *Au tournant d'une rue je vis des matelots*
> *Qui dansaient le cou nu au son d'un accordéon*
> *J'ai tout donné su soleil*
> *Tout sauf mon ombre*[30]

Apollinaire's belief in the significance of sensation formed the basis of his sympathy with the visual arts. Conversely, this sympathy may have influenced the development of his poetry in which Symbolist anti-materialism became weaker as the emphasis on sensation became stronger:

> *J'écris seulement pour vous exalter*
> *Ô sens ô sens chéris*
> *Ennemis du souvenir*
> *Ennemis du désir*
>
> *Ennemis du regret*
> *Ennemis des larmes*
> *Ennemis de tout ce que j'aime encore*[31]

He avoided the doctrinaire because he felt that any sort of generalization weakens the reality of individual experience. 'At a time when scholars and thinkers are abandoning systems,' he wrote in 1911, 'one would not expect artists to devote themselves to such dangerous games.'[32] He found true consciousness in the intensity of the unique experience, and this mode of experience is embodied in the very structure of his poems, which are like constellations of separate images unconnected by the sequential links of rationality and whose only unity is that of Apollinaire's unmistakable voice. The nature of such poetry is best expressed by Valéry's comment that Mallarmé's language 'enjoins upon us to come into being much more than it stimulates us to understand'.[33] However, even if the meaning of Apollinaire's poems is obscure, the emotion which brought them into being is clear and intense, and even if they have no rational continuity, they have an internal consistency given by the mysterious associations between images and by their unique incantatory rhythms. The poems were thus embodiments of the poet's belief that the word brings consciousness into being at the same time that it creates a 'universe' subject to the laws of that consciousness.

Apollinaire made the same assertion about pictorial constructs when he identified the 'voice of light' with 'line'. He did not conceive of such light as a pictorial property, but as a metaphor of the artist's power to create new form. This was the meaning of his words, 'I love the arts of the young painters because I love light above all else . . .'.[34]

Apollinaire's writings on art

1 *Apollinaire and early Cubism* 1908–9

In June 1908, Apollinaire wrote an article, 'Les trois vertus plastiques' for the catalogue to an exhibition at Le Havre. Although the exhibition consisted of Symbolist, Neo-Impressionist, and Fauve paintings, Apollinaire later used the article to open his book, *Les Peintres cubistes: Méditations esthétiques*, and he considered it a sound definition of the principles of Cubism.[35] It shows very clearly how Apollinaire's ideas on the visual arts derived from his poetry, and how his criticism was influenced by the same deliberate mystery that is found in his poems: 'Those who unveil the mysteries of Art and Literature', he wrote in 1914, 'are not its real initiates'; the public should be seduced 'but without understanding, above all, without understanding'.[36]

The theme of the essay is again that of the artist who becomes 'inhuman' because, like God, he creates a new world free from the prosaic limitations of the natural one. Thus, if he is to attain the 'three pictorial vitures, unity, purity, truth', he must exclude all non-pictorial naturalistic elements. This is the meaning behind Apollinaire's obscure invocation:

> *Flame is the symbol of painting and the three*
> *pictorial virtues radiate in flames.*
>
> *Flame has that purity which will tolerate nothing*
> *foreign to it; it cruelly transforms that which*
> *enters it.*
>
> *It has such magical unity that, when it is divided,*
> *each tongue of flame is identical with the unique*
> *flame.*
>
> *Finally, it has from its light that sublime*
> *truth that no one can deny.*[37]

Apollinaire's statement is not original, for the Symbolists had long since emphasized that the painter must transform 'nature' in the creation of the new world of the painting, and his ideas were similar to those which Matisse had put forward in late 1908:

A work of art must be harmonious in its entirety; for superfluous elements would ... encroach upon the essential elements.

Underneath this succession of moments which constitutes the superficial existence of things ... it is yet possible to search for a truer, more essential character ...[38]

Matisse expressed himself more directly than Apollinaire, but he too emphasized that the painting has its own unity which 'will tolerate nothing foreign to it'. There is one significant difference between the two statements, for Matisse wished to express the truth beneath the transience of nature, whereas Apollinaire was fascinated in the phenemenon of transience:

In vain one binds the rainbow, the seasons quiver, crowds rush to death, science makes and unmakes that which exists, worlds move forever beyond our consciousness, our mobile images recur or revive unconsciously, and the colours, smells, and sounds by which we are guided, astonish us and then disappear from nature.[39]

His images themselves are mobile and transient, and ceaselessly flow, melt, and transform themselves into other images. Apollinaire found stability in the creative act, but he did not believe that the work of art, whether poem or painting, should *be* static for this was to him the equivalent of death.

Apollinaire was more straightforward in his next important article, the introduction to the catalogue of Braque's exhibition in November 1908. Again he identified the painter as a semi-divine creator: Braque, he said, 'became a creator ... by drawing from himself the elements of the synthetic motifs which he represents': he was thus able to make each painting 'a new world with its own specific laws'.[40]

His words outstripped the reality of the paintings of that date, but Braque later acknowledged that the two articles of 1908 were true to his own and Picasso's aspirations and that they shared Apollinaire's belief in the necessity of the artist's freedom from the limitations of nature.[41] In his own poetry, Apollinaire showed the possibility of discarding the traditional connections between images, denying fixity of any kind, and affirming the supreme power of the artist to create new structures with their own internal structure, while Braque and Picasso were making their first steps in a similar direction. One tends to forget that the first Cubist paintings seemed to be infinitely mysterious: even the Fauves had accepted traditional relationships between figure and space, solid and void, ground and sky, but Braque and Picasso had begun to break these down. In *Le Port* of 1909 (Pl. 118), Braque made space solid (comparable to Apollinaire's 'solide espace' in a poem of mid-1909[42]); he forced solids into explosive centrifugal movements which destroy their separate identity; he eliminated the ground-plane and background space, and thus created a new structure: a curious oscillating relief in which the luminous planes melt into one another in constant fluidity. Apollinaire's visions—with their soaring movements, abrupt plunges into the past, swoops across space, their brilliant lights and sensuous colours—could not have been further removed from the grave colours and naturalistic subjects of Braque and Picasso's early

Cubist paintings; but their disregard for naturalistic restrictions in the creation of *new* forms was similar in kind, even if the Cubists' more limited subjects made the tension between nature and the created object more concrete and intense than in the visionary poems.

II *Apollinaire and Cubism*, 1909–12

Apollinaire rarely had the opportunity to write about the paintings of Braque and Picasso since they did not exhibit in France after 1908, but when he did write about them—or rather, about Picasso—he continued to use the obscure language of the poems and articles of 1908. A passage written on Picasso in 1912 shows that he continued to make use of the image of light: 'Then he severely questioned the universe. He grew familiar with the immense light of its depths. And sometimes he did not disdain to confide actual objects—a two-penny song-sheet, a real postage-stamp, a piece of oil-cloth patterned like chair-caning—to the clarifying light.'[43] Taken literally, the passage is nonsensical, for the Cubists were not concerned with light as were Delaunay and Kupka. However, Apollinaire was using the image as he had used it before: to symbolize the artist's transformation of matter to create form. The painter's almost magical power of transformation is, indeed, seen most strikingly in Braque's and Picasso's collages in which a scrap of newspaper, for example, can assume the semblance of something other than itself: it may 'become' a bottle or a musical instrument, and yet remain newspaper. Apollinaire did something analogous in poems like 'Les Fiançailles' or 'Zone', when he juxtaposed impressions of contemporary Paris with more abstract visionary images, for his vivid images of Paris retain their own reality and yet are simultaneously transformed into the new reality of the poem.

Apollinaire could thus recognize in Cubism the qualities which he recognized as essential to his own poetry. Cubism, he wrote, 'is not an imitative art, but a mental art which seeks to attain the level of creation'.[44]

Apollinaire moved from Montmartre to Auteuil in 1909 and remained there until 1912. He experienced a renewed interest in the contemporary life of Paris, and although he was reworking his visionary poems, his new poetry tended to be more straightforwardly lyrical. This period coincided with the development of naturalistic Cubism which he began to defend in 1911. Apollinaire became a regularly employed art-critic in 1910, and, since the readers of reviews of the great Salons demanded information rather than mystification, his criticism became more concrete and expository.

Moreover, instead of having the occasion to write about the work of Braque and Picasso, he generally had to review the work of the naturalistic Cubists which was easier to deal with in plain prose.

Apollinaire was originally suspicious of the Cubist paintings of Gleizes and Metzinger and their group. In late 1910, he ridiculed those who saw a 'plastic metaphysic' in their work, which he described as a 'jackdaw clothed in peacock's feathers' and a 'pale imitation' of the work of Picasso. However, he gradually became more appreciative, and in mid-1911 accepted the name 'Cubist' for a motley group of painters who were trying 'to return to the basic principles of drawing and inspiration'.[45]

He seems to have tried to come closer to the specific formal qualities of the paintings he discussed. About Metzinger's painting he wrote: 'without renouncing the benefits of perspective, this cinematic art ... aims to show us plastic truth in all its guises'—a sound characterization of Metzinger's rather mechanistic juxtaposition of view-points in a more or less traditionally constructed space. He may also have considered a problem previously obscured by the grandiloquence of his language: how the 'univers nouveau' created by the artist could impose itself, and how it attained 'that unity which made it necessary'. The problem was intimated, although not pursued, in his comments on Gleizes' portrait of Nayral: 'it is a good likeness and yet, in this impressive canvas, there is not one form, not one colour that has not been invented by the artist'.[46]

Apollinaire did not use the image of light in these more sober articles, and his only reference to it was factual, as when he described 'the contrast of dark forms and light areas' of naturalistic Cubism.[47] However, in 1912 light again became central to his criticism, and when he spoke of the Salon des Indépendants of 1912, he spoke as a prophet with the gift of illumination:

for seven years, I have spoken truths about contemporary art ... which no one else has dared to say. These truths were as blinding as a truth which is too bright. However, I had the satisfaction of knowing that they enlightened an élite. One soon became used to the clarifying light. My flames have even ignited other torches. Today I am no longer alone in defending the discipline of the new French schools.[48]

III *Apollinaire's definition of pictorial Orphism:*
'Orphisme, peinture pure, simultanéité' 1912–14

Apollinaire sought meaning at the heart of transience: he tried to embody the mobile, the passing, and the unresolved, and he avoided the expression of coherent theories which would impose a fixity on the infinite mobility of the mind. His most important work on art, *Les Peintres cubistes: Méditations esthétiques*, was conceived in this way, for the 'meditations' are both fluid and discontinuous, and the themes of the new painting—purity, musicality, simultaneity, mysticality—flicker into life and then disappear into the flux. Such themes assume a certain fixity when they are analysed, but this was not the condition in which they were conceived. Apollinaire later said that he was trying to write poems which one could not read 'without immediately conceiving the simultaneity of what they express', and he evidently formed the 'meditations' in the same way in order to create a Simultanist art-criticism in which the 'past, present, and future' are simultaneously present in the reader's consciousness.[49]

Apollinaire composed *Les Peintres cubistes* in the summer of 1912. It is a collage of articles which includes his Symbolist evocation of Picasso's early works of 1905; the 'trois vertus plastiques' of 1908; the manifesto articles on 'la peinture pure' of 1912, and chapters on individual painters based on conversations of that summer. Apollinaire incorporated new material—including the definition of 'Orphic Cubism'—in the proofs in October. Clearly he had no intention of describing the evolution of the new art or giving a coherent interpretation of it, but was trying to give an impression of all that passed in his mind as he meditated on the new art during that summer of 1912; meditated on the past phases of that art, on its future development and on the many different creations and ideas that were evolving at that very time. Apollinaire intended the book to be like his 'conversation-poems' in which 'the poet, at the centre of life, somehow registers the surrounding lyricism'.[50] Apollinaire himself said that the book should not be regarded as 'a popularization of Cubism', but simply as a 'meditation'; his friend, Raynal, remarked that 'in this sort of poem on painting ... his essentially poetic nature excuses him from commenting on and explaining painting as such'.[51]

In late 1911 Apollinaire had been imprisoned for a few days on suspicion of having stolen the *Mona Lisa* from the Louvre. This was a traumatic experience, which confirmed his sense of alienation from a hostile society where his only true friends were the artists and writers who lived on its fringes, and his release was almost immediately succeeded by a series of activities in which he embraced the idea of a modern poetry and a modern art more decisively than before. He wrote a number of revolutionary articles on art in his journal, the *Soirées de Paris*, and he began to write poems which had features in common with his visionary poems of 1908–9. However, Apollinaire was no longer really interested in expressing mystic obscurity: he was inspired more directly by everyday experience, and employed a more conscious modernist imagery, using the Simultanist techniques of the juxtaposition and fusion of diverse images with greater personal immediacy. He was clearly returning to his earlier interest in the creative act, as is shown by his poem 'Zone'—a powerful expression of the poet's power of transcending localized space and sequential time, in which an everyday conversational tone co-exists with more exalted visionary language, and ancient mystery, childhood memory, and modern image are fused together so that each adds its dimension to the new 'time' of the poem.[52]

Apollinaire also made use of the resonance of the past in his writings on art. Thus, in his first significant article of 1912, 'Du Sujet dans le peinture moderne', he used a classical source—the story of Apelles' line—to justify the contemporary developments towards an art of 'pure aesthetic pleasure'.[53] However, his most conspicuous, subtle, complex—and most questionable—use of this principle occurred in his invention of the term 'Orphism'.

I quote here the statements which Apollinaire made on Orphism between October 1912 and March 1913:[54]

It is the art of painting new structures with elements which have not been borrowed from visual reality, but have been entirely created by the artist, and which have been endowed by him with a powerful reality. The works of the Orphic artists must simultaneously give pure aesthetic pleasure, a structure which is self-evident, and a sublime meaning, that is to say, the subject. It is pure art. The light in Picasso's works contains this art which Robert Delaunay for his part is inventing and towards which Fernand Léger, Francis Picabia, and Marcel Duchamp are also struggling.

(October 1912)

Soon new tendencies showed themselves within Cubism. Breaking with the conceptualist formula, Picabia gave himself—at the same time as Marcel Duchamp—to an art which is no longer limited by any rule. Delaunay, for his part, was, in silence, inventing an art of pure colour. Thus we are tending towards an entirely new art which will be to painting what, until today, one had imagined music to be to poetry. This will be pure painting. (October 1912)

Much has already been said about Orphism. This is the first time that this tendency has been shown. It unites painters of quite different characters all of whom have, by their researches, arrived at a more subjective, more popular, more poetic vision of the universe and of life. (March 1913)

Apollinaire has here returned to the ideas of a pictorial structure independent of visual reality which he first formulated in 1908, and, as usual in this context, he has used the image of light (this is his pretext for including Picasso in the group of Orphic Cubists). He also introduces several new ideas: that of a 'non-conceptual' art; that of the relationship between the purity of music and the potential purity of painting; that of the 'sublime meaning' or 'subject'.

Apollinaire's ideas on the 'subject' are curious. He used the word in a relatively straightforward way in his article of February 1912, when he said that 'the subject now has little or no importance', and claimed that: 'the new painters will provide their admirers with artistic sensations by concentrating exclusively on the creation of harmony by means of unequal lights.'[55] He was probably thinking of Delaunay's theories of colour-construction, and possibly of his nearly abstract *Fenêtre sur la Ville. n° 3*, painted in December 1911 and January 1912, and perhaps also of some of Kupka's contemporary works like the *Amorpha* studies (Pls. 132 and 14). In March, Apollinaire still used the word 'subject' in its usual sense in his praise of Delaunay's modern allegory, *La Ville de Paris* 'Now', Apollinaire wrote, 'the artists of the new schools will dare to face up to subjects and to interpret them plastically'.[56]

However, as can be seen particularly clearly in *Les Peintres cubistes*, Apollinaire used the word 'subject' in a more obscure way to indicate the 'new universe' created by the artist. Thus in the material which he wrote during the summer, he criticized both Picabia and Léger for not having confronted the 'true subject'; they, however, were painting works like *Danses à la source I* and *La Femme en bleu* (Pls. 224 and 195) which have precisely what would normally be considered a 'subject'.[57] Apollinaire's meaning becomes slightly clearer if one examines another mysterious comment in his article, 'La Peinture nouvelle' of April–May 1912 in which he stated that the new school of painters: 'wishes to embody the beautiful, independent of the delight which man causes man ... The new artists must [create] an ideal beauty which is no longer simply the prideful expression of the species, but the expression of the universe so far as it has become human through light.'[58] He was again using light as an image for the creative force which makes human meaning of the universe, a meaning which has nothing to do with the depiction of human life. In this sense, Kupka's *Amorpha, Chromatique chaude* and Delaunay's *Fenêtres* could be seen as an 'expression of the universe so far as it has become human through light', while Léger's *Femme en bleu* and Picabia's *Danses à la source I* were still human-centred subjects— subjects which encourage the spectator to examine the relationship between themselves and their models, rather than to become conscious of their own independent life and the creative act by which the artist transforms inert material into a 'new universe'.

Apollinaire was impressed by Delaunay's ideas on the new paint- ing, which were themselves influenced by his reading of Leonardo da Vinci's notebooks. Delaunay conceived of his paintings of light as microcosms of the universe, and he used Leonardo's phrase about an 'eternal subject' which could attain sublimity to give some idea of the profundity of meaning he found in such paintings. These ideas influenced Apollinaire's concept of the 'sublime meaning [or] subject', that is, of painting which was no longer dependent on the human world and which could awaken consciousness of a new kind.

Apollinaire made other statements in mid-1912 which shows that he was thinking about an art that communicated directly without a verbal subject. He claimed that Duchamp had raised the possibility of an art which was based not on 'intellectual generalizations' but on forms and colours which have not been 'translated' into conceptions.[59] In October—perhaps influenced by Picabia's more abstract recent works, like the *Danses à la source II*—he stated that Picabia was 'breaking with conceptualist formula'. Thus, following Delaunay's lead, Apollinaire used Leonardo's words to give substance to his own belief in the work of art as a unique structure which communicates directly with the inner mind by means of its own physicality and without the intermediary of rational concept.

Apollinaire could also have been influenced by an article by Auguste Joly, published in Belgium in July 1912 and reissued as a broadsheet by the Futurists. Joly suggested a relationship between Futurism and contemporary philosophy, particularly that of Bergson which was, he stated, based on opposition to the 'idea'; he traced the conflict between the idea and direct experience back to Plato and to 'the first orgiasts and the first mystics, the Orphics, Pythagoras, many Alexandrians'—precisely the writers who fascinated Apollinaire. He continued: 'the adherents of the "direct sense" of things and of life should truly be called mystics', concluding in Apollinairean tones: 'the painting should no longer resemble nature, it should resemble itself and should [thus] confer its own authenticity.'[60]

Since the development of pure painting was strongly influenced by the example of music, which communicates profound emotion without having a recognizable subject, it is not surprising that Apollinaire should have chosen a word with strong musical associations to characterize the new art. However, although he did write about the relationship between painting and music, he did not do so in his published statements on Orphism, perhaps because of the painters' antagonism to superficial analogies between the arts.

Apollinaire first put forward the idea of a pure painting in 'Les trois vertus plastiques' in 1908: 'Flame has that purity which will tolerate nothing foreign to it; it cruelly transforms that which enters it.' At this stage, he did not identify pure painting with abstract painting. However, in February 1912, he wrote: 'We are... moving towards an entirely new art which will stand in relation to painting, as envisaged until now, as music stands to literature. It will be 'pure' painting.'[61] This is the first time that Apollinaire explicitly mentions the relationship between the two arts. Although the idea was being revived in Paris at this time—notably by Kupka and Picabia—Kupka was then the only painter in Paris to have painted fully developed pure 'musicalist' works (see Pl. II). Apollinaire was probably also influenced by Kandinsky's *Ueber das Geistige in der Kunst*, to which Delaunay may have drawn his attention and which contained the most developed theory of the relationship between non-representational art and music. Kandinsky distinguished between melodic and symphonic form, and Apollinaire made the same distinction in an article on the Futurist exhibition, in which he suggested that the French painters had developed only melodic form and that they could learn from the Futurists' ideas on 'symphonic form'.[62] Although Delaunay speculated on the relationship between painting and music in the first months of 1912, by spring or early summer he was following the precepts in Leonardo's notebooks and began to discriminate between the visual and auditory arts, claiming that only the former could embody 'simultaneity', the essence of life.[63] Apollinaire's interest in Simultanism would have attracted him to this concept, and during the summer he too began to distinguish between the arts, claiming that Picabia's art was closely related to music, although music operated by suggestion, while painting communicated its meaning directly.[64] Many of Picabia's works of that summer—*Tarantella*, *Musique de Procession*—had musical associations, and, particularly in the *Danses à la source*, he attempted to use colour freely in a musicalist way. Apollinaire also discussed the relationship between the two arts with Picabia's wife, Gabrielle Buffet, who claimed that she influenced Apollinaire's choice of the word 'Orphism' for the new movement because she had stressed the relationship between the purity of music and the potential purity of painting. In any case, she was a musician, and since she was the only one of the three who knew anything about music, she may have clarified their ideas about its specific properties.[65] Apollinaire may also have learnt to be cautious about too close an identification of the two arts through Kupka's apparent objections to the way in which the poet had stressed the musical qualities of his painting.

Apollinaire stated in *Les Peintres cubistes* that Duchamp's art, 'which strives to give aesthetic form to musical perceptions of nature, forswears the caprice and the inexpressive arabesque of music'.[66] The comment is puzzling, for Duchamp was never interested in the musical analogy, but it was one of Apollinaire's most truly Orphic statements since Orphism was founded on the belief that all existence is animated and united by an inner life, soul, or essence which is regulated by 'rhythm' and 'number' (the belief underlies the myth of Orpheus' power over animals and plants). It would have appealed to Apollinaire because of his fascination by the question of what it is, in words or paint or sounds, that can give the artist power over his world; hence it is possible that the phrase 'musical perceptions of nature' refers to the artist's awareness of the inner life of form. This seems to have little to do with Duchamp, who was certainly not a mystic although he was interested in the power of form to express wordless inner experience; but Apollinaire may simply have used the ambiguous phrase in his characteristic way to draw the imagination to explore a dense web of obscure intimations.

It is possible that Apollinaire used the term 'Orphism' for the new painting because the purest example of that painting—Kupka's *Amorpha, Fugue en deux couleurs* (Pl. II)—had musical associations (there may even have been an association of ideas between the words 'Amorpha' and 'Orphism'). Kupka exhibited his painting at the Salon d'Automne which had opened only eleven days before Apollinaire allegedly used the word in front of his works at the Section d'Or. Since Kupka was interested in the relationship between music and painting, he may have tried to dissociate himself from Apollinaire's classification because he felt that the impact of his painting would be diminished if it were considered simply as an equivalent for music, without being seen as having its own specific meaning.[67]

It must have been all these uncertainties which persuaded Apollinaire to omit the musical reference from his definition of Orphism as it appeared in *Les Peintres cubistes* (although he may also have been following his custom of elimating explanatory matter in both his poetry and his criticism). Nevertheless, the analogy between the two arts confirmed the possibility of a visual art which communicated some inner meaning without conceptual subject-matter. Once this had been recognized, it became equally important to explore the specific mode of expression of each art. Thus, the assertion of the relationship between painting and music led to a new emphasis on *pictorial* matter, which Apollinaire reflected in a comment in 1913: 'Form and matter are the objects and the subjects of the best today's painters who do not need to trouble themselves with movement, evolution, and other fluidities which are appropriate only for music.'[68]

When, in late 1912, Apollinaire extended his definition of Orphism to include the concept of Simultanism, he was again directly influenced by Delaunay. Apollinaire had always expressed a 'simultaneous consciousness' in his poetry, but, with one exception, he did not discuss Simultanism in the visual arts until 1912, when he himself began a more conscious exploration of poetic Simultanism. The exception occurred in 1908 when Apollinaire was writing those visionary poems in which he most clearly transcended the normal limits of time and space. He then wrote that, if an artist is to create a work which will embody his 'divinity', he must 'embrace the past. the present, and the future in a single glance'.[69] There is a hint here of the psychological experience which Apollinaire found in Simultanism, the creative transformation of past experience into present consciousness.

In 1914 Apollinaire asserted that Braque and Picasso had been interested in Simultanism since 1907, and that it had preoccupied Léger and the Futurists. He continued: 'It was then that Delaunay declared himself its champion and made it the basis of his aesthetic. He contrasted the simultaneous to the successive and saw in it the new characteristic of all modern art.'[70] Apollinaire became interested in Delaunay's painting at the very time that the painter himself was moving from the figurative to the non-figurative expression of simultaneity. He greatly admired Delaunay's programmatic expression of figurative Simultanism, *La Ville de Paris* (Pl. 136) (which may have influenced his 'Zone'), and when Delaunay followed it with his first nearly abstract works, the *Fenêtres*, (Pl. I), Apollinaire embodied his response in the poem 'Les Fenêtres' which was written in the last months of 1912, when he was staying with the Delaunays and sleeping in the studio where Delaunay was painting his *Fenêtres*.[71] He was also editing Delaunay's article, 'Réalité, peinture pure', in which the painter explained why figurative painting could not embody simultaneity.

The poem has a sensual directness and a colouristic brilliance which was unprecedented in Apollinaire's work but which was, of course, characteristic of Delaunay's painting.[72] It opens with the line 'Du rouge au vert tout le jaune se meurt'. Apollinaire has transformed a physiological observation into a musical evocation. Red and green are complementaries which, when placed together, intensify each other so that they attain a high degree of purity and seem to vibrate, expand, or contract at their point of contact; Delaunay exploited such reactions by playing on the way each colour modifies those adjacent to it so that his paintings seem to be in a continual process of being formed from ceaselessly changing colours. Apollinaire commented on Delaunay's ideas on these colour structures in a lecture of January 1913: 'Delaunay believes that if a simple colour really influences its complementary, it does so, not by decomposing light, but by creating all the colours of the prism at the same time. This tendency could be called Orphism.'[73] Delaunay believed that absorption in the mobile colour structure of his paintings could turn the mind towards itself, towards consciousness of its own simultaneity, whereas Apollinaire's experience of the brilliant planes of fluctuating colour set his mind ranging through time and space to embrace the whole world:

Du rouge au vert tout le jaune se meurt

.   .   .

Tu souleveras le rideau
Et maintenant voilà que s'ouvre la fenêtre
Araignées quand les mains tissaient la lumière
Beauté pâleur insondables violets

The self-generating fluidity of such imagery—the way in which each image opens out into, merges with, and creates the next image—is comparable to the way that Delaunay's colour planes generate one another. Apollinaire, of course, used specific images, while Delaunay's expression resided primarily in the abstract colour planes. The difference was appropriate to their material, for the verbal image could suggest multiple meanings without any one of them becoming the static focus as the specific image does in painting (as happened in Delaunay's *Équipe de Cardiff F.C.* (Pl. 151) which he began to paint in late 1912 and which may, in its turn, have been influenced by Apollinaire's figurative Simultanism). Apollinaire used his images to create a multi-layered movement in which each image appears as a melting facet of the poem's colour structure. In the earlier visionary poems, there was an implied continuity—that of Apollinaire's psychological descent into himself—which was often deliberately obscured; the mobile ambiguity of 'Fenêtres', however, seems a more natural expression of the mobility of consciousness. Apollinaire was no longer concerned with the expression of private states of mind, but with the expression of the unreflecting joy of the senses, of consciousness, of creation, in which the poet seems to seize upon the vivid associations which flash through his mind before they are generalized into concepts. The poem is an ambiguous structure in which each image enfolds others; thus a line like 'Araignées quand les mains tissaient la lumière' suggests the infinitude of the poet's consciousness in a single moment of awareness. In terms of Apollinaire's definition of Orphism, such a structure is 'self-evident': it is comprehended, not simply through reference to an external model, but through immersion in the sensually direct yet abstract words. These words have the power to create new existences, as in the image 'Beauté pâleur insondables violets', which is rooted in sensual experience and which yet has it own inner reality. Apollinaire thus fulfilled his early ideal: the creation of 'a new universe'.

The poem owes much to Apollinaire's understanding of contempory painting. It becomes a unity only if the reader participates in its movement, just as the unity of a Cubist or Orphist painting is created by the spectator. This was, however, already a feature of Apollinaire's poetry before he had had any real contact with painting, and his deepest debt to it lay in his realization that the mind could attain a very profound experience through absorption in a simple sensual experience. This absorption could reflect consciousness back on itself, so that it becomes aware of its own being and of its own relation to the external world. This realization enabled Apollinaire to abandon his obscure visionary language and to draw upon his sensations of the light and colour of the natural world to create new and unique structures.

Each of the Orphic painters had his own conception of Simultanism, but it was only Delaunay's that Apollinaire discussed at any length. He did, however, recognize another form of Simultanism—the psychological Simultanism he mentioned in the chapter on Duchamp in *Les Peintres cubistes*, when he stated that all the experiences we have had 'have left traces in our memory' which can be represented.[74] Apollinaire himself had always tried to find a means of expressing the relationship between the individual self and the experiences which have composed it. This was the theme of his poem 'Cortège':

> *Un jour je m'attendais moi-même*
> *Je me disais Guillaume il est temps que tu viennes*
> *Et d'un lyrique pas s'avançaient ceux que j'aime*
> *Parmi lesquels je n'étais pas*
> .   .   .
>
> *Le cortège passait et j'y cherchais mon corps*
> *Tous ceux qui survenaient et n'étaient pas moi-même*
> *Amenaient un à un les morceaux de moi-même*
> *On me bâtit peu à peu comme on élève une tour*
> *Les peuples s'entassaient et je parus moi-même*
> *Qu'ont formé tous les corps et les choses humaines*[75]

He then opposed this fragmented self to the wholeness he experienced in creation. Apollinaire's ideas on the power of memory to regenerate the past have something in common with Bergson's ideas on the creativity of memory, but, more profoundly, they were drawn from his own psychic experience, which made him sensitive to the fact that Duchamp too was trying to embody something similar—for example, he suggested his complex awareness of his sisters by multiplying their images in *Yvonne et Magdeleine déchiquetées* (Pl. 219), while in his *Le Roi et la reine entourés de nus vites* (Pl. 236) he found a more suggestive way of embodying the sinister images into which the subconscious mind has converted personal memories. These 'traces' of past experience certainly do have a 'personality'—of a most threatening kind—but Duchamp did not make them specific. The painting thus awakens haunting, half-formed associations, analogous to those aroused by Apollinaire's deliberately obscure images. Picabia developed this psychological

Simultanism in paintings like *Je Revois en souvenir ma chère Udnie* (Pl. 251).

After the publication of *Les Peintres cubistes* in May 1913, Apollinaire wrote no more of his obscure but prophetic articles on pure painting. He devoted his critical energies mainly to literary polemic, and when he did interest himself in art, his interest in the expression of mental experience drew him increasingly to the surrealistic work of artists like Chagall and de Chirico; he thus turned away from the pure sensual concentration that he had found significant in Orphist painting, towards 'the most modern of stimuli, surprise' that he now found significant in de Chirico's plastic enigmas'.[76]

It was through his understanding of his own poetry that Apollinaire was able to understand the new painting, for his own sense of inner meaningfulness acquired in the process of shaping matter into personal form made him sensitive to the concept of a work of art as a unique structure with its own physical laws which could communicate directly to the inner consciousness without the need for conceptual formulation or recognizable subject. His own experience gave him faith that the spectator or reader could in imagination participate in the act of creation as embodied in form. However, his sense of the very interiority, the inexplicability of creation also led to the obscurity of his utterances on art, for he intended that they should draw the imagination to awareness of the mysteries of art, without explaining it in a way which would destroy the mystery.

Although Apollinaire was fully aware of the implication of non-figurative art, it is difficult to believe that he was really sympathetic to its specific embodiments; this may explain the many inconsistencies of his comments on individual works, and the fact that, after early 1913, he more or less abandoned Orphism to others. Orphism, however, contined; the art that he had illuminated in such brief, fitful, yet magnificent flashes must now be examined more closely in its own terms.

Section II   The Orphist painters

33 Frank Kupka, *Le Bibliomane*. 1896–8 (95 × 152).

34 Frank Kupka, *L'Âme du lotus*, 1898. Coloured drawing and gouache
(38·5 × 57·7).

Chapter 1 Mystical Orphism

FRANK KUPKA (1871–1957)

Kupka became the first artist to exhibit fully developed non-figurative paintings when he showed the *Amorpha* paintings (Pls. II and 82) in the Salon d'Automne of 1912 and the *Plans verticaux* in the Indépendants of 1913 (see Pl. III[1]). They were the first large-scale paintings which were not abstracted from a natural scene or object, and it must have been a shock to come on those huge, inexplicable works which stood out from the other paintings in the Salons by reason of their uncompromising purity.

Most critics reacted with derision or seemingly embarrassed incomprehension, and it remains true that Kupka's originality has never been sufficiently acknowledged—perhaps because his style, with its coarse colours and its lingering debt to Art nouveau, is not a sympathetic one; however, when one is able to see a group of his paintings together, there is something moving in the queer consistency and the sheer physicality of his form of expression. Kupka thought profoundly about the nature of art, and before the First World War he wrote a treatise on it which rivalled the ambition and scope of Kandinsky's *Ueber das Geistige in der Kunst* of 1912. He went further than Kandinsky in considering the nature of the creative process, and in particular the role of the subconscious and the conscious in this process. However, although he began it before the First World War, his treatise was published only after the war, and in Czech, so that he was never able to provide a basis for the understanding of the new art as did Kandinsky and Mondrian.[2]

There is, indeed, something mysterious in Kupka's art and in his life. In his early paintings he often concealed symbolic meaning behind a natural façade, and some of his abstractions seem to have been motivated by his desire to conceal the literal subject of the work. Even the dating of his works is difficult. Most of them are post-dated in an erratic way (partly because Kupka tended to work on his paintings for a very long period or to return to them many years later), and although two recent studies have established a fairly convincing sequence for his works, the precision one would wish for is perhaps not possible to achieve.[3] His life also had its mysteries. He lived in seclusion and it is difficult to know much about him as a person, beyond the fact that he was of great integrity and utterly devoted to his painting. Even his funeral—as recently as 1957—is an example of the mystery that enshrouds him, for it was carried out at a secret place by a secret society.[4] Interpretation of his art is thus difficult and necessarily tentative.

Kupka was deeply interested in the meaning of life, and his attitude may be summed up in the title of an early work, *Quam ad causam sumus* also called *La Voie du silence* (Pl. 35), in which a lonely figure dwarfed by the mysterious sphinxes and the starry skies seems to contemplate the enigma of being. Kupka believed that the true reality was a spiritual one and that it was the function of art to restore consciousness of this reality.[5] Since this reality was immaterial and invisible, he felt it could not be expressed naturalistically. Thus he wrote: 'The organic laws of nature have nothing in common with the laws of the work of art. Nature follows its own evolution, the work of art is the expression of the human soul, or rather of the mind which is itself superior to the evolutionary stage of the material world.' At the same time, he was fully aware that he had to express

35 Frank Kupka, *Quam ad causam sumus* (or *La Voie du silence*), 1900. Etching and aquatint (34·7 × 34·8).

the immaterial by means of the materiality of paint. He approached this dilemna in two antithetical ways. On the one hand, he had had a thorough academic training which encouraged him to express the immaterial allegorically by using forms as equivalents for ideas which can be decoded. On the other, he came to believe that non-representational form could awaken consciousness of the nature of being without needing to be translated into conscious meaning. For much of his life, his painting was to oscillate between 'pure' abstraction and 'code' abstraction. He showed that he was aware of this distinction when he wrote, 'before I was seeking to give form to the idea, now it's the idea of the form which I seek.'

Kupka had a lust for knowledge which ranged from the ancient Indian religions to modern physics, from spiritualism to science (he was at one time a medium), from telepathy to microscopy. The one belief shared by all the thinkers, and systems in which he was interested (by Baudelaire, Leonardo da Vinci, Bergson, Redon, Theosophy, the Veda, astrology, alchemy, and spiritualism) was the belief in a spiritual essence permeating all being and uniting man to the cosmos. He described this as 'a correspondence between the general activity of the universe and the psychic and cerebral activity of a man'. He found this belief confirmed in scientific discoveries about the structure of matter, for unlike Kandinsky he did not turn his back on modern science, and believed that 'the observation of the surrounding world is one of the necessities of becoming conscious of the self.'

He sought a synthesis between the mystic and the scientific, just as Apollinaire sought a synthesis between ancient mystery and the modern world. Indeed, in the range and nature of his non-pictorial interests and in his intentional seeking of mystery, Kupka was closer to Apollinaire than were the other Orphist painters, which makes Apollinaire's omission of Kupka from his public pronouncements on Orphism hard to explain.[6] Kupka exploited the relationship between music and painting which Apollinaire encapsulated in the word Orphism; he was fascinated by the imagery of light, and was the only Orphic painter to share Apollinaire's interest in the antique. In about 1909, at least two years before Apollinaire proclaimed Orphism, Kupka depicted Prometheus holding a flaming sphere composed of concentric circles; since this was a study for his illustrations to Aeschylus' *Prométhée*, and since Apollinaire was interested in the revival of illustrated books, he may have known it.[7] There is also a significant parallel between Kupka's illustration of the demi-god who brought fire and light to man and Apollinaire's words: 'I love today's art because I love light above all else and all men love ... light, they have invented fire.'[8] I have explained that Apollinaire was referring to the artist's divine power of creating 'new worlds' with their own structure and internal meaning; his ideas were related to one of the most important themes of Kupka's writings: how the artist might 'raise himself to the divine' in realizing internally coherent structures which obeyed their own physical laws and not those of nature.

Light was one of the major themes of Kupka's pre-war paintings. Most of the systems of thought in which he was interested were based on the image of light as the primordial form from which all specific forms emerge. Kupka seems to have shared this belief, and painted his first works representing pure light in 1911, giving them structures formed either from circular movements or from vertical planes (Pls. 81 and 96). It is significant that these structures were foreshadowed by configurations in his early nature-based paintings, where they presumably did not have the mystic connotations which they later acquired (see Pls. 46 and 55). Since Kupka emphasized that the painter discovers both the means and the ends of his expression in the act of painting, he probably discovered the emotional significance of pure light in this way, and his experience of the innerness of the discovery would have confirmed his belief in an existence more fundamental than that found in the material world. His belief would have been strengthened by the various spiritual systems which he studied. Thus the image of light had for him a meaning similar to that which it had for Apollinaire: it was an image of the artist's experience of finding inner coherence in the act of creating form. In Kupka's case it is interesting that he continued to paint circular and vertical configurations after he had ceased to paint the image of light, for this confirms the suggestion that the structures themselves had some inner relevance for him.

Even if one cannot fully understand the meaning of Apollinaire's Orphist poetry, one can sense the emotion which makes it meaningful; by contrast, however, it is more difficult to understand Kupka's art. Apollinaire found meaning in the act of creation rather than in the enunciation of a coherent ideology, but it is hard to know from his paintings whether Kupka was trying to translate esoteric doctrine into paint or whether he trusted form to convey its own peculiar wordless meaning.

There is little doubt that Kupka was thinking of himself when he wrote of:

a man who is a revolutionary, at the borders of all that is established ... And does not every man who stays outside the routine course of things and of lives, have some confort—the secret hope of doors open onto new ways which will permit us to escape the heavy social encumbrance with which we struggle.[9]

Kupka was deeply influenced by both spiritualism and anarchism. He was more actively involved in anarchism than were those of his fellow artists who were interested in it (he illustrated books by the anarchists, Kropotkin and Élisée Reclus, and he was friendly with other active anarchists).[10] Anarchism is an extreme form of individualism which maintains that only the destruction of the machinery of the State will allow the full and free development of the individual living in harmony with other individuals. Kupka's early Parisian drawings were a ferocious attack on the injustice, cruelty, and hypocrisy of society (Pls. 37–40), and it is not improbable that he believed that his non-representational works could also have a function in the erosion of the State by awakening consciousness of the individual self in its relation to the whole. His art would thus have a role not unlike the Utopianism of Mondrian or the apparent Nihilism of Malevich.[11] Kupka did not put forward any specific ideology, probably because he believed that this would be to substitute one dogma for another. His spiritualism also, led him away from specific doctrine, for if he wished to express the ineffable, he could not do so in images which anchored the mind to material reality. Thus the primary function of his art was to awaken consciousness, not to transmit particular ideas, and he came to believe that abstract forms could do this in such a way that 'the artist will no longer need to subject himself to the servitude of a programme or even a specific intention'.[12]

There were, however, factors which militated against Kupka's realization of this aspect of his art and which contributed to his life-long struggle between his belief that form contains meaning and his uneasy need to support (and weaken) it by spelling out its implications. He was conditioned by his long academic training, and his many years as an illustrator, to consider that the visual arts should *illustrate* more or less definable concepts. Thus he wrote as late as 1921:

In principle, the art of painting is to articulate a proposition which can be read by means of combinations of graphic and plastic signs and light and colour effects...

Joys are fountains of round and undulating lights. Pleasure; mother-of-pearl ... tickling of lascivious curves, melting warmth. Grief quivers in broken lines; revolt, hatred; angular contrast. Cold falls abstract in mute verticals...[13]

He was influenced by nineteenth-century theories on the possibility of using pictorial qualities as predetermined equivalents for specific ideas or emotions, and he seems to have found it hard to divest himself of the academic procedure of working out the form and content of a work before actually beginning to paint it, as is suggested by his recommendation in the same article that the artist should first study nature in order to find appropriate linear structures and should only then explore colour, the 'mirror of states of mind'. The use of colour as an emotional embellishment to a predetermined naturalistic structure, rather than a constructive element, can be seen particularly clearly in the *Plans par couleurs* and *Plans verticaux (Cathédrale)* (Pls. 103 and 109). Yet Kupka could also criticize this kind of structure on the grounds that it kept attention on the material world, could write of the dangers of codification of the symbolic meaning of colour and line, and could emphasize the necessity of developing non-naturalistic internally coherent structures which would communicate subconscious meaning.

These contradictions in his theory are echoed by contradictions in his paintings. The 'plastic characters' described by Kupka ('lascivious curves', 'undulating lights', 'mother-of-pearl') were strongly influenced by Art nouveau's *stylized naturalistic form*. In his painting, Kupka came surprisingly late to Art nouveau, for its fluid curves and transparent space were at their strongest in his work in certain stylized figures of *c.* 1910–11 (Pl. 106)—after he had developed a form of expression influenced by Fauvism and based on the constructive use of colour (Pl. 59). His non-figurative art was to alternate between this constructive expression and a kind of abstract illusionism based on the naturalistic relationships between light and shade, object and space that are found in Art nouveau. Thus, although the latter kinds of painting do not represent the natural world, they tend to make the spectator strain to decipher them in naturalistic terms, and thus divert his attention from their own being; they simply do not have that concentrated materiality necessary for convincing non-figurative expression. Since these are the works by which Kupka is best known, and since the toughest of his non-figurative paintings (the *Amorpha, Fugue en deux couleurs* and *Plans verticaux III*) are both difficult to see and much diminished by reproduction, they explain why Kupka has never had his due as the painter who took the first uncompromising step into the unknown future of non-representational art.

Kupka's figurative works. The mid-1890s to the late 1900s

Kupka was born in 1871 in Opočno in eastern Bohemia, a region which 'had produced other self-taught thinkers and rustic mystics'.[14] He had a conventional academic training in Prague (1887–91) and Vienna (1891–3), and was the only Orphist painter to have had such a training. As a youth, he was impressed by the Baroque art of his native Bohemia whose illusionism seems later to have influenced his style. In other things than art, Kupka was self-taught: in Prague and Vienna he read voraciously—his reading included the *Veda*, Plato,

Kant, Nietzsche, Schopenhauer, and books on astrology, alchemy, chemistry, and astronomy. He was introduced to spiritualism in Prague and became a medium in Vienna. Few paintings of Kupka's Viennese period have survived. Some of their titles—*Vers les hauteurs éthérées* and *L'Hymne à l'univers*—suggest a symbolic content and introduce themes which were to preoccupy him for many years.

Kupka visited Paris in 1894, settled there in 1895, and attended classes at the École des Beaux-Arts and the Académie Julian. His paintings of the period *c*. 1895 to *c*. 1906 were didactic, symbolic, or allegorical, and were painted in a rather heavy academic style with lumpy forms and coarse bright colour. However, he devoted most of his time to illustration. Until about 1905 he did drawings for anarchist or satirical journals like the *Canard sauvage* or the *Assiette au beurre* (for which he designed whole issues, 'La Paix' and 'L'Argent' (1904), and to which Villon and later Gris contributed); these reveal his disgust at the values of contemporary society. He also did

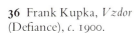

36 Frank Kupka, *Vzdor* (Defiance), *c*. 1900.

illustrations for symbolist journals and for some of E. A. Poe's mystic stories (Pl. 36). In 1903 or 1904 he was commissioned to design the chapter-headings and tailpieces for Élisée Reclus's immense work, *L'Homme et la terre*, a geographical and historical survey of the development of man, published in six volumes between 1905–8; prolonged contact with this work turned Kupka from his absorption in the mysteries of the past, and made him more aware of the present about which Reclus was lyrically optimistic.

Kupka gradually gave up journalistic illustration, and in 1905–1910 devoted himself to the illustration of luxury editions of the classics: the *Cantique des cantiques*, Leconte de Lisle's *Les Érinnyes*, Aristophanes' *Lysistrata*, and Aeschylus' *Prométhée*. Under the influence of Art nouveau and archaic Greek art, these illustrations became increasingly stylized, with curious shadows which harden into separate forms bearing no relation to the volume of the body. Even so, they tended to be conservative in style and content.

The didactic character of Kupka's illustrated cycles was reflected in his early paintings. For example, in *L'Argent* (*c.* 1899) (Pl. 37), he pointed a ferocious moral in the contrast between the young woman

37 Frank Kupka, *L'Argent*, 1899 (81 × 81).

38 Frank Kupka, 'Not a bad business', illustration for *Religions*, special number of *L'Assiette au beurre*, Paris, 7 May 1904.

39 Frank Kupka, 'It won't last long', illustration for *L'Argent*, special number of *L'Assiette au beurre*, 11 Jan. 1902.

40 Frank Kupka, 'Brotherhood', illustration for *L'Argent*, special number of *L'Assiette au beurre*, 11 Jan. 1902.

and the repulsive old man with a transparent belly swollen with gold. Kupka also created more ambiguous symbolist works like *Ballade/Joies* (1901–2) or *L'Origine de la vie* (1903) (Pls. 43 and 47). The striking thing about these works is the literalness with which Kupka attempted to express very complex ideas, and, since similar ideas inspired his non-figurative works, and he often carried certain images (like the interlinked circles in *L'Origine de la vie*) from his figurative to his non-figurative works, one is again confronted with the problem of deciding whether Kupka assimilated certain forms in such a way that they became a natural expression of inner meaning, or whether he used them in a more objective symbolic way to denote a fixed meaning.

In *Ballade/Joies* Kupka combined an intimate personal meaning with a more general one. He depicted the female figure confronted by natural elements like the sun or the sea in a number of early works (Pls. 45 and 50), and he was, I think, representing the human materialization of the life-force. He may have been expressing a similar consciousness in his early painting *Méditation* (Pl. 45). When it was reproduced in his *Album* of *c.* 1907, Kupka gave it the caption 'Meditation: when mountain and valley are one'. The literal meaning of the image is found in Kupka's use of reflections, but the role of the meditator (surely a self-portrait) suggests that Kupka was trying to express a more profound, universal unity. He was impressed by Reclus's aphorism 'man is nature becoming conscious of itself' (he did an illustration for it which is also based on the motif of interlocking circles).[15] The idea that man and nature are one, and that man is separate from nature only in being endowed with consciousness, was common to all the mystic beliefs of the period, and was to be of central importance in Kupka's development of non-figurative art.[16] Kupka wrote that in this painting:

> I want to express something of what I felt when I used to sit alone on the sea-shore ... The sea-shore and the clouds are humming with some unknown joy ... All of us have a desire for joy, for some pure immaterial feeling of well-being. I want everyone who sees the picture to experience such feelings.[17]

Kupka clearly intended that the painting should make the spectator conscious of and at one with the mysterious joyful vibrating life that pervades all being.

Kupka's art of this period had a markedly sexual character, and many of his works seem to have an autobiographical character. Thus in *Ballade/Joies* he apparently depicted both his current mistress (the brunette) and his ex-mistress, a Dane who had died in 1896.[18] The

41 (*left*) Frank Kupka, drawing for an illustration to A. Sova, *Balada o jednom člověku*, Prague, 1907. Ink and white body-colour (30 × 21).

42 (*right*) Frank Kupka, design for a cover for a journal, *Europa, c.* 1900–4. Pen and ink (31·5 × 23·7).

43 Frank Kupka, *Ballade/Joies*, 1901–2. Oil on wood (83·5 × 126·5).

autobiographical content seems to be maintained in *Soleil d'automne* of 1906 (Pl. 48), where the Dane has been joined by a woman very like Eugénie Straub whom Kupka married and who, in a clear reference to Eve, the temptress, is about to pick an apple. The sexuality of both women is strongly emphasized, and gives tension to the provocative glance of the woman on the left and the flaunting stance of the one on the right.

Female nudes played a central role in Kupka's *œuvre* until *c.* 1908. He depicted them either as highly lascivious (as in a number of carnival scenes with young women embracing ugly old men, or in scenes of a witches' sabbath with naked crones astride their broomsticks), or as symbols of truth or innocence (Pls. 41–2). Perhaps the only objective representations of the nude are a group of highly explicit depictions of a copulating couple, etched or painted in water-colour between the mid-1890s and about 1905 (Národní Galerie, Prague); unlike these figures absorbed in their own activity, the nudes in *Soleil d'automne* and *Ballade/Joies* blatantly offer themselves to the spectator—and to the artist. A double meaning is suggested in *Ballade/Joies*, where the blonde seems to offer herself to the natural forces of sun or water (the pose is more explicit in studies for the painting in the Národní Galerie), and the theme of sexual impregnation is also implicit in *La Vague* of 1902 (Pl. 44).

Other works of this period show that Kupka was interested in the generation of life. The most important is the coloured etching, *L'Origine de la vie* (Pl. 47). Their source was the coloured drawing, *Âme du lotus* of 1898 (Pl. 34), in which a spirit in the form of a nude woman rises from a lotus which gives off a brilliant light. The lotus and the figures in Indian dress suggest that the drawing was inspired by one of the Indian religions which Kupka studied and in which the lotus often had sexual connotations as a generator of life; for example, in Tantric Buddhism the lotus was believed to be the feminine principle from whose union with the thunderbolt, the masculine principle, the phenomenal world comes into being.[19] *L'Origine de la vie* suggests that this could well be the source of Kupka's image, for he there substitutes a foetus for the spirit-figure of *L'Âme du lotus* and links the halo containing the foetus to a brilliant illumination which would represent the thunderbolt and which hovers above a faint mist emanating from the lotus. The theme of temptation, and of the opposition between the pure and the lascivious, appears again in *L'Âme du lotus* where the prince pushes aside the dancing women to contemplate the spirit.

These sexual themes are obvious enough, but it is difficult to know what personal meaning Kupka found in them, for the curiously literal images give nothing away. For the moment I can do no more

44 Frank Kupka, *La Vague*, 1902. Water-colour and gouache (41 × 50).

than note the presence of a preoccupation with sexual temptation in Kupka's paintings, and to suggest that he dealt with it in two apparently incompatible ways. Firstly, in early works such as *L'Âme du lotus*, by using the nude as a symbol of the opposition between spirit and matter. Secondly, in conceiving it as part of the life-force, attached to the theme of the generation of life as seen again in *L'Âme du lotus*. This image of the nude was to be absorbed into non-representational paintings on the theme of the generation of life and the evolution of matter which were to preoccupy Kupka until the early 1920s in the important *Création* series of *c.* 1911 to *c.* 1920 (Pls. 70, 72–3, 75).

In early paintings like *La Vague*, Kupka depicted woman and nature as separate, but in later works like *La Baigneuse* of *c.* 1907–8 (Pl. 50),[20] he showed the solid forms of the body being absorbed by the natural element—the circular ripples of water which are very like those in *Ballade/Joies*. Kupka indulged in a sun-cult in which he and his wife (who was the model for *La Baigneuse*) and his step-daughter (the *Petite Fille au ballon*) 'exercised naked in the garden, took cold baths, and bathed in the sun'[21] (see also *Méditation*, Pl. 45). This may have been part of his moral preparation for becoming a great painter, but it is also likely that he was trying to attain the sensation of oneness with the forces of nature, and above all, with the life-giving forces of

45 (*left*) Frank Kupka, *Méditation*, 1899.
46 (*right*) Frank Kupka, *La Femme dans un miroir*, 1903 (55 × 46).

47 Frank Kupka,
L'Origine de la vie (or *Les
Nénuphars*), 1903.
Coloured etching and
aquatint (42 × 40).

the sun that he tried to express in *La Baigneuse*. He then developed the
representation of the human body being dissolved into energy, in his
drawings of his step-daughter playing with a ball (Pls. 61–4) of *c.*
1908–10 and in his pastels of the *Femme cueillant des fleurs* (Pls. 91–4) of
c. 1910–11.[22]

In *Ballade/Joies* Kupka added an apparently contradictory dimension by painting the two curious shadows in the left foreground.
They are curious because they cannot be the shadows of the visible
figures. The image of the shadow or reflection of a bodily form was
of some importance to Kupka: he had already, in 1895, painted a
work called *L'Ombre* (private collection, Prague), in which he
depicted a substantial and wholly unshadowy nude which suggests
that Kupka believed the bodily form to be a shadow which hides
some more essential form—a belief common to the many forms of
mysticism in which he was interested. Moreover, if he *experienced* sun
as the life-giving principle, shadow (the absence of light) would
represent a lower, less intense level of life. He referred to shadow in a

48 (*left*) Frank Kupka,
Soleil d'automne, 1906
(103 × 117).
49 (*right*) Frank Kupka,
Deux danseuses, 1905–6
(38 × 46·5).

note said to have been written in 1911: 'seated on the beach in the theatre of nature ... I hear a man rustling ... his shadow slides on the sand like the shadows of Plato's stars. This shadow has something about it that is mysteriously alive.'[23] Kupka first read Plato in the early 1890s, and this passage suggests that he was impressed by the allegory of the prisoners in the cave of material existence in which Plato described how the freed prisoners turned

from the shadows to the images and to the light ... from the underground cave to the sun, while in his presence they are vainly trying to look on animals and plants and the light of the sun, but are able to perceive even with their weak eyes, images in the water which are divine, and are the shadows of true existence ...[24]

It is unlikely that Kupka was influenced by Platonic Idealism as such, but Plato's vivid images would have confirmed his sense of invisible levels of being and may have strengthened his belief that the images of painting could act as intermediaries to these levels of being. He may thus have used philosophical images with as much freedom as did Apollinaire, integrating them with images drawn from other, strictly incompatible, systems of belief—for example, he could have found an echo of Plato's image of material things as shadows of the divine in the central belief of the *Vedanta* in the spirit of life as a transcendant light manifested in specific forms: 'Life comes from the Spirit. Even as a man casts a shadow, so the Spirit casts the Shadow of life and a new life comes to this body'.[25] Kupka saw no conflict between these ideas, for he was less concerned with what they meant in themselves than with what they suggested to him.

It is thus apparent that the meaning of *Ballade/Joies* has to be decoded, for the painting appears naturalistic but contains discrepancies which suggest that it is not, and which nag the mind for explanation.[26] Kupka's message—that bodily forms are unreal shadows and that the shadows on the water are reminders of true existence—can be spelt out. However, although the work was intended to convey 'immaterial joy', it is determinedly material and it is impossible to divert one's attention from the extremely earthy forms of the women.

Kupka went through a period in the early years of the century when he found it difficult to paint or even to see a reason for painting. This may have been in 1904 for he painted little in that year. His 'black period' is said to have been influenced by a tour of the Paris studios which Kupka made in 1903 under the guidance of Jacques Villon (his neighbour in Montmartre), and which apparently shook his confidence in his art.[27] It is difficult to see why this should have been so, since the most advanced styles he could have seen—stylized Impressionism, Neo-Impressionism, Synthetism, and proto-Fauvism—were all fundamentally naturalistic and not very different from his academic naturalism, but he may have been disturbed by the

50 Frank Kupka, *La Baigneuse*, 1907–8 (63 × 80).

51 Frank Kupka, *Divisions et rythmes de l'histoire, c.* 1905. Final drawing for illustration for Élisée Reclus, *L'Homme et la terre*, Paris 1905–8, v. I. Chinese ink heightened with white gouache (31 × 38·6).

52 Frank Kupka, *Autoportrait*, 1905–6 (65 × 65).

fact that most French artists were depicting the life and objects around them, while he was still involved in a complex and contradictory symbolism.

During his 'crisis', Kupka began to read Bergson, which caused him to rethink his idealist philosophy, to reread his scientific books, and to recognize that 'nothing is immobile in nature'. He also began to attend courses on physiology and biology.[28] It was at this time that he began his long task of illustrating Reclus's *L'Homme et la terre*, and this too made him more aware of the real and the contemporary. Some of the illustrations give a clue to his own dilemma, torn as he was between the past and the present, the mystic and the scientific, between direct experience and speculation. In one he depicted an old man bent over his desk and surrounded by bookshelves labelled 'Speculativen', 'Platoniker', 'Materialisten', and 'Neuplatoniker', while a stream of sunlight pours unregarded through a window. Kupka was updating his painting, *Le Bibliomane* (Pl. 33) of 1896–8, a conventional depiction of the conflict between the active and contemplative life, but the new illustration suggests something of the conflict in Kupka's own theory-burdened mind, and this suggestion of an autobiographical element is strenghthened by the fact that Kupka had done a second version of *Le Bibliomane* as a self-portrait.[29] In another illustration Kupka juxtaposed the image of a scientist with telescope and microscope with that of an aged woman in a robe covered with the signs of the zodiac whose body shields the light of a candle from the starlit sky (Pl. 53). This was title design for the chapter, 'La Religion et la science', whose theme was that of the perfectibility of society through education and science. Such ideas

53 Frank Kupka, *La Religion et la science, c.* 1905. Final drawing for illustration for Reclus, *L'Homme et la terre*, v. VI. Black chalk, Chinese ink and white wash (48 × 62·6).

may have induced Kupka to try to reconcile ancient belief with modern science in his continuing search for transcendence. Kupka's changing ideas are best expressed in the passage where Reclus enunciated the theme of his great work:

It is the study of the Earth which explains to us the events of History and this, in turn, leads us to a more profound study of the planet and towards a more conscious solidarity of our individual self—at the one time so small and yet so great—with the immense universe.[30]

This idea was, I believe, of central importance for Kupka. The assertion of the interdependence of the inner self and the external universe freed him from elaborate symbolism of the kind found in the *Ballade/Joies*, for it suggested that personal meaning was inherent in whatever he depicted. The influence of such an idea would have been the stronger, since it has curious similarities to recurrent passages in the *Vedanta* on the relationship between the universal principle and the individual consciousness:

Concealed in the heart of all being is the Atman, the spirit, the self; smaller than the smallest atom, greater than the vast spaces.

.   .   .

We should consider that in the inner world Brahman is consciousness; and we should consider that in the outer world Brahman is space.[31]

Kupka's own words show that he reflected on such relationships: 'It is by sounding the microcosm of our own being that we will find ways to extend the means of unveiling the most subtle states of the human soul: by 'we' I mean the collective self.'[32]

Kupka illustrated Reclus's passage on the microcosm with an image of figures looking out at a star-studded sky, and his other illustrations for Reclus frequently contained representations of light—the light of fire, sun, or stars; circles or waves of light in space. The latter sometimes suggest immense passages of time or immense movements in space (Pls. 54–5), but they often have no precise illustrative function. These configurations were foreshadowed in Kupka's earlier works (in the starry heavens of *Quam ad causam sumus*, the radiant light of *L'Âme du lotus*, or the circular eddies caused by light and tide in *Ballade/Joies*) as if they had some inner meaning for Kupka which was strengthened by images he found in contemporary science or philosophy, or in ancient texts. Thus his sweeping abstract movements in space are reminiscent of the images used to evoke the nature of the universal spirit in the *Bhagavad Gita* and the *Upanishads*:

Even as the mighty winds rest in the vastness of the ethereal space, all beings have their rest in me.

.   .   .

Thus through my nature I bring forth all creation, and this rolls round in the circles of time.[33]

54 (*left*) Frank Kupka, *Progrès, c.* 1905. Final drawing for illustration to Reclus, *L'Homme et la terre*, v. VI. Chinese ink with white gouache (48 × 31·8). **55** (*right*) Frank Kupka, *Internationales, c.* 1905. Final drawing for illustration to Reclus, *L'Homme et la terre*, v. V. Black chalk, Chinese ink and white wash (47·7 × 62·7).

Kupka's mystic belief in the indivisible unity of being was enriched by the scientific discovery that molecular energy was the basis of all matter. He was inspired by a vision of the whole cosmos in constant movement, from the tiniest particle to the largest star, and since man is part of this movement, Kupka may have believed that any representation of the movement of the universe could give the experience of the 'conscious solidarity of our individual self ... with the immense universe'.

Kupka did not begin to express the visionary aspects of his new ideas until about 1910. In the meantime—in the second half of the decade—he painted contemporary life in a direct, non-symbolic way; since he also explored the expressive qualities of colours (which he had never done before, for when he painted his symbolic works he tended to neglect the *physical* properties of paint), it seems as if Kupka had decided on the study 'of the Earth' before tackling 'the immense universe'. He may again have been influenced by the *Bhagavad Gita* in which it was stated that the man who understood the forces of nature would not be their slave, and he himself emphasized that 'the observation of the surrounding world is one of the necessities if one is to become conscious of the self'.[34]

In 1905 or 1906 Kupka and his family moved to Puteaux which was then a rural suburb of Paris and more suited to a sun-cult than was Montmartre. Kupka's retreat from Paris, and his curious austere life, could have been determined by the ethic of the *Bhagavad Gita* which emphasized the need of 'retiring to solitary places, and avoiding the noisy multitudes', and of seeking meaning in work and not in its reward.[35]

56 Frank Kupka, *Dans le Bois de Boulogne, c.* 1907–8 (65 × 65).

Kupka's paintings of contemporary life—such as *Dans le Bois de Boulogne* of 1907 (Pl. 56)—were inspired by Impressionism. It is, however, significant that even in his early works the shadows tend to harden into flat planes of colour which almost seem to detach themselves from the volumes which they should describe. This tendency is stronger in *Dans le Bois de Boulogne*, where the strong, firm verticals of the trees and shadows are curiously combined with the soft broken colours of the figures. The dissociation between colour and volume can be seen even more clearly in the Fauvist studies of Montmartre low life which Kupka painted at the end of the decade (Pl. 59), and in which he at last escaped from his rather cramped stylization of light and began to represent it not by imitation but by force of colour. He no longer attached colour to bulk, as he had tried to do in *Ballade/Joies* or *Soleil d'automne* (Pl. 48) and began to use it with a new freshness and freedom. His interest in experimenting with the intrinsic properties of colour can be seen most clearly in the *Portrait de famille* of 1910 (Pl. 58) which is still fundamentally naturalistic in structure, but which contains so many different ways of using colour that it is impossible to experience it in a coherent naturalistic way. Kupta juxtaposed broken Impressionistic colour with non-representational blocks and dabs which derive from late Neo-Impressionism; he painted radiating bands of mosaic-strokes (not unlike Delaunay's *Paysage au disque*, Pl. 114), and created new kind of space which contrasts oddly with the carefully observed, three-dimensional dog; he employed crude oppositions of pure colour, seen in a striking way on the red shadows and lights on the blue dress of the reclining woman. These oppositions are not used to give substance to the figures, for they have been applied over a naturalistic structure in such a way that they seem to detach themselves from the figures and float on the surface of the painting. Interestingly enough, Kupka used a similar configuration in the *Amorpha, Fugue en deux couleurs* of 1912 (Pl. II) in which the red and blue pattern floats diagonally over a white ground.

57 Frank Kupka, *Étude pour Dans le Bois de Boulogne, c.* 1907–8.

58 Frank Kupka, *Portrait de famille*, 1909–10 (103 × 112).

59 Frank Kupka, *L'Archaïque*, 1910 (110 × 90).

The development of abstraction through the expression of movement

Kupka believed that movement was the fundamental principle of life, and claimed that 'movement, the sensation of movement, determines that of life'.[36] He was fascinated by movement in all its manifestations: by the movement of the body and of thought, and by the invisible movement which animates all matter; he created images which embodied the movement of the mind as it associates different experiences, and painted the ceaseless movement and transformation of evolving matter.

Kupka's first representations of movement date to 1905 when he painted the *Deux danseuses* (Pl. 49), a conventional depiction of a frozen moment; he also did some studies for his illustrations to *Lysistrata*, in which he seems to have tried to suggest the continuity of movement by representing its different phases. However, these were isolated examples, and it was only in the second half of the decade that Kupka began his systematic examination of movement: in about 1907–8[37] he executed at least two drawings of horsemen (Pl. 90), which inaugurated his attempt to embody movement by means of the repetition of vertical planes which indicate the phases of earthbound, horizontal movement, and a year or two later he did a series of drawings of a girl playing with a ball which marked the beginning of his experiments to represent non-gravitational movement in space by means of curving trajectories. Kupka developed the themes of circular and horizontal movement simultaneously: sometimes he united them; at other times he fused them with different themes and motifs; but on the whole, he tended to purify them until he had taken them to the point of abstraction in 1911.[38] These abstractions were the immediate predecessors of the 'circular' *Amorpha* paintings of 1912 and the *Plans verticaux* series of 1912–13.

1 *Circular and curved movement* 1908–12

In 1908 Kupka painted a naturalistic study of his stepdaughter playing with a red and blue ball (Pl. 60). The painting is quite static and nothing indicates that either the girl or the ball have moved, but Kupka then began a series of drawings of the movements of the girl as she bounced and threw the ball which also turned as it moved, representing these movements by curving lines which suggest that the forms left trails in space and which gradually absorbed the solid forms. The drawings are little more than scribbles, but they are suggestive of the way in which Kupka felt his way into the movement and absorbed himself in it. He developed these scribbles in a series of over fifty studies and about a dozen paintings, in which he explored further aspects of circular movement. In one of these

60 Frank Kupka, *La Petite Fille au ballon*, 1908–10 (114 × 70).

61 (*top left*) Frank Kupka, *Study after La Petite Fille au ballon*, 1908–10. Coloured and graphite pencils (20·6 × 13·3).
62 (*top right*) Frank Kupka, *Study after La Petite Fille au ballon*, 1908–10. Pencil (27·3 × 18·7).
63 (*bottom left*) Frank Kupka, *Study after La Petite Fille au ballon*, 1908–10. Pencil (21·2 × 14).
64 (*bottom right*) Frank Kupka, *Study after La Petite Fille au ballon*, 1908–10. Coloured and graphite pencils (21 × 20).

drawings Kupka depicted the girl's head several times in order to represent the continuity of its movement; in another, he repeated the circles representing the ball and linked them by lines which indicate their path in space (Pls. 61–4). Kupka could have been influenced by photographic studies of the phases of movement; these, however, represent movement only on one plane, whereas Kupka was trying to indicate a complex series of movements in space. His awareness of the complexity of movement may have been stimulated by Leonardo da Vinci's analysis of movement.

Kupka deeply admired Leonardo whom he included in his group of 'big blokes' which also contained the anarchist Kropotkin, Baudelaire, the Czech poet Machá—and himself.[39] He was probably moved by Leonardo's exaltation of light and movement as

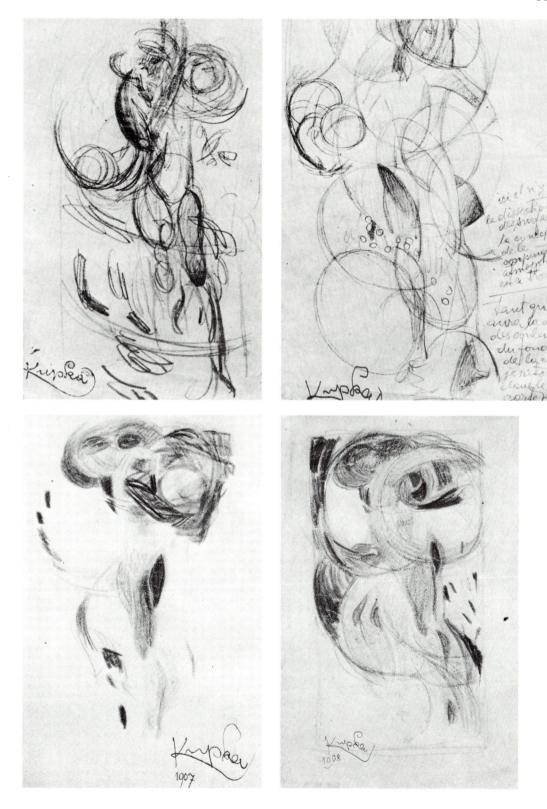

'the cause of all life';[40] Leonardo's ideas on the relationship between the physical movement of the universe and the inner movement of the soul would also have confirmed Kupka's faith in the meaningfulness of representing movement.[41] He probably read Péladan's translations of Leonardo's *Trattato della pittura* and selected texts from the notebooks. Since he had studied the anatomy of the human eye, he would have been particularly interested in Leonardo's analysis of its functioning, which Péladan included in the *Textes choisis* of 1907 and repeated in his in 1910 translation of the *Trattato*. Both contain Leonardo's analysis of movement, accompanied, in the *Trattato*, by a diagram of the movement of the eye as it follows a moving object, and, in both editions, by drawing of a horse and rider whose actions have been multiplied to suggest movement (Pl. 65); although they are not very similar, it is possible that Leonardo's drawings influenced the conception of Kupka's *Cavaliers*.[42] Leonardo drew attention to the complex operations of perception in his analysis of the movements of the eye when it follows the movement of a hand: 'since a continuous quantity is divisible to infinity, the movement which the eye makes as it watches the hand and moves from A to B can be divided to infinity; now the hand which makes this movement changes position and aspect at each movement.'[43] This kind of observation seems very apposite to the earlier drawings in the *Petite Fille au ballon* series (Pl. 61); however, as the series progressed,

65 Leonardo da Vinci, *Cavalier.*

Kupka ceased to represent the separate stages of movement and began to represent the continuity of movement by means of dynamic swinging unbroken curves (Pl. 64). He probably discovered that these abstract forms could express movement through pictorial experiment, but his discovery may have been quickened by Bergson's ideas on movement. Kupka, it may be recalled, read Bergson about 1905–6 and was profoundly impressed by him, and in his *Évolution créatrice* of 1907, Bergson discussed movement in words which read like a critique of Leonardo's analysis, stating that, although the movement of a hand 'from A to B' can be divided into an infinite number of phases, these cannot represent the experience of movement which, when 'felt from within, is a simple indivisible act'.[44] It would thus be impossible to represent the inner continuity of movement by means of a sequence of static images as Kupka tried to do in the *Cavaliers* and the first *Petite Fille au ballon* drawings. Kupka seems to have been influenced less by Bergson's philosophical speculation than by his own experience of painting, for he stated that, although in reality movement is constituted by a sequence of successive presences, these do not accord with 'the single presence of forms and colours in a painting'.[45] It was thus his absorption in movement during the act of drawing, and his observation of how one perceives movement in the picture, that led him to a more synthetic and abstract embodiment of movement.

Small, firm, flat disks appear in some of the *Petite Fille au ballon* drawings; in one, they are generated by the curve of the girl's arm; in others, they represent the ball's movement. They were the source of the forms in the strange little painting, *Le Premier Pas* (Pl. 66) of *c.* 1909–10, whose title (added later) indicates that Kupka regarded the work as decisive in the development of his new art.[46] Although the two overlapping disks and the circle of smaller disks derive from the drawings, Kupka purified them so that they no longer refer to the game of a young girl, but suggest the movements of a solar system in which planets turn on their own axes and revolve around the solar disk (these movements are indicated by the doubling of the solar disk and by the faint halos around the planetary disks). Kupka probably had no precise astronomical theme in mind, for he seems to have been improvising on a motif which had long interested him—the interlocked circles and 'solar' disk seen as early as 1903 in *L'Origine de la vie*.[47]

There are certain similarities between Kupka's *Premier Pas* and Redon's lithographs, *Éclosion* and *Germination* (Pl. 67). *Éclosion* contains the double disks and planetary forms with trails in space; *Germination*, the white orbs on a black ground which are also found in Kupka's painting. About the middle of the decade Kupka painted a tiny gouache (Museum of Modern Art, New York), which

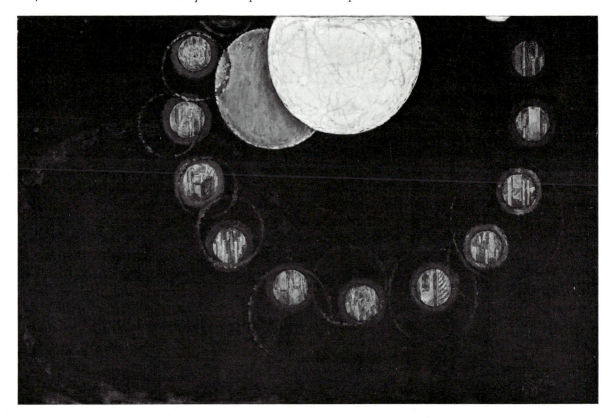

66 Frank Kupka, *Le Premier Pas*, c. 1909–10 (81 × 127).

confirms his interest in Redon for it contains moon-like globes and a curious organic shape like a skull or weathered wood which float in darkness as they do in Redon's lithographs. Kupka shared Redon's fascination with the mysterious origins of life and the formation of matter, and both artists had the problem of expressing mystic intuition in material form:[48] Redon did so by creating mysterious forms which prey on the imagination, while Kupka's painting is so curiously non-committal that one scarcely knows how to look at it.

Kupka had used the motif of two interlocking circles in a drawing for a book-plate for his wife, probably executed during 1905–10 shortly after they were married, which suggests that he gave some intimate meaning to the image he had used in *L'Origine de la vie* to represent the generation of life.[49] He employed overlapping disks or orbs to represent the earth in space in some of his illustrations for Reclus, and the motif of a sphere composed of concentric rings of light appears in one of his studies for *Prométhée*. In fact, the circle appears again and again in Kupka's work—in his most formal oils as in his least conscious scribbles—and it seems to have arisen quite spontaneously, as if it possessed some inner quality which Kupka found meaningful. At times Kupka gave it a specific symbolic meaning, but most often he left its content undefined and open to the imagination. He believed that 'even a scrawl, a daub without importance, will have a meaning',[50] so perhaps the spontaneous emergence of circular configurations gave him faith in the inner significance of his non-representational forms.

The little painting possesses a new kind of space created by the overlapping of the two planes on the flat ground so that they appear to move forward from it. This 'flat-field' painting makes it possible to present pure shapes unaffected by perspectival distortion or atmospheric blurring, and is the basis of the purest form of non-representational painting, because its structure is uninfluenced by the structures of the natural world. Kupka recognized the significance of such pure structures in his comment that, since 'lighting' gives an illusion of modelling and depth, the suppression of lighting was a necessary condition for the return to the basic principles of art; perspective, he claimed, was a trick, and space should be represented by line and colour alone.[51] *Le Premier Pas* was indeed, his first painting in which illusionist lighting and linear perspective were eliminated. Such a structure may concentrate attention on itself and not on its relationship to the external world, and may thus awaken a

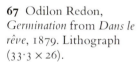

67 Odilon Redon, *Germination* from *Dans le rêve*, 1879. Lithograph (33·3 × 26).

peculiarly intense form of consciousness. This does not occur in *Le Premier Pas* because its internal structure is rather loose and the detail is fussy. The only precedent for its structure is to be found not in painting, but in illustrations to a theosophist treatise, *Les Formes-pensées*, in which the authors attempted to reproduce the forms which they believed were projected by certain mental or emotional states.[52] One illustration (Pl. 69) in the chapter on 'Forms Seen in those Meditating' represented 'The Logos pervading All' and consisted of a yellow disk floating on a flat black ground: this is similar to Kupka's composition of disks on a black ground. The greater complexity of Kupka's painting may have been due to the fact that he was, as I have suggested, trying to represent very complex ideas about the cyclic evolution of life. His work remained close to its original inspiration because he had not troubled to develop a *pictorial* structure; however, by the time he had begun to paint *Amorpha, Fugue en deux couleurs*, he had been working for some time on the pictorial problem of combining different circular motifs, so that he was able to make it a structurally intense work which could deeply involve the consciousness in a way that *Le Premier Pas* could not do.

Kupka developed the circular theme in two directions in and after 1911: one led to the pure abstraction of *Amorpha, Fugue en deux*

68 'Un accident dans la rue', illustration in Annie Besant and C. W. Leadbeater, *Les Formes-pensées*, Paris 1905.

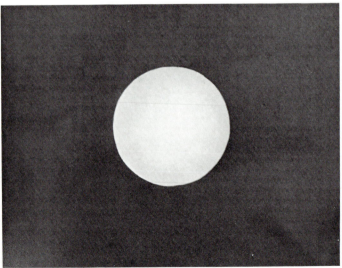

69 'Le Logos pénétrant tous', illustration in Besant and Leadbeater, *Les Formes-pensées*.

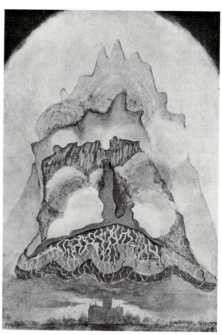

70 (*left*) Frank Kupka, *La Création*, 1911–20 (115 × 125).
71 (*right*) 'Wagner', illustration in Besant and Leadbeater, *Les Formes-pensées*.

couleurs; the other was a more explicit exploration of the theme of the creation and evolution of life. The most important works in this series were *Création* (Pl. 70) and *Printemps cosmique I* and *II* (Pl. 72–3) which were painted between 1911 and 1920 but whose basic structure was realized before the war.[53] Also included in this group were *Naissance* (probably the painting known as the *Ovale animé*, Pl. 79), *Évolution* (now lost), and the *Conte de pistils et d'étamines* (Pl. 75) for which most of the studies were done before 1914, although it was actually painted after the war.[54] The illusionist structure of these paintings suggest that Kupka had been deeply influenced by the Baroque arts which he had admired in his youth in Bohemia, as he used sweeping arabesques which curve into a vortex or swirl outwards over a sphere to express his grandiloquent theme: the creation of form from the formless. Although the works are abstract, Kupka employed illusionistic lighting to suggest modelling and depth in such a way that one is drawn to 'read' them in illusionistic terms, and they thus reveal how strongly Kupka was inclined to illustrate a theme even when he theoretically rejected such an approach.

Printemps cosmique I and *II* are like abstract narratives which owe much to Kupka's study of biology and geology, This debt can be seen particularly clearly in studies for the paintings in which Kupka gradually abstracted natural themes, reducing them to organic shapes so general that they can absorb the forms of mountains, waves, and human heads. In the paintings Kupka created an illusion of globes

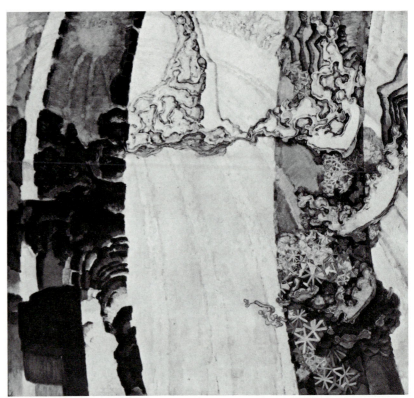

72 Frank Kupka, *Le Printemps cosmique I*, 1911–19 (115 × 125).

73 Frank Kupka, *Le Printemps cosmique II*, 1911–20 (115 × 125).

turning in indefinable space. In *Printemps cosmique I*, he transformed the outer rings of the luminous globe into tiny crystals and forms like molten or weathered rocks, which derive from studies he had done in Brittany a few years before (Pl. 76). He made these suggestions more complex in *Printemps cosmique II*, in which the curved bands which swing over the globe fragment into crystalline shapes like coral or stars, or melt into forms which simultaneously suggest lava, clouds, cells, primeval plant-life, sponges, or fungi. Some configurations suggest human presences—these can be seen more clearly in *Printemps cosmique I* where fleshy pink human forms emerge from the cellular ones. The connection between the evolution of matter and the sexual generation of man is made more explicit in the association between writhing, embracing human forms, foetal shapes, and unspecific organic structures in the *Conte de pistils et d'étamines* (Pl. 75) (itself a suggestive title). Kupka clearly speculated on this relationship, as is indicated by his scribbled note 'phallic forms in humans and in flowers',[55] and his imagination may have been stirred by Redon's graphic meditations on evolution in his suite *Les Origines*, and in particular by lithographs like *Quand s'éveillait la vie au fond de la matière obscure* (1882). As I have pointed out, many of Kupka's early

74 Odilon Redon, *Au Fond de la mer, c.* 1905 (58·5 × 48·3).

75 Frank Kupka, *Conte de pistils et d'étamines I*, 1919–20 (110 × 100).

works were erotic, and ranged from detailed depictions of intercourse to symbolic works suggesting the impregnation of woman by natural forces like the sea or sun.[56] Other paintings are reminiscent of past representations of mythological themes of sexual impregnation—the studies for *Plans par couleurs: Grand Nu* (Pl. 77) remind one of representations of Leda or Danaë—while a later abstraction (Pl. 78) suggests the impregnation of a female figure by the sun.

The greater explicitness of many of the studies for the *Création* series suggests that Kupka's development towards abstraction was partly motivated by a need to conceal a profoundly intimate and overwhelmingly powerful obsession. However, the sexual theme was also fundamental to Kupka's conscious preoccupations, and he would probably have maintained that human generation is but one aspect of the generation of life which the spectator could experience if he imaginatively absorbed himself in the continuous generation of form represented in the paintings. It is significant that in the *Printemps cosmique* paintings, the areas where the small associative forms emerge seem to have been reserved, as if Kupka had planned the major structural parts of the painting but had allowed the smaller forms to emerge while he worked, as suggested by the configurations of the paint. This mode of working again suggests a relationship with Redon, whose pastel *Au fond de la mer* (Pl. 74) is particularly apposite—for its half-formed organisms evolved spontaneously from Redon's manipulation of colour: thus his process of creation was analogous to his conception of the creation of the material world. Kupka's absorption in the generation of form may have been similar, although his creative process was a more complex interaction between the conscious and the subconscious (a central theme of his

76 Frank Kupka, *La Grotte de Théoule, c.* 1905–7. Water-colour (24·5 × 30·2).

77 Frank Kupka, *Étude pour Plans par couleurs: Grand Nu, c.* 1909. Black chalk (24 × 31·2).

78 Frank Kupka, *La Colorée*, 1919–20 (65 × 54).

theoretical writings). He planned his structures carefully, and seems deliberately to have sought ambiguity: in *Création*, he used light and dark illusionistically, so that the heavy opaque red and blue shapes act as gravitational forms which seem to stand below and in front of the lighter one; however, he countered this effect by weaving other colours between the two zones so that no simple naturalistic reading is possible. These ambiguities draw the spectator into the painting, and into further exploration of the ambiguities of the smaller forms which suggest a multitude of associations but which never stabilize into any final form.

Kupka's studies for the *Création* series, in which the figure is absorbed in abstract forces, are closely related to his Reclus illustrations. In one (Pl. 51) he depicted a wave sweeping individual figures into its movement to illustrate Reclus's' evocation of the processes of history:

Men and peoples 'make a turn and then disappear', but they go on to return in an ever vaster circle. From the beginnings of recorded time, the amplitude of the oscillations has never ceased to grow, and the thousands of small local rhythms have gradually merged in a more ample rhythm: the more general oscillations of nations succeed the tiny movements of the life of cities, then comes the great world-wide oscillation which makes the entire earth and its peoples vibrate in a single movement. And while the expansions and contractions swell in size, another palpitation develops in the opposite direction; it takes each individual as centre and regulates his life more harmoniously with the greater circles of the cities, nations, and world.[57]

Kupka's illustration was of a theme seen from the outside, a relatively conventional allegory. However, in the *Création* series, he transformed the theme by absorbing man in the energies of the universe so that his human form is almost lost. Apollinaire wrote that: 'Greek art had a purely human conception of beauty... The art of these new painters takes the infinite universe as its ideal',[58] although at the time he wrote this, in April 1912, Kupka was the only Orphist painter of which it could be said.

Reclus' book concerns the evolution of man in time and in relation to the universe, a theme which Bergson developed in a more abstract way in his *Évolution créatrice* of 1907. He described evolution of life as: 'an immense wave which spreads outwards from a centre and which, on almost the whole of its circumference, is stopped and converted into oscillations...'[59] There is strong similarity between this image and the compositions in the *Création* series, particularly in *Printemps cosmique II*, where spreading waves radiate outwards and are cut by returning ripples which are those which begin to take on specific form. Bergson used the image to embody his contention that evolution had ceased to move forward except at one point—that of man's consciousness—and that man could therefore be conscious of all the stages of evolved matter as simultaneously present in his mind. Bergson's book dealt with two matters which were of fundamental importance to Kupka: evolution and consciousness. If one can see Apollinaire's *Les Peintres cubistes* as a Simultanist book embodying all the poet's ideas, images, and memories of the evolution of the new art as present in his mind in the summer of 1912, one can also see that Kupka's *Création* series embody the consciousness of the evolution of matter that he had acquired through his study of science, history, literature, religious doctrine, and, perhaps most basically, through his creative experience. Indeed, his imagination seems to have been open to anything which confirmed his inner experience. Thus he was struck by the theosophists' theory of cyclic evolution, for he copied out Blavatsky's assertion that everything which evolves returns to its starting point, but with a higher degree of consciousness; this kind of thinking may have influenced *Le Premier Pas*. He himself wrote: 'Every astral body formed by rotations... every movement gives a form to matter, chemical action in minerals, marine plants, land plants, fishes, insects, birds, quadrupeds, and bipeds.'[60] Behind this lay a characteristic mixture of exact science and mystic belief, for Kupka also quoted the theosophist doctrine of the evolution from mineral through plant, animal, and human to spiritual life. A similar emphasis on constant change occurs in Bergson's *Évolution créatrice*:

'The universe endures. The more we study the nature of time, the more we shall understand that duration means invention, creation of forms, continual elaboration of the absolutely new.'[61] The notion of continual creation was deeply fascinating to Kupka, and can be seen most significantly in his process of working in sequence or series in which he could absorb himself in the continuous process of evolving form, a process in which, as he emphasized in his writings, he became ever more aware of form and of its connection with the depths of his inner being.

Because of his concern with this connection, Kupka was deeply influenced by the theory of correspondences and had undoubtedly read one of the most powerful formulations of it in Baudelaire's *L'Art romantique* (Kupka, it will be recalled, greatly admired Baudelaire and ranked him as high as Leonardo da Vinci). Baudelaire, too, speculated on the mystery of the relationship between the one and the many in vivid words which recall Kupka's images of the simultaneous development of different states of matter:

Are the world of the heavenly bodies and the world of the souls finite or infinite? Is the genesis of beings permanent in the great as it is in the little?... The germination, genesis, flowering, the successive or simultaneous, the slow or sudden, continuing or completed eruption of the heavenly bodies, stars, suns, constellations, are you simply the [individual] forms of divine life...?[62]

Baudelaire's question was echoed by Kupka's, 'Isn't there a relationship between the constellations and the structure of organisms in our world?'[63] and would have reinforced his belief in the relationship between the processes of the universe and the processes of creation.

Kupka's interest in the generation of life appeared as early as 1903 in *L'Origine de la vie*. He seems to have found deep meaning in the motif of the interlocking circles which he used in this painting, for in 1909 he transformed it into the basic structure of *Le Premier Pas*. *Naissance* or *Ovale animé* (Pl. 79) is a further stage in this development, and is a more powerful image which makes stronger demands on the imagination than do earlier works. Kupka translated the theme of interlocked circles into three dimensions, so that the flat circles become transparent white or coloured spheres which emerge from radiant depths and are surrounded by dark circling planes which suggest deep space. The ascending movement of the spheres is continuous and without end. It is impossible to determine the scale of the work, since, despite the 'naturalism' of the space, there are no signs to indicate whether Kupka was representing vast or tiny forms. It would indeed by truer to say that he was not representing forms but the genesis of form—a form general enough to evoke both the

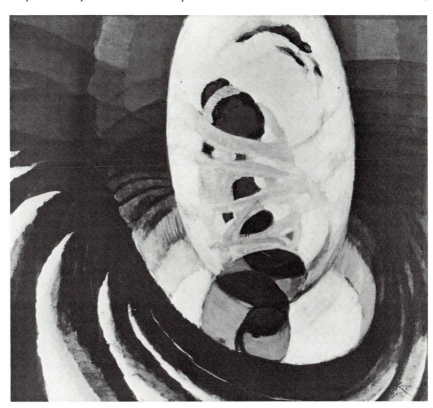

79 Frank Kupka, *Ovale animé* (or *Naissance*), 1911–12 (72 × 80).

heavenly world and the human world without stabilizing into the specific forms of either. As in Kupka's paintings on the sexual generation of life, *Naissance* conceals an explicit theme, for the egg-shape contains a strange dark organic shape which has some relationship to the foetus in the circle in *L'Origine de la vie*. The painting thus seems to reflect ever more complexly Baudelaire's question 'Is the genesis of beings permanent in the great as in the little?' It also reveals something of the complex genesis of Kupka's images, in which ideas from a wide range of sources came to adhere to forms which Kupka had found personally meaningful and thus created an ever more dense web of associations.

The studies for the *Création* series are related not only to Kupka's Reclus illustrations and to his more literal works on the origin of life, but also to the studies for the *Amorpha* series.[64] They may thus throw light on the less explicit content of the *Amorpha* paintings. This series—which includes the two great finished works, several preparatory oils, and over fifty pencil, crayon, and gouache studies—contains both illusionistic and pure works: works which evoke multiple associations and those which discourage specific associations. Some are densely material and have an immediate physical impact, while others are insubstantial and almost retreat from the spectator: the former derive from his Fauvist studies, the latter from his renewed study of the immateriality of light. Kupka began visiting churches in order to study light coloured by its passage through stained glass (one such study he called *Notre-Dame*), and since such light is both sensual and formless, since it makes energy visible and reveals the immaterial, it must have been a source of deep emotion for Kupka. However, the works inspired by this emotion are weak in expression, for Kupka was trying to create an illusion of light, and in so doing he almost destroyed the substance of his paintings.

Kupka's study of the effects of light coming through glass was related to his study of theories of the structure of light and the properties and nature of colour. He studied Chevreul's theories, constructed his colour-wheel, and made observations on his ideas on simultaneous contrasts; he probably also knew something of Maxwell's analysis of the optical mixture of colour, and of Henry's theories of the expressive values of different colour combinations.[65] However, despite his knowledge of the physical properties of colour, Kupka's use of it is generally subjective rather than constructive, and it seems that his *Disques de Newton* series of 1911–12 were not simply explorations of the physical properties of colour, but were symbolic of the structure of the universe.

Les Disques de Newton: Étude pour la Fugue en deux couleurs (Pl. 80) in the Musée National d'Art Moderne is probably early in the series, for it is a rather obvious demonstration of Newton's experiment in which spinning disks composed of prismatic colours are used to produce the impression of white. Kupka painted four main disks, including the mysterious black one behind the coloured ones. The disk is composed of the prismatic colours, red, orange, and yellow; then comes a blue-green, but the blue which should come next in the sequence of prismatic colours is replaced by a violet and is made into a background colour. Other bands are composed of variations on the prismatic colours; they curve over a grey disk which might represent the stage when a disk turns but does not move fast enough to give the impression of white. However, the grey disk finally gives way to the white.

Kupka perhaps felt that this painting was rather static, as he made the Philadelphia *Disques de Newton* (Pl. 81) much more dynamic by eliminating black and grey, so that the colours are purer and more brilliant. The rings are less material and are no longer attached to flat disks, and emerge from a depth which is also formed from spinning rings of colour; thus the sensation of white light emerging dazzling from this dynamic movement is much stronger than in the Paris painting.

Kupka was probably concerned with the spiritual signification of light, since the beliefs in which he was interested used white light as a

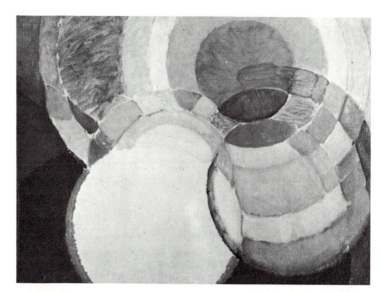

80 Frank Kupka, *Les Disques de Newton: Étude pour la Fugue en deux couleurs*, 1911–12 (50 × 65).

81 Frank Kupka, *Les Disques de Newton*, 1911–12 (100 × 73·7).

symbol for the primordial unity. A Vedic text referred to God transforming 'his white radiance into his many-coloured creation', and the same image was used by the theosophists.[66] Kupka seems to have made a distinction between natural light and essential light, when he referred in his notes to the difference between the lighting which can create an illusion of modelling and of depth, and light in itself which 'becomes an objective element independent of form and colour'.[67]

The rings of colour in the Philadelphia *Disques de Newton* were prefigured by the rings of water in *La Baigneuse* (Pl. 50), where the movement of the body creates ripples which radiate outwards in widening circles, just as the movements of the planets were foreshadowed by the movements of a child's ball. Kupka was obviously receptive to the image of circular movement as an embodiment of the continuity of being, and he may well have been impressed by Leonardo's formulation of this idea: 'Water struck by a stone makes circles around the spot which has been struck. At a long distance, the voice in the air. Still more in fire. Finally [even] more, the spirit in the universe.'[68] Thus *Les Disques de Newton* may have represented the primordial light which consumes all individual form. If this is so, one must also inquire into the significance of the black disk in the Paris *Disques de Newton*, which has a curious power simply because it seems out of place in a painting of pure light. It is possible that this contrast between light and unexplained dark has a meaning similar to that implied in the contrast between sunlight and the unexplained shadows in *Ballade/Joies* and that it suggests that the sun is only an image, a shadow, a reflection of the light of the invisible spirit. This was an image often used by the French mystic poets of the nineteenth century.[69] Kupka's imagery of a light which consumes material forms has some striking similarities to Apollinaire's imagery (particularly in its ambiguity and its wealth of associations). However, once again one is uncertain how to approach Kupka's paintings, for he gave no information as to their possible esoteric meaning, and must therefore have believed that if one contemplated their curiously immaterial dynamism, one would intuitively become conscious of their internal meaning, conscious, that is, of the unity of all existence.

This must also have been the meaning of the *Amorpha, Chromatique chaude* (Pl. 82) which derives more directly from *La Petite Fille au ballon* series, and retained strong traces of its naturalistic origins, for Kupka still used the conventional means of representing form in space: he employed light and shade to create a tonal substructure over which he applied colour in such a way that the relation of form to space is that of traditional nature-based painting, so the picture gives the impression that it is a depiction of an external

82 Frank Kupka,
*Amorpha, Chromatique
chaude*, 1912 (108 × 108).

structure (and in fact it was simply an abstraction of the movement of
the red and blue ball). This prevents the spectator's involvement in
the paintings's inner structure, and presumably blocks the deeper
experience which Kupka tried to communicate. He himself noted
that the moment such lighting was used it gave an impression of
'objectivity'. The *Amorpha, Fugue en deux couleurs* (Pl. II) gives no
such impression because it contains no illusionistic lighting and is
thus independent of the external world. It is also impressive in scale
(being almost seven feet square), and gives a striking proof of
Kupka's daring in presenting this first example of the new, radically
pure art, for it could neither be tucked away in a corner of the Salon
nor explained away as a study for a larger painting, and must have
been the more striking since the works which Kupka had previously
exhibited had been relatively conventional stylized representations
of the external world.

The title, *Amorpha, Fugue en deux couleurs*, suggests that Kupka
intended it to have some musical connotations, but this must be seen
in the light of his attempt to escape Apollinaire's definition of his
work in musicalist terms. His apparent inconsistency was com-

83 Frank Kupka,
*Amorpha, Fugue en deux
couleurs*, 1912 (211 × 220).

pounded by a comment he made in 1913: 'I am still fumbling in the
dark but I think I can find something between sight and hearing and
that I can produce a fugue in colours like Bach has done in music.'[70]
It is clear that he was interested in the relationship between the two
arts, but at the same time he probably wished to be sure that his
painting would not be considered a mere equivalent of music because
it had its own internal structure and its own mode of communication. He was interested in music not only because it suggested
alternatives to the structure of illusionist painting, but because of its
spiritual connotations.

The relationship between music and painting had become almost a
commonplace in Symbolist-influenced art, but Kupka may have
been specifically interested in theosophical ideas on the relationship
between sound and colour.[71] The theosophists believed that all
existence was ordered into planes composed of 'atomic' matter of
increasing fineness, which ranged from the physical plane, the world
of objects, to the highest spiritual plane whose existence can only be
assumed since it escapes normal human consciousness; that intermediate 'mental' planes were accessible to those with spiritual
'sight', and that thoughts and feelings manifest themselves as 'forms'

which can be perceived by those who have developed the capacity to do so. Since music is a mental or spiritual capacity, it too can be 'seen'. Besant and Leadbeater claimed that 'sound produces form as well as colour and ... every piece of music leaves behind it an impression of this nature, which ... is clearly visible and intelligible to those who have eyes to see.'[72] They illustrated their claim with diagrams of the coloured forms 'produced' by different kinds of music. The music of Wagner (Pl. 71) was depicted hovering over a cathedral like a cloud composed of forms which Besant and Leadbeater compared to mountain ranges of brilliant 'flickering, corruscating, scintillating' colour: these forms and colours are so similar to Kupka's *Création* (Pl. 70) as to suggest a direct influence. Besant and Leadbeater explained such phenomena in terms of the vibrations which are emitted by an individual and which transmit his emotions or ideas (expressed by the composer with the help of the musician) to which those who are spiritually aware can respond. Kupka referred to such beliefs in a section of his projected book on 'telepathy, psychopathy, and psychomotricity' where he claimed that 'the mind has the capacity to intercept the waves which another sends into space.' Kandinsky's early theories were deeply influenced by the theosophist concept of 'thought-forms', and Kupka may have read them in *Ueber das Geistige in der Kunst* after its publication in January 1912. He certainly read Blavatsky's *Doctrine secrète* and Steiner's works, for he refers to them in his notes. The strange title, *Amorpha*, may also derive from such sources, for the root of the invented word is obviously *amorphe*, formless, and since the theosophists made a distinction on the mental plane between *rupa* ('having form') and *arupa* ('formless'), *arupa* may well have suggested the new word for Kupka.[73] Thus the title of his work would refer less to the 'material' form of music than to the higher consciousness which it engenders.

One cannot be certain whether Kupka actually believed in particular theosophist doctrines, but the idea that sensation could awaken profound experience on other 'spiritual planes' must have been important to him. He had in fact been a medium, and was still in contact with others interested in such matters, including several members of the Puteaux group, in particular, his friend Alexandre Mercereau who was an important contributor to the spiritist journal, *La Vie mystérieuse*; in 1911 and 1912 the journal contained drawings by mediums; it also published an article 'Le Médiumisme et l'art' on Henri Rousseau (with a reproduction of his *Charmeuse de serpentes*, at that time owned by Delaunay's mother); and photographs of 'les rayons humains'—one of which is very like a Redon.[74] 'Transcendental photography' had been discussed in recent publications in Paris, and had formed the subject of experiments by Professor Baraduc who used photography to 'prove' the connection between 'the human vital force' and 'the living forces of the Cosmos', basing his experiments on the 'impressions of invisible waves, regarded by him as of the nature of light in which the soul draws its own image'.[75] Kupka was pursuing such ideas when he wrote that there is 'a correspondence between the general activity of the whole universe and the psychic and mental activity of man'.[76] However, he also emphasized that this 'correspondence' did not necessarily operate consciously; he could, therefore, abandon any literal and conscious symbolism in order to concentrate on the development of his painting, trusting that such meanings as his paintings contained could operate on an unconscious level.

Kupka did over fifty studies for the *Amorpha*, in which we can follow his complex creative process. Most are in gouache and crayon, and are dominated by the crude vermillion, the hard bright blue, the black and white of the finished work. They are very varied but they are nearly all devoted to the exploration of different kinds of movement or growth, as in the studies for the *Création* series: Kupka suggested the temporal movement of music in a study entitled 'fugue in two colours' in which he repeated two complex shapes like two 'voices' (Pl. 84); another study is like an abstraction of the dynamic circle of figures in Matisse's *Danse* exhibited in 1910 (Pl. 85); another contains a chain of vaguely human forms inscribed 'the arteries', while in another Kupka painted great swirls of broken brushstrokes which recall the celestial movements of the Reclus illustrations (Pl. 86); others suggest plant-growth, sea-spume, or the movement of microscopic forms (Pl. 87). Kupka did not make these associations

84 (*left*) Frank Kupka, *Étude pour Amorpha, Fugue en deux couleurs*, 1912. Gouache (21·2 × 19·7).
85 (*right*) Frank Kupka, *Étude pour Amorpha, Fugue en deux couleurs*, 1912. Gouache (12·5 × 13).

 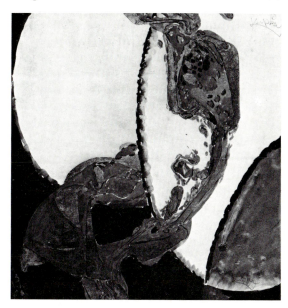

86 (*left*) Frank Kupka, *Étude pour Amorpha, Fugue en deux couleurs*, 1912. Gouache and ink (36 × 37·8).

87 (*right*) Frank Kupka, *Étude pour Amorpha, Fugue en deux couleurs*, 1912. Gouache and ink (36 × 37·8).

explicit because he believed that the same principle animated them all.

Kupka thought deeply about the processes of creation, and in his projected treatise he wrote at length about the relationship between the subconscious and the conscious in the creation of a work of art. He maintained that the subconscious 'furnishes itself' from the observation of nature, and he insisted on the importance of study in developing understanding of the world and of the self. Such studies are, of course, conscious, but they may be absorbed by the memory and transformed into 'cerebral' images which, Kupka stressed, are the more 'dear' and the more 'obsessive' because their origin is unknown. However, he emphasized that 'subconscious creation', based on the accumulation of subjective images, was inferior to a work created from a knowledge of form which the artist could acquire through his use of studies. Kupka stated that the first studies in the creative process were too close to the 'cerebral image', and that the artist 'must proceed by [using] sketches ... plumbing the original image deeper and deeper in order to understand the elements on which his given image was founded.'[77] This part of the process was analytical, but Kupka warned that the 'fundamental first image' might be weakened by too much speculation. Kupka stressed the significance of the subconscious sources of individual forms, but laid no less emphasis on the inner necessity of developing a structure, of finding 'functional' relationships between forms, and thus of creating what he called a 'morphological unity'.

The psychological realism of his account of the process of creation can be observed, first of all, in the extraordinary continuity of certain of his formal configurations (such as the circle motif or the floating red-blue structure seen in both the *Portrait de famille* and the *Amorpha, Fugue en deux couleurs*). These configurations developed from his studies of the external world, but seem to have entered his mind as significant forms whose origins he may not have known. In the second place, this process can be observed in the evolution of *Amorpha, Fugue en deux couleurs*. He had a rich experience of different kinds of form, and his memories of them naturally coloured the many studies for the *Amorpha* with figural, celestial, biological, and musical associations. However, he gradually reduced these associative elements by clarifying his basic forms and eliminating illusionistic effects (Pl. 57). He gradually 'found' his basic forms—the flat black ground and white disks of the *Le Premier Pas*, and the intertwining red and blue motif in the *Portrait de famille, Le Premier pas* (Pls. 58 and 66), and many other works. He discarded atmospheric qualities, and represented space not by means of transparent colour but by means of the strong contrast between the pure colour, the white disks, and the black ground. He was thus able to create a complex temporal experience based on the different kinds of attention demanded by the absolute stillness of the black, the calm concentrated forms of the disks, and the dynamic movement of the colours. That the idea for this structure may have been prompted by the way in which music combines melodic and harmonic form, is suggested by the *Solo d'un trait brun* (Pl. 89) where Kupka developed

88 Frank Kupka, *Étude pour Amorpha, Fugue en deux couleurs*, 1912. Gouache and ink (21 × 22·2).

89 Frank Kupka, *Solo d'un trait brun*, 1912–13 (70 × 115).

the idea in a much more literal way; but the difference between the two paintings shows how important the long genesis of form was for Kupka. There were very few studies for the *Solo* (they are unlikely to have been lost, since Kupka preserved even his tiniest, most illegible scribbles), so the original motif was not transformed into a satisfying, pictorial structure: its composition is diffuse and its temporal structure unpictorial, whereas the more concentrated structure of the *Amorpha* really does make one aware of the simultaneous development of different themes.

Although Kupka worked out the structure of *Amorpha* before he began, he made significant alterations to the structure while he was painting it. Since he also made changes to it some time later, the following observations are based on close examination of the painting in comparison with a photograph of it in its original form.[78] Kupka seems to have enlarged the disks, to have moved them sideways, and to have extended their white over the blues so that they play a more important role than he had conceived in the smaller studies and expand more forcefully outwards and against the reds and blue. The red and blue motif was originally more complex and broken by many more small shapes than now exist, but Kupka painted them out as if he had originally intended that the painting should contain more incident but had only gradually become aware of the power of the great, simple forms as he painted.

Kupka thus used the entire process of painting as a means of exploring the significance of form. The emotion he found in creating pictorial form was similar to that which Apollinaire found in creating poetic form—it is, in fact, interesting that he refers 'pure' poetry when he speaks of his experience. Since his words (written in rather breathless note-form) express something of what he found in creation, they are worth quoting at length:

This perception of form itself, the will towards clear exteriorization, is an apprehension of the universal will. There, the artist is raised to the divine in ordering rhythm, proportions, logical and organic relationships for himself, becoming conscious of his means of expression, of the ends towards which he puts the whole process into movement—of the means which he has created for himself, like the man who creates the word. Edgar A. Poe and Mallarmé have understood this and allow the harmony of their words to sound alone ...[79]

Kupka consciously used the image of radiating circles as an image of the nature of existence, and of the expansion of consciousness beyond the individual self to consciousness of unity with the cyclic movement of the universe. He may have discovered in the long process of creation that the expansion of consciousness occurred through the concentration of consciousness—in his case, through concentration on the evolution of forms which had some mysterious centrality for him. This was the experience behind his transformation of complex associative and symbolic images into a strange non-referential 'new universe'.

II *Vertical planes c.* 1907–13[80]

Kupka's representations of sequential movement by means of the repetition of vertical planes began at much the same time as his studies of circular movement. However, these were conscious experiments, and it is significant that vertical configurations occurred in earlier works just as did the circular ones: for example, the quivering reflections in *L'Autre Rive* of *c.* 1895 (Pl. 99) are similar to the hatched planes in the *Autoportrait* of 1905–6 (Pl. 52); these planes were painted with the greys, the pale and navy blues found in *Nocturne* and *Plans verticaux I* and *III* (Pls. 101, 107, and III); the structure and colours of *Plans verticaux III* can be seen in the mirror in *Femme dans un miroir* of 1903 (Pl. 46). Some of these configurations derive from Kupka's studies of natural effects, but others cannot be so explained. Thus, in a number of very different works, the shadows harden into flat verticals which contrast strongly with the dominant illusionism of the work. These vertical configurations occur so often and in such a wide range of works, in insignificant detail as well as in more prominent structural positions, that they would seem to be the result of an unconscious formal tendency rather than a conscious image or formal element. This background needs to be taken into account when considering the nature of Kupka's representation of movement by means of repeated verticals.

Les Cavaliers (Pl. 90) is probably the first of these experiments, since it can probably be dated to *c.* 1907–8 in view of its relationship to the drawings and etchings of the Bois de Boulogne, in which Kupka stressed the repeated vertical of the trees, the figures in profile, and the shadows; the rather stylish riders could have been those who paraded in the Bois. The *Bois de Boulogne* group has been dated to 1904–8, but *Les Cavaliers* would probably have been executed closer to the later date, for in the other studies of the Bois, Kupka was trying to capture a casual moment in an Impressionistic way, while in *Les Cavaliers* he was clearly interested in the expression of duration, and made the tree-trunks transparent so that they do not interrupt the sequential movement of the riders; he also doubled or trebled several profiles to give an effect of vibratory movement. Although Kupka was probably influenced by mechanical devices for the study of movement such as Marey's chrono-photographs, he could also have been impressed by Leonardo's depiction of the phases of movement of a horse and rider (Pl. 65). Here, however, he was not interested in the implicit circularity of Leonardo's moving forms, and it is significant that he should have used the transparent repetitive vertical and echoing profiles which he had evolved in contexts where he was not concerned with movement.

Kupka's next experiments of this kind, the lovely pastels of the

90 Frank Kupka, *Les Cavaliers, c.* 1907–8. Chinese ink (40·5 × 54).

Femme cueillant des fleurs (Pls. 91–4 and 105), were more imaginative and more pictorial. Kupka showed the woman in profile rising from her chair and bending over the flowers, and he indicated the displacement of her body by shadowy forms like after-images linked by transparent areas slightly darker than the surrounding space. The pastels were probably executed between 1910 and 1911, for they lead directly to the *Plans par couleurs* (Pl. 103) which was painted in late 1911 or early 1912. In the first pastel (Pl. 91) of the series, Kupka made the silhouette of the standing woman dominant and merely sketched the other phases of the movement with fluid Art nouveau contours. He analysed the phases of movement in a more systematic way in the second pastel (Pl. 92) by dividing the action into smaller parts, and perhaps followed Leonardo's observation that a quickly moving body 'seems to tint its course with its own colours' by linking the different phases of movement by blurry passages.[81] This pastel is rather more explicit than the others, and seems to indicate that the figure is unclothed (this is confirmed by a drawing in the Museum of Modern Art where the seated woman is very similar to the nude in the *Plans par couleurs. Grand Nu*, Pl. 102). Kupka divided the background into transparent vertical planes which he strengthened in the next two pastels (Pls. 93–4) so that they almost absorb the shadowy forms of the figure. By merging the separate phases of movement, he was able to suggest the movement of a body through space which is conceived not as a void but as a fluid substance. This characteristic could have been influenced by the Futurists' description of the way a moving object creates 'waves in space'—as

91 (*left*) Frank Kupka, *Femme cueillant des fleurs, c.* 1910–11. Pastel (43·5 × 53). **92** (*right*) Frank Kupka, *Femme cueillant des fleurs, c.* 1910–11. Pastel (45 × 47·5).

93 (*left*) Frank Kupka, *Femme cueillant des fleurs, c.* 1910–11. Pastel (48 × 49·5). 94 (*right*) Frank Kupka, *Femme cueillant des fleurs, c.* 1910–11. Pastel (48 × 52).

they put it in their 1910 manifesto—for it was not present in the staccato forms of *Les Cavaliers*.

The pastel *Ordonnance sur verticales* of *c.* 1910–11 (Pl. 95) is the final development in this exploration of movement, for its transparent planes are identical to those in what is probably the last *Femme cueillant des fleurs* (Pl. 105), except that they no longer contain the human shadow. Through his exploration of this theme, Kupka probably discovered that he could express movement by means of the shifting tissues of colour. He himself commented on the eye's habit of focusing on the human figure, so he was presumably aware that splitting the figure's movement into separate phases thereby resulted in a further fragmentation of 'the fluid continuity of the real'.

In 1909 Kupka painted the *Touches de piano/Lac* (Pl. 97) in a style reminiscent of Kandinsky's early romantic paintings. It is an important work in that it resumes early themes which were to recur in future work. Thus it contains the water, boat, and figures of a painting of 1902, *Le Lac*, although Kupka seems to have transformed the early romantic figures into coupling pairs like those in the *Création* series. Both *Le Lac* and *Touches de piano/Lac* are related to a painting said to have been executed in 1895, *L'Autre Rive* (Pl. 99). Although this painting seems straightforwardly naturalistic, it is possible, since Kupka was interested in concealing symbolic meanings in naturalistic forms, that he used the slightly enigmatic title and the curiously empty scene to suggest a deeper meaning— perhaps intending that reflections in water, like shadows on land, should symbolize the unreality of the material world.[82] The distant

95 Frank Kupka,
Ordonnance sur verticales, c.
1910–11. Pastel (48 × 50).

bank, trees, and reflections are also found in the *Touches de piano/Lac*, but it has less of the soft dreaminess of the earlier works, partly because of its hard, coarse colours, and partly because of the sharp tension between its abstract elements and its representational structure.

At the bottom of the painting, Kupka depicted a hand playing a chord and suggested the reverberations of the sound by long vertical strokes which simultaneously resemble the reflections of the keys on the side of the piano and reflections in the water. They merge with the reflections of the trees and lights, with the trailing leaves of the willows, and with the ripples created by the boat to create complex perceptual ambiguities in which one is never certain what plane of reality one is perceiving. Kupka thus opened up the self-contained image so that it absorbs other images and creates a multiple, dream-like association of ideas. The relationship between the radiation of sound and the ripples of water again recalls Leonardo's phrase, 'water struck by a stone makes circles around the spot which has been struck. At a long distance, the voice in the air.' The union between the visual and the musical is a form of Simultanism, for the chord is played in an instant in time, but evokes another order of time—that of an implied narrative. Kupka was thus expressing the mind's experience of the interdependence of different states of conscious-ness, when it is aware not only of its own continuity but of the infinite complexity of memories, feelings, and thoughts contained in the single moment. The *Touches de piano/Lac* is a rather literal demonstration of the very fugitive form of consciousness that he later tried to embody in *Amorpha, Fugue en deux couleurs* by contrasting the continuity of the 'musical' form with the still concentration of the disks, just as he contrasted a linear motif with a centripetal structure in the *Touches de piano/Lac*.

Kupka took up the theme of descending or ascending notes in a number of works which led him towards abstraction—for example in the sketch for *Nocturne* (Pl. 100) which retains the structure of the keyboard and the rising notes; *Nocturne* (Pl. 101) of *c*. 1910–11 in which the notes remain but their literal source has been disguised; *Ordonnance sur verticales en jaune* and *Plans verticaux I* (Pls. 96 and 107). In the *Nocturne* sketch Kupka distinguished three planes of foreground, middle ground and background, but united them by the repetition of darker strokes across the surface. Beside the sketch he wrote 'dissection du repoussoir', indicating that he was trying to eliminate perspective depth, and in the finished picture there are only the faintest traces of naturalistic space—a few touches indicate a horizon and the heavier tones at the base of the painting suggest gravity—but essentially the sensation of space is created by the 'movement' of the paint strokes.

96 Frank Kupka, *Ordonnance sur verticales en jaune, c.* 1911–13 (70 × 70).

97 (*left*) Frank Kupka,
Touches de Piano/Lac, 1909
(79 × 72).
98 (*right*) Luigi Russolo,
La Musica, 1911–12
(218 × 165).

In the *Touches de piano/Lac*, Kupka represented the movement of thought figuratively, while in the *Nocturne* he dispensed with any figurative references; even so, the painting does evoke a mood by means of the dominant scales of cool blues and greys. It evidently had a close relationship to the *Nocturne* illustration of 1900, but is also said to have been inspired by the memory of a moonlit garden, which suggests that he was influenced by the Synthetists' insistence on the necessity of painting from memory, so that the mind retains only the simplified forms and colours which express the essence of the object as transformed by the artist's subjectivity. Such an idea was probably in his mind when he wrote in 1905: 'I paint only the conception, the synthesis; if you like, the chords',[83] thus suggesting that the dominant colours were the result of the associative and synthetizing powers of the mind. The elaborate '*correspondances*' of *Touches de piano/Lac* were probably a necessary stage in the evolution of a non-representational expression of mood, for Kupka probably realized when he was painting the 'abstract' musical structure that figures and landscape were not necessary for the expression of mood. Perhaps the association with the earlier *Nocturne* occurred during the act of painting as the strokes formed into falling verticals. The title gives depth to the little painting, for the ambiguous blending of the visual, musical, and verbal can draw the mind into an 'infinite reverie'.

99 Frank Kupka, *L'Autre rive*, 1895 (46 × 38).

Although paint strokes had begun to assume a life independent of the demands of representation in Kupka's earlier paintings like the *Portrait de famille*, the *Nocturne* was the first work in which the paint strokes took over the entire painting, and were determined, as Kupka said, 'less by the need of objectification than by the symorphic order of the painting'.[84] The application of small regular strokes (which derived ultimately from Neo-Impressionism) was significant in the evolution of non-figurative painting, for it concentrated the painter's attention on the way in which abstract touches of colour combine to create form, and thus lessened his interest in the relationship between painting and the external world.

Kupka's art was very different from that of the Cubists, but it is possible that he learnt something from it. There is no direct evidence that he ever saw Braque's and Picasso's paintings, but it seems unlikely that an enquiring painter such as Kupka would have ignored Kahnweiler's gallery (and he may have known Picasso when he lived in Montmartre, for he apparently used a model whom Picasso also employed[85]). He was seeking a way of eliminating the distinction between 'the colours of background and flesh' (written on *La Petite Fille au ballon*, Pl. 62) and he could have found it in the way Braque and Picasso used the angular junction of small planes to articulate their paintings. The rhythmic distribution of light and dark planes in

100 Frank Kupka, *Étude pour Nocturne, c.* 1910–11. Pencil (20·5 × 13).

101 Frank Kupka, *Nocturne, c.* 1910–11 (66 × 66).

their analytic Cubist works (Pl. 5) may have helped Kupka free himself from the naturalistic ordering of light and shade, so that he could gradually develop paintings with their own internal structures (as opposed to structures abstracted from naturalistic ones). The new kind of space that he then developed can be seen more clearly in *Ordonnances sur verticales en jaune* (Pl. 96) of *c.* 1910–13, where he used the contrasts between colours, and between transparent and opaque, flat and angled planes, to create a fluctuating relief. The main difference between this sort of painting and analytic Cubism is that the latter embodies object-sensations through the use of tone, while the former uses colour, and that the latter contains linear signs which allude to the external world, whereas Kupka's painting contains naturalistic fragments which draw attention to themselves and prevent any real appreciation of the abstract structure. Once he had freed himself from these, Kupka moved quickly into the pure abstraction which was anathema to Braque and Picasso.

Cubism may also have influenced the *Plans par couleurs* group. In his *Plans par couleurs. Le Grand Nu* (Pl. 102) of *c.* 1909–11 (Salon d'Automne 1911), Kupka attempted to give firmer geometric form

102 Frank Kupka, *Plans par couleurs:Le Grand Nu, c. 1910–11 (150 × 180·8).*

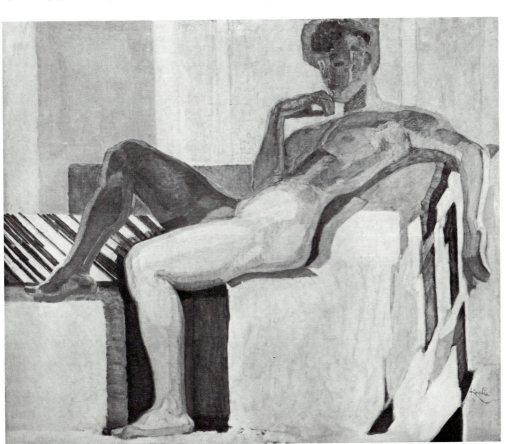

to the curious Fauvism of works like the *Portrait de famille*.[86] Kupka
wrote about the representation of light: 'We who have the conquests
of the Impressionists behind us will enlarge their pointillism into
colour-planes—we know light isn't in black and white but in more
or less scientific complementaries of colour.'[87] He also stated that
light is not obtained by the opposition of shadows, but by the use of
prismatic or near-prismatic colours. His words imply criticism of
Cubism, and yet his combination of prismatic colour and planar
structure suggests that he wished to combine Impressionistic and
Cubistic modes of expression. It is logical, therefore, that his closest
relationship with Cubism was with Jacques Villon's Impressionistic
Cubism, as is shown by the *Plans par couleurs* (Pl. 103) which was
probably exhibited in the Salon des Indépendants of 1912. The pastel
study for the work (Pl. 104) shows that its origins lay in the *Femme
cueillant des fleurs* series (Pl. 105), since Kupka represented the left arm
in different positions as if to register its movement, and showed the

103 Frank Kupka, *Plans
par couleurs, c.* 1911–12
(110 × 100).

104 (*left*) Frank Kupka, *Étude pour Plans par couleurs*, *c.* 1911–12. Pastel (56 × 45·5).
105 *right*) Frank Kupka, *Femme cueillant des fleurs*, *c.* 1910–11. Pastel (42 × 39).

way the body was dissolved by light and how it created ripples in the atmosphere. In the oil-painting, Kupka imposed a geometric framework over these eddies of light; he constructed the figure from vertical or triangular planes which lie parallel to the picture surface, and created depth by overlapping planes of differing degrees of transparency. The angular planes and wedges which he used are very similar to Villon's Impressionistic geometry.

Kupka's painting is more mysterious than Villon's, and, like the *Amorpha, Chromatique chaude*, is immaterial, enigmatic, and withdrawn. The light which emanates from the interior of the *Amorpha* suggests the presence of some unknown form; similarly the figure in the *Plans par couleur* is like a shadow both revealed and obscured by the light which radiates from behind it.

I have already suggested that Kupka used shadows to symbolize the unreality of the natural world in the *Ballade/Joies*. He had continued to be fascinated by shadows and by the 'imprint' or reflection which a figure left in the atmosphere or in water: there are strange shadows cast by the frozen profiles in the *Bois de Boulogne* series (Pl. 57) which are far more assertive than they could be in a 'sous-bois' setting and which draw attention to themselves in a curious way; the 'imprint' or reflection can also be seen in *L'Autre Rive* of *c.* 1895, *L'Âme du lotus* of 1898, *La Baigneuse* of *c.* 1907–8, in *Touches de piano/Lac* of 1909, in *Le Miroir ovale* of *c.* 1910–11 (Pl. 106), and in many other works. The *Petite Fille au ballon* studies and the

106 Frank Kupka, *Le Miroir ovale, c.* 1910–11 (108·2 × 88·6).

Femme cueillant des fleurs series represent the substantiality of space which takes the imprint of the forms passing through it and which transforms them into ever-widening ripples. Shadows or imprints are even found in some of the illusionist non-figurative works—in *Amorpha, Chromatique chaude,* in *Ordonnances sur verticales en jaune,* or in *Printemps cosmique I* (Pls. 96 and 72) where the darker of the two bands crosses and throws a shadow over the sun-form.

Kupka was fascinated by all that modern science could suggest concerning the transcendental signification of matter. He acknowledged the influence of science on painting, and referred to the significance of X-ray studies of tissues; presumably his early X-ray studies would have confirmed his belief that matter is pervaded by the same energies that pervade space.[88] The theosophists drew an analogy between X-rays (which reveal objects 'not visible by the rays of the ordinary spectrum') and the clairvoyant's power of seeing the patterns caused by thoughts and feelings in the higher levels of matter. This idea was reflected by the Futurists, who claimed that their new perceptive powers could 'give results analogous to X-rays' and that their new sensibility 'permitted them to perceive the obscure disclosures of mediumistic phenomena'.[89] Thus Kupka may have been using the image of figures melting into light to express the relationship between the spiritual and the material world. He did this in an almost diagrammatic way in *Plans par couleurs,* indicating the 'material plane' on which the figure exists by overlapping luminous planes so that their transparency becomes opaque and so that they block light in such a way that the figure is composed of an absence of light and is, in fact, a shadow. This suggests that Kupka may again have been expressing his belief that material form is only the shadow of true being. At the same time, light is latent in the figure, which seems as if it were about to melt back into the vibrating light which animates all being.

Kupka painted shadows and reflections until, in mid-1912, he began to paint pure non-figurative works which cannot, of course, contain light and shadow. The fact that he abandoned images which he had found deeply personal must be taken seriously, and indeed it seems probable that he conceived of his pure non-representational paintings not as representations of the unreality of the material world, not simply as embodiments of subjective experience, but as direct intermediaries to true being.

The *Plans verticaux*, which Kupka painted after the *Plans par couleurs*, were of two kinds: those with a flat ground-plane on which more or less flat planes were arranged (Pls. 107–8 and 111); and those with planes jutting into the picture-space and meeting with other planes so that they suggest abstract architectural constructions (Pls. 109–10). Once again his work oscillated between illusionist and purer structures. For example, in *Plans verticaux (Cathédrale)* of 1913, Kupka translated physical characteristics of the cathedral into abstract pictorial equivalents; we can thus decipher its soaring heights, the contrasts between opaque masonry and transparent windows, between white and coloured glass. The naturalistic structure obscures the pictorial one, so that the source of our emotion is not the painting but the conventionalized evocation of the cathedral. That Kupka intended this kind of emotive effect is indicated by a comment he made on a closely related drawing: 'too much the cathedral, it is necessary to draw synthetic form and the essence of nobility from it'.[90] In other words, he was looking for expressive equivalents of the specific emotion aroused by the cathedral. He was, however, wary of such precise equivalents and wrote on another, very obscure, drawing of the period 'too much an equivalent of thought-forms'. This was the phrase used by the theosophists to indicate the forms which the mind projected in the 'mental plane'; thus Kupka's reservations on this point suggest that he felt (as Kandinsky did) that if a mental image were too specific, it would simply draw the mind to a consideration of the known world instead of opening it out on to the unknown (indeed, the theosophists' own illustrations of 'thought-forms' are ludicrously literal).[91]

This may be the reason why Kupka made other *Plans verticaux* less

107 Frank Kupka, *Plans verticaux I*, 1911–12 (150 × 94).

evocative. Thus, in the *Plans verticaux* (*Architecture philosophique*) (Pl. 110) (painted in 1913–23, but realized before the war), Kupka transformed the architectural forms into simple planes of opaque colour to create a work of commanding physical presence. He turned the planes sharply into the picture space and made them meet at right-angles, although they do not dissolve the picture-plane—as they do in *Plans verticaux* (*Cathédrale*)—since they can also be 'read' as planes parallel to the surface. This central ambiguity—which is analogous to that found in Cubism—makes the spectator actively explore the painting. There is no such ambiguity in the *Plans verticaux* (*Cathédrale*), which refers the spectator directly to an external model in such a way that his experience of the painting is

108 Frank Kupka, *Plans verticaux III*, 1912–13 (200 × 118).

109 Frank Kupka, *Plans verticaux (Cathédrale)*, 1913–14 (180 × 150).

relatively passive. One has no idea of the scale of the planes in *Plans verticaux* (*Architecture philosophique*), and this factor too isolates the painting from any external model and allows it to impose its own scale and space. Thus if it is evocative of contemporary architecture (or rather, prophetic of future architecture), this is because there was a relationship between the architect's and the painter's experience of space, not because Kupka set out to imitate architectural constructions.

Kupka probably painted the *Plans verticaux I* (Pl. 107) in the later months of 1912, and the *Plans verticaux III* (Pls. III and 108) in the winter of 1912–13. They were the first of the *Plans verticaux* series constructed from pure pictorial elements which were not abstracted from nature, but were derived in complex ways from the other *Plans verticaux*; their large planes may have derived from the *Plans par couleurs*; their contrast between long hanging or standing opaque planes and a more atmospheric ground can be seen in the *Ordonnances sur verticales en jaune*; while the shimmering insubstantiality of these works has been replaced by the opaque blue, mauve, grey, and white planes of *Nocturne*. This change, from the surface continuity of the earlier works to a composition based on isolated rectangles on a flat ground, parallels the development from the interwoven shifting facets of analytic Cubism to the larger planes on a flat ground of synthetic Cubism (Kupka may have found the detached planes of collage particularly suggestive; see Pl. 194).

In *Plans verticaux I* Kupka arranged the planes so that they lie parallel to the flat blue ground or at a slight angle to it. They form a descending scale (deriving from *Nocturne*), which enters the canvas at the top and flows out at the base and thus creates a movement which continues beyond the finite bounds of the paintings. Although the forms are simple, Kupka arranged them so subtly and ambiguously that the structure cannot be immediately apprehended: he emphasized the flatness of the painting, but simultaneously filled it with space by placing the planes at an angle and suggesting that they grow smaller as they float higher; then he placed the darkest plane on top of the white which seems to push forward from behind the constricting recessive blue. Kupka thus created an unresolvable tension between manifest flatness and infinite indefinable space. He scribbled notes on a drawing related to *Plans verticaux I* which indicate that he was quite conscious of his effects: 'the *repoussoirs* suggest differences in depth / the vertical order calms (silent displacement if need be) ... beware of the appearance of the representation of slabs, too much precision will lead me to this / the intention is to abstract everything...' In other words, he created ambiguity in order to prevent the spectator from finding object-forms in the composition, because he believed that 'the sole presence of forms and pictorial elements is sufficient and must impose itself'.

The composition of *Planes verticaux I* is similar to *Amorpha, Fugue en deux couleurs* in that Kupka had abandoned his earlier attempts to weave 'object' and 'ground' together so that he could present simple undistorted shapes and deploy a mobile theme over a more tranquil one. However, the *Plans verticaux I* is simpler than the *Amorpha* and is the first work in which Kupka gave his forms room to breathe and come slowly to our awareness. Thus, although the 'musical' association is still present, the very simplicity and isolation of the single descending notes gives them a curious significance. The new pure structure concentrates attention on itself and creates a kind of stillness around itself, in such a way as to make the spectator aware of his own consciousness within this stillness. Kupka himself wrote

110 Frank Kupka, *Plans verticaux (Architecture philosophique)*, 1913–23 (143 × 112).

about the *silence* of these paintings. He jotted a few notes on a sketch for the *Plans verticaux III* (Museum of Modern Art, New York): 'The expectation of the / The event of the / Silent vertical planes; and: 'Expectation because there is only the necessary evocation.' Presumably Kupka meant that the painting creates a sense of expectation in the spectator because the associative content is sufficient—but only sufficient—to engage him in looking at the painting. As he looks, he becomes involved in the *pictorial* 'expectation', for the abstract planes are silent and make no verbal communication.

The *Plans verticaux III* is far more austere than *Plans verticaux I*; here Kupka eliminated any subjective reference, any musical association, any hint of movement (as he wrote on an unidentified contemporary drawing, 'there's no movement or any other subjective quality. The presence of the elements constitutes the construction.') Kupka framed the work with austere grey vertical planes which prevent the forms from continuing beyond the painting; he no longer diminished the size of the central planes, so that there is no suggestion that they ascend in space; he replaced the scumbled atmospheric blues and radiant mauves of the earlier work with flatly painted, opaque, sombre colours. He thus created a calm and perfect balance which he kept alive and tense by introducing just the suggestion of depth and movement through overlapping the radiant white by the deep blue plane, and through placing the purple plane at an angle. The resulting painting has an impressive stillness and a dominating presence.

Kupka also wrote 'vertical symorphy by planes' on one of the drawings: the invented word suggests that he saw some link between the *Plans verticaux* and *Amorpha* series, and indeed another note on a sketch for the *Plans verticaux* shows that he considered the circular and vertical compositions as complementary. Another drawing contains both kinds of compositions, which indicates that they were contemporary in conception. Kupka used the word 'symorphy' to refer to the pictorial synthesis of different forms—as a symphony is a synthesis of different sounds.[92] It is difficult to see the relationship between this word and the possible theosophical meaning of the word 'amorpha', as referring to those higher planes of being where matter is not corrupted into specific form. However, Kupka wrote on another contemporary drawing (whose subject I cannot identify): 'Synthesis—the pre-existent form / The elemental through vertical planes / force-planes: / verticals / verti[cal] symorphy'. In the notes for his treatise, he commented that each form contains 'a pre-existent subjective element' whose content is uncertain but which is sufficient to create emotion. As I have pointed out, the vertical planes, like the circular forms, were prefigured in Kupka's earliest work, and he

111 Frank Kupka,
*Localisations des mobiles
graphiques*, 1913
(200 × 200).

explored the theme in depth, gradually isolating and purifying 'the pre-existent form' for something like three years. During this long process, he must have discovered that certain forms have an emotional resonance of their own ('a pre-existent subjective element') which he believed had an elemental significance (much as the horizontal-vertical grid structure of Mondrian's mature works was prefigured even in his early naturalistic work, and was interpreted in a universalizing way by Mondrian). It was thus that he acquired faith in the inner meaning of pure form so that he could say quite simply 'the sole presence of forms and pictorial elements is sufficient and must impose itself'. Evidence suggests—though it does not prove—that Kupka's creative process resulted in an increasing secularization of his thought. Like Mondrian and Kandinsky later, he seems to have turned from the expression of doctrines which purport to convey fundamental truths about the nature of existence, and to have become concerned with consciousness itself. In this context, it is relevant that he did not give the title 'symorphy' to his *Plans verticaux III* when he exhibited it. He thus avoided the suggestion of enigmatic meaning given by the title 'amorpha' and allowed the painting to operate on the spectator as '*silent* vertical planes' whose meaning is not accessible to words.

Conclusion: Illusionist abstraction and pictorial abstraction

Kupka's *Plans verticaux* and *Amorpha, Fugue en deux couleurs* were the first large-scale geometric works to be painted, preceding the developed geometric style of Malevich, Mondrian, and Kandinsky by some time. However, Mondrian took many years to reach this purity, while Kupka's development of pure form was quite rapid; once Mondrian had attained purity, he made it even more absolute until he had eliminated the least trace of naturalistic space and movement, while Kupka's paintings of pure forms were accompanied by symbolist works on creation, by musicalist works, and abstract illusionist works, and in fact had no successors until the late 1920s (it is fair to add that Mondrian developed his mature abstraction in neutral Holland during the war, while Kupka did no painting because he fought at the front, was wounded, and then devoted his time to the Czech war effort).

The development of the non-figurative art of Mondrian, Malevich, Kandinsky, and Kupka was profoundly influenced by their mystical beliefs, but there is considerable difference in the coherence with which they developed their ideas. They all believed that the function of art was to develop man's consciousness by directing it away from the specific forms of the material world. Kupka was aware that this could only be done by excluding such forms from his paintings, but he did not always do so. He drew his ideas from an extraordinary range of sources, whose one common factor was a belief in life as a single essence (conceived either spiritually or scientifically), and as he tried to integrate such ideas into his own system of belief, he seems to have swung between idealism and vitalism, the spiritual and the material, the mystic and the scientific. These apparent changes of direction are reflected in his unusually complex and ambiguous works: in some, he symbolized the unreality of material form; in others, he depicted the absorption of the individual form in light, the spiritual force which penetrates all being; in yet others, he represented the creation of individual form from the formless. In these paintings, he tended to use abstractions of the natural world to illustrate his beliefs, and he gave an account of the genesis of such paintings in which he explained how the linear structure could be suggested by specific motifs in nature, and how colour and tone should be added to this linear structure. He did not therefore fully separate the structure of the pictorial world from that conventionally used to depict nature, so that one's relationship to the painting has analogies to one's relationship to nature. For example, *Amorpha, Chromatique chaude* is an abstraction based on the movement, light, and space of the natural world in which the spectator may, in imagination, absorb himself and thus lose that consciousness of his own separateness by which he defines his being.

The experience demanded by *Amorpha, Fugue en deux couleurs* and *Plans verticaux III* is different because their structures are not analogous to natural structures, and they put a distance between themselves and the spectator who cannot absorb his separate being in theirs. Kupka maintained that there was a form of consciousness different from emotional consciousness which he called the 'super-conscious', and believed that this consciousness could be attained through contemplation of his pure pictorial structures. He also asserted that it is no use trying to communicate specific ideas (for no one can think in the way another thinks), but that pictorial forms can put the spectator in a state of mind in which he can develop his own ideas. This suggests that when he made *Amorpha, Fugue en deux couleurs* and *Plans verticaux III* non-referential, he was aware that the consciousness they evoke could only be silent, and therefore could only refer back on itself, so that the spectator would become aware of his own separate inner being. In a slightly different sense, this was Kupka's own experience: he explained how he became aware not only of his means but of his purposes during the act of painting, and he found the act of creating form so significant that, like Apollinaire, he described it as 'divine'. I have shown how this process consisted of his 'finding' the forms that had been meaningful for him, and of ordering them in increasingly pure and tense structures. His words show that his pictorial form gradually revealed itself to him in a way that made him conscious both of its separate life, and paradoxically of the life of his own 'superconsciousness'. It is significant that he should refer to the purest of his works as 'silent', for it was only in silence that he could attain this heightened, wordless, objectless consciousness.

However, these pure works were rare and most of Kupka's early works illustrated verbal conceptions in semi-abstract form. Thus although he has a clear claim to be considered an Orphist, one can understand Apollinaire's apparent ambivalence towards his art, for, to use Apollinaire's terminology, Kupka rarely transcended his ideas to create new worlds 'with their own laws'.

One must, however, recognize his courage in painting and exhibiting the huge and uncompromising *Amorpha, Fugue en deux couleurs* and *Plans verticaux III*, and acknowledge the fact that, although many of the younger Orphists exploited themes which he had developed (such as the representation of serial or circular movement and of pure light, the expression of Simultanist mental experience, and the development of musical abstraction), they very rarely equalled the extraordinary purity of his major works.

Chapter 2 **Perceptual Orphism**

Delaunay and Léger had laid the foundations for their non-figurative painting by mid-1912 when Léger began painting what he called 'the abstract series of pictures in pure contrasts' and Delaunay was developing his paintings based on pure colour relationships. However, their development of such an art was no more consistent than Kupka's, since they did not foresee abstraction but reached it as a result of trying to express certain forms of consciousness which they also attempted to reach in other ways. Léger's *La Femme en bleu* and Delaunay's *2ᵉ Représentation. Les Fenêtres. Simultanéité. Ville. 1ʳᵉ partie. 3 motifs* (Pls. 195 and 145) were by no means as pure as the abstractions which Kupka painted in the summer and autumn of 1912. Although the natural object still played a part in their compositions, the *structure* of these works is not naturalistic, for Léger and Delaunay had eliminated naturalistic devices for the representation of space or light, and used objects less for their own sake than as elements which add to the physical tension of the works. Then, in certain works of 1913, they excluded even these vestigial objects and created independent pictorial structures 'from elements which have not been borrowed from visual reality, but [have been] entirely created by the artist', according to Apollinaire's definition of Orphism. These pure works were accompanied by figurative ones whose structure was, however, no longer naturalistic.

The Orphism of Delaunay and Léger differed from Kupka's because they were concerned above all with the inner experience of sensation. They were deeply influenced by the Impressionists as well as by Cézanne: that is, by artists who found the deepest personal meaning at the heart of perceptual experience; whereas Kupka was most affected by stylized forms of illustrative naturalism, and was completely uninfluenced by Cézanne and only marginally by Cubism, both of which gave the art of Delaunay and Léger its structural strength and physical density.

Unlike Kupka (and most other important pioneers of non-figurative art), Léger and Delaunay were not inspired by any kind of mystical belief. They both believed that profound experience could be found through perception, and that pure painting could so deeply involve the spectator in its physical being that it could give him an intense consciousness of the essence of life, of its movement, energy, and dynamism. For Delaunay, this consciousness could approach the mystic consciousness of the imminent dissolution of the self in the impersonal movement of the universe, but his experience was a lived and intuitive one, with nothing of Kupka's rather intellectual mysticism. Léger totally repudiated intellectual or metaphysical speculation, and derived his form of expression from his awareness of modern life. Kupka was interested in modern science and technology, but saw them with eyes veiled by the mysteries of the past; while Delaunay and Léger had a whole-hearted delight in the potential of new discoveries to free man from the traditional confines of time and space. They believed in a new realism which took account of what they felt to be an essential mode of consciousness—consciousness of the self's existence, a consciousness found in perceptual experience unclouded by conceptual, learnt experience.

ROBERT DELAUNAY (1885–1941)

Delaunay was always fascinated by the immaterial energies of light, and his search for a way of embodying them led him towards non-figurative painting. In his earliest works he depicted objects made insubstantial by light which gradually absorbed objects in its curving eddies and which later became the sole inspiration of Delaunay's non-figurative paintings of circular forms—forms which were foreshadowed in his early works, just as the formal configurations of Kupka's non-figurative works were foreshadowed in his naturalistic works. Delaunay's sense of the significance of this evolution lay behind his passionate belief in light as the essence of being.

His early themes were those of the Impressionist tradition—landscapes, portraits, and still-lifes—but in 1909 he began to explore two modernist subjects: the city and the Eiffel Tower; through this exploration, he became aware of more profound aspects of modern life and of a new form of consciousness: Simultanist consciousness. Delaunay's change to modernist themes could have been influenced by Sonia Terk, an extremely intelligent woman who seems to have been more receptive to new ideas than he. Movingly, when he was dying in 1941, he called her his 'animatrice' and it is certain that she gave him lifelong encouragement—perhaps even at the cost of subordinating her own gifts as a painter. She made their home an exciting environment—where, as Apollinaire said, they woke 'talking painting'—sharing their love of colour, their enthusiasm for the modern world, and their belief that they could create a new form of expression for that world. This environment was stimulating not only to Delaunay's immediate followers, but to creators as original as Apollinaire and Cendrars. It is more difficult to estimate Sonia Delaunay's contribution to pictorial Orphism, but it would be true to say that Robert Delaunay's evolution as a painter was rather self-contained. His art was, in a sense, less developed than Sonia Terk's when they first met in 1908 or 1909, but it was potentially more constructive, for he had begun to master the discipline offered by Cézanne which never touched Sonia Delaunay, particularly since she seems to have given up painting during the crucial years of 1909 to 1912. It was this discipline which taught Delaunay to think pictorially, to 'reason' from what he saw develop on the canvas, and from one canvas to another. It was through the actual experience of painting that he became aware of new forms of consciousness—and it was perhaps at that stage that Sonia Delaunay encouraged him to interpret his discoveries in more specifically modernist terms.

Seuphor later described Delaunay's curious naïvete:

this man assaulted one with commentaries and demonstrations, repeating the same citations from Apollinaire, the same studio-clichés twenty times over... He had a way of knocking one out with simple truths—'the world is round, old chap, the world is round'—which left one mentally in ruins, paralysed, and without reply. Moreover, a reply would have been useless: Delaunay was incapable of hearing it, so strong a noise did his conviction, his simple idea, make in him.[1]

This is, of course, only part of the truth, for this simple man during four years created an unbroken sequence of beautiful and revolutionary paintings, and it is clear that he thought not intellectually but pictorially. His friend, Maurice Princet, wrote of him in 1912: 'When Delaunay discusses, argues, compares, and deduces, he always does so with palette in hand... He expresses himself in volumes and colour-values; he defends his earlier works with new ones which explain the preceding ones...'[2]

In his first individual works, Delaunay exploited the dynamism inherent in the painting of Cézanne and the Cubists; he was then influenced by the literal modernism of his contemporaries, and sought to express Simultanist experience through the juxtaposition of separate viewpoints or images in more or less traditional illusionist space. However, the non-representational colour-structure of his paintings gradually became stronger as he became more deeply involved in the process of creating form. His experience of the generation of form was so absorbing, so profound, and so intense that he came to believe that it was generated by some universal principle and that it put him in touch with the 'simultaneous movement of the universe'.

Through this experience, Delaunay acquired insight into the way an objectless art may be a means of attaining self-awareness through awareness of the physical as something other than the self.[3] However, he did not consistently pursue this realization, perhaps because his intellectual weakness made him more susceptible to contradictory ideas. He was inadequately educated, and unable to develop his conception of the relationship between contemporary life and art with any consistency. For example, although he was fascinated by contemporary poetry, he used it as a source of vivid but curiously dissociated images when they seemed to echo his own fragmentary ideas, rather than as a means of developing and strengthening these ideas. In this way, his attraction to literary images frequently led him back to figurative art, and to betray his unequivocal statements of 1912 that only pure colour-painting could give a sense of the essence of life.

Delaunay's figurative paintings from the early 1900s to the completion of La Ville de Paris in early 1912

Delaunay had no formal training (although he did work for a time in a studio of theatrical design), and taught himself by exploring the same gamut of styles as most of his contemporaries: Impressionism, Post-Impressionism, Neo-Impressionism, Fauvism, and Cubism. In his early works he represented the luminosity of light by making the paint seem almost transparent and by dissolving the surface of the picture in a manner characteristic of late Impressionism (Pl. 112), but he soon became interested in styles which exploited the materiality of paint. Their influence can be seen in works like *Le Marché* of 1905 (Pl. 113) in which forms are reduced to flat planes and heavy squiggles of opaque paint, and light is represented by the violence of colour

112 (*left*) Robert Delaunay, *Les Bords de la Yèvre (Berry)*, 1903 (72·5 × 91·5).
113 (*right*) Robert Delaunay, *Le Marché*, 1905 (39 × 46).

contrasts. The brilliant colour and sensual handling suggest that Delaunay knew something of Fauvism. Neo-Impressionism was probably even more important for Delaunay, as it suggested a way of representing the brilliance of light through contrast of colour, and of reducing the volume of objects by breaking them down into flat patches of colour which are no different in substance from the patches used to represent space. In this way Delaunay was able, in the *Paysage au disque* of *c.* 1906 (Pl. 114), to represent the pulsing vibration of bright light unbroken by any solid form, while in *Le Fiacre* of the same date (Pl. 115), he showed how the sparkling chains of light leap across space and dissolve objects into their swirling movements.[4] The two paintings show how important the abstract properties of Neo-Impressionism were for Delaunay, in that they

114 Robert Delaunay, *Paysage au disque, c.* 1906–7 (55 × 46).

115 Robert Delaunay, *Le Fiacre, c.* 1906–7 (43 × 58).

enabled him to place his strokes directly on to the canvas without being slowed by the more detailed demands of naturalistic coherence, in such a way that he could swing them into the rhythms of his excitement. In this way the technique allowed him to transpose his feelings for specific effects of light directly into paint, and absorbed him in the process by which the abstract patches of colour generate a new structure. During the pre-war years, Delaunay was always to respond to light in a spontaneous, improvisatory way, in which his initial sensation gave way to his involvement in the dynamic of the painting process during which certain characteristic configurations emerged. His involvement in the materiality of pigment—which was strengthened by his experience of Cubism— was the basis for the sensual intensity of his non-figurative works.

Delaunay may have seen Picasso's pre-Cubist geometric experiments, for he had contact with his circle by 1907 and some of his works of that year (Pl. 116) have a structural bias similar to his— although it could also be attributed to their shared interest in Cézanne. Delaunay was sent to Laon for military service in late 1907, and did not paint there; however, when he returned to Paris in the autumn of 1908, he painted his first significant works, his *Autoportrait* of 1909 (Pl. 6), and his series of interiors of the church of Saint-Séverin which were influenced by Cézanne and by early Cubism.

Delaunay was one of the first painters to appreciate and make use of the way in which Cézanne conveyed sensations of distance, mass, and gravity by means of small patches of colour. For example, in his

116 Robert Delaunay,
*Nature morte: Vases et
objets,* 1907 (43 × 34).

Autoportrait he employed planes of contrasting green and pink to create mass and space, and at the same time to break up the self-contained solidity of the head by linking its coloured planes to those of the ground. He used colour in a similar way in the *Saint-Séverin* series (Pl. 117), contrasting warm pinks and ochres with cool greens and blues to represent the advance and recession of form. However, the constructive properties of colour are prevented from functioning with their full strength by the firm linear structure which creates a curving movement into depth in opposition to the 'relief' structure created by colour. Delaunay later commented on this contradiction:

one can see the desire to construct, but the form is conventional ... The light breaks the lines in the vaults and near the ground. Despite the attempt not to copy nature objectively, the colour is still chiaroscuro which makes the construction a perspectival one ... The colour relationships lead to the linear structure.[5]

Delaunay's perspective does not recede towards a single vanishing point, for he used many viewpoints which record the movement of the eye as it follows the curving aisle into depth, falls to the floor, or soars up the columns of the vaults. The distortions in the columns represent the disorientation experienced when one follows the upward movement of a single column while also attempting to see it in relation to its immediate surroundings. He may have been influenced by the way the Fauves distorted the space of an interior in order to represent the physical sensations of being inside that interior; but he had a much firmer control over spatial movement, which he probably derived from study of the ways in which Cézanne had tried to embody the movement of the eye. However, the swaying, restless instability of the *Saint-Séverin* paintings was very different from the solemn mass and gravity of Cézanne's paintings, being more characteristic of Braque's paintings of 1909 such as *Le Port* (Pl. 118). The crystalline structure on the floor of *Saint-Séverin. nº3* is found in *Le Port*, and since Delaunay limited his colours to blues and greens, it seems as if he intended to follow Braque and Picasso in restricting the range of his colours.

117 Robert Delaunay, *Saint-Séverin nº 3*, 1909 (112·5 × 88·8).

118 Georges Braque, *Le Port*, 1909 (81·3 × 81·3).

Cubism influenced Delaunay in contradictory ways: in his transitional works of 1909–12, it helped him to break down the self-contained structure of objects so that he could integrate them in the dynamic rhythms of his paintings. However, the Cubists sought to express the tangible sensations of the objective world by means of the tactile qualities of painting, and this had a disturbing effect on Delaunay: he had been happy to dissolve the object in veils of light or chains of colour, but when he tried to express the relationship between solid and space, the object asserted itself with a prosaic actuality which he could not absorb in the structure of the painting. The Cubists' objectives demanded that they should paint small-scale subjects with which they had an intimate relationship, whereas Delaunay wanted to represent huge spaces full of light and movement. These were the reasons why Cubism was most significant to Delaunay when he abandoned his attempts to represent the world of objects and tried to express the immaterial, and to do so, moreover, by means of surfaces which are intensely sensuous and yet do not evoke any sensation of tangibility. In fact Delaunay had seized on this quality when he first saw Cubist works and cried, 'but these chaps paint with cobwebs!'

Although the city and the Eiffel Tower were favourite literary symbols for Simultanist experience, Delaunay probably did not originally consider them as such, for both images contained vast stretches or vast heights of light-filled space, and, since the eye has to make huge movements to take in such space or height, Delaunay may have taken up these themes as part of the exploration of visual movement that he was carrying on in the contemporary *Saint-Séverin* series, which of course had no modernist implications.[6] Delaunay continued to explore the movement of light and the movement of perception until he reached near-abstraction in 1912, having used the *Ville* series as a vehicle for experiments in constructive colour, and the *Tour Eiffel* series for the representation of linear dynamism. It seems probable that Delaunay embarked on the two series because he was fascinated by the pictorial challenge they posed, and that he only gradually became conscious of their symbolic implications when he came into contact with, or became aware of, people who were interested in the epic character of 'la vie moderne': the poets and artists of l'Abbaye, Jules Romains and the Futurists in 1910–11, Apollinaire in 1911–12, and Cendrars in 1912. Perhaps *Le Dirigeable et la Tour* of 1909 (Pl. 120) suggests that Delaunay was more conscious of the specifically modernist connotations of his subjects, but he did not actively explore them until 1912, when in *La Ville de Paris* (Pl. 136) he developed a more complex theme which demanded more than the perceptual awareness evoked by the earlier *Ville* and *Tour Eiffel* series. Thereafter, between 1912 and 1914, Delaunay oscillated between complex figurative works (including the *Équipe de Cardiff F.C.* and the *Hommage à Blériot* (Pls. 151 and 172), and those which depended purely on perceptual experience.

119 Robert Delaunay, *La Ville n° 1*, 1909 (80·5 × 67·5).

120 (*left*) Robert
Delaunay, *Le Dirigeable et
la Tour*, 1909 (34·8 × 26·8).
121 (*right*) Robert
Delaunay, *La Tour.
Première étude*, 1909
(46·2 × 38·2).

The earliest paintings of the city and the Tour Eiffel (Pls. 119 and
122) were influenced by the tendency towards sobriety of colour and
simplication of form which succeeded the Cézanne retrospective of
1907, and were simply straightforward views composed from static
blocks or silhouettes. In *La Tour Eiffel* in the Arensberg collection,
Delaunay made the tree swing across the tower and merge with its
profile, so that the tower is dragged on to the frontal plane and into a
heavy surface rhythm. He had probably observed this device in the
paintings of Cézanne, or the Cézannist paintings of Braque and
Picasso; for example, in Picasso's *Paysage, La Rue des bois* of 1908 (Pl.
123). By using this device, Picasso was able to integrate different
objects into a complex rhythm which develops in depth and on the
surface, but Delaunay did not succeed in doing this because the
separate elements are forced apart by the assertive perspective.
However, in the next paintings of the Tour Eiffel, Delaunay was able
to generate a more dynamic relationship between the tower and the
surrounding space by abandoning deep space and creating staccato
movements in and out of shallow space. Thus, in what was probably
the earliest of the dynamic representations of the Tour Eiffel, *La Tour
Eiffel aux arbres* of 1910 (Pl. 124),[7] Delaunay broke the continuous
closed contours of his earlier works so that he could use multiple
viewpoints in a more dynamic way. He depicted the tower from
several different levels and splayed out its trunk in a tangle of broken

shapes which echo the central image in a series of paler planes like an after-image. He thus showed that light is not simply a passive mode of illumination but an active force which bursts into and shatters solid objects. Braque had used light dynamically in his *Paysage, La Roche-Guyon* of 1909 (Pl. 125) in which he opened out the forms of objects and broke them into freely placed patches of light and shade so that they create a violent, unstable, surface rhythm. Delaunay attempted to do the same thing by splitting the ground and foliage into planes of rhythmically distributed tonal contrasts. However, Braque was developing a new pictorial structure in which the distinction between positive volume and negative space is eliminated, and the painting becomes like a relief from and into which forms seems to emerge and sink in continuously fluctuating ambiguity, while Delaunay retained a distinction between object and space. Thus his depiction of light is like a diagram of naturalistic effects very different from Braque's pictorial embodiment of the way the eye feels its way into form. The difference was partly due to the fact that Delaunay was attempting to represent an object of enormous size, and unlike the few earlier painters of the Eiffel Tower, he was viewing it from very close as it towered above him, and he depicted the way the eye grasps the whole vast bulk by

122 (*left*) Robert Delaunay, *La Tour Eiffel*, 1909 (95 × 69·4).
123 (*right*) Pablo Picasso, *Paysage: La Rue des Bois*, 1908 (92·6 × 74·3).

creating an equivalent for the movement of the eye as it soars upward, swoops down, or turns into depth.

Delaunay transformed this rather schematic representation of temporal and dynamic processes into something pictorially much more exciting in *La Tour Eiffel* exhibited in the Indépendants of 1911 and in those of the *Tour* series painted later in 1911 (Pls. 127–9); he framed the open space with buildings which narrow the area in which the linear movements act and thus intensified pictorial conflicts in that area. He strengthened the sharp, angular shapes which represent the forces of light and showed them piercing the tower, bouncing back into the buildings, tossing images of earth-bound forms into the sky and splintering solid forms.

It is significant that Delaunay worked in series, and also that he worked from memory. The dynamic paintings of the Tour Eiffel were begun during the months April to September 1910 which the Delaunays spent in the country, and were mental images of Delaunay's visual experience of the tower. He was thus free to

124 Robert Delaunay, *La Tour Eiffel aux arbres*, 1910 (124·4 × 91).

125 Georges Braque, *Paysage: La Roche-Guyon*, 1909 (92 × 73).

126 (*left*) Robert
Delaunay, *Étude pour La
Tour*, 1910 (116 × 81).
127 (*right*) Robert
Delaunay, *La Tour Eiffel*,
1910–11.

develop his composition as he painted, drawing instinctively from
his previous pictorial experience so that he could respond immediately to the growth of form on the canvas. This process can be
observed in *La Tour Eiffel* (*Champs de Mars*) of 1911 (Pl. 129), in
which he prepared the canvas with an intermediate tone of warm
beige which unifies what is, in effect, a large sketch drawn in a very
summary way. He clothed the linear structure with the colours he
had evolved earlier in the series, but he made them richer and more
complex as he painted, for example, intensifying the orange-red of
the tower by strengthening the complementary green of the planes of
the sky, and thus creating a colour movement which counteracts the
recession suggested by the naturalistic structure. As the painting
developed, it generated increasingly complex and contradictory
readings, which make the pictorial structure denser and remove it
further from the source, as can be seen in his use of transparent planes
which 'read' as flat rectangles creating directional movements on the
surface, or as the sides of three-dimensional transparent forms which
create movement into depth. The painting thus becomes a structure
composed of conflicting movements which jostle across the surface
or melt into indefinite depth. Such movements are discontinuous, so
that one has to choose how one shall read them; this makes one

128 Robert Delaunay, *La Tour Eiffel*, 1910–11 (198·7 × 136·2).

intensely conscious of the movement of the eye as the dynamic planes force it to the ground, allow it to soar upwards to meet the yellow clouds which pour forwards from the painting, and send it curving around the tower into depth. These changing relationships absorb the spectator in such a way that he becomes conscious of nothing beyond the experience of sight, just as Delaunay seems to have become absorbed in the evolution of pictorial form which increasingly dominated over his need to depict objective forms.

Delaunay's use of transparent planes owed much to the Cubists's practice of melting foreground into background by sliding transparent planes one over the other. However, the texture of Cubist painting is so continuous that objects cannot be seen as separate from space whereas Delaunay broke up the object by diagrammatic thrusts of light which function in what is still naturalistic space. Delaunay's image suggests that he could have been influenced by the Futurists' ideas on the way that light and movement can dynamically penetrate solid bodies. Delaunay later said that in *La Tour Eiffel*: 'Light deforms everything, breaks everything, no more geometry, Europe collapses.

129 Robert Delaunay, *La Tour Eiffel* (*Champs de Mars*), 1911 (162·5 × 130·5).

Waves of madness (Futurism before the theory); dislocation of the "successive" object. Planetary waves ...'[8] It is an open question whether the fragmented *Tour Eiffel* did represent 'Futurism before the theory', for there is no evidence that any of the series were painted before the publication of the 'Manifeste des peintres futuristes' in May 1910: all that is known is that the first two dynamic representations of *La Tour Eiffel* were painted between April and September, the months which Robert and Sonia spent at Nantua near Paris (Pls. 124 and 126),[9] and that Allard criticized Delaunay for following Futurist principles in *La Tour Eiffel* which he had exhibited in the Indépendants of 1911 (Pl. 127).[10] It is clear that Delaunay shared important ideas with the Futurists, and although these may have originated in their common sources, it is possible that the vehement clarity with which the Futurists advanced such ideas made Delaunay more fully conscious of their presence in his own work. Like Delaunay, the Futurists were interested in the dynamism of light, while their idea that painting should represent not 'a fixed *moment* in universal dynamism' but 'the dynamic sensation itself' described what Delaunay had been trying to do since he began the *Saint-Séverin* series in 1909. They also suggested that the spectator should be placed at the centre of the picture: the linear structure of Delaunay's *Tour Eiffel* of 1910–11 does just this.

Whereas Delaunay depicted light as a dynamic destructive force in the *Tour Eiffel* series, in the *Ville* series he developed a structure in which transparent veils of colour submerged solid form and brought together the near and the far on a single fluctuating surface. Colour played little constructive part in the paintings of the Tour Eiffel, whose compositions were primarily linear, but it became the primary means of expression in his representations of the city.

Delaunay painted the first of the *Ville* series in 1909 (Pl. 119), basing them on a postcard view taken from the Arc de Triomphe across a tangle of buildings to the Eiffel Tower in the distance.[11] The postcard does not show the ground plane and has a peculiar oblique perspective; Delaunay simply repeated this unpromising view, accentuating the slight tilt in the buildings caused by photographic distortion. The houses bulge and sway with no substance of their own and the perspective thrusts the closely packed divergent forms out of the side of the canvas. Braque's *Paysage, La Roche-Guyon* (Pl. 125) has a similar oblique perspective thrusting out of the picture, and a counter-movement which thrusts forward from the picture plane and which is also found in Delaunay's painting. Braque's composition seems about to be split apart by the divergent movements, but he brought them into a tense balance, whereas Delaunay was more closely tied by the composition of the photograph and did not succeed in creating a convincing pictorial structure. He was conscious of this failure, and in succeeding works he tried to strengthen the composition by framing and partly veiling the view with the gauze curtain of an implied window. In *La Ville. nº 2 (étude)*, which may have been shown in the Salon des Indépendants of 1911 (Pl. 130), he suggested the way light glances off the curtains by stippling them with small squares of green and grey with a few touches of red. He extended this technique in *La Ville. nº 2* (shown in the Blaue Reiter exhibition in late 1911) (Pl. 131) by carrying the square strokes across the painting and enriching the colours with brighter greens, red-browns, mauves, and purples which create vibratory movement and suggest both the intensity of rays of direct light and the vivacity of the motes of light which animate shadow. Delaunay had used small mosaic strokes in his Neo-Impressionist paintings, but was more probably influenced here by the small rectangular strokes of grey, brown, ochre, and white used by the Cubists in 1910–11 (Pl. 146). They used them in conjunction with transparent planes and an ambiguous linear scaffolding to melt all solid forms into a continuous, fluid, luminous surface. Delaunay also

130 (*left*) Robert Delaunay, *La Ville nº 2 (étude)*, 1910–11 (146 × 140).
131 (*right*) Robert Delaunay, *La Ville nº 2*, 1911 (145 × 112).

tried to fuse solid and space, the close and the distant, into a new surface structure composed of a transparent screen of dots, but this structure only partially absorbs the separate blocks of the architecture, so that the two modes of construction—the naturalistic and the pictorial—exist in uneasy juxtaposition. Delaunay was probably aware of this contradiction, for in the next painting in the series, *La Fenêtre sur la Ville. nº 3* (Pl. 132) which he began in December 1911, he strengthened the abstract colour-structure at the expense of the naturalistic one. He later commented that in the *Ville* series 'all the spaces were broken up, reduced to an infinitesimal size. It is a dynamism which dissolves all; the liquidation of all traditional artistic means . . . line, values, volume, chiaroscuro, etc . . .'[12] He now constructed the entire painting from small rectangular strokes and reduced the cityscape to insignificance, merely suggesting the presence of the buildings by simple planes like shadows behind a vibrating screen of colour.

He painted the small squares in all the colours of the spectrum instead of the greys, greens, and occasional reds and purples of the earlier city paintings. Delaunay's change to prismatic colour was probably influenced by the recent revival of interest in the Neo-Impressionism of Seurat, Signac, and Cross, for he stated in 1912 that Seurat had discovered 'simultaneous contrasts', and that 'the

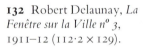

132 Robert Delaunay, *La Fenêtre sur la Ville nº 3*, 1911–12 (112·2 × 129).

133 Paul Signac, *Le Palais des papes, Avignon*, 1900 (73 × 92).

simultaneous contrasts which function in all later representations' first appeared in *La Fenêtre sur la Ville. nº 3*. However, he criticized Seurat's use of 'simultaneous constrasts', claiming that he could not use them constructively because he was hampered by the naturalistic demands on his paintings. Indeed, Neo-Impressionist paintings do have a naturalistic structure to which colour adheres like a skin (Pl. 133), while Delaunay was trying to find a way of using colour so that it could function independently of natural structures. He may now have studied Chevreul more closely, for Chevreul's analysis of the simultaneous interaction of juxtaposed colours was the ultimate source of late nineteenth-century experiments in the constructive use of colour.[13] Moreover, Chevreul's elegant diagrams functioned without reference to the world of objects and may have suggested to Delaunay—as to many another early twentieth-century painter— that pure colour structures could exert their own fascination (the fact that page after page of his book was composed of radiant disks of colour may have been of particular fascination to Delaunay). However, Delaunay did not use simultaneous contrasts in any doctrinaire way, for, as he said in 1913, 'I'm mad about the forms of colour, but I don't look for their scholastic explanation.'[14] He seems to have improvised his colour structure as Kupka had improvised his *Nocturne*, allowing the brush strokes to develop their own rhythm which overwhelmed the traces of the observed scene, and watching the way juxtaposed strokes of closely related or sharply contrasted colour interact to create sensations of dynamic thrust or more passive recession. He wove together these colour movements and thus created a dense surface structure which almost seems to pulse and to rise and fall in ever-changing movement.

Although some of the diagonal movements in the painting suggest the flow of light, the colour relief is independent of the objective world, for Delaunay had found a new way of representing light by using colour in such a way that light seems to emanate from the painting as a whole, thus freeing him from the necessity of indicating its presence by showing its effect on objects. It was therefore the first painting in which Delaunay almost dispensed with the object—and Apollinaire was probably thinking of it when he wrote in February 1912, 'the new painters will provide their admirers with artistic sensations created entirely by the harmony of unequal lights'.[15]

By the end of 1911 Delaunay had arrived at near-abstraction by seeking a means of using colour to represent light and by 'allowing' colour to generate structure. However, in the first quarter of 1912, he swung back to figurative painting: he spent January in Laon where he painted a number of works 'from nature', as he had not done for some time, and he then painted *La Ville de Paris* (Pl. 136), a work of considerable iconographic complexity through which he tried to express Simultanist experience. However, although *La Ville de Paris*

134 (*left*) Robert Delaunay, *Les Tours de Laon*, 1912 (162 × 130).
135 (*right*) Robert Delaunay, *Les Trois Graces*, 1911 (209 × 160).

136 Robert Delaunay, *La Ville de Paris*, 1912 (267 × 406).

was figurative, it was a turning-point in Delaunay's development of a non-figurative art, because it made him realize that the mere multiplication of images could not create Simultanist consciousness; immediately it was finished he began to paint the *Fenêtres*. Their figurative content was minimal, but Delaunay believed that their sensual concentration could give the spectator an intuitive consciousness of the simultaneity of being.

It is not certain exactly when *La Ville de Paris* was painted. It has been suggested that it was completed before Delaunay went to Laon in January, but this seems unlikely, since Delaunay had begun to use the flat planes of transparent colour used in *La Ville de Paris* in his paintings of the cathedral at Laon (Pl. 134). Moreover, *La Ville de Paris* seems to have been influenced and even inspired by the Futurist exhibition and manifesto which burst upon the Parisian scene on 5 February 1912. Delaunay is said to have executed it in less than a month, and this could have been true despite its huge size (about eight and a half by thirteen feet), because Delaunay painted it very thinly like an enormous sketch and pieced it together from several earlier paintings. He could, then, have painted it between the Futurist exhibition in early February and mid-March when it was exhibited in the Salon des Indépendants.[16]

Delaunay probably intended it to be seen as a specifically French response to the Italian claim that French painting was 'passéiste' because it ignored the modern urban world. He took up Futurist ideas on the expression of the 'simultaneity of states of mind', and with consciously French elegance he evoked the past, present, and future of Paris by fusing a number of images associated with it. The painting was also a synthesis of Delaunay's past work (as its dating to '1910–12' may indicate) and perhaps, as Apollinaire suggested, a summary of 'the total intention of modern art'.[17]

Delaunay divided his picture into three parts which remain distinct although he linked them with transparent colour planes. The probable final study for the work (Pl. 137) shows that this effect was intentional and not due to Delaunay's inexperience in working on a large scale, so that the critic Granié's description of the painting as 'a kind of unified triptych' is very apt.[18] Delaunay could have got the idea of a triptych from Boccioni's programmatic *Stati d'animo* (Pls. 138–40) which was shown in the February exhibition. This is a real triptych composed of separate canvases in which Boccioni represented the different emotional reactions to the departure of a train by means of contrasting lines and colours, while Delaunay used the triptych in order to juxtapose images which are naturalistically unrelated but associated with the concept of the 'City of Paris'. Each image has a characteristic linear structure, and the contrasts between them are analogous to the contrasts between Boccioni's different

137 Robert Delaunay, *Étude pour La Ville de Paris*, 1912. Ink, pencil on tracing paper (74·5 × 100·5).

canvases: the left-hand image of the city is divided by horizontals and verticals into static units; the verticals of the central group of figures are penetrated by the circular rhythms which explode out of the dynamic right-hand section. Each image expresses a different aspect of the city. Thus, in the left-hand section of his painting, Delaunay combined the view over the rooftops he had used in the *Ville* series with a view from the studio he had occupied at the Quai du Louvre until 1909–10. Part of this view, and the flatly painted quay, foot-bridge, and boat are also found in Rousseau's *Portrait-Paysage* (1899), then owned by Delaunay, and since Rousseau had been a friend of Delaunay until his death in 1910, Delaunay may have conceived of this section as a homage to the older painter, as well as a reference to his own artistic past. However, he replaced Rousseau's self-portrait by the rather incongruous group of *Les Trois Graces*, a subject which he seems to have taken up in late 1911 or early 1912 (Pl. 135) and which he adapted from a photograph of a Pompeian wall-painting. Delaunay's idea of representing the totality of the city—and of doing so with this specific view of Paris and the three symbolic women—may well have been inspired by Zola's *L'Œuvre*. This is the more likely, since allegory was foreign to Delaunay, and since all his major subject paintings were dependent on literary sources. Zola's ill-fated hero, Claude Lantier, was obsessed by the idea of representing the very essence of Paris, and Zola described how he studied all aspects of the life of the city, at all hours, in all weathers, so that he became aware of 'twenty different cities'. Lantier wished to

138 Umberto Boccioni,
Stati d'animo: Gli Adii,
1911 (70·5 × 96).

139 Umberto Boccioni,
*Stati d'animo: Quelli che
vanno*, 1911 (70·7 × 95·7).

140 Umberto Boccioni,
*Stati d'animo: Quelli che
restano*, 1911 (70·7 × 95·7).

represent modern Paris but, as he evolved his great composition, the three women bathers at the centre of the composition gradually assumed a symbolic character with the one magnificent nude embodying 'the very flesh of Paris'. Delaunay took his view from practically the same point as Lantier's, but faced down the river away from the city itself and towards the Eiffel Tower, symbol of modern life and embodiment of the Simultanism not just of the city but of the universe. He also retained the group of three women—perhaps to make a reference to the Judgement of Paris—but even the antique reference may have been suggested by Zola, who spoke of 'this Venus born from the waters of the Seine'.[19]

The Simultanism of *La Ville de Paris* was quite different from that of Delaunay's earlier works, in which he was concerned simply with sensation and in which he tried to synthesize successive visual experiences (in the *Ville* and *Tour Eiffel* series, he expressed the movement of the eye as it looks steeply down, sweeps up the vast heights of the tower or across the roofs of the town, soaring into the sky or plunging into distance). In actuality these visual experiences develop sequentially in time, but Delaunay tried to ensure that they were experienced simultaneously, so that while the spectator follows one movement, he is peripherally aware of the rest of the painting. He was not fully successful, as each part of the painting is so strongly defined that it becomes separate from the others. In *La Ville de Paris* Delaunay tried to synthesize mental images of something which cannot be comprehended in purely visual terms, and since this change was a change of direction rather than a result of the internal development of Delaunay's painting, it must have been influenced by some external source. The fact that Delaunay tried to fuse images related to the past with others which clearly refer to the dynamism of the present, suggests that he may have been influenced by Bergsonist ideas on the way the past is transformed into present consciousness by memory, particularly since such ideas preoccupied the poets with whom Delaunay was acquainted. In the more immediate pictorial context he may have been interested in the Futurist's interpretation of such ideas. Delaunay was becoming increasingly friendly with Apollinaire, and it is possible that he was influenced by his suggestion that French painters could learn something from the Futurists' ideas on synthetic painting and from their Unanimist titles.[20] Cendrars later described Delaunay's evolution in terms which suggest that he was influenced by Unanimism. He stated that Delaunay:

finally found a new subject which allowed him to apply all his discoveries ... the Great City. A multitude of new problems arose; analogies, correspondences, spiritual and physical contrasts, questions of perspective, technical questions, abstract questions such as unanimism and synthesis. And the whole personality of Paris entered into him.[21]

In his Unanimist works, Jules Romains attempted to express how the individual consciousness may become one with the dominant energy of a group or place. He was particularly interested in urban themes, and tried to evoke the rhythms which characterize different aspects of urban life in *La Vie unanime* and *Les Puissances de Paris*. The latter book was published at the very end of 1911, and is particularly relevant for an understanding of Delaunay's *Ville de Paris*; in it Romains evoked specific localities, events, and aspects of Paris in terms of dominant rhythms, just as Delaunay gave each of his images of the city a different rhythm.[22] The sensations which Delaunay embodied when he depicted the circular energies which spin out from the Eiffel Tower and eddy into the group of nudes are similar to those in Romains' description of the Place de l'Ètoile: 'turning so powerfully that it drags a part of heavy city with it ... the desire of turning makes distant houses lighter'.[23]

Delaunay had used circles and curves to represent the radiance and energy of light in early works like *Le Fiacre* and the *Paysage au disque*, but did not use them again until *La Fenêtre sur la Ville. n⁰ 3* of late 1911, in which some of the strokes and patches of colour form tentative curved movements which suggest eddies of light. Delaunay made these abstract curving movements stronger in *La Ville de Paris*, by representing the movement of light as it refracts from the surface of the building on the right in a series of circular eddies which decrease in energy as they ebb away from the building. Boccioni used similar curving movements in his *Stati d'animo: Gli addii* (Pl. 138) to represent the energies which pulse through space and fuse individual forms in their dynamic rhythms. Delaunay later said that he had tried to create 'rhythmic harmonies' between the 'landscape, woman, and tower' and that he had attempted unsuccessfully to apply the 'simultaneous contrasts' he had discovered in *La Fenêtre sur la Ville. n⁰ 3*.[24] He was unsuccessful because he retained the local colour of the figures, cityscape, and tower and returned to a Cézannesque construction of space through contrast of warm and cool colours, painting the background in transparent blue and green planes which push forward the opaque pink, red, and yellow planes of the women and the tower. He attempted to give the painting unity by using the transparent planes to link the brighter opaque ones: for example, he merged the transparent body of the woman on the left with the staccato movements of the city section, and the woman on the right with the brighter colours and sharper definition of the tower. However, his attempt to create unity through colour is hampered by the hard linear skeleton, by the distracting contrasts between opacity and transparency, and by the fact that the specific details make one focus on them to the detriment of one's appreciation of the continuity of the colour structure. He himself later criticized this aspect of the painting, noting how the 'fragmentation effectively obstructs the rhythm, movement and dynamism—the result is jerky and the areas of colour are broken by chiaroscuro. The whole is grey. It is only in certain passages that one can foresee the abstract period of the *Fenêtres*.'[25]

La Ville de Paris is thus an uneasy juxtaposition of allegorical idea and pure pictorial expression, and of the descriptive and the abstract. Delaunay himself said that it was transitional between his 'destructive' and 'constructive' paintings: that is, transitional between paintings with a fragmented linear structure derived from the external world, and paintings in which colour was used to create a new unity independent of the external world.[26] However, the very fact that it contained contradictions was important for Delaunay, because it made him aware that figurative elements prevented one from attaining the inner consciousness of the self's relation to the whole; this realization caused him to return to his exploration of perceptual experience and to create works which would excite the sense of sight alone, for he came to believe that sight could attain the state of consciousness which he had tried to express by conceptual means in *La Ville de Paris*.

The 'Fenêtres' of 1912

After the Salon des Indépendants had opened in late March, Delaunay wrote to Kandinsky about the similarity of their pictorial explorations. 'This research into pure painting', he wrote, 'is the current problem. I do not know any painters in Paris who are truly in search of this ideal world. These things are still not harmonious enough for me.'[27] He was probably referring to the *Fenêtres* which he began in April 1912. He had completed at least thirteen paintings by mid-January 1913, but executed most of them during the summer of 1912 which he spent in the country near Paris.[28] Delaunay believed that they represented a new form of expression, and described them as 'windows opening onto a new reality'.[29] They were nourished by a number of sources new to Delaunay, which ranged from the writings of Leonardo, to Mallarmé's poem, 'Fenêtres', and perhaps to Goethe's *Farbenlehre*; also, since this was the time when Delaunay was closest to Apollinaire, his paintings of pure light probably owed something to the poet's image of light as the supreme constructive power. These rich sources may have given Delaunay confidence in pursuing the representation of light alone and in the transformation of his earlier rather literal modernism to an almost mystic one. The transformation is reflected in the two articles, 'La Lumière' and 'Réalité, peinture pure', which Delaunay wrote during the summer and in which he criticized the Cubists and

Futurists for basing their art on the world of objects.

Delaunay wrote in his letter to Kandinsky: 'I will soon speak to you about the subject in painting, about a fascinating conversation with Apollinaire who is beginning to believe in our search. The coincidence with your letter underlines all this—that is so frail, yet so alive.' The fascinating conversation with Apollinaire probably centred on the ideas which Apollinaire expressed in his February article, 'Du Sujet dans la peinture moderne', in which he stated that the emotion given by a painting resides in its pictorial structure, not in its resemblance to the objects of the external world. Delaunay later commented on the originality of his *Fenêtres* and added:

The first time that I came upon a suggestion of this idea was in the notes that Leonardo da Vinci wrote on the difference between the arts of painting and literature, but this appreciation deals only with the question of the eye. He tries to prove the intellectual superiority given by simultaneity, by our eyes, *windows of the soul*, over the auditory and successive function of hearing. In the painting of the *Fenêtres* ... it is a question only of *colour* for *colour's* sake.[30]

Delaunay took notes from Péladan's translation of Leonardo's notebooks—probably in the first part of 1912 before he wrote his articles which are full of phrases from the notebooks. Leonardo's praise of the eye, the 'window of the soul' which communicates the beauties of the world—above all, light—to the mind, encouraged his faith in an art based on sight alone; Leonardo's metaphor of the window as a mystical illumination would have given added measure to the transformation from the prosaic view of the *Ville* to the emotional intensity of the *Fenêtres*.

Because Delaunay was to use Leonardo's words over and over again I quote his notes at length:

Para. 358. The eye, which is called the window of the soul, is the principal means by which the mind can consider, largely and in their splendour, the infinite works of nature ... because poetry speaks to the imagination with letters, *while painting truly puts before the eyes an image whose similarities he (the poet) perceives as if the things were natural*...

Para. 365. ... In the beauty of any fictitious thing by the poet, it happens that the fact of giving the parts separately in successive time prevents the memory from perceiving harmony.[31]

The following extract from 'La Lumière' shows how deeply Delaunay was influenced by Leonardo:

The eye is the noblest sense: it is the one which communicates most directly with *our mind, our consciousness*. The idea of the vital movements of the *world* and its *movement is simultaneity*...

Auditory perception is not adequate for our knowledge of the universe; it has no depth . . . Its movement is *successive*, it is a sort of mechanism, its law is the *time* of *mechanical* clocks which, like it, has no relationship with our perception of the *visual movement of the Universe*.

It has the parity of geometrical things.
Its nature brings it close to the *geometrically conceived Object.*
The *Object* is not endowed with *life, with movement.*
When it *simulates movement* it becomes *successive, dynamic.*[32]

Delaunay used Leonardo's words to criticize an art which based itself on the object, and which he therefore felt must be 'geometric', 'successive', 'mechanical', and thus unable to express the essential simultaneity of existence. He may have found confirmation of Leonardo's rejection of the successive in favour of the simultaneous in Bergson's claim that analytic methods of describing reality could not grasp the mobility which is the essence of the Simultanist consciousness.

   Leonardo's words give meaning to an otherwise almost incomprehensible essay which Delaunay wrote as a conversation between a Cubist, a Futurist, and a commentator who is presumably himself, and which he clearly based on Leonardo's debate on the superiority of painting over the other arts.[33] Delaunay's commentator asserted that neither the Cubists nor the Futurists could represent the vital unity and movement of the world if they painted the object, and that the Futurists' attempt to represent movement through multiplication of the moving object (which he described as 'sauter un object succesivement') could not represent *real* movement. 'By starting with the object,' he wrote, 'you fragment the universe.' He himself suggested no clear alternative, and merely concluded by quoting Apollinaire's phrase: 'J'aime l'Art d'aujourd'hui parce que j'aime avant tout la lumière.'[34]

   For Apollinaire, light was a metaphor for the artist's power of creating meaning from the chaos of experience; Delaunay found it no less profound, although he believed that its meaning lay in its sensational existence. The intensity of his feeling for its beauty was strengthened by his belief that it was the essence of life, so that consciousness of it would give consciousness of the very nature of being. He wrote in his essay, 'Réalité, peinture pure':

Our eyes are the essential intermediary between nature and our soul. It is through our eyes that the Present and consequently our sensibility exists. We can do nothing without our sensibility, hence nothing without light. Consequently our soul exists in a state of harmony, and harmony is only engendered by the simultaneity with which the measure and proportions of light arrive through our eyes to our soul . . .[35]

He took his words from Leonardo's 'Do you not know that your soul is composed of harmony which is engendered only by the simultaneity with which the proportions of objects are seen and heard?'[36] He seems, then, to have used Leonardo's concept to confirm his sense that he could attain consciousness of his inner self only by integrating consciousness of external forms into his present consciousness. Thus his notion of Simultanist consciousness has something in common with Apollinaire's realization that he could acquire a sense of inner wholeness by transforming his memories of his past self into the living present through poetic creation.

Delaunay believed that, since light is composed of prismatic colour, pure colour painting could be a 'representative harmony', a microcosm of the larger harmony of being; following Leonardo, he called this 'representative harmony' the 'eternal subject'. He thus claimed a very profound meaning for non-figurative painting as an embodiment of the relationship between the individual and the whole. He also insisted that this meaning transcended verbal modes of consciousness: he quoted Leonardo's comment that 'painting has no need of any words to interpret it', and emphasized that its meaning could be found only by intensifying one's *visual consciousness* of the painting.

Leonardo may even have suggested a means of studying light, for he discussed experiments in letting a limited amount of light penetrate into a darkened room through a small hole (the principle of the *camera obscura*) and Delaunay, as Cendrars describes, made a hole in a shutter so that he could investigate the structure of light:

a ray of sunlight filtered into the darkened room, and he began to paint it, to analyse its constituents of form and colour ... He worked thus for months, studying the pure light of the sun, attaining sources of emotion beyond any subject. Then he enlarged the hole in the shutter a little and began to paint the play of colour on a transparent, fragile material like a pane of glass. Reflections, breaks, his little canvasses took on the synthetic appearance of jewels.[37]

Leonardo's device was not, of course, unique; since Delaunay used it more for studying light itself than lighted objects, he would probably have been more interested in Newton's investigation of the structure of light, isolating a ray by making a tiny opening in a shutter into a darkened room, and decomposing it into its constituent colours by means of a prism. It may have been Kupka—who had already painted his *Disques de Newton*—who drew Delaunay's attention to these experiments. Goethe used similar devices to study light, and Delaunay seems to have been influenced by his writings on colour by 1913 at the latest and perhaps as early as the spring of 1912.[38] Whatever the source of his experiments, Delaunay used them less as a means of knowledge than as a way of penetrating to the heart of his feeling for colour, for his realization that white light is composed of marvellously pure and intense colours would have confirmed his belief that colour was the very essence of life.

Delaunay began painting the *Fenêtres* in April. The first may have been those painted in mauves, violets, pinks, pinky-ochres, cloudy blues, and greens (Pl. 141), as these were the dominant colours of *La Fenêtre sur la Ville. nº 3* and *La Ville de Paris*. However, in the same month, Delaunay also began using pure bright oranges, yellows, blues, greens, and violets of a brilliance unprecedented in his work (Pl. 144). In *Les Fenêtres sur la ville. 1ʳᵉ partie 2ᵉᵐᵉ motif nº 1* (Pl. 141), which was probably painted early in the series, Delaunay loosely juxtaposed the flat blurry planes of colour on a horizontal-vertical

141 Robert Delaunay, *Les Fenêtres sur la Ville. 1ʳᵉ partie 2ᵉᵐᵉ motif nº 1*, Apr. 1912. Oil on card (39 × 29·6).

grid and dissolved the previously obtrusive architectural blocks by using a slurred impressionistic brush-stroke. A few firmer planes are all that remain of the original architecture, and these act as flat shapes which do not interrupt the movement of the non-representational planes for Delaunay no longer used linear perspective to separate the 'near' and the 'far', and instead created *pictorial* space through the interaction of colours of 'unequal intensity'. This kind of space was probably influenced by Cézanne's late works in which he used transparent planes of warm and cool colours to give sensations of space and depth.[39] However, there is a strong sense of nature's space in even the most abstract of Cézanne's late paintings, whereas in the *Fenêtres*, the planes are firmly tied to the surface of the painting and space is created by the superimposition of transparent planes which always lie parallel to the surface. Delaunay's new emphasis on the picture-surface may owe something to Monet's recent works, such as the *Palazzo da Mula* (Pl. 142) which was exhibited in Paris in May and may have been in Durand-Ruel's gallery earlier than that.[40] Delaunay's colour-scheme (blue dominant with green, mauve, rose, and touches of ochre) is like a variant of Monet's; both painters used darker colours which seem to scoop into the surface, and lighter ones which seem to vibrate outwards from it; using strong horizontals and verticals, both artists created strong geometric compositions, though Monet painted the lower part of his picture as a single horizontal plane, while Delaunay broke his into smaller planes. But Monet's combination of luminous colour and material pigment would have been even more important for Delaunay, for he used the shimmering insubstantiality of the colours to dissolve the surface, while simultaneously reinforcing it by his sensual handling of the paint.

142 Claude Monet,
Palazzo da Mula, 1908
(62 × 81).

Impressionism helped Delaunay to move from his rather literal Cubism. In Cubist painting, as in Delaunay's *Ville* and *Tour Eiffel* series, there is always a central core or area of activity in which recognizable forms or signs are concentrated, and which acts as a kind of focus, a pause which helps one become aware of the ambiguous relationship between the objective subject and the pictorial structure. However, neither Monet's late works nor Delaunay's *Fenêtres* have a centralized structure, for, although the Eiffel Tower is, of course, central, it is simply a colour plane among other colour planes and does not act as a focus (Delaunay has also altered its real colour from red-brown to green so as to reduce its separate identity—he may have been influenced by Kandinsky's suggestion that the artist should transpose the colour of natural objects as a means of effecting the transition from naturalistic to abstract painting[41]). Since Delaunay's new paintings were no longer centralized, he could extend them indefinitely—as he did in works like the oval *Fenêtres simultanées* (Pl. I). Monet's *Nénuphars* (Pl. 167) was also without focus or boundary and suggested the unbroken continuity and pervasiveness of light.

Delaunay had a deep emotional attachment to Impressionism because it meant for him 'the birth of Light in painting',[42] but his own attitude to light was quite different: the Impressionists based their paintings on the *observation* of light, while he sought abstract pictorial equivalents for light considered as a general force animating all nature. Thus Monet's painting has an even, diffuse radiance inspired by the radiance of a specific scene, while Delaunay's painting was based on schematically conceived movements of light (for example, the diffuse light of the central area, or the ray of light from the upper right) which were gradually transformed into a new and abstract structure during the painting process.

Delaunay wrote in 1913: 'Although I do not agree with the little Cubists, I have been enlightened by their theories of light founded on geometry.'[43] He was probably referring to the discussions that took place at Puteaux in preparation for the Section d'Or exhibition. Cubist painting was constructed from patches of light and shadow whose position was determined by the internal rhythmic or geometric structure of the painting, and not by the laws of scientific naturalism. Gleizes and Metzinger wrote at this time in *Du Cubisme*: 'Loving light, we refuse to measure it, and we avoid the geometric ideas of focus and ray which imply the repetition ... of light planes and dark intervals in a given direction.'[44] Delaunay distributed light more or less naturalistically in his *Ville*, *Tour Eiffel*, and *Laon* series, and showed it coming from a dominant source, illuminating objects and casting shadows in a fairly regular way. Picasso and Braque, on the other hand, distributed light according to the free rhythmic structure of the painting: Delaunay adopted this mode of lighting in his *Fenêtres* by superimposing transparent and opaque planes of contrasting tone to give the effect of an ambiguous shifting relief. However, in Cubist painting one is made aware of the space by its tactile qualities, by the sensation that it advances towards one, and that one could run a finger over its recessions and projections, whereas Delaunay's painting melts away from one because of his use of transparent colour. In his letter to Kandinsky he said that his experiments with transparency of colour had led him 'to discover the movement of colours'. He had tried to create movement in depth in *La Fenêtre sur la Ville. n° 3* by superimposing a transparent screen composed of small strokes of colour over shadowy opaque planes. But these opaque planes restricted depth, and in the *Fenêtres* he created limitless depth by interweaving transparent planes of colour so that light seems to glow from within the painting. He had used planes of transparent colour for the first time in the paintings of Laon cathedral of January 1912 (Pl. 134), but here the colour could not act constructively because the planes were too closely tied to the architecture, to perspective space, and to naturalistic light and shade. Delaunay also used transparency of colour in *La Ville de Paris* in order to unify the surface and suggest depth, but was unsuccessful because he had to interrupt the continuity of colour with the graphic detail and chiaroscuro necessary to define the figures and objects.

Delaunay could have learnt something from Kupka's representation of the immateriality of light, for although the mysterious moody subjectivity of his painting would have repelled him, he may have been interested in the way Kupka excluded tactile sensations and suggested depth by superimposing layers of transparent colour so that light seems to emanate from the depths of the painting. He could have observed this effect in the *Plans par couleurs* (Pl. 103) which was shown in the same Salon des Indépendants as his *Ville de Paris*, before he began painting the *Fenêtres*.

Kandinsky exhibited *Improvisation 23* (Pl. 15), *24*, and *25* at the same time, and although they are totally different from Delaunay's painting, Delaunay may have been struck by seeing that another painter had managed to suggest space without relying on the tactile qualities of light and shadow. Delaunay did, in fact, call attention to the similarity of their researches, and said that Kandinsky's paintings in the Salon had been discussed by a 'toute petite élite': it is possible that the freedom with which Kandinksy arranged his bright transparent colours to give a sense of movement in immeasurable space could have shown him the possibility of detaching colour from objects so that it could be used to express movement. Kandinsky had sent him *Ueber das Geistige in der Kunst* in early 1912, and Delaunay was probably stimulated by his assertion that it was necessary to destroy the 'single surface' in order to create an 'ideal plane', and by his discussion of how colour can advance or recede and how it can therefore be used to construct 'suspended non-material form'—a phrase which could be used to describe the *Fenêtres*.[45] Even if Delaunay was helped by Kupka and Kandinsky, his art was very different from theirs: he was concerned with the perceptual experience of light, and they with its symbolic meaning.

Delaunay had never been really interested in the physicality of objects, although when he was influenced by Cubism (between 1909 and 1911) he was necessarily drawn to represent the tangible qualities of objects, and it seems that his new awareness of Impressionism and his encounter with the non-tactile art of Kupka and Kandinsky helped him to use Cubism to realize his more fundamental concern with the immaterial. He was thus able to create a synthesis which was deeply influenced by both Impressionism and Cubism, but which was profoundly different from both: from Impressionism he learnt to use colour to construct paintings without the object-tension of Cubism; from Cubism he learnt to improvise without being restricted by the forms of the external world and to interweave light and dark, transparent and opaque planes so that they create fluctuating movements which develop simultaneously across the surface and into depth. Delaunay retained this mobile, ambiguous structure even after he had declared his independence of Cubism in October 1912, and had banished any reference to objective form in the *Formes circulaires* of 1913.

The comments of Gleizes and Metzinger on colour may also be relevant for an understanding of Delaunay's development. They criticized the Neo-Impressionists' attempt to represent light through optical mixture, because the result was less luminous and intense than its components:

Loving colour, we refuse to limit it ... we accept all the possibilities contained between the two extremes of the spectrum, between the cold and the warm tone. Here are a thousand tints which escape from the prism, and hasten to range themselves in the lucid region forbidden to those who are blinded by the immediate.[46]

Delaunay too, criticized the Neo-Impressionists (in the person of Seurat) on the grounds that their naturalism prevented the constructive use of 'simultaneous contrasts'; he therefore enlarged the small neo-Impressionist strokes he had used in *La Fenêtre sur la Ville. n° 3* into small intensely luminous planes which overwhelm the vestigial hints of naturalistic space—the short diagonals of the window-frame, the sides of houses, and the tower. Delaunay wrote in 'Réalité, peinture pure' that the only real way to structure a painting was by means of: 'The simultaneity of colour through simultaneous contrasts and all the unequal intensities arising from the colours, according to their expression in their representative movement.'[47] He was, of course, continuing to exploit Chevreul's suggestions on the interactions between juxtaposed colours, and was creating a complex pictorial structure by observing the effects of colour relationships which developed as he painted. The importance of this mode of working can be observed in the contrast between the intensity of colour of *Les Fenêtres simultanées* in the Hamburg Kunsthalle (Pl. 144) and the weakness of the colour-structure in the unfinished *Fenêtres* in the Kunstsammlung Nordrhein-Westfalen (Pl. 143). Delaunay painted the latter work with a relatively simple sequence of flat rectangular planes intersected by two triangular ones and a few curves, while in the Hamburg picture he modulated the original flat planes by painting layers of contrasting or closely related colour over them, making the darker colours more resonant and the lighter ones more luminous, and all the time intensifying the ambiguous mobility of the whole. For example, where there is a simple sequence of thinly painted planes in the Dusseldorf painting, there is an extremely complex series of shifting relationships in the painting in the Guggenheim museum—a green plane is shot with orange so that it can be seen either as projecting forward from the darker blue and green planes on either side, or as the side of a rainbow-coloured transparent cube; the yellow plane below is

143 Robert Delaunay, *Les Fenêtres simultanées*, 1912 (64·4 × 52·4).

144 Robert Delaunay, *1er Représentation. Les Fenêtres simultanées. Ville. 2e motif 1re partie*, 1912 (46 × 40).

touched with a thin layer of orange; it gleams forward but is simultaneously pushed into depth by the transparent blue descending from the darker blue heights of the central triangle; it can also be seen as the side of a cube formed by the blue-green plane to the right of it, or as a transparent glass-like plane through which light shines. The whole painting is formed from these relationships which alter as the eye moves, and since it can find no point of rest, no moment in which the colours settle into stable form, it becomes absorbed in the ceaseless movement.

These are purely physiological reactions, yet to Delaunay they were something more. He constructed his paintings so that no colour can be perceived in isolation and can only be seen 'simultaneously' with all the others; he believed that absorption in this pictorial simultaneity could give an intuitive grasp of the simultaneity, the unity of all existence. Even the basic relationship between the primary colours and their complementaries had for him a profound significance, for such colours contain all potential colours and thus embody the interrelatedness of all being. Apollinaire's enthusiasm for these works was probably due to his realization that Delaunay had succeeded in creating a 'new universe' by means of his power to transform the external world—the 'luminous power which constructs as it pleases'—by using light (by means of colour) to fuse individual forms into a new, fluid unity.

In June, Delaunay fused three single windows in a long narrow format (Pl. 145) in such a way that he introduced a new dimension of time into his painting which, as he later said, 'develops in time while being perceived simultaneously in a single glance'.[48] When one looks at one of the paintings of a single window, one's mind oscillates between awareness of the movement of colour across the surface and the movement of colour into depth, for although one can 'see' all the colours which give these contrasting sensations, one cannot interpret them simultaneously because the information they give is not consistent. By extending the painting laterally, Delaunay made the discontinuity between depth and surface more extreme; thus when one seeks to comprehend them, one becomes increasingly aware of the independent reality of the painting, increasingly aware of what one is seeing, and increasingly aware of the indivisible continuity of one's own experience.

Gleizes and Metzinger suggested that the fusion of multiple viewpoints of objects could be used to express 'the fourth dimension of time', yet Delaunay believed that each viewpoint demands that the spectator should focus on it in such a way that his consciousness is fragmented into a sequence of separate 'moments'.[49] Delaunay expressed his belief in Bergsonian terms, but he probably arrived at it through his own experience of creating mobile form and observing

145 Robert Delaunay, *2ᵉ Représentation. Les Fenêtres. Simultanéité. Ville. 1ʳᵉ partie 3 motifs*, 1912 (34 × 89).

146 Georges Braque, *Les Toits de Ceret*, 1911 (81 × 64).

how figurative details interrupted it. He did not then give different viewpoints of the Eiffel Tower, but reduced it to a flat plane which has no more substance than any other plane, and by repeating this simple silhouette, he reduced the objective reality of the motif even further. However, the very ambiguity of the tower makes one more aware of the reality of the painting, since the more one attempts to interpret it in objective terms, the more one becomes aware of the way it is assimilated into the movement of the colours—sometimes affirming itself, sometimes acting simply as a coloured plane or as the curved edge of a transparent one, Its function is that of a leitmotiv which awakens one's consciousness of the way colour themes develop across the surface or into depth, the way certain shapes reappear in different contexts in stronger or weaker or contrasting colours, or the way in which certain colour areas break down into smaller ones or expand and absorb others.

Delaunay first used the word 'simultaneous' for the titles of his works in the catalogue for his Berlin exhibition of January–February 1913, where he entitled his tripartite window, *2ᵉ Représentation. Les Fenêtres. Simultanéité. Ville. 1ʳᵉ partie 3 motifs* (Pl. 145).[50] Such a title suggests that he was painting variations on a theme in a musical way, and this may be confirmed by his statement to Kandinsky about his discovery of the relationship between transparent colours 'comparable to musical notes' and the movement of colour, for he used transparency to relate themes which developed across the surface to the layers of colours which sink into the depths of the painting, in a way that is analogous to the development of harmonic and melodic structures. It is possible that he mentioned such ideas to Klee when the latter visited him in April 1912 or when they corresponded about the translation of 'La Lumière' for *Der Sturm*, for Klee later made a comment on the serial *Fenêtres* which throws some light on Delaunay's ideas: 'Polyphonic painting is ... superior to music in that the time element is more spatial. The idea of simultaneity would then appear even richer ... Trying to make the time-element prevail on the model of a pictorial fugue, Delaunay chose a format whose length was impossible to take in at a glance...'[51] Delaunay may also have been interested in Kupka's efforts to paint themes which developed on different levels and at different 'speeds', and which culminated in the *Amorpha, Fugue en deux Couleurs* of mid-1912. However, unlike other early non-figurative artists, Delaunay did not continue to make use of musical analogies in such a specific way, probably because he was impressed by Leonardo's evaluation of the different arts on the basis of their degree of simultaneity and by his claim that music was inferior to painting because its harmonies supersede one another, whereas in painting all is simultaneously present.[52] In these terms, the time embodied in the *Ville* and the *Tour Eiffel* series was sequential, for as the eye moves from one viewpoint to the next it loses what went before. In *La Ville de Paris* Delaunay next tried to express the mind's experience of time by fusing images with different temporal implications, but he was not successful since each of the images represented a moment of comprehension in which time was frozen. It is possible, then, that the musical analogy suggested a means of awakening consciousness of the continuity of mental experience—particularly since Bergson had used the image of music to illustrate how memory transforms the past into the Simultanist present.[53] But Leonardo's comments made Delaunay conscious of the specific properties of his medium, which demanded

147 Robert Delaunay, *2ᵉ Représentation. Les Fenêtres. Simultanéité. Ville. 2ᵉ partie 5 motifs*, 1912 (51·5 × 206·5).

148 Robert Delaunay, *Les Trois Fenêtres, la Tour et la Roue*, 1912–13 (132 × 196).

that a theme which developed in time should also be integrated into the pictorial structure in such a way that the spectator would be aware of its wholeness in the present. This is the reason why he avoided the unbroken sequential movement of works like Kupka's *Solo d'un trait brun* (Pl. 89), and concentrated on developing structure on surface and in depth in the multiple *Fenêtres* and the *Soleil, Lune. Simultané* paintings (Pls. 164 and 166).

The *Fenêtres* became more intense and more subtle as Delaunay animated the horizontal-vertical grid by introducing curving movements which add to the complexity of movement in space and in depth. He also introduced details from the world of appearances as in the *2ᵉ Représentation. Les Fenêtres. Simultanéité. Ville. 2ᵉ partie 5 motifs* (Pl. 147), or the *Trois Fenêtres, la Tour et la Roue* (Pl. 148) which was painted in late 1912 and early 1913. This is the largest and most complex of the *Fenêtres* series, and since its colours are more opaque than the transparent colours of the small jewel-like *Fenêtres*, it has a more commanding physical presence. It is possible that Delaunay's use of denser, more material colour owed something to his wife who seems to have resumed painting at about this time. Her first new paintings had none of the colouristic vitality of her Fauve works, but in her collages for bookbindings (Pls. 150 and 154) and posters, the

149 (*left*) Sonia Delaunay, coverlet, 1911. Mixed fabrics (109 × 81).

150 (*right*) Sonia Delaunay, cover for the proofs of Guillaume Apollinaire's *Alcools*, 1913. Oil on leather.

colours were more dense and opaque than Robert's, and indeed, he later emphasized the significance of the fact that her use of colour was not influenced by Cubism. In 1911 she made a patchwork quilt for their baby son (Pl. 149), and realized that its structures suggested an alternative to Cubism which they began to apply to other objects and to paintings.[54] The use of fabrics showed how sensations of projection and recession could be suggested by contrasts of colour alone, so that the sensual impact of colour would not be weakened by any other space-creating device. However, because she had been deeply influenced by Gauguin and Fauvism, Sonia Delaunay's work was always characterized by a stronger linear structure than Robert's, so that although her colours were bright, she found it difficult to develop independent pictorial structures, and tended to abstract her works from certain themes which she linked with abstract colour rhythms (Pl. 157). However, Sonia Delaunay's influence was undoubtedly crucial at this stage of their career because of her infectious enthusiasm for colour. Apollinaire described how, when they woke, the Delaunays 'talked painting ... obsessed by the new expression of colours'; this obsession resulted in the flowering of Sonia Delaunay's decorative objects and the increasing colouristic intensity of Robert's paintings.[55]

The physical density of *Les Trois Fenêtres, la Tour et la Roue* also shows how much Delaunay had learnt from his colour improvisation in 1912, for the range of effects is greater than in any earlier work. He laid in the major colour areas fairly simply, but transformed them by overlaying them with layers of transparent paint, with dry scumbles which allow the lower planes to glow through, short impressionistic strokes which take colour from one plane to the next, and heavy, rather inert, opaque planes. He used a very wide range of colours, but if one examines the fortunes of even a single colour, one can begin to comprehend the complexity of the whole. There is a green in the left-hand colour wheel which eddies towards the centre in planes coarsely streaked with brown, purple, and blue, which give way to more luminous planes which seem to melt into an infinite depth in transparent layers. As one follows this movement into depth, one is also aware of the echoing green planes on the far left, and if one concentrates on this relationship, one slowly gets the impression of a large transparent plane swinging across the whole painting from the upper left and making one 'see' that the planes—which one had previously seen as recessive—push forward from the canvas. These are only a few of the interpretations suggested by the green, and the green itself is only one element in a structure composed of varied oranges, reds, purples, blues, yellows—colours too many and too subtle to enumerate.

It is disconcerting to find that Delaunay now depicted fragments of the objective world after he had made very pressing arguments against such depiction, for although he tried to integrate them into the colour structure (for example, by giving the wheel an alternative reading as another abstract colour circle) he was not successful, since the recognizable objects act as focal points which interrupt the colour-movement. Like *La Ville de Paris*, the painting is tripartite, and as the parts range from the non-figurative on the left to the figurative on the right, it is possible that Delaunay was trying to express Simultanist experience as he had done in the earlier painting, for, if *La Ville de Paris* summed up Delaunay's past experience of painting as he saw it in early 1912, *Les Trois Fenêtres, la Tour et la Roue* sums up his experiences of 1912 itself. Moreover, its abstract section looks immediately ahead to the *Formes circulaires* of 1913. However, the painting itself confirms Delaunay's own assertion that if one fragments the object 'one fragments the universe', and it does not attain the deeper symbolic unity of the non-referential *Fenêtres*.

The paintings of 1913 and 1914: the figurative and the non-figurative

Delaunay probably began painting his first non-figurative works, the *Formes circulaires* or *Soleil, Lune* series, in the late winter or spring of 1913.[56] Slightly earlier, in the winter months of 1912–13, he was painting his figurative works, the *3ᵉ Représentation simultanée: L'Équipe de Cardiff F.C.* and the study for it (Pls. 151–2). It is possible to be over-pedantic about the purity of non-figurative art, but these

151 Robert Delaunay, *Troisième Représentation. L'Équipe de Cardiff. F. C.*, 1912–
1913 (326 × 208).

works show that in Delaunay's case there was a fundamental opposition between the figurative and the non-figurative pictorial constructions—as he himself had already stressed in his theoretical writings.

The *Équipe de Cardiff* was the first of Delaunay's developed colour structures to be exhibited in France, and, as Apollinaire indicated in his review of the 1913 Salon de Indépendants, it signalled a general tendency towards the more constructive use of colour in French painting. Delaunay described it as:

the first great example of colour construction applied to a large area. It is no longer like *La Ville de Paris* which was fragmentary and broken. The surface of the painting is living and simultaneous; the whole of the painting is an ensemble of rhythms. The modern elements, the poster, the great wheel, the tower, take part in the game of the footballers, of the bodies which weave together in life. Their relative spaces, their movement are a part of the general movement of the painting; there are no dead, no descriptive parts.[57]

The consciously modernist subject-matter links the painting with Delaunay's other Salon 'machines', *La Ville de Paris* and *Hommage à Blériot* (Pl. 172), but it is more straightforwardly modern than *La Ville de Paris* for Delaunay excluded its 'passéiste' allegorical

152 Robert Delaunay, *L'Équipe de Cardiff. F. C. Esquisse*, 1912–13 (196·5 × 130).

references. The modernist references are clear: sport was seen as a manifestation of the vitality of modern life (Gleizes and Boccioni also painted soccer and rugby players at this time); the Eiffel Tower with its wireless transmitters was used as a Simultanist image for the unity of the universe; the aeroplane enabled man to transcend past limitations of time and space; names of cities were used in contemporary poems like Apollinaire's 'Fenêtres' and Cendrars's 'Prose du Transsibérien' to suggest the poet's Simultanist consciousness of widely separate places;[58] the brilliantly coloured poster was seen to embody the dynamic life of the modern city;[59] finally, the Great Wheel, like the Eiffel Tower, was considered a supreme example of the triumphant power of modern construction and used as an image of the circular movement of the entire globe.

L'Équipe de Cardiff was transitional between the figurative structure of *La Ville de Paris* and the pure colour structure of the *Formes circulaires*. Delaunay said that it was: 'more significant in its expression of colour, less broken than *La Ville de Paris*. The yellow poster in the middle of the canvas contrasts with the blues, the greens, the orange; it is a measure of colour which functions as colour.'[60] He no longer applied pale colour transparencies over a tonal structure as he did in *La Ville de Paris*, but evolved specific images (like that of the poster) from the abstract colour areas in a way that was similar to

153 Sonia Delaunay, *Contrastes simultanés*, design for a poster, 1913–1914. Water-colour (64 × 49·2).

what Braque and Picasso were doing in their Synthetic Cubist works. Delaunay made the colour planes of the *Équipe de Cardiff* larger, simpler, and more opaque than those in the *Fenêtres*, so that the reactions between colours was more forceful. However, he still used the same principle of developing a continuum from the physiological reactions between colours (this is what he meant when he wrote that the surface of the painting was 'simultaneous'). Apollinaire commented on the colour structure of the *Équipe*, saying: 'Each colour calls forth and is illuminated by all the other colours of the prism. This is simultaneity'. His words suggest that Delaunay knew something of Goethe's belief that complementary contrasts evoke the whole spectrum. A friend of Cendrars said that the 'poet wished to make Delaunay, this *gamin* of Paris, a philosophical painter. He spoke to him of the controversies of Schopenhauer and Goethe on colour problems.'[61] If Delaunay did know of Goethe's ideas on colour, he showed as little regard for their real content as he had shown for those of Leonardo, but he would probably have been captivated by Goethe's sparkling descriptions of light and colour, by his emphasis on the creative role the eye plays in the perception of colour, and by his insistence that light is fundamental to our perception of the world. Goethe's belief that 'the eye may be said to owe its existence to light', and that 'colours are acts of light', has many echoes in Delaunay's writings. Goethe wrote:

the eye especially demands completeness and seeks to eke out the colorific circle in itself. The purple or violet colour suggested by yellow contains red and blue; orange, which responds to blue, is composed of yellow and red; green, uniting blue and yellow, demands red... When in this completeness the elements of which it is composed are still appreciable by the eye, the result is justly called harmony.[62]

Goethe's theory would have substantiated Delaunay's experience that the eye creates visual continuity, and may have encouraged him to think that, in works like the *Équipe*, the spectator could appreciate the recognizable images while, at the same time, weaving them back into the 'depths' and 'movements' of the colours. He was unsuccessful in achieving this effect because he based the group of players on a newspaper photograph and used the dark tones of the figures in the photograph so that they suggest naturalistic space and gravitational weight which conflict with the fluctuating non-gravitational space created by colour. The figures focus attention on themselves and freeze one's perception of the colour structure. The painting does not, therefore, attain the discontinuous unity which Delaunay sought, and falls apart into a number of 'dead and descriptive parts'; however, in the large oil 'sketch' (Pl. 152), Delaunay was able to integrate figures in the abstract colour rhythms

because he abandoned the use of black to situate the figures in space and translated all form into colour. Delaunay sent a photograph of the painting to Franz Marc who strongly expressed his disappointment: 'If this is one of your most recent pictures, then I must confess that I expected a development diametrically opposed to its style. This is actually the sheerest Impressionism, instantaneous photographic motion.'[63]

Delaunay's return to figuration was probably influenced by Cendrars, since the *Équipe de Cardiff* was painted in the excitement of the early stages of their friendship, when Cendrars was writing his first straightforwardly modernist poem, the 'Prose du Transsibérien et de la Petite Jeanne de France', in which he brought together different dimensions of time and place by sharply juxtaposing vivid images in a staccato discontinuous structure. He was expressing the way the mind assimilates the chaotic sensations which beat in on it, weaving them into its own being by means of memory and association. Cendrars clearly did not think much of Delaunay's non-figurative painting, for he said that Delaunay *returned* to a 'proper subject-matter' in works like the *Hommage à Blériot* or the *Drame politique* (Pl. 173), and that Delaunay used the Simultanist technique when he worked with figurative images—with 'the tower, bridges, houses, man, woman, toys, eyes, windows, books, New York, Berlin, Moscow...'.[64] Delaunay was sufficiently impressed by Cendrars's words to incorporate them in his own writings.

The *Équipe de Cardiff*, like the serial *Fenêtres*, incorporates different kinds of time—the single moment of the game and the continuous movement of colours (embodied in the image of the wheel). The 'Transsibérien' also functioned on different temporal levels, with the continuous time of the journey cut by flashes of memory to the past or by associations to the present existence of distant Paris. Sonia Delaunay added to this temporal complexity when she designed a pictorial edition of the poem with Cendrars later in 1913 (Pls. 154–5). The poem was printed on a narrow vertical strip, with expressive typography in different colours interwoven with patches of abstract colours, and accompanied on one side by a band of curving, brilliantly coloured, abstract shapes from which images of the Eiffel Tower from time to time emerge. Cendrars and Sonia Delaunay explained that 'the simultaneous contrast of colours and text form depths and movements of colours' in such a way that the poem can be *seen* as a whole, while one is simultaneously aware of its sequential development.[65] Their discussions on these matters may have persuaded Delaunay that specific images need not destroy Simultanist consciousness. However, there were significant differences between his medium and Cendrars's which he does not seem to have taken into account: Cendrars evoked specific images with

155 Sonia Delaunay, detail of 'La Prose de Transsibérien'. © by A.D.A.G.P. Paris, 1978.

154 Sonia Delaunay, coloured edition of Blaise Cendrars's 'La Prose du Transsibérien et de la petite Jehanne de France', 1913. Single folded sheet, 2 m long.

words which are *mental* signs and which thus have a free life in the mind, while Delaunay's specific images were concrete and focused attention on themselves rather than sending the mind ranging across time and space as Cendrars's did. This is why whenever Delaunay accepted a direct literary or verbal suggestion—as in *La Ville de Paris*, *L'Équipe de Cardiff*, and *Hommage à Blériot*—his Simultanism becomes enumerative and successive.

On 2 June 1913, Delaunay wrote to Macke from Louveciennes: 'I am in the country now, working a great deal, my last picture is the *sun*. It shines more and more brightly the more I work on it. From now on, all my new synchromies will be born out of this motion. The window pictures marked their beginning.'[66] In some of the *Fenêtres* of late 1912, the colours form circular movements created by the 'shafts of light': meeting the more abstract horizontal-vertical structure of the planes, they form structures like the segments of a colour wheel. The same configuration can be seen in details of the *Ville* and *Tour Eiffel* series (Pls. 132 and 129), in *La Ville de Paris* and in *L'Équipe de Cardiff* where the great wheel forms a colour circle which is also the upper part of a great 'S', of which the lower part forms a less obvious circle. Delaunay eventually developed these fragmentary curving movements into independent works, to which he gave strange titles like *Contraste simultané, Mouvement de couleur profondeur. Prisme. Soleil. 1.* Such titles do not imply that Delaunay was depicting the sun as an objective form external to the painting, but that the paintings were expressions of the principles which animate light and which are manifested in specific form in the sun and moon. This explains how he could write, 'I am painting the sun which is nothing but painting.'[67] He also said that in these paintings 'colour is *form and subject*', meaning that, since light is composed of prismatic colour, the pure colour structure of painting could embody the fundamental structure of reality, and could awaken consciousness of this reality.[68]

Circular or curving movement can be observed in Delaunay's earliest paintings—as in the concentric circles in the water and the curving movements of the foliage in *Les Bords de la Yèvre* of *c.* 1903 (Pl. 112); curving chains of movement animate *Le Fiacre* (Pl. 115), while in the *Paysage au disque* (Pl. 114) of *c.* 1906, Delaunay represented the radiation of light by a series of circles concentric to the light source—as did the Neo-Impressionists and the Fauves. The

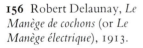

156 Robert Delaunay, *Le Manège de cochons* (or *Le Manège électrique*), 1913.

157 Sonia Delaunay, *Le Bal Bullier. Mouvement couleurs profondeur Danse Bullier*, 1913 (97 × 390).

Saint-Séverin series are made dynamic by the curving perspective and columns which always draw one's attention back to the vortex centre of the painting (Pl. 117).[69] The same curved perspective can be found in the *Tour Eiffel* series, and in the torrents of small, transparent forms in the sky, the *Formes circulaires* can be observed in embryo (Pl. 127); just as one can see them in the dynamic eddies of light in the *Ville* paintings and in *La Ville de Paris*. However, all these works were based on naturalistic gravitational structures, and it was not until Delaunay abandoned this that he could develop his circular forms more fully. Kupka led the way, in making the circular movement of light the subject of major paintings, and since he exhibited impressive examples in the Salon d'Automne of 1912, a few months before Delaunay began to paint his *Formes circulaires*, it is possible that he encouraged Delaunay to isolate and strengthen the circular movements which had already appeared in his painting.

It is probable that Delaunay was not conscious of the early evolution of the circular or curving forms in his works, that he only gradually became aware of their significance and that he found confirmation in the works of writers who used the image of the circular radiation of light as an image for the fundamental structure of reality and for the functioning of consciousness and perception. I have, for example, discussed how poets like Romains used the image to evoke the universal energy of which all things are part:

> *Et l'âme que diffuse en vapeur incolore*
> *Le mélange des chairs, des âmes, des maisons,*
> *Forme un vague halo qui nimbe ma raison.*[70]

Delaunay used strikingly similar imagery in the letter he wrote to Macke in 1913, in which he emphasized how he found it necessary to study light and the movement of colour in nature:

It is only in this way that I have found the laws of the complementary and simultaneous contrast of colours which nourish the very rhythms of my vision... It is there alone that the Spirit can evolve, by comparing the antagonisms, the struggles, the movements from which is born the decisive moment, when man becomes aware of himself on earth... Above all, I always see the sun! Since I wish for identification of myself and others, there is everywhere a halo, halos, movements of colours. And I believe that this is the rhythm. To see is a movement. Vision is the true creative rhythm; to discern the quality of rhythm is a movement and the essential quality of painting is representation, the movement of vision which functions by becoming aware of reality.[71]

Delaunay's words suggest that he experienced painting both as a means of self-realization and as a means of participating in the vital rhythms of nature. He found this inner experience confirmed by the fact that he could see the rhythms of nature emerging spontaneously and unsought in his paintings.

Sonia Delaunay described how they were both inspired by the 'multicoloured halos' which surrounded the electric lamps then being installed in the Boulevard Saint-Michel: 'Thus there came to Delaunay the idea of observing the moon; there he found the same halos; then the midday sun; there he still discovered forms in the shape of disks. Then he passed from the prismatic colour of the famous series of *Fenêtres* to circular forms, to end up finally with pure disks.'[72] Both Sonia and Robert did a number of studies of 'electric prisms' in 1913–14 (Pls. 158–9 and 171) which culminated in her large *Prismes électriques*, shown in the Indépendants of 1914, and his *Manège électrique* (Pl. 156, destroyed), exhibited in the Herbstsalon of 1913.[73] They spent the spring and summer months of 1913 at

158 (*left*) Sonia Delaunay, *Étude, Boulevard Saint-Michel*, 1913–14. Pastel (27·5 × 18·2).
159 (*right*) Sonia Delaunay, *Étude pour Prismes électriques*, 1914. Crayon (22·5 × 21·5).

Louveciennes, where Delaunay studied the light of the sun and the moon; indeed, there are details in some of the *Formes circulaires* which suggest that he occasionally represented the optical effects caused by looking at a strong light: for example, there are rounded shapes like after-images in *Soleil, Lune. Simultané 2* (Pls. IV and 166).

Goethe's *Farbenlehre* may have inspired Delaunay to look at such phenomena, or at least may have confirmed his sense of the significance of what he had observed. In his study of the physiological activity of the eye, Goethe examined the concentric halos of colour which appear round a source of light, and compared them to the 'undulating' circular movement created by a stone thrown into water, and continued:

If we have ever remarked the concentric rings which appear in a glass of water on trying to produce a tone by rubbing the edge; if we call to mind the intermitting pulsations in the reverberations of bells, we shall approach a conception of what may take place in the retina when the image of a luminous object impinges on it, not to mention that as a living and elastic structure, it has already a circular principle in its organisation.[74]

Elsewhere, in his examination of 'apparent' colours (transient effects of colour caused by such phenomena as refraction and reflection), he wrote:

If the sky is white or luminous around the sun owing to the atmosphere being filled with light vapours; if mists or clouds pass before the moon, the reflection of the disk mirrors itself in them; the halos we then perceive are single or double, smaller or greater, sometimes very large, often colourless, sometimes coloured.[75]

His study of light as it passes through a hole in a shutter convinced him that light was not composed of *rays* of colour (as Newton believed), but that it was somehow circular in structure: 'We might rather consider the splendour of the sun or of any light', he wrote, 'as an infinite specular multiplication of the circumscribed luminous image,' and he described how light passing through a small hole produced 'double shadows of bodies' which 'follow each other in light and dark coloured and colourless circles, and produce repeated, nay, almost innumerable halos'.[76] This imagery is strikingly similar to the *Soleil, Lune* series, and recalls Delaunay's phrase 'there is everywhere a halo, halos, movements of colour'. Goethe's theories would have confirmed Delaunay's sense that the underlying structure of reality was based on circular movement—and they would have done so with added force because they repeated Leonardo's comparison between the radiation of ripples in water, the radiation of sound, and of 'the spirit in the universe'.

In the summer of 1913, Delaunay explained how he used colour to express movement, the fundamental principle of life: 'There are

160 Robert Delaunay, *Soleil 1*, 1913 (100 × 81).

qualities of movement of colour of all intensities: *slow* movements, complementaries; *fast* movements, dissonances. This has nothing to do with the *descriptive* movement of the Cubo-Futurists which the painters call *dynamism*.'[77] He thus based his construction on the fact that different colours set up optical vibrations which the eye experiences as movements of different speed. He explored the relationship of complementary colours in *Soleil 1* and *Soleil 2* (Pls. 160–1). The *Soleil 1* was probably the first of the series, since it contains traces of the horizontal-vertical grid of the *Fenêtres*, whereas *Soleil 2* and *Lune 1* (Pl. 162) are composed only of circular forms. *Soleil 1* is formed from a ring of mainly complementary colours which rotates around a circle of yellow turning to white—an arrangement which might have been inspired by Kupka's *Disques de Newton* (Pl. 81). The painting has a peculiar discontinuity, as if each colour was asserting its separateness: it is this which makes one aware of simultaneous movement, for one is made to concentrate on the single colour, but at the same time, one is peripherally aware of other colours expanding and contracting in relation to it.

The *Soleil, Lune. Simultané 1* (Pl. 164) probably also came early in

161 Robert Delaunay, *Soleil 2*, 1913 (100 × 68).

162 Robert Delaunay,
Lune 1, 1913 (65 × 54).

163 Sonia Delaunay,
Contraste simultané, c. 1913
(45·5 × 55).

the series, for the right-hand portion still retains a hint of the horizontal-vertical pattern of the *Fenêtres*, and it is clearly a fulfilment of the half-realized circular movements of *Les Trois Fenêtres, la Tour et la Roue*. Delaunay's use of contrasting focal areas, based on motifs from earlier paintings, would also have derived from that painting. However, one's experience of *Les Trois Fenêtres, la Tour et la Roue* is still determined by the vestigial gravitational structure created by the naturalistic fragments, whereas *Soleil, Lune. Simultané 1* is composed of fully non-gravitational colours. It is possible that Delaunay's new compositions were influenced by Kandinksy, as he had developed the abstracted landscapes, which Delaunay saw in the Indépendants of 1912, into non-centralized, non-gravitational, multi-dimensional compositions, which Delaunay may have seen in the Sturm gallery when he visited Berlin in January 1913. There is a relationship between the structure of works like Kandinsky's large oil study for *Avec l'arc noir* of 1912 (Pl. 165) and Delaunay's *Soleil, Lune. Simultané 1*, although it is obscured by the multiplicity of tiny shapes scattered over the larger forms in Kandinsky's painting. He formed his painting from curved, brilliantly coloured shapes which clash together to give an impression of swift rotatory movement, and intensified this movement by superimposing opaque and transparent planes of contrasting hue and intensity. The way these movements fluctuate from depth to surface and from surface to depth is similar to the way movement develops in Delaunay's painting, even though the surface of the latter is more dense and material than Kandinksy's.

Delaunay divided his painting into two colour areas, one of which is dominated by the warm red-orange-yellow half of the colour circle, the other by its cool blue-green-violet half, but he introduced smaller areas of colour from each half into the other in order to animate the colours, to relate the two halves, and to create complex spatial movement. The discontinuity between the contrasting parts of the painting is very marked and was probably intentional, for Delaunay used it as a means of awakening Simultanist consciousness. The other Orphist painters also combined different forms of movement so as to embody complex temporal experience, as can be seen in Kupka's *Amorpha, Fugue en deux couleurs*, Léger's *Contrastes de formes*, and Picabia's *Edtaonisl* (Pls. II, VI, VIII, 83, and 248). The unity of such works is not immediately apparent, for it depends on the willingness of the spectator to explore relationships in time.

Delaunay painted the 'moon' area of *Soleil, Lune. Simultané 1* in rings of closely related colours, which expand slowly from the ethereal milky pink disk until they come into collision with the dissonant contrasts, the hot colours, and broken movements of the 'sun'. However, he made the movement more complex by introducing contradictory colour information into each part of the

164 Robert Delaunay, *Soleil, Lune. Simultané 1*, 1913 (64 × 100).

painting. Thus he painted a red band in the 'moon' area which is repeated by the broken reds of the 'sun' and which counteracts the recessive tendency of the more passive blues and greens; the pink moon-disk is echoed by a smaller, more intense pink, almost submerged in the dynamic spiral created by interwoven blues, greens, and purples, oranges, reds, and yellows in the 'sun' area. Delaunay thus created a physically dense structure by exploiting the way colours emit forces of different intensity, and since it is dependent on the relationship of forces which alter as the eye moves, it appears to be in a state of ever-changing movement.

In the *Soleil, Lune. Simultané 2* (Pls. IV and 166) Delaunay made the circular movement of colour stronger by discarding the last traces of the horizontal and vertical, and by adopting a circular format so that the painting is no longer like a slice cut out of space, but turns endlessly, expanding and contracting so that it seems to draw space into itself. Delaunay may have got the idea of using this format from Monet's circular *Nénuphars* of 1907 (exhibited in Durand-Ruel's gallery in 1909) (Pl. 167), in which the floating lilies occupy the same position as the sun and moon in Delaunay's painting. Monet's painting has the same capacity to draw the spectator's attention to its empty centre, so that as he becomes aware of this emptiness his gaze then moves to the isolated, unrelated circular shapes and to the circular boundary, in such a way that he also becomes increasingly aware of the paradox of a unity composed of discontinuity, and of a structure which is enclosed but limitless—paradoxes which make it impossible to grasp the work easily, and which make one intensely aware of one's relationship to it.

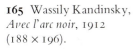

165 Wassily Kandinsky, *Avec l'arc noir*, 1912 (188 × 196).

166 Robert Delaunay, *Soleil, Lune. Simultané 2,* 1913 (133 cm diam.).

Delaunay kept the discontinuous structure of the earlier work, but tried to interrelate the two parts more closely by reducing the violent contrasts between the two colour areas, by emphasizing the rhythmical relationship between different colour shapes, and by using brush strokes to give greater continuity. In this way he created a unity in which 'sun' and 'moon' are *separate*, but can be perceived *simultaneously*: if one focuses on the turbulent, broken rhythms of the 'sun' area, the calmer colour forms of the 'moon' can still be perceived distant and mysterious so that they stabilize and intensify the 'sun'; alternatively, if one concentrates on the cool blues and greens of the 'moon', the reds and oranges turn and vibrate at the edge of one's gaze, and the blues and greens become stronger until the whole painting is dominated by them.

Delaunay did not plan these relationships: he found them as he painted, by modulating simple colour areas with striations, patches, scumbles, and glazes of contrasting or related colour. The resulting structure is based on interwoven sensations so complex and so changeable that they cannot be described in words. Delaunay found the central experience of Simultanism—the sense of the unity between individual consciousness and the universe—through his absorption in the process of creating forms in which the rational, verbal consciousness with which he defined his individual being was replaced by his consciousness of the growth of form which seemed to develop without intellectual premeditation. His feeling of the profound significance of this improvisatory activity was probably intensified by the spontaneous emergence of those circular forms which many believed represented fundamental aspects of existence. Thus he felt that he was being absorbed in the processes of growth, in the movement which animates the universe, and, as he said, 'became aware of himself on earth'. Since he left his painting process visible, he may have felt that the spectator would be able to participate in the generation of form and through this to attain consciousness of the unity of being.

The *Disque* (Pl. 168)—which was probably painted in mid-1913[78]—was the seemingly obvious climax to Delaunay's non-figurative researches, but was without sequel until the late 1930s, and was the only work of his early period in which he entirely excluded any metaphorical reference to a natural phenomenon or state of

167 Claude Monet, *Les Nénuphars*, 1907 (80 cm diam.).

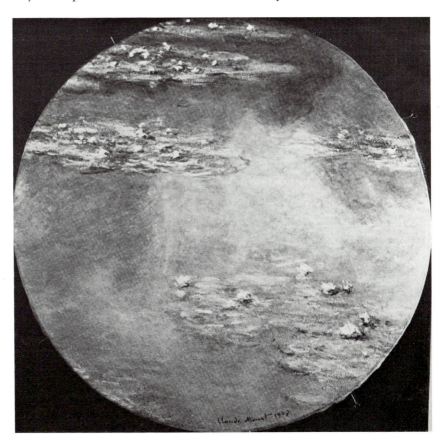

168 Robert Delaunay,
Disque, 1913–14 (134 cm
diam.).

being. It consists simply of seven concentric circles cut into four
segments on a circular canvas about four and a half feet in diameter.
In contrast to the exuberant brushwork of the *Soleil, Lune* series, the
rings are flatly painted in matt colours and are separated by a narrow
line of unpainted canvas which adds to the geometric clarity of the
whole. Since the painting makes no reference to anything outside
itself, it demands involvement in its unique being—in the expansion,
contraction, and movement of its colours. In this way, like Kupka's
earlier *Plans verticaux III*, it creates a stillness around itself in which
the spectator can be aware of nothing but the slow radiation of the
colour structure. It is possible, then, that Delaunay believed that this
concentrated stillness could create the condition in which the mind
could open out into awareness of itself in relation to the whole.

While he was painting the non-figurative *Formes circulaires* and
Disque, Delaunay was also painting the figurative *Soleil, Tour,
Aéroplane. Simultané*, a second version of the *Manège électrique* (since
destroyed), and the *Disques solaires simultané forme; au grand
constructeur Blériot* (generally called the *Hommage à Blériot* and

exhibited in the Salon des Indépendants of 1914). Slightly later he painted a curious and very uncharacteristic subject—the *Drame politique* (Pl. 173), based on a newspaper illustration of a political scandal in which the wife of a prominent politician shot and killed the editor of *Le Figaro*.[79] It has been suggested that Delaunay conceived his *Formes circulaires* merely as studies for the colour structure of his figurative works, but there is little evidence to support this view. He did not exhibit them in Paris, but this, I think, was due to his strong personal fear of criticism rather than to any lack of belief in them as paintings, since he did exhibit them as definitive works in Berlin where he felt confident of having a more appreciative response than in Paris. Moreover, since he had put forward strong theoretical justifications for non-figurative painting, it is his return to figuration that needs to be explained. Cendrars may again have persuaded him to return to a 'proper subject', perhaps convincing him that objects could function in the colour structure, just as in the external world smaller specific incidents participate in the 'universal movement'. Delaunay was most successful in doing this in *Soleil, Tour, Aéroplane. Simultané* (Pl. 170), the most beautiful of his figurative Simultanist works, showing him in full command of his technical resources so that he could for the first time express what he described as 'the poetry of the tower which communicates mysteriously with the whole world. Rays of light, symphonic waves of sound.'[80] The work is successful because Delaunay was able to make the objective forms part of the experience of colour, rather

169 Robert Delaunay, *Sculpture simultanée. Cheval prisme, Soleil, Lune*, 1913. Painted wood (*c.* 70 cm high).

170 Robert Delaunay, *Soleil, Tour, Aéroplane. Simultané*, 1913 (132·2 × 131·2).

than an obstacle to it, by representing the aeroplane with colour planes as richly modulated as those in the abstract colour areas, and by representing the Eiffel Tower with stabbing strokes of black paint which acts as a colour rather than as line or shadow (as in *L'Équipe de Cardiff*) and which can thus be integrated into the rich colour structure composed of thickly encrusted accretions of scumbles and glazes. Delaunay's use of black suggests that he may have learnt something from Léger's criticism of his colour structure as an updated Impressionism in which contrasts were lost in atmospheric continuity; his creation of a perilous unity from forms requiring different modes of visualization has something in common with the semi-figurative paintings in Léger's contemporary *Contrastes de formes* series (Pl. V). Delaunay used these different modes of visualization to emphasize the separate identity of the different parts of the painting, while uniting them by echoing and interweaving scales of colour from one part to another. One is thus made to concentrate on a single area, while being simultaneously kept aware of the complementary existence of the others: if one concentrates on the radiant transparencies of the sun area, the tower area hovers in dark tension below; if one concentrates on the tower, one is made more conscious of the glowing luminosity of the warmer area; if one concentrates on the aeroplane, one becomes aware of the dynamic forward movement of the 'sun', and, by contrast, with the light soaring tones of the sky and the sombre colours and retractive movement of the tower.

Delaunay was less successful in creating a Simultanist structure in the *Hommage à Blériot* because it was based on too strong a contrast between the abstract colour structure and the illusionist space structure. The latter is given by the aeroplane which establishes a foreground, by the Eiffel Tower which suggests distance since it is softened by atmospheric perspective and diminished by linear perspective, and by the light colours of the sky which reinforce the gravitational structure. The recognizable objects enable us to measure space by experiencing, for example, the vastness of the flight between the telescoped images of the tower and the aeroplane. Following Bergson, Delaunay had asserted in his 1912 articles that such measurements interrupted the continuity of consciousness,[81] and in the *Formes circulaires* and the *Disque* he had created fluctuating relationships with which one cannot identify, and which one cannot stabilize or measure. However, in the *Hommage à Blériot* he tried to express human bodily sensations of the kind he had embodied in the *Tour Eiffel* series, and which Romains had expressed in *La Vie unanime* in lines like 'Entre les marroniers ... Le soleil roule, et je roule vers le soleil'.[82] Romains wished to express the nature of the individual's human consciousness before it is fused with impersonal collective energies, and it is possible that Delaunay was trying to do something similar when he juxtaposed specific images with abstract ones. There is, however, no interrelation between the recognizable images and the abstract circular forms. These are composed of concentric bands of opaque colour like the *Disque*, but although they are geometrically stronger than the earlier *Formes circulaires*, they cannot counterbalance the perspectival and gravitational information given by the aeroplane, tower, and sky. The painting thus demands two quite incompatible visual responses, so that one either examines the colour structure and tries to ignore the inassimilable objects, or one attempts to decipher what is going on in naturalistic terms—in which case the abstract circles are simply a distraction. The *Hommage à Blériot* was probably inspired by literary sources for Apollinaire wrote in *Les Peintres cubistes*: 'Just as a work of Cimabue was carried in procession, so our century has seen the triumphal procession... of Blériot's aeroplane, charged with humanity, with the efforts of centuries, with necessary art.'[83] Delaunay had become interested in the idea of a universal style applicable to all the arts, so he may have been interested in Apollinaire's ideas on 'necessary art' and

171 Sonia Delaunay, *Prismes èlectriques mouvement couleur 'Simultané'*, 1914 (250 × 250).

the implicit assumption that the functional object was essentially similar to the pictorial object. Barzun and Cendrars also wrote on the theme of the aeroplane; following Apollinaire, Cendrars wrote in his poem 'Contrastes' in October 1913: 'L'aérodrome du ciel est maintenant, embrasé, un tableau de Cimabue.'[84] Barzun combined the image of the aeroplane with that of radio waves emanating from the Eiffel Tower, using them as metaphors for the total inclusiveness of the poet's consciousness and for the power of his words:

> *Je m'élève, Aérien, poussé par ses hélices,*
> *Planant majestueux au-dessus de la ville,*
> *Annonciateur des triomphes prochains.*
>
> *J'irradie, invisible, au Sommet de la Tour,*
> *Fluide portant l'espoir au navire en détresse*
> *Enveloppant la terre de mes ondes*
> *Clamant la Verbe et l'Heure au monde.*[85]

André Salmon greeted the painting enthusiastically and described how Delaunay grinds and decomposes light with the propeller of the triumphant aerial craft; he tries to suggest to us the idea of movement itself. Beyond the luminous zones born from this movement, the sterile immobility of a glider; in the halo corresponding to the horizontal rhythm, the flight— which is slower because more distant—of a *dirigeable*. Finally, the absolute immobility beyond any luminous matrix—the Eiffel Tower so dear to the heart of the painter.[86]

Salmon's words show that the content of this painting can be quite adequately translated into the verbal medium because it was itself a pictorial translation of verbal images. However, Delaunay was seeking to embody non-verbal consciousness, as shown by his evocation of what he wished to express in this painting: 'Creation of the constructive disk ... Depth and life of the sun. Constructive mobility of the solar spectrum; growth, fire, evolution of aeroplanes. All is roundness, sun, earth, horizons, fullness of intense life, of poetry *which one cannot make verbal*...'.[87] The *Formes circulaires*, on the other hand, were not translations of verbal ideas. Delaunay believed in the 'constructive mobility of the solar spectrum' as a principle of life; hence he also believed that he was following the

172 Robert Delaunay,
Hommage à Blériot, 1914
(250·5 × 251·5).

principles of nature when he created his pure colour structures. He found his own experience confirmed by Leonardo's words, which he copied out: 'Painting therefore does not need any language to interpret it ... it satisfies the human spirit immediately, as does everything produced by nature.'[88] Delaunay believed that sight could attain a profound consciousness which would only be obscured by verbalization, and he felt that when it was engaged in the pure, concentrated world of painting, it could give the individual a sense of his own inner being and of its relationship to the external world where 'all is roundness, sun, earth, horizons, fullness of intense life...' This is the sense of the conclusion to his essay on light: 'Our understanding is *correlated* to our *perception. Let us try to see.*'[89] He thus glimpsed the essential function of non-figurative art: the awakening of consciousness through contemplation of non-referential form, and he indicated that this was the experience that he himself found in painting when he wrote: 'form is the sole witness of our being ... our sole verification of reality on earth'.[90]

173 Robert Delaunay, *Drame politique*, 1914. Oil and papier colle on card (88·7 × 67·3).

ROBERT DELAUNAY

FERNAND LÉGER (1881–1955)

Léger was unlike the other Orphists, in that he was concerned with the physical reality of the external world; but he believed that changes in contemporary life had so transformed perception that reality lay in sensation rather than in comprehension of specific objects (as an example, he drew attention to the way in which speed makes objects flash into one's awareness as telescoped physical shocks which are not differentiated as objects). Thus although he drew the subject-matter of his mature works from the external world, he subordinated it to the pictorial conflict between line, colour, and volume in such a way that any associated ideas or emotions are overwhelmed by raw sensation.

The other Orphists shared Léger's preoccupation with un-differentiated sensation as opposed to intellectual knowledge of the world of things, but they found metaphysical meaning in such experience and were attracted by systems of belief which confirmed this meaning, while Léger rejected any such speculation; hence his work is distinguished from theirs as a single-minded expression of violent sensation. However, like the other Orphists, he created unique new structures which, despite their apparent simplicity, can never be simply interpreted, for, as one attempts to identify their shapes, colours, and lines as objects, these same shapes, colours, and

174 (*left*) Fernand Léger, *Le Jardin*, 1905 (46 × 38).
175 (*right*) Fernand Léger, *Le Village de Belgodère en Corse*, 1906–7 (55 × 46).

lines separate themselves from objects and break back into the fluctuating movement of the whole. Thus the 'meaning' of these paintings lies in our consciousness of their unique physicality, not in our identification of their specific subject.

Delaunay derived the intensity of his belief in light as the principle of life and central theme of painting from his experience of its centrality in his own work, Léger discovered the inner significance of his work in a similar way, for his earliest works contain strong pictorial contrasts which he developed with remarkable consistency, until he became aware of them as the basic structural principle of art, and, in 1913, declared them to be the essence of modern life and thus the fitting subject of his art.

The development of Léger's painting until mid-1912

Léger destroyed most of the works he had painted before 1909, but he said that his first ones were Impressionistic.[1] This is what one would expect from someone of his generation, and it is more interesting that his early Impressionist works reveal his individuality; for example, *Le Jardin* of 1905 (Pl. 174) has a material density very different from the immaterial luminosity of Delaunay's Impressionist works (Pl. 112). Léger painted the circular lawn and flower-bed so solidly that they become almost volumetric and clash

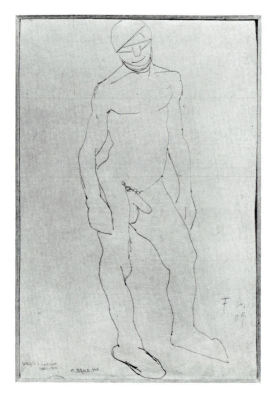

176 Fernand Léger, *Académie d'homme*, 1909. Pen and ink (33 × 25).

sharply against the path. At the same time, the thick flecks of colour detach themselves from the objects and lie scattered over the surface like confetti. Curiously, the same contrast between hard volumes and fragmentary colour was basic to Léger's *Contrastes de formes* of 1912–14; however, between *c.* 1906 and 1911, he concentrated on the expression of volume at the expense of colour. Thus the paintings he did in Corsica between 1906 and 1907 (Pl. 175) have solid block-like forms which owe much to the geometric firmness of Cézanne's classical period and which represent a reaction against Impressionist diffuseness.[2]

Léger continued this tendency in works which reflect the general movement towards geometric condensation and more sober colouring which had succeeded Fauvism by the end of the first decade of the century. The first of these works were a series of drawings of the nude done between *c.* 1908 and 1910 (Pl. 176) in which Léger disarticulated the parts of the body, reduced them to their simplest form, and boldly juxtaposed them in order to create powerful dynamic effects. The drawings have something in common with the slightly earlier works of Matisse in which he tried to express volume with the almost coarse directness seen in his *Nu bleu* (Baltimore), which was shown in the Salon des Indépendants in 1907. Apollinaire said that Léger's early compositions suggested the influence of Matisse (he was presumably talking about the works which Léger destroyed): such an influence would have strengthened Léger's expression of strong physical sensation, a form of expression which was to distinguish him from the Salon Cubists whom he met in 1910.[3]

Léger intensified the expression of volume in his first major work, *La Couseuse* of 1909 (Pl. 177), making the woman appear like a robot by the disarticulating of the body into mechanically precise parts. Léger crudely adapted Cézanne's mode of representing changes of light, by confining each change of tone to a single, clearly defined zone, and in this way he firmly attached light to volume, as he continued to do in all his pre-war works in strong contrast to the way Delaunay freed light from form. Léger's procedure was similar to the way Picasso represented light and shadow with strongly defined tactile planes in his primitivist figure-paintings like *La Paysanne* of 1908 (Pl. 178), but Léger made the zoned transition from light to dark more regular and more machine-like. His reduction of the hands to mechanical shapes could have been suggested by the same painting, although he carried the suggestion of powerful machine-like pistons further. It is not certain when Léger first saw Cubist paintings, but he could have known their work through Delaunay who had visited Braque's exhibition in 1908 and had entrée to Uhde's collection of Cubist paintings; his *Le Pont* of 1909–10 (Pl. 179) suggests that he did have early knowledge of Cubist paintings,

177 Fernand Léger, *La Couseuse*, 1909 (72 × 54).

for it is not simply a geometrization of a landscape, and in its abstraction it has close affinities to the landscapes which Picasso painted at La Rue des Bois (Pl. 123) and Braque painted at Estaque in 1908.[4] Like them, Léger split the landscape forms into small angular planes with a rather arbitrary distribution of light and shade, and continued this fracturing right up the surface of the painting, making the distant forms as hard and physically dense as those in the foreground. He was thus able to give his painting its own internal structure which was based on the forceful contrast of forms which thrust into one another.

178 Pablo Picasso, *La Paysanne*, 1908 (90·2 × 56·2).

In *La Couseuse* and *Le Pont* Léger was already interpreting the external world in an individual way, and one feels that they were the result of a deliberate process rather than of a spontaneous reaction to the external world. Léger could have been encouraged in this approach by Cézanne's words as they were published in 1907:

the painter ... gives concrete shape to his sensation and perceptions. One is neither too scrupulous, nor too sincere, nor too submissive to nature; but one is more or less master of one's model, and above all, of one's means of expression. Go to the heart of what is before you and continue to express yourself as logically as possible.[5]

Léger freely acknowledged his debt to Cézanne in these early works:

At that time I wasn't interested in anything except Cézanne ... my interest in him came at the same time as the need to exaggerate volumes. With all my strength I went to the opposite extreme of Impressionism. I became obsessed—I wished to dislocate the body. I took two years to struggle with volume in the *Nus dans un paysage* which I finished in 1910. I wished to push volume as far as it would go.[6]

Léger's *Nus dans un paysage* (Pl. 180) created a sensation when it was exhibited in the famous Salle 41 of the Salon des Indépendants of 1911, and it must have stood out even beside the works of Le

Fauconnier, Gleizes, and Metzinger (who exhibited in the same room) as a large-scale, fully and confidently realized work in a new style whose originality even Picasso recognized.[7]

Léger had come into contact with the Salle 41 group and the writers associated with them by mid-1910, and later in the year he participated in their regular discussions. They had been influenced by the epic modernism of the Abbaye de Creteil community, and were very conscious of their avant-garde mission in creating awareness of the complex totality of modern life. However, even though he was closely associated with them, Léger maintained his independence, for, as he emphasized, he was then 'not interested in anything except Cézanne', and refused to get involved in their speculations.[8] Thus, although he was probably influenced by contemporary ideas on Simultanism, for example, it is primarily in his 'struggle with volume' that one must seek the meaning of his art. Although there are similarities between his *Nus dans un paysage* and other works shown in Salle 41 such as Metzinger's *Deux nus*[9] or Le Fauconnier's *Abondance* (Gemeente Museum, The Hague), Léger had begun his painting before coming into contact with them, and it is more complex than their geometric paraphrases of naturalistic structures.

Léger disarticulated the figures and landscape into small curved shapes, modelled by the bands of light and shade he had first used in

179 Fernand Léger, *Le Pont*, 1909–10 (92·5 × 72·5).

180 Fernand Léger, *Nus dans un paysage*, 1909–11 (120 × 170).

La Couseuse, so that the whole painting (rather than just the figures) is composed of small, firmly defined shapes. Picasso was the only contemporary who could have influenced Léger, for in figure paintings of 1908–9, like the *Nu dans la forêt* (Pl. 181), he dismembered the body into angular shapes modelled by sharply defined zones of light and shade. Léger's originality lay in his use of curved planes, while in 1909–10 Braque and Picasso began to employ flat planes which detach themselves from the surface of the object and make the relationship between the object and space extremely ambiguous. Léger's curved forms were lit fairly consistently from above and defined clearly by line, so that it is easier for one to identify the figures and the elements of landscape; however, at the same time, the fragmentation of form is so extreme that figures seem almost on the point of being lost in the restless jostle of bulbous shapes. Apollinaire called attention to the way Léger also used colour to unify the painting, describing how 'the colour of the whole partakes of that deep greenish light which falls from the branches'.[10] In his *Nu dans la forêt*, Picasso emphasized the relationship between the figure and the green depths of the forest by modelling the figure with the same green. Léger used a similar technique, but while Picasso's colours were firmly attached to tangible forms, Léger, as Apollinaire suggested, created space full of green light which was more closely related to Impressionist atmospheric light than to Cubist monochromatism. In fact, although Léger claimed that his expression of volume took him to 'the antipodes of Impressionism', he tried to reconcile strongly defined volumes and atmospheric continuity until mid-1912, when he began to seek other means of relating sensations of touch and light. He also learnt much from observing how the Impressionists' attempt to express sensation reduced the importance of the specific subject, and in 1913 he pointed out that their 'research into real atmosphere is already relative to the subject: trees and houses are mixed together and are closely linked, enveloped in a coloured dynamism which their methods did not yet allow them to develop'.[11] Although the cool silvery greens of the *Nus dans un paysage* are quite different from the whiter light of most Impressionist paintings, one can see that light does in fact unite the bulging forms. It was Cézanne who showed Léger how to create a sensation of volume, without breaking atmospheric unity, by using continuous scales of colour to build into *curving* volumes so that one's perception oscillates perpetually, making the planes stabilize in volumes or breaking them into a fluctuating relief space.

Léger was perhaps the only major painter to understand Cézanne's advice to 'treat nature by the cylinder, the sphere, and the cone', and it enabled him to retain unity while exploiting the tensions between highly plastic forms.[12] Gleizes and Metzinger also noted that

181 (*left*) Pablo Picasso, *Nu dans la forêt*, 1908 (186 × 107).
182 (*right*) Paul Cézanne, *Les Trois Baigneuses*, 1879–1882 (58 × 54·5).

Cézanne had shown how to express dynamism,[13] but they tried to do so by using planes with slurred or broken contours so that their forms tend to melt together, while Léger tried to express dynamism through the active conflict between well-defined forms. He saw in Cézanne's painting an 'uneasy sensitivity to plastic contrasts'.[14] and understood that it was not straightforwardly harmonious but that it was a magnificent resolution of disharmony, imbalance, and conflicting forces. This is particularly true of Cézanne's series of nude bathers which must have profoundly impressed Léger. A number of these paintings were exhibited in the Cézanne retrospective of 1907 and in the Bernheim-jeune exhibition of 1910; Léger may also have known of *Les Trois baigneuses* (Pl. 182), owned by Matisse, which could also have influenced his *Baigneuses à la tortue* of 1908 and Picasso's *Demoiselles d'Avignon* of 1906–7. All three painters seem to have reacted to the tension and ambiguity of Cézanne's figures. In Léger's painting, as in Cézanne's, it is difficult to know what the figures are doing and what is their relationship to one another. Cézanne made his figures anonymous by representing them from the back or obscuring their faces: Léger also did this, using two of Cézanne's favourite poses, the seated figure and the figure with its arm crooked over its head, both seen from behind. Cézanne created tension within the figures by cramping their bulging forms with heavy contours, and intensified the strain by making the shallow space of the landscape far too shallow to contain the strongly modelled figures and by hardening the distant trees and clouds so that they press forward against the figures. Léger used the same devices, and made them more extreme so that the whole painting appears to be made of hard expansive forms pushing so forcefully against one another that they seem to press forward from the picture plane. Even if Cézanne's painting contains considerable tension, it is still full of a radiant light, but Léger transformed this into something sombre, just as he hardened the soft bodies by modelling them with mechanical regularity (Picasso's stark *Trois nus* of 1908–9, in the Hermitage, Leningrad, may have shown a way of disciplining Cézanne's softer and more luminous forms). He reduced his figures to small shapes like standardized, interchangeable, machine parts (which may have been suggested by the lay figure which he had in his studio, as is seen in the *Essai pour trois portraits*, Pl. 183). The movements of the figures also remind one of machines, for they suggest the interaction of separate parts which notch into one another and crank into activity in a way that is quite different from the smooth continuity of human movement. Although there is no external evidence to suggest that Léger was conscious of the machinist character of his painting, it is so consistently developed that it seems likely that he was influenced by the widespread contemporary analogy between the new man and the

183 Fernand Léger, *Essai pour trois portraits*, 1911 (196 × 115).

machine, and by the belief that the rhythms which pulse in machines animate the rhythms of contemporary life and throb in contemporary man.[15]

The almost surreal character of Léger's early figure-paintings has not been sufficiently recognized, because they have been too readily interpreted in the light of his later painting—the direct painting of the violent physical forces of modern life. These early paintings certainly have an insistent physical presence, but this is caused not merely by the pressure of form against form, but by the rather threatening implications of such forms—as was recognized by some of Léger's contemporaries. For example, in his paintings of the *Nu descendant un escalier* begun later in 1911 (Pls. 226 and 234), Duchamp followed Léger in creating sinister images in which the female nude is transformed into a mechanical construct and flesh made hard and metallic. Apollinaire, too, recognized this quality, and noted in his review of the Salon that Léger had 'the least human accent' in Salle 41.[16]

Léger accentuated this mysterious tension in his next major figure-painting, the *Essai pour trois portraits* (Pl. 183), which he may have painted during the summer of 1911 at his home in Normandy. Gleizes commented that, although the *Essai* was 'much less savage' than the *Nus dans un paysage*, Léger's 'absolute determination only to express himself plastically, gives his composition an aspect which is, at first, rather disturbing'.[17]

There is some irony in the way Léger developed a very radical stucture for a traditional portrait group composed of figures with highly individual faces and lively expressions posed formally in the artist's studio (perhaps a temporary studio in an attic or barn on his family's Norman farm, for the interior seems to be made of heavy planks and beams), surrounded by the characteristic studio paraphernalia—a sculpture-stand, bowl of fruit, pot-plant, an African carving, and the lay figure he must have used for the *Nus dans un paysage* which here wittily underlines the artificial dismembering of the human figures. Léger reduced all the figures and objects to tiny cylinders, spheres, and ribbons, modelling them so smoothly as to suggest they are all made of a shiny metallic substance. He also eliminated even the minimal perspective depth still existing in the *Nus dans un paysage* so that the firmly modelled forms project from the surface to create a dense relief similar to the relief structure of analytic Cubism, but composed of tangible curved forms rather than melting flat planes. He was thus able to create a curious fluctuating space in which the tiny bullet-shapes establish a background plane which pushes forward the larger cylinders and soft 'cloud' forms.

Léger was quite arbitrary in his treatment of the figures, and broke down the solid cores of their bodies probably because they would be too stable, merely indicating their position by the placing of the limbs. He also detached the heads from the bodies so that the head of the woman floats far above and to the right of her shoulders, and that of the man is crushed down between his arms. This arbitrariness is made more disturbing by the extreme realism of the heads, which struggle to assert themselves against the overwhelming dynamism of the abstracted forms. Léger also fractured the limbs of the figures into smaller tubes which meet at sharp angles like pistons. Similar fractures are found in Delaunay's *Tour Eiffel* series, but Delaunay broke the vertical thrust of the tower so as to make the eye conscious of vast movements in space, whereas Léger broke his forms so as to create pictorial density. For example, he repeated the tubular shapes of the limbs elsewhere in the composition without any representational function, as if to ensure continuity of the cranking mechanical rhythms. He intensified these mechanical movements by multiplying the rake-like hands so as to suggest the phases of their movement and to set up small zigzag movements which amplify the staccato rhythms of the larger cylinders. Into these complexly interlocked rhythms, he then wove other movements composed of the luminous softly expanding 'clouds'.

These free-floating curved shapes were an important element in Léger's mature style. They existed in an embryonic form in the small hillocks of the *Nus dans un paysage* which are lighter than one would expect in their context. Léger then exploited curved shapes in the *Fumées sur les toits* series, a group of small experimental works which he began in 1911 and in which the curved shapes again derived from visible facts, in that they were abstracted from the plumes of smoke billowing over the city.[18]

184 Fernand Léger, *Maisons et fumées*, 1911.

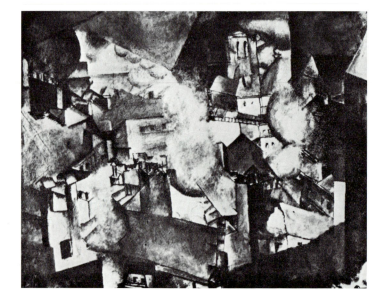

185 Fernand Léger, *Les Fumées sur les toits*, 1911 (60·3 × 96).

The view over the city was as important for Léger as it was for Delaunay, since for both painters the solution of the problem of representing its enormous size and its dynamic physical life contributed to their development of non-figurative expression. Although Léger stated that he did not paint from the motif, the linear structure of his painting was based on the view from the window of his studio in the rue de l'Ancienne Comédie, and he synthesized different aspects of his visual experience—the experience of looking down steeply on to the nearest roofs and into the chasms between them, and of looking across the distant buildings to Notre-Dame; just as Delaunay had shown a view deep into the street below and then across roof-tops to the Eiffel Tower. Although the city was a favourite Simultanist image, Léger was not interested in expressing any complex mental content: all he sought to do was to create pictorial equivalents for the movement of the eye as it tries to grasp relationships between forms in space—as Cézanne had done.[19] The *Maisons et fumées* (Pl. 184) was probably one of the earliest of the series because it is close to the observed scene. The Minneapolis *Fumées sur les toits* (Pl. 185) would also have been painted fairly early in the sequence, for its contrasting forms are straightforward simplifications of the soft plumes of smoke and angular buildings. Léger may have felt that such compositions were rather passive, for he introduced non-representational forms, transformed the smoke forms into hard geometric shapes, and eliminated atmospheric blur, so that the contrast between pictorial elements became harsher and the painting denser and more material (Pl. 187).

Léger's cityscapes could have been influenced by Braque's and Picasso's earlier studies of buildings; comparison between his *Fumées*

186 Fernand Léger, *Les Fumées sur les toits*, 1911 (46 × 55).

sur les toits (Pl. 186) of 1911 and Braque's *Les Toits de Céret* of 1911 (Pl. 146) shows how Léger developed the tensions inherent in Cubist painting into absolute conflict between the flatness of the abstract shapes and the volumes of the identifiable objects. Braque broke the contours of his planes so that solid form melts into surrounding space, while Léger wanted to express the physicality of objects, and hence emphasized their tangible substance with heavy shading and firm unbroken contours. Since the abstract shapes were no less firmly defined, the two orders of reality are equally powerful. It is therefore impossible to apprehend the gravitational naturalistic structure without one's attention being short-circuited into an awareness of the rotatory movement of the floating triangles, trapezoids, and circles.

In 1913 Léger asserted that contrasts of form provide the most effective means of expressing the intensity of modern life.[20] The *Fumées sur les toits* series shows that he developed such contrasts most strongly in small experimental works, rather than in his larger subject-paintings, for the series enabled him to study the effect of certain form-combinations more immediately, and to observe how sharply contrasting forms could be used to embody physical intensity. A similar empirical process had led Delaunay from paintings of the solid forms of the city to paintings in which these forms were dissolved by the immaterial energies which *he* believed

187 Fernand Léger, *Les Fumées*, 1912.

to be the essence of life.

Léger's use of contrasts in the *Essai pour trois portraits* was less straightforward. The cloud-forms were partly derived from the external world (as in the light which pours through the window or seems to fall on the back of the chair), but they also assume their own life, independent of visual reality, and one can sense that Léger was fascinated with what he could do with them—he made them gleam out of the sombre blue-greens like a quivering transparent substance, so that they seem to ooze from behind the harder forms; he used them to establish soft movements which throw the sharper movements of the machine-forms into relief and which simultaneously unite and intensify the metallic shapes. But whichever way he employed them, they add to the hallucinatory effect of the strange figures.

The painting is hauntingly mysterious. Its parts are clearly defined, but their colours are soft and full of light, and melt as one looks at them; the formal portrait disintegrates into restless fragments; the human figure takes on the substance of metal and makes movements characteristic of a machine; and the whole painting seems to be in continuous movement, in perpetual transformation so that it seems impossible ever to grasp it.

Léger expressed the unity between the figures and their environment by reducing them to a single substance, and it is possible that he was influenced by Romains's attempts to express the unity between man and his ambiance, and between the individual and the collective.[21] Léger was resolutely opposed to the use of specific literary themes in painting and was no less hostile to philosophic speculation about it; however, he also believed that the artist should express his own age, and clearly his consciousness of contemporary life would have been influenced by his colleagues' discussion of the dynamic synthetic character of modern life. The Salon Cubists were interested in Bergson, and the mode of consciousness embodied in Léger's painting could be described as Bergsonist, for Bergson's ideas on the unbroken continuity of every manifestation of life could be reflected in the serial movement of the hands and limbs, and in the curious way that the bodies seem about to melt into the surrounding forms.[22] Bergson's theme of the perpetual transformation of matter is paralleled in the ceaselessly changing forms of the *Essai*. These qualities ensure that one's experience of the painting is an experience that develops in time, giving one an ever-deepening consciousness of the physical being of the painting and of one's own relationship to it. This experience of a consciousness that develops in time but is simultaneously gathered up in the single physical being of the painting is again Bergsonian. However, it would be uncharacteristic if Léger had set out to paint a Bergsonist painting in a programmatic way, and it is more probable that he arrived at a painting which embodies such complex forms of consciousness through the actual

188 (*left*) Fernand Léger, *Le Compotier*, 1911–12 (83·8 × 98·7).
189 (*right*) Fernand Léger, *Dessin pour une abondance*, 1911–12. Pen and ink (30·5 × 20).

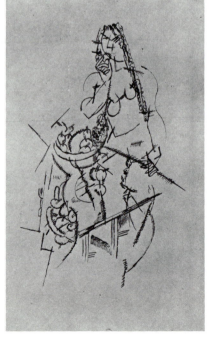

experience of painting. His initial conception was of a relatively conventional grouping of people in rigidly frontal poses, but his need to express physical intensity led him to break the figures into smaller and smaller fragments, pushing 'volume as far as it would go', and trying to make his composition both physically dense and dynamic. Once he had freed himself from the conception of the human figure as a continuous volume (as he had begun to do in his earlier drawings and in the *Nus dans un paysage*), he was free to develop the density of his composition and to do so over a period of time, and this process—perhaps inevitably—resulted in a form of expression which could be called Bergsonist (particularly since Léger incorporated details like the multiplied hands which suggest a specific theoretical influence).

It is quite possible that Léger's painting was analysed in Bergsonist terms by Léger's colleagues—for it was exhibited in Salle 8 of the Salon d'Automne with works which were more obviously inspired by philosophic concepts[23]—and such analyses may have led Léger to a more conscious exploration of such ideas in his subsequent paintings, *La Noce* and *Le Fumeur* (Pls. 190 and 192), for they are based on an intricate interweaving of figures and urban landscape in a way that suggests that Léger was trying to express something more complex than he had done in his previous works.

There is some doubt about the dating of the two paintings, but I think that *La Noce* was executed first, and that it can be identified with the *Composition avec personnages* exhibited at the Salon des Indépendants of 1912. The considerably smaller *Le Fumeur* (which is 126 cm. high, while *La Noce* is 257 cm. high) would have been painted shortly after, as it seems to me to be transitional between the complexities of the early figure-paintings and the new geometric simplicity and directness of *La Femme en bleu*, painted during the summer of 1912 and exhibited in the Salon d'Automne.[24]

It is possible that *La Noce*—like Delaunay's *Ville de Paris* (Pl. 136) and Gleizes' *Baigneuses* in the same exhibition—was conceived as a major Unanimist or Simultanist statement, for one of the major themes of Romains's Unanimist poetry was that of a crowd of people united by a festive occasion and animated by lively rhythms which pervade the figures and their surroundings, and Léger was clearly expressing something very similar. Léger undoubtedly took longer to paint his work than Delaunay did to execute *La Ville de Paris*, and perhaps for this reason he was more successful in uniting different orders of reality. He again dismembered the figures, but he dissociated their heads and limbs even further from their bodies and made them less plastic, so that they fuse more easily with other tiny patches of colour or with the soft cloudy areas of colour. These confetti-like fragments only solidify into recognizable forms (faces, top-hats, hands, dresses, houses, trees, furniture) when one focuses

190 Fernand Léger, *La Noce*, 1911–12 (257 × 206).

on them, and they dissolve back into kaleidoscopic movement when one looks elsewhere. Léger made the cloud-forms more luminous so that they interpenetrate and fuse the tiny shapes. Although their shapes derive from the smoke or light in earlier works, they no longer have any basis in observed reality, and Léger used them for purely pictorial effect. He may have observed how, in 1911, Braque and Picasso began to use large stable planes amidst the small fluid ones, to create a new form of space which seems simultaneously to emerge from the picture's surface and to sink back into it. Léger developed this kind of space, but made it richer by moulding his large planes with transparent layers of colour until they were almost sculptural (as, for example, the folded and scooped planes on the right). He thus created complex non-gravitational space by cutting into the picture's surface or by shaping forms which press forward from it. He awakened sensations of touch, suggested the volume and weight of objects, but at the same time detached such sensations from specific objects. The Cubists, too, broke down the physical sensations attached to the specific object in order to create a painting which was intensely physical in itself. However, Cubist paintings are always small, whereas Léger's *La Noce* is over eight feet high, so that the spectator is more completely immersed in the painting and in its intricate interwoven movements. These movements function across the surface or in and out of depth in an extraordinarily complex way—the small bulbous shapes create a chaotic circular movement, and the abstract shapes radiate forward from the centre of the painting, form three verticals which move across the surface, and swing slowly into a rotatory movement which is intensified by the tubular arms which act like the pistons of a machine in movement. There are similar complex movements in Delaunay's *Ville de Paris*, but Léger was able to interlock them so that they create a dense structure which draws one into its complex life, while, paradoxically, it also retreats from one's apprehension. Delaunay was less involved in the development of a pictorial structure, for he was trying to realize a literary concept, whereas Léger was concerned, above all, with the creation of a new physical reality.[25] Moreover, his painting was probably inspired by his friend André Mare's wedding (at which he was present: he appears in a wedding photograph which he may have used for the composition), so it embodied something he had himself experienced—the sensation of being part of a crowd united by a common sentiment of joy. *La Ville de Paris*, on the other hand, was not based on direct physico-emotional experience (except in certain parts), and it may be no coincidence that its structure was less intensely worked than Léger's.

La Noce is in many respects similar to Severini's *Danse du Pan-pan à Monico* (Pl. 12), shown in the Futurists' exhibition six weeks before

Léger exhibited his work in the Indépendants. Severini's was a huge work which had taken over a year to paint, and since they moved in the same circles, it is quite possible that Léger could have seen Severini's work while it was being painted, either before or after he began his own work. Severini also represented a festive occasion—a crowded night-club animated by the interlocking and contrasting rhythms of different dances—and he fragmented the figures, the interior, and all the accessories, so that they form part of the interwoven movements. Léger also tried to express the experience of being in an animated crowd which absorbs everything in its excited rhythms so that only details—hands, top-hat, a laughing mouth—momentarily catch the attention and are then reabsorbed into the multiple movements. Léger's conception is remarkably similar to Severini's, and the unusual mobility and lyrical colours of his painting may also owe something to *La Danse du Pan-pan*.

Léger inserted diagonal splinters of a townscape into the figure-composition as if to suggest the turbulent intermixture of images in the mind. In this respect, the painting has some similarities to Boccioni's *Quelli che vanno* (Pl. 139) in the *Stati d'animo* triptych, in which transparent fragments of houses penetrate the heads. The triptych was shown in the Futurists' exhibition in February 1912, and since Léger seems to have painted the fragments of the townscape when the work was quite advanced,[26] it is possible that he decided to strengthen the dynamic interpenetration of forms after seeing Boccioni's painting. However, this would have been no more than a change in emphasis, for Léger's boldly-worked study for *La Noce* (Pl. 191) shows that he had from the beginning conceived the juxtaposition of separate realities—the wedding group, the fragments of landscape, and the abstract shapes. The major difference between the study and the finished work is that Léger originally represented fewer figures and gave them solid, coherent bodies, arranging them in vertical bands separated by abstract bands, with none of the complex interpenetrating rhythms of the finished work. The dense physical substance of the finished work seems to have developed as Léger painted and as he transformed his specific sources into something new and strange.

With its haunting juxtaposition of dense physicality and quivering green or roseate light, of thrusting metallic shapes and soft evocative ones, *La Noce* is indeed a curiously enigmatic painting. It has a real relationship with Duchamp's *Portrait* (*Dulcinée*) (Pl. 9) which had been hung in the same room as the *Essai pour trois portraits* in the Salon d'Automne. Duchamp represented the figure of a woman in so insubstantial a manner that she seems about to melt into the immaterial space surrounding her, and in this way he seems to suggest that she has no reality apart from her existence in his mind.

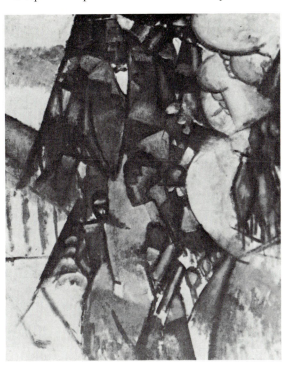

191 Fernand Léger, *Étude pour La Noce*, 1911 (81·3 × 68).

By depicting her change from a clothed to a naked state, he was trying to represent the 'processes of desire' and the mind's power of transforming reality. Similarly, Léger seems to have been representing not only the physical experience of being at a wedding, but the memories, feelings, and associations which it evoked. Thus the soft fleshy pinks and rounded forms of the central shapes suggest a woman's naked hips and thighs and—whether or not Léger intended it—clearly such an image is as much part of a wedding as the top-hatted gentlemen. The sexual association was made by a contemporary critic who described the painting as: 'a conglomeration of soap-bubbles which represent, higgledy-piggledy, quarters of faces, an assortment of profiles and of unattached eyes; the whole is sprinkled most harmoniously with breasts, thighs, and stomachs.'[27] Léger's images change continuously and are so unstable and indeterminate that they ceaselessly melt into other forms, thus recalling Bergson's account of the perpetual flux of mental images as they are transformed by memory and emotion. Léger would certainly have been aware of Bergson's ideas, for they were discussed by his friends; yet although his *awareness* of mental processes may have been influenced by Bergson, Léger is unlikely to have been directly influenced by him, for he arrived at experience through painting, and his understanding of mental processes derived more profoundly from his own creative processes. By this time, he allowed the picture to grow as he painted it, freely elaborating his broadly realized, relatively simple, original conception and responding to the associations aroused by the evolving forms. Thus although literary Unanimism may have suggested the idea of representing a collective event, and although other paintings may have suggested different ways of doing so, ultimately the real meaning of the painting derives from Léger's pictorial experience.

Paintings of pure sensation 1912–14

After painting *La Noce*, Léger seems to have made a deliberate decision to abandon complex subject-matter and to clarify his formal structure by eliminating the atmospheric effects found in his paintings of 1910 to early 1912. *Le Fumeur* (Pl. 192) played a significant role in the transition from complex figurative paintings to simpler, more abstract ones. It has none of the mystery of *La Noce* or the *Essai*, for Léger was interested only in expressing intense physical sensation. Shortly after, in *La Femme en bleu* and the first of the *Contrastes de formes* (I have given this title to the whole series, though some have more specific titles), Léger simplified his subjects even more radically so that he could concentrate entirely on the expression of sensation. The works which he then painted, between the summers of 1912 and of 1914, ranged from ones where no subject can be seen, to ones in which the subject is very clear.

It is possible that this change was influenced by Léger's reaction to the Futurists' paintings. He was interested in many of their ideas, but was probably not sympathetic to the blurred atmospheric qualities of the paintings he saw in their February exhibition, and his reaction may have led him to be more critical of similar qualities in his own painting. When the Milan Futurists visited the Salon d'Automne in late 1911, they saw Léger's *Essai pour trois portraits*. Since it would have been the most dense and forceful painting they saw there, it may have contributed to the emphatic statement they made about pictorial conflict in their Parisian catalogue in 1912: 'every object influences its neighbour... by a real competition of lines and a real conflict of planes'.[28] However, the works they showed in their exhibition still tended to veil conflict in atmospheric haze. Léger's expression of contrasting forms was more forceful, even though he still softened some transitions with cloudy forms; but, in *Le Fumeur* and the slightly earlier *Compotier* (Pl. 188),[29] he began to harden the soft shapes and to bring them into direct conflict with the smaller representational forms. His reaction against Impressionistic continuity can also be observed in his use of separate viewpoints in *Le Fumeur*, where he sharply juxtaposed the implied space of an interior with a wide urban vista, jammed a figure against the landscape, inserted a still-life fragment which was presumably in the interior, and, without any atmospheric transition, piled up a tangle of planar

192 Fernand Léger, *Le Fumeur* [*Les Fumeurs*], 1911–12 (21·4 × 96·5).

roofs and heavily modelled oval trees. These harsh juxtapositions are quite different from the fusion of different elements in *La Noce*.

The use of the picture plane as a window looking on to a cityscape was a fairly common means of representing simultaneity, for it enabled the painter to fuse the near and the far, the individual and the collective, the small and the vast, the detailed and the generalized; but when Léger had previously depicted a view from a window, he did not present the simultaneous interpretation of interior and exterior as he did here. Delaunay had tried to do so in *La Ville. n⁰ 2* (Pl. 131), but had indicated the window in only the vaguest way so that the eye glides imperceptibly from the window into the depths of the painting, whereas Léger's staccato construction seems designed to make one aware of the movement of sight from the near to the far. Léger's interest in such visual sensations may have been aroused by a passage in the Futurists' catalogue:

In painting a person on a balcony, seen from inside the room ... we try to render the sum total of visual sensations which the person on the balcony has experienced ... This implies the simultaneousness of the ambient, and, therefore, the dislocation and dismemberment of objects, the scattering and fusion of details, freed from accepted logic, and independent from each other.[30]

This passage clearly refers to Boccioni's *La strada entra nella casa* (Pl. 3), which was shown in the 1912 exhibition and which contains a figure in the foreground on a balcony high above the street which acts as an intermediary between interior and exterior. This conception may well have influenced Léger's, although Léger embodied the complex visual sensations of being in a room and looking out from it, instead of depicting the sensations of the figure on the balcony. Apart from this, there are strong similarities between the two paintings: for example, his still-life plays the same role as Boccioni's balcony-rail in indicating the simultaneity of interior and exterior, and his figure, like Boccioni's, is juxtaposed with spiralling fragments of an urban vista. However, Boccioni tended to soften these juxtapositions with his vibrant, Impressionist colour, while Léger slammed them into one another.

Léger's doubling of the head to suggest its movement in space could also have been influenced by Boccioni's repetition of his figure. He had already used serial images in the *Essai* and *La Noce*, but only in details and as much to animate the composition as to represent movement, whereas the serial movement of *Le Fumeur* is central to one's experience of the painting, for Léger used it to create the visual movement necessary for one to grasp the discontinuous forms by making the doubled head turn into the painting, so that it draws one's eyes with it and makes the whole cityscape turn in a series of inter-locking movements (Delaunay, as has been said, had used similar devices in the *Saint-Séverin* and *Tour Eiffel* series).

Le Fumeur has a physical immediacy which was new in Léger's work. He accentuated the tactile separateness of individual objects by means of modelling and strong local colour, and at the same time strengthened the non-representational forms which derived from the plumes of smoke in earlier works, but made them so hard and firm that the derivation is no longer obvious. Léger inserted some of these geometric planes behind the objective forms, so that they press the smaller forms forward and shatter the continuity of the cityscape. One is thus most fully aware of the sensations of weight, tangibility, and movement, while recognizable images only flicker into one's awareness without ever settling into static, clearly identifiable form.

Léger wished to embody the form of consciousness most appropriate to the modern age of the power and intensity of its physical being. He was also concerned with pre-conceptual consciousness, for he shared the view of many of his contemporaries that intensity of experience is weakened if the intellectual process intervenes to classify sensations into objects. He asserted that, since painting is visual, it should not be 'psychological' and should reflect 'external conditions'.[31] Thus, after the *La Noce*, he stopped trying to represent complex physico-mental experience, and concentrated on realizing pictorial structures whose objective content was overwhelmed by powerfully conflicting forces. These new paintings—which include *La Femme en bleu* and the *Contrastes de formes* (Pls. 195 and 203–7)—are paradoxically both representational and non-representational.

Léger painted the first *Contrastes de formes* in the second half of 1912, that is, at the time the other Orphists were evolving non-figurative forms; he would have participated in the discussions on the subject at Puteaux; he would also have seen Kupka's non-representational works, and have observed Delaunay's approach to pure painting in the *Fenêtres simultanées* and known about his ideas concerning non-representational art. He could have observed that the figures in Picabia's *Danses à la source I* and *La Procession, Séville* (Pls. 224–5) are swallowed up by the movement of colour in a way that was paralleled by his own paintings, and he could also have read Apollinaire's comments on the new art. His new works fitted naturally into the tendency towards pure painting and justified Apollinaire's assertion that Delaunay, Léger, Picabia, and Duchamp were 'struggling in the same direction'.[32] He realized his most abstract *Contrastes de formes* in mid-1913, at the same time that Delaunay painted his *Soleil, Lune* series and that Picabia executed his first fully non-representational paintings[33].

Léger's paintings of this period are less densely structured and thickly worked than his earlier ones, and, in this respect, even the two works he painted for the Salons—*La Femme en bleu* (Salon d'Automne, 1912[34]) and the *Nu dans un atelier* (Salon des Indépendants, 1913, Pl. 196)—were closer to the *Contrastes de formes* than to the earlier Salon paintings. Léger's change to small, roughly painted, experimental works may have owed something to the fact that he signed a contract with Kahnweiler in 1913, and was thus absolved of the need to paint eye-catching Salon pictures.[35] Green has also convincingly suggested that Léger's change to an experimental series was related to 'the new dynamic view of reality', and it does seem probable that he shared the belief of many of his

193 Fernand Léger, *Étude pour La Femme en bleu,* 1912 (129·5 × 100·3).

contemporaries, including the Orphists, Kupka, Delaunay, and Picabia, as well as Apollinaire, that authentic experience is to be found in the *process* of creating form rather than in embodying pre-existent ideas in a planned structure. The same rejection of the final and the static can be seen in the sketchy lines, scrubby paint, kaleidoscopic surfaces, unresolved movements, broken rhythms, discordant shapes, and unstable combinations of conflicting forms of the whole *Contrastes de formes* series.

The last time in the pre-war period that Léger used an oil-study in the traditional way as a means of clarifying a structure was in the study for *La Femme en bleu* (Pl. 193), probably painted in the early summer of 1912. Thus before he had begun to paint the final work, he had already worked out a highly abstract structure composed of hard geometric forms, painted in flat opaque colours with heavy contours, and had fragmented the figure of the woman into such unspecific shapes that only the hands give a clue to its presence. The few changes that Léger made between the study and the final work served to strengthen pictorial contrast; for example, Léger shattered what was left of continuity of surface in the study by strengthening the opacity of the planes and eliminating atmospheric luminosity from all but peripheral areas. He had first used coloured abstract planes in *Le Fumeur*, but although they contrast with the small representational forms, they also form continuous rhythms with them since they are fused by blurred contours and transparent planes. However, in *La Femme en bleu* there is real conflict between the two orders of reality, for the abstract planes fragment the continuity of the objective forms and threaten to overwhelm them altogether. Léger could have been influenced by the way Braque and Picasso used collage to contrast material and representational realities (Pl. 194), but took the principle of contrast much further by using the abstract planes to counteract our very conception of the human figure: he transformed the rounded forms which he had previously used to represent parts of the body into *flat* planes of sharply contrasting tones, and made the great blue plane slice into them, scattering them sideways so that any sense of the figure as a solid existence in space is lost. In this way, the sensations of tangibility, of physical volume, and weight which would normally appertain to the figure were taken over by the painting as a whole.

Léger later explained that in order to liberate himself 'from Cézanne's domination' and 'from Impressionistic melody' he had to go 'as far as abstraction' in *La Femme en bleu* and *Le Passage à niveau* (Pl. 13).[36] He believed that the mode of expression suited to the Impressionists' age was that of an unbroken atmospheric continuity, but that since modern life was violent, fragmentary, and dissonant, he should develop a style based on violent and discontinuous contrasts and dissonances.[37] Many of his contemporaries also used contrasting images and pictorial elements as a means of expression, but when they did so, they also found means of weaving the contrasting elements together, as when, for example, Delaunay modulated the contrasting images and colours of *L'Équipe de Cardiff F.C.* in such a way that the eye slips easily from colour to colour. Léger was very critical of Delaunay's 'Impressionist colour relationships', and tried to eliminate such continuities by avoiding the juxtaposition of complementaries which create optical mixtures so that he could 'arrive at colours which isolated themselves—a very red red, a very blue blue.'[38] The separation of pictorial elements in *La*

Femme en bleu creates a conflict between one's apprehension of the picture's surface structure and one's experience of its depth, and also makes it impossible to 'see' the figure as an integral whole, for, as one seeks to reconstitute it, it disintegrates into conflicting planes. Léger carried discontinuity even further in *Le Passage à niveau*, by replacing the continuous modelling he had used in the representational forms in *La Femme en bleu* with sharply contrasting bands of light and dark, and by separating colour from line by isolating bands or patches of colour within the areas bounded by line. The painting gives the impression of kaleidoscopic colour, animated but not delimited by heavy lines, and only temporarily stabilized by the harder geometric planes. Léger had painted no pure landscapes since *Le Pont* of 1909–1910, probably because he found it easier to express contrasts in the literal contrast between architectural solidity and the indeterminate forms of smoke; but perhaps he now had greater confidence in his new mode of expression and wished to demonstrate its universal applicability. He believed that since 'all this research comes from the modern environment', any subject was suitable for the new mode of expression.[39] The new subject may have helped him to break from his reliance on the object which had still determined the structure of *La Femme en bleu*, for it was probably more difficult to disregard the peculiar properties of a figure than the less emotive forms of a

194 Georges Braque, *Compotier et verre*, 1912. Papier collé and charcoal on paper (61 × 44·5).

195 Fernand Léger, *la Femme en bleu*, 1912 (194 × 130).

196 Fernand Léger, *Nu dans un atelier*, 1912–13. Oil on burlap (127·8 × 95·7).

landscape, and since a landscape is less tangible and less immediate to the eye than a figure, Léger must have realized that he had to *introduce* contrasts to intensify the structure, rather than abstract them from existing forms. However, he had no intention of maintaining formal distinctions between different subjects, and applied the same divisive technique to any subject.

The *Nu dans un atelier* (Pl. 196), exhibited in the Salon des Indépendants in 1913, was Léger's first major work in his new style. It is characteristic of his fresh approach that, although it is quite a large painting (152 cm. high, compared with the 194 cm high *Femme en bleu*), it is much more sketchy in execution and appearance than his earlier work; thus, while *La Femme en bleu*, *La Noce*, and the *Essai* contained beautiful areas of painting, Léger almost scrubbed the paint on to the roughly primed canvas of the *Nu dans un atelier*— perhaps in order to call attention to the paint as a *substance* and to stress its non-imitative character. This enabled him to reduce all forms to the same degree of abstraction, and to eliminate the sharp distinction between representational and non-representational form that was the basis of *La Femme en bleu*. The painting thus has greater surface continuity which, paradoxically, made it easier for Léger to develop dynamic clashes between opposing movements. He reduced the body to a series of interlocking, ambiguously curved planes

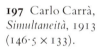

197 Carlo Carrà, *Simultaneità*, 1913 (146·5 × 133).

198 (*left*) Carlo Carrà, *Nuda di donna*, 1912. Pen and ink (81 × 35·5). **199** (*right*) Fernand Léger, *Femme nue*, 1913. Pencil (49 × 32).

which swing down the centre of the canvas; he inserted a few angular planes into the curves, so that the 'body' is broken down into the angular planes on either side of it; and he reinforced the smooth central movement with echoing curves on the right-hand side of the painting. In this way, Léger succeeded in establishing the continuity of the figure, while simultaneously emphasizing its discontinuity by means of the lateral displacement of angular and curved planes.

There are interesting similarities between Léger's painting and Carrà's *Simultaneità* of 1912–13 (Pl. 197), for Carrà also built up the body of a female nude from curved planes with metallically smooth modelling and broke the continuity of the figure by thrusting angular house-forms and abstract 'lines of force' into it (just as Léger's nude is penetrated by red and white zigzag shapes which he often used to represent roofs or steps). Although Léger is unlikely to have seen Carrà's painting, he may have seen some related drawings of late 1912 and early 1913, for they are more staccato and fragmentary than the oil-painting, and are remarkably similar to Léger's drawings of a nude of the same period (Pls. 198–9). The Futurists certainly believed that they had influenced the dynamism of his works of early 1913, and when a lecture in which Léger strongly emphasized the dynamism of modern life was published with a reproduction of an abstracted drawing of a nude entitled *Études de dynamisme linéaire* (Pl. 200) in *Montjoie!* in May 1913, Carrà claimed that Léger misunderstood their ideas and that the drawing was 'passéiste', although Boccioni welcomed the article as 'a real act of Futurist faith' even though he disputed some points in it.[40] However, Léger merely took the relationship between his art and Futurism to be confirmation of the universality of the movement towards the new realism, and would have thought it reasonable to adapt their ideas and forms if he needed them.[41] The Futurists may have contributed to his belief that 'contemporary life, more fragmented and faster-moving than in preceding periods, has had to accept an art of dynamic divisionism as its means of expression', for they had insisted upon the importance of divisionism in the expression of modern life in their 'Technical Manifesto' of 1910, and, as Boccioni claimed in his article, they were the first to insist on divisionism as a 'definitive system'. However, despite their emphasis on the dynamic conflict of pictorial elements, in practice they softened such conflict by continuing to use Impressionistic broken colour which suffused their forms with light, whereas Léger went further and insisted that 'divisionism of colour' must be succeeded by 'a parallel research into the divisionism of form and of drawing'; accordingly he broke every continuous volume, line, or colour into smaller parts and kept them separate, so that one is the more aware of their particular character and each element can function with maximum effect.

The figure in the *Nu dans un atelier* is like a machine, for the modelling suggests the shiny curves of polished steel; the separate

200 Fernand Léger, *Étude de dynamisme linéaire*, 1913.

parts are put together as a machine is put together; and the way energy is transferred from one group of forms to another is more characteristic of mechanical than of human dynamism in which energy flows in continuous movement through the whole body. Léger later described how he, Duchamp, and Brancusi had been overwhelmed by the contrast between the Salon d'Automne and the Salon d'Aviation which they visited when both were held in the same building. He spoke of his enthusiasm for 'the beautiful hard metal objects . . . with pure local colours', and for the way 'steel in its infinite variety played against the vermilions and blues'.[42] He could have been describing his own painting which gives one the physical pleasure of a well-oiled, beautifully functioning machine. His fusion of the human and the machine is celebratory, and has none of the bleak and sinister implications of Duchamp's *Nu descendant un escalier II* (Pl. 234)—it may, indeed, have been partly intended as a comment on Duchamp's pessimistic view of the new world of the machine.

Les Maisons sous les arbres (Pl. 201) shows how Léger used the same forms in different contexts and different combinations like the interchangeable parts of a machine. The combination of curved and angular planes is very similar to that in *Nu dans un atelier*, except that Léger transferred the angular planes to the centre of the canvas, and

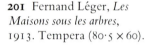

201 Fernand Léger, *Les Maisons sous les arbres*, 1913. Tempera (80·5 × 60).

202 Robert Delaunay, *Soleil*, 1913 (75 × 71).

the more heavily modelled, interlocking curves to the sides. Although the painting represents a landscape, Léger used several devices to make it impossible to read any coherent landscape-space within the painting: for example, he made the green curves swing across the surface, dug the vertical planes into the ground plane which is pulled up to the surface of the painting, and thrust the black and isolated blue planes forward so that they counteract any landscape recession. Without the landscape frame of reference, the painting is very difficult to look at, for its elements contrast so strongly that it is hard to see any relationship between them, and it is only gradually that one begins to appreciate how continuities develop from discontinuities, how shapes, colours, and lines interpenetrate in complex oscillating movement, and how the whole structure ceaselessly renews itself.

Les Maisons sous les arbres was probably painted shortly after the *Nu dans un atelier* for it has a surface-continuity that Léger shattered in the mature *Contrastes de formes*. It would then have been contemporary with Delaunay's early *Formes circulaires*: it is certainly closer to Delaunay's non-figurative paintings than are any other works by Léger, and there is a real relationship between it and the *Soleil* in the Folkwang Museum, Essen (Pl. 202), for Léger's painting had greater colouristic continuity than his later *Contrastes de formes*, and Delaunay used blacks and lines to intensify contrasts rather than relying on pure colour relationships as in most of the *Formes circulaires*. There are similarities in the way the two painters modulated curved forms, made angular planes penetrate rounded ones, and kept their paintings in movement. Léger's painting was, of course, more rooted in sensations of the objective world than was Delaunay's, for his forms obey the pull of gravity, while Delaunay's turn freely in space, and his surfaces are tactile where Delaunay's are immaterial.

However, Léger seems to have felt that the contrasts in works like *Les Maisons sous les arbres* were weak, and his observation of the optical mixture in Delaunay's paintings may have convinced him of the need for strengthening line and isolating colour even further. This conviction was given greater force by Léger's thoughts on the nature of realism. He believed that modern realism originated in the Impressionists' preoccupation with sensations of colour rather than with the specific form of individual objects, pointing out that if they painted a green apple on a red carpet, they would be interested in 'the

203 Fernand Léger, *Contrastes de formes: Nature morte aux cylindres colorés,* 1913 (129 × 193).

relationship between two colours' rather than in the objects themselves.[43] He believed, however, that in limiting themselves solely to colour sensations, the Impressionists were still too close to 'visual realism'—to a passive acceptance of the fact that if one looks 'at objects in their surroundings', one does 'not perceive any line defining the zones of colour'. Léger felt that this passive approach did not allow the artist to express his own individual experience of nature, and he insisted that it was not enough for the artist to remain 'an imitator of the new visual world', for he had to 'achieve a completely subjective awareness of this new state of things'. In order to express this subjective awareness, the artist must invent forms which are not found in a pure state in nature: 'From now on, everything can contribute to an intensity of realism obtained by purely dynamic means. Pictorial contrasts in the purest sense (complementaries of colours and lines, of forms will henceforth be the fundamental structure of modern paintings.' Thus he declared unequivocally that 'the realist value of a work of art is completely independent of any imitative quality'.

Léger claimed that the cinema and popular novel had made 'the visual, sentimental, representational, and popular' subject-matter of traditional painting irrelevant, so that if a painting did have a recognizable subject, it was merely a pretext for 'the simultaneous disposition of the three great plastic qualities: Lines, Forms, and Colours'—as he defined pictorial realism. Léger combined these pictorial elements in many different ways, making no essential distinction between landscape, still-life, and figure paintings, or between representational and non-representational painting (Pls. 203–6).[44] It is striking that he was able to develop so many variants on so narrow a range of themes and with so limited a number of pictorial elements, but in fact these limitations emphasize not only the unity but the diversity of the *Contrastes de formes*, for they demand that one looks closely at them in order to appreciate the subtle variations between them; one thus becomes more and more deeply aware of their unique pictorial being, so that on this level, they function like variations on a musical theme. Léger did not explore these variations in order to perfect a structure—for no *Contrastes de formes* is more 'final' than another—but he used them, partly to demonstrate the infinitive variety of modern life, and, more fundamentally, to deepen his consciousness of it by absorbing himself in the forces which animate it, for he claimed that 'composition by multiple contrasts, using all pictorial means, not only allows a deeper experience of realism, but also ensures variety'. More profoundly again, he painted not simply to give expression to his interpretation of external conditions, but to answer some inner need to create formal structures of a particular kind which he found through the

204 Fernand Léger, *Contrastes de formes*, 1913. Oil on burlap (130 × 97).

processes of painting.[45] It is on this level—that of a deepening consciousness of an individual structural order—that the *Contrastes de formes* may appeal to the spectator.

Comparison between the *Contrastes de formes* in the Museum of Modern Art, New York and *La Femme dans un fauteuil* in the Hanover Niedersächsische Landesgalerie (Pls. V, VI and 205), both of which were painted in 1913, shows how little distinction Léger made between representational and non-representational images: the major compositional difference between the two lies in the way he left the two corners of the representational painting empty as if to suggest the neutral space surrounding the figure, whereas in the non-representational painting, he gave the whole surface equal density. Léger used many devices in *La Femme dans un fauteuil* to counteract any straightforward figurative reading. For example, he split the body into a number of cylinders indicated by painted curved and straight lines, but extended many of these lines beyond the cylinder so that they contradict its three-dimensionality. Then he indicated the colour of each cylinder with two coarse strips of colour separated from each other by a white 'highlight', and from the contours by a strip of bare canvas. In this way Léger gave a summary indication of curved volumes, while drawing attention to the fact that he was using rough patches of paint which destroy any sense of the figure as a continuous volume and which form interpenetrating chains of movement which break down the self-containedness of figurative form. If one follows the lines which compose the cylinders, it is possible to isolate and identify the figure, but the figurative reference disappears if one concentrates on the interlinked movements or echoing patterns formed by the patches of colour and the curved and straight lines, or if one observes the way coloured cubes and wedges penetrate the cylinders. It is thus very difficult to see the figure, even when the title and small clues like the fingers, eye, and nose indicate its presence.

Léger used the same crudely drawn lines and roughly painted patches of colour and white highlights in the non-representational *Contrastes de formes*, but since he was free from the restrictions of figurative form, he was able to develop his interlocking forms to create a more richly interwoven structure. In his 1914 lecture he gave his recommendations for composing a painting by setting 'groups of similar forms ... against other opposing groups', and continued:

If you distribute your colours in the same way, that is, by painting one of these groups of forms with related colours and opposing them to a similar grouping of contrasting colours, you will obtain collective sources of tones, lines, and colours acting against other contrasting and dissonant sources. Contrast = dissonance, and consequently a maximum expressive effect.

One can observe how Léger used conflicting visual information in a way similar to that which he had used in his representational work, undermining the plasticity of the clusters of forms by emphasizing the flatness of the colours so that they do not adhere to the surfaces of the cylinders and wedges. Thus if one interprets what one sees according to the information given by the colours, the plastic forms explode into jostling fragments, but if one accepts the information given by line, one sees the painting in terms of interpenetrating volumes. Then, although these volumes seem to have weight, they obey no gravitational pull, and although they are strongly plastic, there is no space to accommodate them. In the representational works, these conflicts are made more complex by the struggle between one's awareness of the abstract structure and one's desire to isolate those forms which suggest objects, so, paradoxically, the presence of such representational clues contributes to the abstract dynamism. In neither kind of painting, can one assimilate the information given by colour and that given by line into a single stable interpretation, so one's consciousness oscillates between them, and as it does so it becomes increasingly aware of the reality of the painting itself. This is what Léger meant when he asserted that an abstract structure was more 'realist' than an imitative one.

205 Fernand Léger, *La Femme dans un fauteuil*, 1913 (130 × 97).

206 Fernand Léger, *Les Maisons dans les arbres,* 1914 (130 × 97).

Many of Léger's paintings of 1914 were more straightforwardly representational than those of 1913; for example, he painted several variants of the *Maisons dans les arbres* (Pl. 206), where, unlike the Essen *Maisons sous les arbres* of 1913, it is immediately possible to distinguish house-forms from tree-forms. Léger may have chosen to get closer to 'visual realism', in order to demonstrate the power of 'conceptual realism', for when one first looks at the paintings, one does what one's visual habits lead one to do—one identifies the subject; but if one continues to look at the painting, it becomes apparent that the pictorial information does not allow any straightforward or final interpretation. For example, the curious trees appear like trees only if one does not really look at them : if one does, they reveal themselves as rubbery 'balloons' with red tubes thrusting into them which twist up the surface in enchained movements, punch into the flat planes, and completely destroy landscape-space. Thus the figurative *Contrastes de formes* can make one aware of the conflict between what one actually experiences and what one accepts in terms of acquired generalizations. Bergson had called attention to the conflict and had claimed that it was the artist's task to destroy those conventions which prevent one not only from really seeing what one is looking at, but from being aware of one's individual consciousness.[46] However, the conflict had posed specifically pictorial problems ever since nineteenth-century Realists had begun to attack inherited modes of seeing, and Léger was more likely to have become aware of such problems through his understanding of painting—above all, of Impressionism—than through theory.

Léger was probably trying to show how 'composition by multiple contrasts' could overwhelm the specific subject, for he stated in his 1914 lecture:

I have not deliberately chosen so-called modern subjects, for I don't know what is meant by an old or a modern subject; I know only a new interpretation and that's all ... everything is suitable for the application of moving form; all this comes from the modern ambiance. But you would, with advantage, replace locomotives and other modern engines... by the most banal, worn subject—a nude woman in a studio or thousands of others. These things are simply a means to an end; the only interesting thing is the way in which one makes use of them.[47]

He used them to embody his belief that the dynamism of modern life had transformed consciousness in such a way that one received sensations rather than perceived individual objects. He could, indeed, have used lines from a poem Cendrars wrote in February 1914 to express his own interest in the dynamism rather than the specific forms of a landscape:

> *Le paysage ne m'intéresse plus*
> *Mais la danse du paysage*
> *La danse du paysage*
> *Danse-paysage*
> *Paritatatitata*
> *Je tout-tourne*[48]

Léger also continued to paint non-representational *Contrastes de formes*, for example, the richly developed one from the Kunstsammlung Nordrhein-Westfalen (Pl. 207). This painting reveals the paradoxical nature of Léger's *Contrastes de formes* very clearly, for, although Léger made the means by which he achieved his effects fully visible, the structure is curiously elusive, and although it is physically dense, it seems to transform itself before one's eyes and to retreat from one's apprehension. This is partly due to Léger's deliberate use of ambiguity, but also to the fact that he used pictorial devices normally used to represent objective forms when the painting contains no such forms, so that there is no intellectual recognition to enable one to stablize the forms into what one knows and thus to immobilize the continuous movement of one's perceptions.

In his lectures Léger insisted that the new movement in art was not the creation of a few initiates, and that the principle of dynamic pictorial contrasts was 'a universal concept which allows all sensibilities to develop' and 'the complete expression of a new generation

207 Fernand Léger, *Contrastes de formes*, 1914 (80·7 × 65·2).

whose needs it sustains and whose aspirations it answers.' Léger had been associated with writers and artists who were preoccupied with the expression of modern life since 1910, when he met poets and painters who had been associated with or influenced by the ideas emanating from the Abbaye de Creteil group, and began to participate in the discussions at Puteaux and in the activities organized by the consciously modernist group, the Artistes de Passy. It is clear that the excitement of shared ideas, of being in a movement that was revolutionizing art and seeking to make it express the realities of contemporary life, meant a great deal to Léger, yet it is also clear that in some ways he stood alone in these groups. This was largely because he distrusted theory, contenting himself, in Apollinaire's words, with 'quite simple truths', and (according to Ribemont-Dessaignes) refusing to get involved in the 'labyrinths of dialectic' of the Puteaux discussions.[49] There often seems to have been a gap between theory and form in the works of his friends, whereas the two were inseparable in Léger's case, for he drew his theories from his forms. Like him, his friends were preoccupied with the dynamism of modern life, and favoured forceful, dissonant, abruptly contrasted ways of expressing it; yet they tended to soften contrast by using interpenetrating transparent planes and continued to develop complex Simultanist subject-matter, whereas Léger rejected the complex themes of the *Essai pour trois portraits* and *La Noce* and returned to the simple themes of the Impressionist tradition— landscapes, still-lifes, single figures, or small groups of figures— without ever juxtaposing images from separate orders of reality in order to express Simultanist experience as his colleagues were doing. Léger made this change because he believed that specific subjects made it difficult to express the essence of modern life, and that paintings composed of multiple images could not embody Simultanist consciousness because they made the spectator search for what he could recognize, and thus prevented him from becoming aware of the meaning of pictorial form. Delaunay made the same point in the 1912 essays when he too was seeking a pictorial structure which could exist independently of the subject. However, Léger was not seduced by literary images as Delaunay was: he does not seem to have been interested in the written word, but even if he had been, he is unlikely to have been attracted by the writers of the Artistes de Passy group, for although they were interested in the expression of modern life, their vision tended to be cosmic, their imagery enumerative, and their style rhetorical; whereas Léger was concerned with the here and now—with what one can grasp and feel, and with what one can see. He did not believe in synthesizing the arts as many of his contemporaries did, for he believed that: '*Specialization is a modern concept,* and pictorial art, like all other manifestations of the human mind, must submit to its rule; it is logical, for in limiting each such manifestation to its proper aims, it makes it possible to intensify its realisations.'[50] Léger found the meaning of his art in painting, not in external theory, although this is, of course, not to say that he was uninfluenced by it. He was most fundamentally concerned with the realization of a physical consciousness which was independent of conceptual modes of understanding, but he also insisted that the mind played a part in this realization, so his pictorial evolution was the result of intuitive pictorial execution which he then rigorously analysed. Thus Léger discovered the signification of pictorial contrasts through his discovery of their centrality in his painting, but his awareness of them and of their meaning was probably quickened by his discussions with his friends about the nature of modern life and the means that could be used to express its dynamism. Léger's discovery of form was the discovery and clarification of something that was already in his painting, which was there before he had any connection with the avant-garde and which had some intimate—and ultimately indefinable—connection with his inner being. Whatever it was that impelled him towards a pictorial structure based on contrasts, would also determine the way he perceived the external world and would predispose what he defined as essential in modern life. This development explains the marked internal coherence of Léger's style and why he regarded form as more important than subject. It also helps one to understand the profound significance he found in the 'law of contrasts' which he described as 'eternal as a means of creating an equivalent of life'.[51] Cendrars was the only writer for whom Léger had any sympathy—and he insisted that he had not read any of his books. Clearly this was no bar to their exchange of ideas, and, as Léger said, they 'embarked together on the discovery of modern life'.[52] Both sought to express intensity of sensation rather than ideas or sentiments, and to do so by means of sharp contrasts of form. Although such contrasts existed in their work before they met in the second half of 1912, they may have discussed how they could be used as a fundamental mode of expression, for they made them stronger and clearer as their friendship became stronger in 1913. Cendrars gradually suppressed the words which indicate the transitions and relationships between other words and which imply the continuity of a *thinking* consciousness, replacing the thinking, feeling individual who had linked the diverse images of the 'Pâques à New York' of 1912 and the 'Transsibérien' of late 1912 to early 1913, by a self which seems merely to register sensations, images, and associations as they beat in on it. Thus he composed his 'Dix-neuf poèmes élastiques'— which he began to write in mid-1913—of vividly contrasting staccato phrases held together only by rhythm, analogy of sound, and association of image. At the same time Léger broke the surface continuity of his earlier works, and purified his pictorial elements, juxtaposing them in such violent contrasts that the painting often seems on the point of disintegration. Cendrars could have been thinking about the experience embodied in these works when he wrote in his poem 'Contrastes' in October 1913:

> *L'unité*
> *Il n'y a pas d'unité*[53]

Although Léger, like Cendrars, withheld any comment on the human condition,[54] his pure painting is by no means without human relevance, for it celebrates the significance of physical experience, of forms of consciousness which bypass the verbal, and, on a profound level, it demonstrates the artist's power of creating a structural order which is also able to embody the chaos and randomness of contemporary life.

These qualities were so integral to Léger's painting that they survived the changes that war brought to his art. He was called up in August 1914 and served at the Front until he was gassed in 1917. The war was a revelation to him, for he felt that he had returned to realities which he had lost sight of in the Parisian studio-world; he was exhilarated by his comradeship with his 'new friends, miners, navvies, workers in wood and metal', and he became more deeply aware of the marvellous objects produced by modern technology.[55] He was determined not to lose hold of these realities, and decided that it was necessary to return to figurative art to celebrate the life of modern urban man. However, he continued to use the pictorial methods he had developed before the war, and his post-war paintings retain the sheer vigorous delight in physical being that had characterized his pure painting—a quality which inspired Apollinaire's comment 'when I look at a painting by Léger, I feel very happy'.[56]

Chapter 3 **Psychological Orphism**

FRANCIS PICABIA (1879–1953) and
MARCEL DUCHAMP (1887–1968)

Apollinaire's inclusion of Picabia in the Orphist group was logical, for in late 1912 Picabia was beginning to subordinate recognizable form to non-representational colour; but his incorporation of Duchamp was not the least puzzling aspect of the whole affair. There is evidence that he was uncertain how to define Duchamp's position in the modern movement,[1] and his decision makes sense only if one focuses on the situation between the spring and autumn of 1912, when Duchamp was painting works like *Le Roi et la reine entourés de nus vites* and *Le Passage de la vierge à la mariée* (Pls. 236 and 239).

Duchamp later explained, 'I wanted to get away from the physical aspect of painting. I was much more interested in re-creating ideas in painting';[2] his works often had verbal origins and were as much influenced by literature as by painting. Taken literally, these factors would distinguish his art from that of the other Orphists which was essentially non-verbal and anti-intellectual. He also said that 'every picture has to exist before it is put on canvas, and it always loses something when it is turned into paint',[3] and this attitude is quite opposed to that of Delaunay and Léger who believed that the physicality of pictorial form had its own meaning, and is even opposed to the approach of Kupka and Picabia who shared Duchamp's interest in mental experience, but who found significance in the process of creating form. However, Duchamp's statements must be considered in the light of what he practised at the time: he tried to express experiences of a kind which are not accessible to words by using pictorial form, and between late 1911 and mid-1912 he created works of dense and complex physicality. Thus, although he may have been inspired by verbal ideas, they remain mysteriously ungraspable: they lead the spectator into the painting only to confront him with an ideological void and thus to make him aware of the material reality of the work. This remains true despite Duchamp's later denigration of the physicality of painting. He used forms which are so ambiguous that one cannot interpret them in terms of 'intellectual generalizations'—to use Apollinaire's phrase.[4] Thus his paintings of 1912 awaken consciousness of the functioning of the mind rather than communicate definable ideas.

Duchamp shared the other Orphists' interest in the expression of movement and the processes of time, and tried to express psychic movement·as well as physical or perceptual movement; in other words, as Nayral said, he sought to embody 'a double dynamism—subjective and objective':[5] he expressed the movement of thought in *Portrait* (*Dulcinée*) (Pl. 9) and the movement from one state of being to another in the *Passage de la vierge à la mariée*. Like Kupka, he began with rather literal diagrammatic modes of representing psychic or physical movement, but soon developed more concentrated pictorial forms which create awareness of movement by making the spectator aware of his own visual activity as he explores the painting. Thus, like the other Orphists, he began to create forms which have no specific counterpart in the objective world, probably in order to prevent the spectator from seizing on known form and thus fragmenting what Bergson called 'the fluid continuity of the real'. However, unlike Kupka, Delaunay, Picabia, and Léger, Duchamp tended to retain gravitational structures and to separate certain forms from the background, so that one tries to read them as a figuration of 'something', even while one is simultaneously unable to do so because of the contradictory information given by the forms. In this way Duchamp became the first painter to use Cubism surrealistically, by employing its ambiguous object-sensations to evoke disturbing but undefinable states of mind. These paintings conformed to Apollinaire's definition of Orphic Cubism as 'new structures [composed of] elements which have not been borrowed from visual reality, but have been entirely created by the artist'. Apollinaire also said that these new structures contain their own meaning—a meaning which lies in the power of the painting to engage the mind and to awaken consciousness. Apollinaire's classification of Duchamp as an Orphic Cubist is therefore explicable; however, at the very time he made it, Duchamp decided to give up painting, and spent the last years before the war in the complex intellectual speculations which he embodied in as insubstantial way as possible in the *Mariée mis à nu par ses célibataires, même* (1915–23). The roots of these speculations can be found in Duchamp's painting of 1909–12, but they themselves were antithetical to Orphism. I will, therefore, not discuss Duchamp independently as an Orphic Cubist; however, since Picabia's non-figurative painting is almost inconceivable without Duchamp's contribution, I shall discuss Duchamp's role in Picabia's development of an abstract art embodying subjective experience which he described as 'psychological studies [realized] through the mediumship of forms which I created'.[6]

Although Picabia was little older than the other Orphists (he was born in 1879), he was precocious and began his art-studies in the 1890s, and had become an extremely successful Impressionist painter by the early 1900s. The other Orphists spent the first decade of the century exploring the full range of contemporary styles, but Picabia submerged his personality in a conventional academic Impressionism which gave no hint of his future originality. This is the more strange since he was apparently interested in the expression of mental experience at an early age. His grandfather, Alphonse Davanne, a friend of Daguerre and amateur photographer, with whom Picabia lived after the death of his mother when he was aged six, apparently tried to persuade him to take up photography on the grounds that it would supersede painting; but his insistence only succeeded in making Picabia realize that the mechanical process could not reproduce the forms he had in his head.[7] It is curious, then, that Picabia should have attached himself to Impressionism rather than to Symbolism in the 1890s and 1900s, but he may have remained conscious of the problem of expressing inner experience and this probably influenced his sudden rejection of naturalism in 1908, when he renounced Impressionism, declared the possibility of 'un art autre', and began to explore Symbolist modes of expression. However, his painting between 1908 and 1912 was—with a significant exception—so old-fashioned as to justify Salmon's comment in early 1912 that Picabia was a late-comer to Fauvism and content to be so.[8] This was despite his increasing contacts with avant-garde artists in 1911 when he met Duchamp and Apollinaire and was admitted by the Puteaux group. However, in mid-1912 he began to paint more adventurous works like the *Danses à la source I* (Pl. 224) in which he broke down the figure into a surge of abstract colours; he carried this process even further in the *Danses à la source II* (Pl. 235) by shattering the figure and ground into confetti-like particles which are no longer recognizable as objective forms. The structure of the painting was still derived from nature, although very indirectly, but in the spring of 1913 Picabia began to construct paintings whose structure was quite independent of nature.

The rapidity of Picabia's development from the old-fashioned to the most modern was equalled only by the rapidity with which he passed through his non-figurative phase, which lasted just over a year until the outbreak of war forced him to give up painting for a time; when he returned to it in 1915, he abandoned abstraction in favour of machinist Symbolism. These rapid changes have led many to question Picabia's seriousness in his non-figurative works, and since he was, moreover, the prototypical Dadaist, it has been easy to assume that he intended that his abstract works should undermine traditional artistic values in a merely negative way. However, there is evidence to suggest that Picabia was genuinely trying to develop an artistic language which could communicate emotion;[9] perhaps more fundamentally, his formal evolution between 1908 and 1914 had a marked internal coherence in which Picabia isolated and purified certain formal configurations which can be found in his representational paintings and which, by using improvisatory modes of creation, he allowed to evolve freely in his non-representational paintings. I have shown how similar processes operated in the evolution of Kupka, Delaunay, and Léger's non-figurative works, and I have suggested that the continuity of analogous configurations in their *œuvre* implies that the configurations themselves had some deep inner significance for their creators: I see no reason to doubt that this was also true for Picabia. At the same time Picabia *was* drawn to destroy that which he had created and had found meaningful (as is revealed very strikingly in the biographies by two of his three wives); it seems, therefore, that the roots of his nihilism lay deep in his personality and in his strange and lonely childhood, and that it was not cynicism but a personal anguish which caused him to abandon his non-figurative art.[10]

When Picabia rejected naturalistic art in 1908, Symbolist theory suggested an alternative; however, the pictorial form in which the theory had been embodied was essentially that of the illusionist tradition, so Picabia found Symbolism both a help and a hindrance in his development of a new art-form, and between 1908 and 1912 he simply abstracted his forms from naturalistic sources (Pls. 211 and 221). It was probably Duchamp who helped him to understand how avant-garde artists were developing structures independent of nature, for it was only after they met that Picabia began to abandon the naturalistic structuring of form in space and to interest himself in the expression of human emotion. Duchamp could have suggested how he might—in his own words—'paint that which my brain, my soul sees'.[11]

Duchamp and Picabia operated in an emotional sphere quite different from that of Delaunay and Léger, for their irony, their pessimism, their concern for the delicate movements of inner life, were in fundamental opposition to the others' optimistic delight in the world of sensation. Nevertheless, they too shared a deep-rooted suspicion of modes of experience based on preconception, and also created pictorial structures for which there are no verbal equivalents and which demand a new kind of attention from the spectator.

The development of Picabia's painting until late 1911

Picabia studied at the École des arts décoratifs between 1895 and 1897.[12] He had obtained sufficient proficiency to exhibit in the Salon des Artistes français in 1899, but remained in the academic studio of Fernand Cormon and Ferdinand Humbert for a few more years. In 1902 he met two sons of Camille Pissarro, Georges and Rodo, who reported on Picabia's academic methods to their father and who seem to have converted him to Impressionism. Picabia had great technical facility, and was soon able to pander to the upper bourgeoisie's taste for an adulterated naturalism which took the pretty and the evocative from Impressionism while rejecting its revolutionary formal and visual discoveries.[13] Picabia was of this world and he filled the role of a socially pleasing artistic prodigy with ease and style.

The prefaces to Picabia's immensely successful exhibitions at the prestigious galerie Haussmann were written by the fashionable critic, L. Roger-Milès. In the 1907 preface he emphasized the subjectivity of Picabia's landscapes, not seeing that this subjectivity lay less in Picabia's response to a landscape than in his use of stock images for the expression of sentiment from the academic Impressionist repertory, for his paintings give no evidence that he was searching out his own relationship to the landscape (Pl. 208).[14] Roger-Milès' comments on Picabia show how Symbolist or Synthetist ideas on the power of form and colour to convey emotion had become so diffuse

208 Francis Picabia, *Soleil aux bords du Loing*, *Moret*, 1905 (73·7 × 92·7).

that they could be used by the defenders of poeticized naturalism without there being any real change in that tradition.[15] For example, he was clearly influenced by the Synthetists' emphasis on the fact that nature cannot be imitated and that the artist must therefore construct formal equivalents for it: he wrote in the 1907 catalogue that the artist must express the character of nature in 'an expressive living synthesis', and that since one cannot represent the immensity of nature 'it is necessary to detach from it arrangements which can give us a sense of this immensity'. In fact, Picabia's landscapes were nearer to being pastiches of the works of Monet and Sisley than pictorial constructs, but he was eventually influenced by this Synthetist idea. Roger-Milès also stressed the importance of Picabia's drawings, saying that he painted from nature during the day, but that at night he draws 'like a virtuoso seated at the clavier ... who throws himself ... into improvisations ... which follow the movements of his psychic disposition, so Picabia seeks forms, constructions of lines, configurations of spaces which his eye has retained and whose real character his mind wishes to uncover.' The drawings which illustrate the catalogue are very conventional but Roger-Milès may have been talking about different ones, since he said that Picabia was unwilling to show his more abstract drawings; they could therefore have been more developed examples of two surviving scribbled drawings of 1908 (Pl. 210), and were perhaps related to the abstracted drawings which Gabrielle Buffet said Picabia had begun before she met him.

209 Francis Picabia, *Les Bords du Loing*, 1908 (61 × 91·5).

She said that while he talked, he drew 'frightening forms which shaped themselves automatically under his pencil: erotic monsters, half-man, half-animal, an entire hallucinating universe which he carried within him'.[16] Thus Picabia not only drew simplified images from memory, but already improvised hybrid forms like the half-sexual, half-mechanical images in *Je revois en souvenir ma chère Udnie* (Pl. 251). He continued this improvisatory practice throughout his Orphist period, when he would improvise a linear structure and then elaborate a colour structure.

The conclusion of Roger-Milès' long preface has become ironic, for he speculated on whether Picabia's career 'promises us any more surprises ...'. He probably did not know of the crisis that was approaching in Picabia's art, nor, of course, could he have suspected the nature of the surprises which the future would bring.

Picabia seems to have painted very little in 1908, which, in striking contrast to his earlier prolific output, indicates some dissatisfaction with his painting. The works which he did paint—perhaps in the earlier part of the year—show a development from a fluid Impressionistic style towards stronger shapes and firmer, more substantial brush-strokes (Pl. 209). Picabia was apparently deeply depressed and under considerable nervous strain—partly manifested in excessive drinking—which also suggests that he found this kind of painting an inadequate mode of expression.[17] It was at this time that he rejected Impressionism, symbolizing and actualizing this rejection by breaking his profitable contract with the fashionable dealer, Georges Danthon, which had been drawn up for three years in 1907.[18] Since he had considerable private wealth, this break had a more than financial significance, for it left Picabia in a very isolated position with no close artistic contacts—a situation which lasted until 1911.

His marriage with Gabrielle Buffet was undoubtedly of very great significance in Picabia's development. They met in September 1908—when he spoke about his disillusion with painting—and they married the next January, the month that Picabia's dealer had a sale of his paintings to compensate for the breaking of the contract. Gabrielle Buffet was an extremely intelligent woman from an intellectual milieu quite different from Picabia's fashionable one, and she undoubtedly helped him to find an alternative to the art which he now found meaningless: besides being intelligent, she had closer connections with the avant-garde than he, so she was able to sympathize with and perhaps clarify his half-formed ideas about a new form of painting.[19] She was a musician, a pupil of Vincent d'Indy who had been closely associated with the Symbolists, and she had also studied with Busoni in Berlin where she apparently had exciting discussions about a new 'pure' music with her fellow students. It is then probable that she strengthened Picabia's inclination towards purer, non-naturalistic painting, encouraged his interest in Symbolism, and clarified his awareness of the possible relationship between music and painting.

She has given an account of the conversation she had with Picabia when they met, in which Picabia said that he would have given up painting had he not conceived of a new kind of art which would contain 'forms and colours freed from their sensorial attributes' and would be 'situated in pure invention which recreates the world according to its own desires and its own imagination'.[20] Picabia's ideas were deeply influenced by the Symbolist emphasis on the immaterial and on the artist's freedom from the restrictions of the natural world—ideas which were expressed by Apollinaire in his Symbolist article, 'Les trois vertus plastiques', published earlier in the year.

Although Picabia's words have been used to support the contention that he had early conceived of the possibility of non-figurative painting, his contemporary paintings suggest something different, for they show that when he spoke of 'forms and colours freed from their sensorial attributes', he was thinking about simplifying forms in such a way that they could evoke emotion without having to describe a specific physical reality. The Midi *Paysage* of 1908 (Pl. 211) seems to have been conceived in this way, for Picabia probably painted it from memory, a procedure recommended by the Synthetists because memory simplifies the image of the object, rejects inessentials, and retains only those dominant lines and colours which the Synthetists believed embodied the essential structure of the natural scene as well as the mood which the scene had induced in the painter. Thus, when Roger-Milès wrote about Picabia's work in

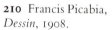

210 Francis Picabia, *Dessin*, 1908.

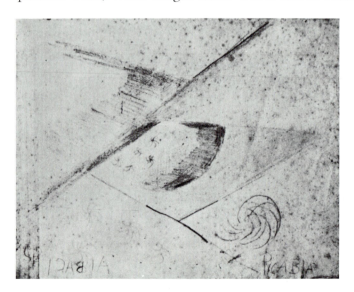

211 Francis Picabia,
Paysage, 1908.

early 1909, his words reflected the reality of his paintings for the first time: 'the clear ideas translated into the simple verb; the synthesis more and more concentrated, tending towards a more explicit and unified art'.[21]

Picabia's paintings of 1909 followed the general movement away from the fluidity of Impressionism towards firmer, more geometric constructions—as can be seen in a comparison between Léger's *Le Pont*, Delaunay's *Tour Eiffel*, and Picabia's *Paysage à Cassis* all painted in 1909–10 (Pls. 179, 122, and 212). However, the comparison shows that Léger and Delaunay were influenced by Cézanne's structural discipline, while Picabia seems to have been more interested in the Synthetists' decorative form and evocative content, for although the 1909 *Paysage à Cassis* is more firmly constructed than the *Paysage* of 1908, Picabia still followed the Synthetists' mode of representing space by means of overlapping planes in such a way that his painting lacks the spatial tension and strong physical presence of the paintings influenced by Cézanne and is relatively 'free from sensorial attributes'.

Picabia painted the enigmatic little picture *Caoutchouc* (Pl. 213) at this time, and it is far more interesting than these abstracted landscapes. In fact a number of writers have seen it as the first step in a fairly consistent progression towards non-figuration and as a confirmation of their belief that Picabia had early conceived of a non-figurative art (supposedly supported by the 1908 statement).

Caoutchouc is so different from Picabia's other works of this period that on merely stylistic grounds I would date it to 1913 (for it has significant similarities to works painted in that year), were it not for the existence of evidence that suggests it was painted in 1908–9: first, it is related to two scribbled drawings, one of which is clearly dated 1908 (Pl. 210), which contain the abstract planes and star-shapes also found in *Caoutchouc*; secondly, Gabrielle Buffet-Picabia states that it—or works like it—existed when she met Picabia in autumn 1908 and that it was abstracted from a still-life, like several other paintings of the period: it does, in fact, have similarities to a stylized *Nature morte* of 1909 (Pl. 214).[22]

Caoutchouc is thus related to Picabia's contemporary works in that it is abstracted from a model (the fact is partly obscured by the curious title, but since Picabia only named it later, he may have wished to hide its origins). However, the painting does differ significantly from Picabia's other abstracted landscapes and still-lifes, for the structure of most of Picabia's paintings up to late 1912 is determined by an external model which one can easily decipher, which is not true of *Caoutchouc*, for even with knowledge of its derivation, one is not tempted to 'read' the work in terms of its original model. This is because the pictorial structure is not naturalistic and is not affected by the laws of perspective space, of gravity, or light-distribution. Picabia made the transparent and

212 Francis Picabia, *Paysage à Cassis, c.* 1909 (50·5 × 61·5).

213 Francis Picabia,
Caoutchouc, c. 1908–9.
Water-colour and gouache
on paper (45·5 × 61·5).

opaque planes create a spiralling movement into depth, which is
countered by the transparent circles which arise from depth and twist
forward from the surface and thus gives the painting its own unique
spatial structure which prevents any simple reading of it as a still-life.
Picabia was not therefore merely giving a simplified version of the
external world, but was creating a new one which engages the
spectator's imagination in a way that none of his abstract landscapes
can.

However, Picabia does not seem to have recognized the
significance of his little painting at the time, for he did not pursue
such formal experiments. The discontinuity of his development is
more apparent if one contrasts *Caoutchouc* with Kupka's *Premier Pas*
(Pl. 66) of approximately the same date, for although the formal
structure of Kupka's work is less interesting than Picabia's, Kupka
explored the theme for the next three years until he was able to create
such powerful and authoritative images as *Amorpha, Fugue en deux
couleurs* (Pls. II and 83), whereas Picabia did not pursue the
implications of his discovery until 1913 when he used the rotatory
movement and complex spiralling depth of *Caoutchouc* in *Udnie,
jeune fille américaine* (Pls. VII and 247). Nevertheless, in the
intervening years he did extend his formal range so that he was able
to make his first non-figurative works both strong and subtle.

Most of Picabia's paintings of 1909–11 were less abstract than those
of 1908–9. He seems to have been uncertain of his direction, since he
pursued a sequence of styles without developing them in any
consistent way. For example, when he took up late Neo-

214 Francis Picabia, *Nature morte*, 1909 (73·7 × 92).

Impressionism, he did not explore its constructive potential as did Delaunay in *La Fenêtre sur la Ville nº 3* and Kupka in *Nocturne* (Pls. 101 and 132), and merely applied the colour-bricks of Signac and Cross over a naturalistic structure (as in *Le Port de Saint-Tropez*, Pl. 215). In other works he continued to simplify landscape into flat planes of bright colour (Pl. 220), and he continued to paint stylized naturalistic works even after he had met Duchamp and the Salon Cubists after mid-1911 (Pl. 223).

Picabia exhibited his first significant figure-paintings in 1911. He showed *Sur la plage* (Pl. 218) in the Salon d'Automne in which Léger exhibited his *Essai pour trois portraits* and Duchamp his *Portrait (Dulcinée)* (Pls. 183 and 9). Léger and Duchamp made use of Cubist fragmentation of form to create ambiguous structures which demand an active response from the spectator if they are to be understood, but Picabia's painting was a casual glimpse of figures caught in movement and rapidly set down: if it owed an allegiance to contemporary painting, it was not to Cubism but to Matisse, for it could have been influenced by the abrupt discontinuities of his figure-paintings of 1908–10. There are similarities between *Sur la plage* and Matisse's *Musique* of 1908 (Museum of Modern Art, New York)—one of the few works in which Matisse represented the figure in movement, just as Picabia's picture was his first attempt to represent the moving figure. The problem of representing movement was henceforth to fascinate Picabia as it had fascinated the other Orphists, and he followed a course similar to theirs when his desire to embody the continuity of movement led him to non-figuration in 1913.

Picabia embarked on another theme which was to be central to his work in *Adam et Eve* of 1911 (Pl. 216), his first erotic painting. Stylistically it was not very adventurous, being close to the decorative naturalism of *Vaches au pâturage* and lacking even the expressive vitality of *Sur la plage*, but it does foreshadow certain characteristics of the non-figurative paintings of 1913–14: Picabia used heavy contours which flow around the figures and unite them to the landscape, and although he modelled the figures they remain

215 Francis Picabia, *Le Port de Saint-Tropez*, 1909 (73 × 60).

curiously immaterial, as if they were floating over the darker forms, and this combination of fluid line, ambiguous modelling, and floating weightless form provided the essential structure of his non-figurative paintings.

Picabia probably became interested in erotic themes through the work of Duchamp. He had very rarely painted the nude, but it had been Duchamp's most important theme since 1910 and he had, moreover, painted this specific subject in *Le Paradis* (Pl. 217) of 1910–1911. There is strong erotic tension in both works, although Duchamp's is characteristically more enigmatic, for his figures look past each other as if alone in their sexuality, while Picabia's interact in a much more straightforward way. In fact, Duchamp had already gone much further than this, and by the autumn of 1911 had painted *Portrait* (*Dulcinée*) (Pl. 9), the first of his paintings of 'the *processes* of desire', whereas Picabia simply depicted a single moment in a narrative sequence, and it was not until eighteen months had passed that he began representing the kind of mental experience that preoccupied Duchamp. Nor in the meantime did he continue to paint the nude, temporarily abandoning the subject with characteristic arbitrariness.

216 Francis Picabia, *Adam et Eve*, 1911 (100 × 81).

217 Marcel Duchamp, *Le Paradis*, 1911 (114·5 × 128·5).

The paintings of 1912

Picabia at last developed a consistent personal style in 1912, at the same time that his relationship with the avant-garde became stronger.[23] He was closest to Apollinaire and Duchamp, who freed his imagination in ways which set him apart from the Salon Cubists—for example, the latter tried to represent the 'fourth dimension' as a physical dimension (albeit experienced by the mind) by the use of multiple viewpoints, while Picabia and Duchamp maintained that the fourth dimension was 'that of the mind' and thus felt themselves free to stimulate consciousness by the use of allusive but mysterious pictorial forms.[24] They probably gave the same twist to the discussions on non-figurative art that took place at Puteaux by emphasizing that non-figurative forms should embody mental experience.

Picabia's paintings have a strange immateriality which is more apparent when they are compared with those of his friends, for although they were more closely based on the forms of external nature than were those of the Cubists, they do not generally contain the tension between the objects represented and the pictorial structure that characterizes Cubist painting. In Picabia's painting this

218 Francis Picabia, *Sur la plage*, 1911.

tension is found only in a few paintings of mid-1912 (such as *Danses à la source I* and *La Procession, Séville*, Pls. 224–5) which were directly influenced by Salon Cubism, but immediately afterwards he returned to the 'non-sensorial' in the ambiguously structured immaterial paintings of 1913–14. These pictorial changes were reflected in Picabia's changing ideas about his art.

His paintings of late 1911 and early 1912 like *L'Arbre rouge* and *Port de Naples* (Pl. 220),[25] were still immaterial, for although the small planes are related to the features of the landscape, Picabia made the relationship ambiguous by emphasizing the sharpness of their boundaries and creating contradictory tonal sequences, so that the landscape is almost overwhelmed by the tiny jostling planes. Picabia probably got the idea of using small planes to eliminate recessive space and to unite foreground and background, solid and space, from studying the works of the Salon Cubists, but the planes themselves were derived from the large planes of his early decorative landscapes, so they do not have the materiality of their Cubist counterparts. The work is important in that it is constructed from the combinations of curved, slightly bulging and angular, flat planes which Picabia used in all his paintings of 1912 to 1914.

The works which Picabia painted after the first months of 1912 were more significantly influenced by Cubism, even though he still followed Synthetist procedures. Most of these paintings were based on scenes he had observed during his long honeymoon in Spain and

Italy in 1909, so they were memory-images in which the scene was simplified and painted in colour scales evoked by the remembered emotion. Thus, while Picabia made increasing use of Cubist devices to structure his works more firmly, he was still abstracting from nature rather than creating independent pictorial structures. At the same time, Cubism enabled Picabia to break down the self-contained forms which had previously dominated his paintings and thus gave him the means of constructing his ambiguous but densely worked structures of 1913–14.

Paris (Pl. 221) was probably one of the earliest of his new paintings, for although Picabia transformed objects into cubic forms, he retained a traditional perspectival stage on which the figures can move: hence—despite the fact that certain planes have become detached from the forms to which they belong so that they begin to make a relief structure which contradicts the perspectival structure—the construction of the painting is fundamentally naturalistic. Thus, if one attempts to 'see' the painting as an abstract structure, all one can perceive is a chaotic jumble; the only way one can really appreciate it as an organized structure is by recognizing that the planes form the cores of figures. *Paris* is, in fact, as close to Impressionism as to Cubism, for Picabia merely simplified the figures and objects of an Impressionistic street scene into geometric shapes, showing that he misunderstood the real nature of Cubism. This

219 Marcel Duchamp, *Yvonne et Magdeleine déchiquetées*, 1911 (60 × 73).

suggestion is confirmed by a statement he made in 1913 in which he said that the Cubists 'were as intent on producing a facsimile of their model, person or landscape, as Gainsborough or Manet. Only they demanded of the observer an impossibility. They demanded that he see reality in cubic form—in the outward technicalities of their painting.'[26]

The *Danses à la source I, Procession, Séville,* and *Figure triste* (Pls. 224–5 and 227)—which were probably all painted in the summer after the exhibition of the Société normande in Rouen in June—were more impressive attempts to make use of the formal devices of Cubism. They are still legible as simplifications of actual figures or scenes, but Picabia was clearly trying to develop them as independent organisms with their own internal structure of colour, shape, light,

220 Francis Picabia, *L'Arbre rouge,* 1911–12 (92 × 73).

221 Francis Picabia, *Paris*, 1912 (74 × 92).

222 Gino Severini, *Le Boulevard*, c. 1910 (63·8 × 92·7).

and shade. They were the first paintings in which Picabia developed an alternative to perspective space—previously he had represented space either by using diagonal lines to create a stage, or by using a sequence of flat, overlapping planes to indicate foreground, middle ground, and background, and he inserted figures or objects into this preconstructed space. The structure of these paintings was rather

223 Francis Picabia, *Le Poulailler*, 1912 (130 × 164).

224 Francis Picabia, *Danses à la source I*, 1912 (120·6 × 120·6).

rigid and made it impossible for him to represent movement, but he now created more mobile structures by breaking down the separation between objects and space: in *Danses à la source I* and *Figure triste* he wove the figures into the surrounding space and created movement which fluctuates in and out of depth by using ribbon-like planes which detach themselves from the central core of the figures and weave into the other forms; in *La Procession, Séville*, he squeezed out background space by breaking all the forms into evenly accented angular volumes which create a uniform relief structure, of which the figures are merely a part.

Since these were Picabia's first large-scale paintings in the modern idiom, it is natural that he should have looked to his contemporaries for help, and he seems to have been particularly influenced by Duchamp, Léger, and the Futurists who had, of course, recently exhibited in Paris. The dynamism of the *Danses à la source I* was quite new in Picabia's painting and probably owed something to Futurism. Apollinaire commented in mid-1912 that Picabia seemed 'to desire an art of mobility' and that he 'should be able to abandon static painting to confront new methods'; he noted that Picabia's colour was 'saturated with energy [so that] its extremities continue

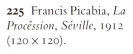

225 Francis Picabia, *La Procéssion, Séville*, 1912 (120 × 120).

226 Marcel Duchamp, *Nu descendant un escalier I*, 1911 (96·7 × 60·5).

into space'.[27] His phrase suggests that he had some knowledge of the Futurist's concept of 'lines of force' which represent the forces within the figure or object and which unite it with the forces which pervade space, and he may have been thinking of the way the narrow planes of the *Danses* break away from the figures to form a dynamic movement which explodes upwards and outwards. Picabia was thus able to express the continuity of movement as he could not do with the static self-contained forms of his earlier works. The hot colours of *Danses à la source I* were closer to those of the Futurists than to those of his French friends. The theme of the dance may even have had a Futurist origin, for it had been one of Severini's favourite themes since 1911, and although Picabia had observed the scene on which it was based in 1909, he did not paint it until after the Futurist exhibition in February 1912 when he could have seen Severini's *Danse du Pan-pan à Monico* (Pl. 12), in which the dancers were similar to his own.[28] After mid-1912, the dancer was as important in his own work as it was in Severini's. There are also similarities between Picabia's *Paris* and Severini's *Boulevard* of 1910 (Pl. 222) which may be significant: Severini's painting was probably influenced by Romains's Unanimism, since, like the poet, he was trying to express the way in which individual consciousness is absorbed in the larger collective emotions generated by the rhythms of a city. Picabia may have intended to express something similar in *Paris* (the central theme of Romains's *Puissances de Paris* of 1911 was of the characteristic rhythms of the different streets, squares, and locations of Paris). Moreover, in *Danses à la source I* and *La Procession, Séville*, he showed how the individual loses his separate being in the group rhythms of a dynamic dance or a religious procession, just as Romains described how the movement of a funeral procession or a street dance breaks down the individual's separate being into larger rhythms.[29] Picabia's interest in such modes of consciousness would have encouraged him to move from the depiction of recognizable human situations to the representation of pure rhythms.

Picabia's paintings were, however, pictorially firmer than those of the Futurists, for instead of using impressionistic broken colour and hazy outlines, he gave his forms firm contours and modelled them so that they are more plastic than in Futurist painting. In this respect *Danses à la source I* and *La Procession, Séville* are more closely related to the way in which Duchamp reduced figures to small, firm, plastic cylinders in his first *Nu descendant un escalier* (Pl. 226). The Futurists suggested movement by splitting it into its separate phases linked with broken colour which blurs the boundaries of form, but Duchamp followed the Cubists' technique of contrasting dark and light to make the spectator actively aware of the dynamic exploratory movement of sight. He later explained this aspect of his work: 'My interest in painting the nude was closer to the Cubists' interest in decomposing forms than to the Futurists' interest in suggesting movement or even to Delaunay's Simultanist suggestions of it. My aim was a static representation of movement with no attempt to give cinema effects in painting.'[30] Picabia was probably influenced by this more abstract mode of representing movement which could have taught him how to create a complex structure from contrasting kinds of movement: for example, in *La Procession, Séville*, the movement of the contrasting light and dark planes forms a relief structure which juts out from the surface and counters the movement of the figures as they pour out of the lower corner of the painting, as they do in *Nu descendant un escalier*. Duchamp separated the figure from the background and thus weakened the physicality of the painting, and Picabia may have observed this since he tried to create continuity between the figures and space. He was not fully successful, for in both *Danses à le source I* and *La Procession, Séville* the figures do stand out against the ground. This may be the reason why Apollinaire added a note to *Les Peintres cubistes* to the effect that the art of Picabia and Duchamp gives 'only the simulacrum of movement ... [and] has not yet a fully realized plastic signification'.[31] He may have been influenced by Delaunay who had frequently criticized what he called 'the simulacrum of movement', by which he meant the splitting of figurative movement into its successive phases, as Duchamp did in *Nu descendant un escalier* and as Picabia seems to have done in *Danses à la source I* and *La Procession, Séville*. However, both artists had already represented movement more abstractly, and Apollinaire's contradictions suggest that he was confused by the fact that in the autumn Picabia and Duchamp exhibited works in which the figure was clearly visible as well as those which were much more abstract, including among the latter Picabia's *Danses à la source II* and *La Source* (Pls. 235 and 1). *La Source* was probably the earlier of the two, for Picabia still composed the painting with a ground plan and forms emerging from a relatively neutral 'background'. However, these forms are simply small tumbling rectangles which suggest falling water only because the title prepares one to search for such a reference. The structure of *Danses à la source II* was based on the figurative version, but Picabia fragmented his figures into such minute parts that they are no longer discernible as figures; he obscured the figure reference even further by carrying transparent planes over the kaleidoscopic particles, so that they fuse into new shapes which counter any figurative interpretation. He succeeded in creating pictorial movement by making the eye fluctuate between the transparent configurations which swing across the surface or sink into depth. This kind of structure—based on visual oscillation between surface and depth, between tantilizing hints of the visible world and abstract colour patterns—is analogous to the structure which Delaunay had developed in *Les Fenêtres simultanées* (Pl. I).

Gabrielle Buffet-Picabia has given several accounts of the discussions which Picabia and Apollinaire had on pure painting during the summer of 1912 and which, she claims, led Apollinaire to modify certain points in *Les Peintres cubistes* which he was writing at the same time.[32] In fact, parts of what Apollinaire wrote on Picabia's ideas are very close to her reports of their conversations. She also implies that the contradictions in Apollinaire's comments on Picabia were caused by his lack of understanding of Picabia's work, but they are just as likely to have been caused by the discrepancies between Picabia's theory and practice earlier that summer, when his ideas were still in advance of his means of expression; the conversations which he had with the poet would have forced him to define his previously rather vague ideas and thus probably stimulated him towards greater abstraction—which may well have taken Apollinaire further than he wished to go. At any rate, Apollinaire's contradictory comments on his friend's painting, and Picabia's oscillation between the figurative and the non-figurative, reveal something of the difference between Symbolism and the new painting and show how both Apollinaire and Picabia were groping towards clarification of an only partially realized idea.

Gabrielle Buffet-Picabia states that Apollinaire was worried by recent developments in Picabia's art which he regarded as 'inhuman' and in danger of becoming merely decorative, and that Picabia countered this charge by claiming that non-representational art contained its own kind of meaning: 'Are blue and red unintelligible?' he asked. 'Are not the circle, the triangle, volumes, and colours as intelligible as a table or a cup?' He was proposing an alternative to the Symbolist theory that forms act as ciphers for invisible truths, which suggests that he had glimpsed a belief that lies at the heart of most western art of the twentieth century: the belief that 'meaning' is less significant than consciousness. Apollinaire was clearly recording Picabia's idea when he wrote that, in Picabia's painting, 'reality is matter', and when he asserted: 'It is nothing to do with abstraction, for the pleasure which these works propose to give the spectator is direct ... Would one say that the scent of a peach is only an abstraction?'[33] He stated that Picabia was developing the Fauves' transposition of light into colour into an art where colours no longer acted simply as a 'colouring' and were no longer 'symbolic', but meaningful in themselves as 'concrete forms'. This is a succinct and meaningful account of Picabia's development, for Picabia had been influenced since 1908 by an idea advanced by the Synthetists, and followed by the Fauves, that light cannot be imitated and can only be represented by an independent colour structure which suggested an equivalent intensity. However, the Fauves still believed that this colour structure stood for natural light, whereas Picabia, as Apollinaire stated, was moving away from the symbolic use of colour and was approaching the idea of an art whose 'meaning' lies in its own physical reality and not in its resemblance to something outside itself. This was the most important idea that Apollinaire and Picabia discussed in the summer of 1912.

However, when Apollinaire corrected the proofs of his book, he was staying with Delaunay who may have persuaded him that Picabia's art was not as pure as he had thought, perhaps by showing him that, although the colours of *Danses à la source I* and *La Procession, Séville* begin to form independent structures, their linear structure is still so closely related to the model that it makes the spectator focus on the identifiable forms and prevents him from absorbing himself in the colour structure. Apollinaire thus changed his comment that 'form is symbolic and colour is formal' to 'form is still symbolic when colour should become formal'.[34] This suggests that in the summer he thought it possible for colour to function formally while forms still had a referential function, but that by October he had come to realize that colour could not be constructive so long as the forms were tied to the structures of the natural world.[35] This is the meaning behind another obscure note which he added to the proofs of his book in October: 'without embarking on new methods, an artist like Picabia denies himself one of the principal elements of painting, the conception. For the artist to be able to deny himself this, colour must become formal in appearance ...'.[36] In other words, if the painter is to realize a work does not have a conceptually accessible subject, he must develop a structure which is strong enough to involve the spectator in its own reality. When he wrote these comments, Apollinaire would have had two images in his mind: the recognizable images of *Danses à la source I*, and the mobile patterns of *Danses à la source II*. In isolation *Danses à la source II* appears fully abstract, but in juxtaposition with *Danses à la source I* its derivation is obvious, and as one looks at it one seeks restlessly to isolate its model. It would thus be true to say that the later work is not fully realized as an independent structure.

Perhaps influenced by Gabrielle Buffet-Picabia, Apollinaire also stated that Picabia's painting was as closely related to music as was possible with an art which used another medium of expression. Picabia's paintings had been described in musicalist terms even before his break with Impressionism, and his lasting interest in the relation between the two arts was confirmed by a statement he made in 1915 when he said that for seven years he had been trying to make painting 'that would live by its own resources, like music. I was trying to make a psychic painting.'[37]

This is a typical Symbolist statement—it is, for example, related to Gauguin's ideas on the relation between musical and pictorial form and the expression of inner experience published as recently as 1910 in the Neo-Symbolist journal, *Vers et prose*, a journal which was certainly read by Apollinaire and his friends: 'In [painting], all sensations are condensed; contemplating it, everyone can ... have his soul invaded by the most profound reflections ... Like music, it acts on the soul through the intermediary of the senses.'[38] Picabia's interest in music was reflected in the dreamy evocative landscapes of 1908–11 with their immaterial, softly rhythmic forms, but the paintings of 1912—*Tarantella, Danses à la source, Musique de Procession, La Procession, Séville*—had more obvious musical associations, as Picabia indicated in a comment of 1913: 'There are no dancers, no spring ... nothing whatever in the way of a visible clue to the feelings I am trying to express. You don't find any of these things in Beethoven Pastoral Symphony, either. There is the title indicating the motif. That is sufficient.'[39] Picabia gave each of these paintings a dominant colour and a dominant movement: *Danses à la source I* is dominated by hot reds, oranges, and browns arranged in an expansive movement which thrusts upwards and outwards, while *La Procession, Séville* is constructed from colder blacks, greys, and blues arranged in steeply descending movement and intensified by the contrasting accents of orange. These different structures express different moods—ebullient and joyful in *Danses à la source I*, solemn and restrained in *La Procession, Séville*. The Synthetists had exploited the idea of using dominant colours and linear directions to express emotion, but it had been revived more recently by the Futurists, as could be seen particularly clearly in Boccioni's triptych, the *Stati d'animo* (Pls. 138–40) shown in their February exhibition and described in the catalogue:

in a pictorial description of the various states of mind of a leave-taking, perpendicular lines, undulating and, as it were, worn out ... may well express languidness and discouragement.

Confused and trepidating lines, mingled with the outlined gestures of people ... will express a sensation of chaotic excitement ...

That Boccioni may have been responsible for introducing such ideas into Picabia's circle is suggested by the strong similarities between his first oil version and drawings for the *Stati d'animo* (in particular, *Quelli che restano* and *Quelli che vanno*, Pls. 229–30) and Duchamp's

227 (*left*) Francis Picabia, *Figure triste*, 1912 (118 × 119·5).
228 (*right*) Marcel Duchamp, *Jeune Homme triste dans un train*, 1912 (100 × 73).

Jeune Homme triste sur un train (Pl. 228) which he painted in January 1912 and in which he too expressed despondency with sombre colours and 'perpendicular lines, undulating and . . . worn-out'. Since he had not used such expressive dominants in his earlier paintings, he may have owed something to Boccioni who could have brought drawings or small canvasses with him when he visited Paris in the autumn of 1911, and who certainly told Apollinaire how he used lines and colours to express the states of mind associated with the departure of a train, since Apollinaire reported his ideas rather dismissively in the *Mercure de France* in November. Duchamp seems to have confirmed this interpretation when he remarked that Apollinaire had described the *Jeune Homme triste* as 'un état d'âme futuriste', but that he had not seen Futurist paintings, and he concluded: 'let's just say that it was a Cubist interpretation of a Futurist formula'.[40] Duchamp used similar emotional dominants in *Nu descendant un escalier* in a way that seems to have influenced Picabia's *Danses à la source I* and *II* and *La Procession, Séville*; in addition, Picabia's *Figure triste* (Pl. 227) has more than a superficial resemblance to the *Jeune Homme triste*.

Picabia's interest in the expression of psychological states gave a new dimension to Orphist painting. He had been concerned with the expression of mood since he had begun painting in a Synthetist manner in 1908, but he then represented external scenes in the hope that these would induce emotion, and it was only in 1911 that he became interested in expressing human situations, and as he did so he

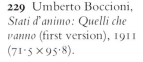

229 Umberto Boccioni, *Stati d'animo: Quelli che vanno* (first version), 1911 (71·5 × 95·8).

gradually turned his mind in on itself rather than out on to the external world. It is no coincidence that this should have occurred after he had become intimate with Duchamp and Apollinaire, for both attempted to embody internal mental processes. For example, when Duchamp summed up the sequential phases of his imagined undressing of a woman in the single image of *Portrait (Dulcinée)*, he was probably trying to represent the way the mind transforms what it sees and transposes its past phases into present consciousness—just as these processes had been described by Bergson. His image is rather literal, as is his use of insubstantial forms to indicate the fluidity and tenuousness of mental images. This rather diagrammatic mode of representing mental experience is found in other transitional works of late 1911—for example, in the study for *Joueurs d'échecs* (Pl. 231), Duchamp set the chess-pieces within the transparent heads as if to show that the moves of the game exist only in the mind. The two versions of *Nu descendant un escalier* of December 1911 and January 1912 are more complex for, as Duchamp stated, they originated in some drawings he had done in 1911 for Laforgue's *Sanglot de la terre*. The relevant drawing is that inspired by the poem, 'Encore à cet astre' (Pl. 233), in which mortals derisively contrast their life with the declining heat of the sun, while it mocks their doomed antics, for even if it caresses them with its warmth, they cannot escape death.[41] Duchamp showed one figure mounting a staircase and another descending, and between them he suspended a head in a position similar to that in the study for *Jouers d'échecs* which suggests

230 Umberto Boccioni, *Stati d'animo: Quelli che restano* (first version), 1911 (72·4 × 90).

231 (*left*) Marcel Duchamp, *Étude pour Portrait de joueurs d'échecs*, 1911. Ink and water-colour (16·5 × 15·6).
232 (*right*) Marcel Duchamp, *Portrait de joueurs d'échecs*, 1911 (108 × 101).

that Duchamp may have intended it to represent the thinking agent, the mind in which the figures exist. If this is so, it would suggest that Duchamp was not depicting two figures but was representing the different phases of movement of a single figure. He may, therefore, have intended that the drawing should express the poet's simultaneous awareness of two inextricable experiences—the challenge and defeat of the mortals who ascend and descend in the eternal treadmill of life. The vision is a profoundly pessimistic one, but Duchamp had clearly not found a way of embodying the emotion and it is possible, as I have suggested, that Boccioni showed how he might do so, for there is a striking difference between these schematic diagrams of mental situations and the emotional intensity of *Jeune Homme triste* and *Nu descendant un escalier* which derives from the use of expressive dominants and the more concentrated pictorial structure. The dark colours and falling lines of the *Nu* convey a sinister, threatening, oppressive mood and suggest that Duchamp had found how he could move from the expression of emotion as something external to himself to the embodiment of something more profoundly felt. This was recognized by Picabia who explained to a reporter in 1913 that in *Nu descendant un escalier*: 'No attempt was made at depiction, at objective presentation. The picture expresses the mood produced in the painter's memory by a view of a nude descending a flight of stairs.'[42] It is clear, however, that the painting did not have such a simple origin, and even if Picabia is right in asserting a specific visual stimulus, obviously the image of the descending nude could evoke many other associations, either to the poetry of Laforgue and Mallarmé, or, perhaps more profoundly, to Duchamp's own earlier images: the immediate source of his work were the *Portrait (Dulcinée)* and the nudes of 1909–10 (in particular, *Le Paradis* of 1910–11). All of Duchamp's major paintings of 1911–12—*Sonate*, *Portrait*, *Yvonne et Magdeleine déchiquetées*, *Portrait de joueurs d'échecs*, and *Jeune Homme triste*—were images of Duchamp's family circle or personal incidents, which suggests that the sinister pessimism of *Nu descendant un escalier* originated in some personal experience of a profoundly private kind which Duchamp later attempted to distance and defuse through the elaborate ironies and intellectual games of *Mariée mise à nu par ses célibataires, même*.[43]

Beside *Nu descendant un escalier* and *Jeune Homme triste*, and, even more, beside *Le Roi et la reine entourés de nus vites* (Pl. 236) which was painted in May 1912, Picabia's *Danses*, *Procession*, and *Figure triste* are innocent and straightforward; nevertheless they do show how

233 (*left*) Marcel Duchamp, *Encore à cet astre*, 1911. Pencil (25 × 16).
234 (*right*) Marcel Duchamp, *Nu descendant un escalier II*, 1912 (146 × 89).

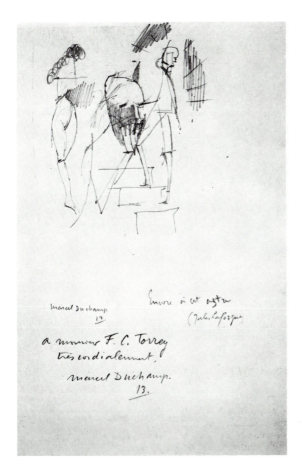

235 Francis Picabia, *Danses à la source II*, 1912 (246 × 251).

Duchamp influenced Picabia's move towards the representation of internal states of mind.

Apollinaire's comment that Picabia's and Duchamp's paintings gave 'only the simulacrum of movement' would not apply to the paintings executed after *Le Roi et la reine entourés de nus vites*, *Danses à la source I*, and *La Procession, Séville*. Thus, when Duchamp painted *Le Passage de la vierge à la mariée* and *La Mariée* (Pls. 239 and 16) during the summer which he spent in Munich, he tried to embody psychic processes and abandoned any attempt to represent physical movement. He created ambiguous structures in which sensations of volume ceaselessly transform themselves into sensations of void, and which therefore cannot be identified as figures as the titles and evocative fleshy shapes invite one to do; in a similar way Picabia destroyed any possibility of interpreting his *Danses à la source II* in terms of figurative movement, by fragmenting the objective forms and by fusing them with transparent planes so that he too created a structure which alters as one watches it.

Apollinaire clearly felt the contradiction between abstract constructions and paintings abstracted from external models, for he added several notes to the proofs of his book to the effect that Picabia's and Duchamp's paintings were not really independent structures; he then crossed most of them out, and finally decided to include them in the category of Orphic Cubists: certainly both had arrived at a degree of abstraction similar to that attained by Delaunay and Léger in the summer of 1912, for Delaunay's *Fenêtres*, Léger's *Femme en bleu*, Picabia's *Danses à la source I* and *II* and Duchamp's *Le Roi et la reine entourés de nus vites* all referred to a specific model which left its imprint on the structure of the painting, although all four painters were becoming aware of necessity of creating autonomous pictorial structures. It is no coincidence that in his *Passage de la vierge à*

236 Marcel Duchamp, *Le Roi et la reine entourés de nus vites*, 1912 (114·5 × 128·5).

308

PICABIA, ART REBEL, HERE TO TEACH NEW MOVEMENT

After Outcubing the Cubists and Setting France Agog, He Turns to America Where He Believes the Theories of the New Art Will Hold More Tenaciously.

The Port of Naples from a Height, Painted in 1913.

*A never-ceasing ... a Cubist.
Picabia's First Leanings Toward the Techni of the New School*

Picabia in His Studio in Paris, at the Right is a Painting in His Early Impressionistic Style. His Latest Work is on the Easel.

One of Picabia's Early Paintings of the Impressionist School Before He Outcubed the Cubists.

Picabia's Latest Manner—A Blaze of Coloristic Personal Impressions with No Attempt to Reproduce the Subject Painted.

LITTLE STORIES OF FACT AND FANCY

A Choctaw Technicality.

Why He Was Popular.

Saved by Stinginess.

Perfume for the Blind.

Sure of a Job.

Nuts to Crack

la mariée Duchamp should have realized the most self-contained structure, for he was inventing evocative forms to express inner experience rather than deriving them from the external world. This was the direction which Picabia took in the lost *Procession* (Pls. 237–8), which he probably painted after the Section d'Or exhibition and after he had visited his wife's home in the Jura with Apollinaire and Duchamp in late October.[44] During this trip they discussed 'the possibilities of a new evolution', and these possibilities may have included further abstraction and the continuing exploration of psychological painting, as well as Duchamp's decision to turn to a more intellectual art. Picabia's painting owes much to Duchamp's *Le Roi et la reine entourés de nus vites*, for it is dominated by a diagonal flow of non-representational shapes not unlike the 'swift nudes' in Duchamp's picture, although it is even further removed from any reference to the visible world. Picabia checked the flow of movement by placing larger and heavier shapes in the 'foreground', and modelled them meticulously, making them rather bulbous in such a way that they seem to represent 'something'—as they do in *Le Roi et la reine*—but it is only the title which indicates the subject of the work. This nagging sense of presence is similar to that given by the evocative forms in Duchamp's paintings.

238 Francis Picabia, *Procession*, 1912.

239 Marcel Duchamp, *Le Passage de la vierge à la mariée*, 1912 (59·4 × 54).

New York. January to March 1913

In January 1913 Picabia and his wife went to New York for three months to attend the Armory Show and to open a studio to teach 'the true method of painting'.[45]

New York exerted a strong influence on the imagination of the European avant-garde which saw it as both symbol and embodiment of modernism. It was the central theme of Cendrars's poetry of 1912, and it was probably Cendrars who inspired Delaunay to write 'DELAUNAY NEW YORK–PARIS' across the *Équipe de Cardiff* and to plan a series of paintings of New York.[46] Delaunay never fulfilled this project, but Picabia did paint a number of pictures of New York, or rather, of his mental image of the city. He was fascinated by its skyscrapers, its luminous signs, its jazz, its cars, and its continuous turbulent dynamic movement, and in an article, 'How New York Looks to Me', published in the *New York American* on 30 March, he commented: 'You of New York should be quick to understand me and my fellow-painters. Your New York is the cubist, the futurist city. It expresses in its architecture, its life and its spirit, the modern thought.' This was the first time that Picabia had showed any interest in modern life, yet despite his enthusiasm for the specific creations of the new civilization, he ceased to represent the objects of the external world, for he believed that artistic expression was 'necessarily related to the needs of the civilization of the time', and his conception of contemporary civilization went deeper than its exterior aspects, being concerned with a change of consciousness.[47]

Picabia must have been disappointed at the negative reception given to his paintings in the autumn exhibitions in Paris, for when asked why he came to America, he replied: 'France is almost outplayed ... I have come here to appeal to the American people to accept the New Movement in Art in the same spirit as they have accepted political movements to which they at first have felt antagonistic ...'[48] This interview was the first shot in a futuristic publicity campaign which lasted the whole of his visit, and it gives a surprising and somewhat inaccurate picture of the revolutionary nature of his previous art: 'PICABIA ART REBEL, HERE TO TEACH NEW MOVEMENT: After Outcubing the Cubist and Setting France Agog, He Turns to America Where He Believes the Theories of the New Art will Hold More Tenaciously ...' The tone was obviously that of the reporter, but the content of the propagandist article was probably determined by Picabia's feeling that anything was possible in the exhilarating atmosphere of New York and that he could indeed outdo the Cubists and set 'France Agog'. He responded with enjoyment to the American press which was prepared to entertain new ideas with a gusto inconceivable in Paris. With his wife as an intermediary (for he did not speak English), he gave interviews, issued public statements, and wrote articles which are an important source for Picabia's ideas about the new painting. His statements were often contradictory, partly because he had to make use of the critical vocabulary of his Synthetist period which no longer accorded with his new work, and—more basically–because he had not yet fully realized his ideas. However, his pronouncements do reveal his struggle to define the new function that he had glimpsed for art.

He and his wife were staying in Greenwich Village, where they were welcomed into its intellectual and artistic circles and met Stieglitz and the artists and writers who gathered in what Gabrielle Buffet-Picabia described as the 'vivifying ambience' of his Photo-Secession Gallery, the temple of the New York avant-garde. A statement by the Picabias' friend, Maurice de Zayas, in Stieglitz's journal, *Camera Works*, reveals something of the confidence of their new acquaintances: 'Being in possession of all the elements of Anthropology, Ethnology, Psychology, and Art ... we are, at last, in a position to clear up ... the complex problem of the evolution of Form, if not of Art.'[49] Picabia's introduction to the catalogue of an exhibition he held in Stieglitz's gallery suggests that he was influenced by his friends' democratic conception of the role of avant-garde art, for he stated that art is a form of communication and that laws could be found to ensure the success of the communication. He admitted that the new art could seem mysterious, but he asserted that this was because its laws were not yet understood and even allowed that objective elements might continue to be necessary to ensure communication during a transitional period.[50] This reasonableness is more characteristic of Gleizes and Metzinger (who also stressed the continuing necessity of objective forms) than of Picabia, who was to assert, a few months later back in Paris, that only an educated élite was capable of understanding the new art.

The Armory Show opened on 17 February, and those who had read Picabia's account of recent French painting in the *New York Times* the previous day must have been surprised at the relatively conventional nature of the works Picabia exhibited; indeed, one critic noted that although they were 'recent in date' they were:

much less abstract than what he is doing today. The *Procession, Séville*, with its hieratic design and the curiously structural look of its close packed units of shape and color, still indicates slightly the natural realities that inspired it.

So in greater measure does his *Souvenir de Grimaldi, Italie ... Paris* is almost realistic, compared with the painter's present standards, but *La Danse à la Source* with its rhythmic lines and its vigorous color throbs approaches nearer the up-to-the-minute ideals of the Cubists.[51]

There was a significant difference between these works and those which Picabia exhibited a month later in Stieglitz's gallery. As soon as he had arrived in New York, he turned his room at the Hotel Brevoort into a studio and painted a series of gouaches on themes of New York, Harlem, jazz, and dance, thirteen of which (with some drawings) were shown in his exhibition which consisted solely of work he had done since he arrived in the United States; during that time he had come into contact with new ideas through the Stieglitz group, and had had a unique opportunity to study different forms of the emergent abstract art at the Armory Show where the whole spectrum of modern art (except that of the Futurists, Kupka, and Delaunay) was displayed. Picabia's exhibition must have been impressive—and perhaps unsettling—for such an ensemble of works had never previously been presented. The paintings benefit greatly from proximity to their fellows, for they are subtle variations on a limited number of themes which range from the sombre colours and elusive movement of the *Chanson nègre* (Pl. 245), to the bright flickering movement of the *Danseuse étoile et son école de danse* (Pl. 240), and to the intense reds and pinks and dynamic movement of *New York* (Pl. 243). The grouping of works in series makes the individual character and mood of each painting more apparent, and gives them a force and subtlety which they lose when seen individually.

The paintings ranged from fully non-representational ones, to those which retained the relationship between painting and the external world that was found in his paintings of 1912. His most

240 Francis Picabia, *Danseuse étoile et son école de danse*, 1913. Water-colour on paper (26·2 × 56).

significant achievement in the former category was to take a decisive
step towards the establishment of multi-dimensional space, in which
he could freely deploy his forms without being restricted by the
pictorial devices which are necessary to separate object from space
and the near from the far, and which still existed—in a very vestigial
form—in the *Danses à la source II*. The forms he used were prefigured
in his earlier works, and once he had freed them from their
representational function, he was able to develop more complexly
evocative structures.

   The horizontal version of the two *New York* paintings (now in the
Art Institute of Chicago, from Stieglitz's collection, Pl. 242), is like a
bird's-eye view of Manhattan in which one can distinguish shapes
which suggest skyscrapers and roads in diminishing perspective, so it
is simply a further development of the approach used in *Paris* in 1912.
However, Picabia asserted that if certain aspects of New York could
be recognized, it was not because he had sought them, but because
they were so vivid that they had become 'a salient part of his
mood',[52] and he also counteracted any straightforward identification
by superimposing transparent and opaque planes over the linear
perspective (in fact, the way such planes invade the base and sides of

241 Francis Picabia,
*Danseuse étoile sur un
transatlantique*, 1913.
Water-colour on paper
(75 × 55).

242 Francis Picabia, *New York*, 1913. Water-colour and gouache on paper (75 × 55).

243 Francis Picabia, *New York*, 1913. Water-colour on paper mounted on board (75·5 × 55·5).

244 *Going North on Fifth Avenue*, 1913.

the composition is similar to the composition of some of Kupka's contemporary works (Pl. 111). The painting thus contains a strong contradiction between the imagined scene and the abstract structure which Picabia resolved in the second *New York* in the Art Institute (Pl. 243). This is a more impressive work which in some ways prefigures Russian abstraction (for example, the way the small wedges impart dynamism to the ambiguous space, or the way small rectangles float in undefined layers of space, suggest both Malevich and Lissitsky). Picabia did a drawing for this work (reproduced by the *New York American* on 30 March with the caption 'Going North on Fifth Avenue Where the Subtle Perfume of Feminity is Impressed on the Brain', Pl. 244). It had a vestigial ground plane and perspective, which Picabia eliminated in the finished work; he also transformed the flat vertical planes which suggest skyscrapers into soft curved shapes. It is clear from these changes that Picabia deliberately created ambiguity by setting up a sequence of contradictory readings. One is accustomed to read space in terms of a sequence of tones, but Picabia interwove light and dark in such a way that it is impossible to define the spatial location of any shape. For example, if looked at casually, the dark planes appear to be superimposed on the lighter ones, yet if one looks longer, they appear to slip behind the lighter planes, and the floating pinks press the greys together, while the black bars draw the shapes into a curious momentary pause which emphasizes the continual fluctuation in one's perception of the whole.

Picabia probably learnt how to suggest multiple readings from Duchamp who manipulated light and shadow in a similar way. Thus, in *Le Passage de la vierge à la mariée* (Pl. 239), what appears as a ground plane can also be read as a plane in the process of becoming concave or as the convex interior of a sectional form. However, Picabia's work is less substantial than Duchamp's and does not evoke any known material forms, while Duchamp simultaneously suggests soft flesh and metallic hardness. This difference was partly due to the fact that Duchamp had a profound understanding of Cubism, whereas Picabia was more deeply influenced by Synthetism and distrusted Cubism as materialistic:

I have come to realise that cubes cannot always be made to express the thought of the brain, the feelings of the soul ... I have got entirely beyond the material, therefore there is nothing materialistic in my studies of New York nor anything sensual. For a picture that is created from the brain cannot be sensual. Art should be pure. When a picture is created from the brain, it is pure.[53]

Picabia thus made sure that the structure of his painting had no resemblance to the structures traditionally used to represent the world, so that his painting has its own life as something which defies any simple identification and which must be experienced as music is experienced—though absorption in its unique life and without question as to its 'meaning'. Duchamp's painting, on the other hand, invites speculation about its meaning.

In his New York articles and interviews Picabia frequently used the example of music to substantiate his ideas on non-representational painting: 'Art resembles music ...' he said. 'To a musician words are obstacles to musical expression, just as objects are obstacles to pure art expression.'[54] Picabia could have seen musicalist painting without representational structures in Paris (Kandinsky's *Improvisations 23, 24,* and *25* were shown at the Indépendants of 1912 (Pl. 15), and Kupka's *Amorpha, Fugue en deux couleurs* at the Salon d'Automne). However, he seems to have believed that musicalist expression was compatible with figurative painting even after he had been in New York for a while, since it must have been he who suggested to a reporter that 'he had been striving to paint music with his brush'.[55] His change may have been influenced by a clever critic of his works in the Armory show who said that his painted music was 'programme music', and thus suggested that there was a contradiction between true musical expression and representation of the visible world.[56] However, Kandinsky's painting and theory probably exerted a more profound influence. He exhibited *Improvisation*

245 Francis Picabia, *Chanson nègre*, 1913. Water-colour on paper (66·3 × 56).

246 Wassily Kandinsky,
Improvisation 27, 1912
(120 × 140).

27 (Pl. 246) in the Armory show where it was purchased by Stieglitz;
the latter may have had other paintings by Kandinsky in his gallery,
and he had published extracts from Kandinsky's *Ueber das Geistige in
der Kunst* in *Camera Work*.[57] Picabia could have been influenced by
the fluctuating space of Kandinsky's pictures, by his improvisatory
mode of painting, by his specific ideas on the relationship between
music and painting, and even by his conception of the spiritual in art.

There are, for example, significant similarities between Picabia's
Chanson nègre (Pl. 245) and the *Improvisations* which Picabia could
have seen, although they are obscured by the fact that Kandinsky
used bright and varied colours, while Picabia created a sombre mood
by the use of more closely related tones ranging from deep blacks and
browns through dusky pinks, greys, watery browns, to near whites.
Both Picabia and Kandinsky used curved transparent shapes which
float in limitless space, making them dynamic with black lines which
dart over the surface. They also animated their larger forms with a
multiplicity of smaller forms—arcs and curves, thin lines embedded
in the larger planes, and small arrow-like wedges—which sink into
suggested depth whilst they are simultaneously pushed forward by
the larger softer planes. The relationship between sequential and
simultaneous pictorial experience is very important in both paintings. For example, in Kandinsky's paintings one can follow the

structure of the dark lines as they move across space, and one becomes increasingly aware of the way they change direction, become thick and strong or thin and delicate, fade into depth and thrust forward. If one focuses on them, one is simultaneously aware of the presence of the colours, but it requires an active change in concentration to *see* how the colours act in relation to one another. Kandinsky was probably influenced by the combination of the successive and simultaneous, the melodic and harmonic, in musical form. Picabia also structured his new paintings in this way, although he tended to retain a vestigial ground plane while Kandinsky's forms float freely over the picture surface. Picabia could have observed that Kupka had been developing similar musicalist compositions—he may have seen his *Solo d'un trait brun* (Pl. 89) which he must have been finishing when Picabia left Paris since he exhibited it at the Indépendants at the same time that Picabia was showing his *Chanson nègre* in New York. Kupka too attempted to combine 'harmonic' and 'melodic' forms by using superimposed transparent planes and a separate linear motif, but the *Solo* is pictorially rather thin, while *Chanson nègre* is more closely related to the study for *Amorpha, Chromatique chaude* (Pl. 14) with its complexly interwoven transparent planes. Transparency was, in fact, a common device to fuse different temporal experiences, as can be seen in works as diverse as the *Chanson nègre*, the *Amorpha* study, Delaunay's tripartite *Fenêtres*, and Duchamp's *Jouers d'échecs* (Pls. 145 and 232).

Picabia described how he observed New York with its great buildings, its hurrying workers, its crowds, its movements, and continued:

I absorb these impressions. I am in no hurry to put them on canvas. I let them remain in my mind, and then when the spirit of creation is at floodtide, I improvise my pictures as a musician improvises music. The harmonies of my studies grow and take form under my brush as the musician's harmonies grow under his fingers. His music is from his brain and his soul just as mine are from my brain and soul.[58]

Elsewhere he explained the analogy between painting and music, claiming that if a musician is inspired by a landscape, he does not describe it, 'he expresses it in sound waves, he translates it into an expression of the impression, the mood. And as there are absolute sound waves, so there are absolute waves of colour and form.'[59] His words suggest that he—like Kandinsky—may have been influenced by the theosophist belief that every animate and inanimate form emits vibrations which express its 'personality' and which can be perceived by those endowed with spiritual sight.[60] This belief seemed to be confirmed by synaesthesia, about which the theosophists wrote and which both Kandinsky and Picabia experienced;

it is well known that Kandinsky 'heard' Wagner's *Lohengrin* in terms of his childhood memories of Moscow: 'I saw all my colours in my mind's eye,' he wrote in 1913. 'Wild, almost insane lines drew themselves before me.' Picabia experienced 'purple as the inevitable and dominant hue' when he heard a black singing in Harlem, and this inspired his *Chanson nègre*.[61] The 'theory of correspondences' rested on this kind of experience: many believed that the spontaneous occurrence of such psycho-physical experience confirmed the existence of a spiritual realm which was independent of individual human life, even though human life partook of it. However, Picabia did not have any real spiritual belief for, unlike Kandinsky, he could have no faith in the existence of a fundamental order which would transcend his sense of the fragmentation of life, the isolation of the self, and the fundamental absurdity of existence. It seems, then, that he felt that those profound sensations—which others saw as confirmations of spiritual being—bore witness only to his own inner being.

I do not know if Picabia had any specific knowledge of theosophy, but a number of his acquaintances were interested in spiritualism, and in the way that scientific hypotheses about the 'immateriality' of matter seemed to confirm belief in spiritual essence, and they may have influenced his conception of the way sound and colour 'waves' transmit emotion.[62] Moreover, in 1913 Picabia spoke about the difference between painting drawn from the objective world and painting which was independent of it, in terms which suggest that he knew something about the theosophists' structuring of existence into planes of different degrees of purity, ranging from the material to the purely spiritual and ineffable: 'Look at a canvas "d'origine matière pensée"; and you have a "fixité"; so there is a limitation. Look at one of mine. Naturally you could not find any "fixité", because it is infinite, just as my emotions are. It expresses a "pensée pure" which evidently blends with the infinite.'[63] His terminology may have been influenced by the theosophist's 'mental' planes—those intermediate between the material and the spiritual planes, in which material forms could be perceived as mental images, or mental activity could assume material form (Pls. 68–9 and 71). In his Synthetist works, Picabia had represented his mental impressions of the material world (these were his canvases 'd'origine matière pensée'), so his words suggest that he felt he had transcended such a stage.[64] However, all that one knows of Picabia suggests that he would not have taken theosophist doctrine very seriously, and that theosophist imagery would have done no more than assist him when he began to turn his consciousness in on himself and to become aware of those aspects of personal being which are undeniably real but which, since they escape verbalization, can be *felt* as 'infinite'. Thus, while Kandinsky and perhaps Kupka were influenced by specific theosophical images, there is no trace of such images in Picabia's art.

Gertrude Stein later made an enigmatic comment about Picabia's paintings of this period which also indicates that, rather than giving him any doctrinal belief, spiritualist ideas suggested how he might try to embody his own consciousness: 'Picabia had conceived and is struggling with the problem that a line should have the vibration of a musical sound and that this vibration should be the result of conceiving the human form ... in so tenuous a fashion that it would induce vibration in the line forming it. It is his way of achieving the disembodied.'[65] She explained 'the emotion of the object' creates a vibration which determines the character of the line. In 1913 Picabia was reported to have said that he was attempting to represent 'the emotion produced in our minds by things': he may have been referring to the processes on which Gertrude Stein commented.[66]

The New York paintings were inspired by specific scenes, events, and encounters which excited Picabia in some way (for example, the *Danseuse étoile et son école de danse* (Pl. 240) is said to have been inspired by his meeting with an exotic dancer[67]). However, the emotion communicated to the spectator is not a straightforward one, probably because Picabia worked in an improvisatory way, allowing the painting to generate its own structure so that the final work was not simply the expression of a remembered emotion but something more complex and elusive. His comment that he improvised like a musician suggests that he may have been interested in Kandinsky's ideas on musicalist improvisation; indeed, his paintings of 1913 can be divided into categories which correspond to the 'Impressions, Improvisations and Compositions' which Kandinsky discussed in *Ueber das Geistige in der Kunst*, for his exhibition contained both improvisations (like *Chanson nègre*) and works which were closer to the scene which inspired them, corresponding to Kandinsky's 'impressions'. Kandinsky defined his improvisations as 'a largely unconscious, spontaneous expression of inner character, non-material nature' which may be compared with a reporter's account of how Picabia 'cut loose from cubism ... with entirely unfettered, spontaneous, ever-varying means of expression in form and colour waves, according to the commands, the needs, the inspiration of the impression, the mood received'.[68] Moreover, Picabia intended to use his New York paintings for a more formal work when he returned to Paris, and in fact he did so in *Udnie* and *Edtaonisl* which could thus be equated with Kandinsky's compositions.[69]

Picabia's improvisation developed in two stages: he first drew a linear structure—perhaps while thinking about the dancer, about New York, or the black singing—but without using the lines to suggest a particular grouping or scene as he had done in *Paris* or

Danses à la source I. He then improvised from this linear structure, either affirming it by filling in the areas bounded by line, or breaking it down by continuing a colour over a boundary, by overpainting earlier shapes, or by fading one plane into the next, but always taking care that the abstract linear substructure remained visible. Although his forms were very different, he probably derived this mode of painting and its resulting ambiguity from the Cubists, who also improvised from a linear substructure related to the external model. Picabia had followed this practice in 1912, but he now began to invent the substructure and here again he may have been influenced by Kandinsky. In this way Picabia, like the other Orphists, became increasingly involved in the self-generating evolution of a painting, and as he did so he became increasingly confident that form and colour could embody inner experience which did not need to be translated into the sphere of verbal consciousness.

Like all the painters who were interested in the relationship between painting and music, Picabia was interested in the expression of subconscious experience, and this interest may have been intensified by the fact that a number of his friends in New York were interested in psycho-analytic theory.[70] Picabia was the great-nephew of the celebrated Dr. Charcot with whom Freud had studied in Paris in the 1880s and whose studies of hysteria and hypnosis were important in the genesis of Freud's theories, and one wonders if Picabia knew of this connection and whether it would have aroused his interest in psycho-analysis. This is speculation, but it is true that certain critics discussed Picabia's work in terms which show that such ideas were current in American artistic circles. The article written by Hapgood—which was based on conversations in French with Picabia—gives an idea of the rather general way such ideas had percolated artistic conceptions. Picabia had talked about how he tried to express 'soul states' (the product of the artist's personality, experience, mood) through 'the arrangements of line and colour in such a way as to suggest the equilibrium of static and dynamic qualities of rest and of motion, of mass and balance'. Hapgood said that he found this suggestive, 'for I find that any intense effort of expression in any art means that by means of a few simple devices we suggest ... the spiritual picture of our soul, and its wealth of subconscious detail'.[71] Inspired by a memory, an impression, or a mood, Picabia would improvise, and in so doing he became less and less conscious of the literal meaning of what he painted and increasingly absorbed in establishing an 'equilibrium' of pictorial elements. Thus the finished painting was no longer directly dependent on what had originally inspired it, yet still contained evocative forms which suggest some presence and which haunt 'the fringes of consciousness'—a phrase of William James which

Hapgood quoted. The forms which evolved during this improvisatory process were ones which had evolved spontaneously in Picabia's previous paintings, and this probably confirmed his belief that the forms had some connection with his inner self.

In his preface to the exhibition, Picabia stated that it was no longer possible to express 'the new consciousness of nature' by objective means and continued: 'the resulting manifestations of this state of mind which is more and more approaching abstraction can themselves not be anything but abstraction. They separate themselves from the sensorial pleasures which man may derive from man or nature (impressionism) to enter the domain of the pure joy of the idea and consciousness.'[72] His reference to a 'state of mind ... approaching abstraction' does, I think, confirm the suggestion that he was seeking to penetrate to those wordless levels of being which lie at the centre of the self.

Paris. The paintings of 1913–14

Almost immediately after his return to Paris in May 1913 Picabia began to paint his most significant works, *Udnie, jeune fille américaine (danse)* and *Edtaonisl (ecclésiastique)* (Pls. VII, VIII and 247–8), in which he revealed the power of his new expression and which show how, since mid-1912, he had moved from something accessible to something closed and private—just as Duchamp had done between mid-1911 and mid-1912. It was at this time that Picabia first began to show signs of mental disturbance, manifested in bouts of depression and exhaustion.

Udnie and *Edtaonisl* were Picabia's first large-scale non-figurative works. They were intended as companion pieces, for they are the same size and complement each other in colour, composition, and mood: *Udnie* is an expanding dynamic composition painted in airy floating blues, while the composition of *Edtaonisl* is inward-turning and claustrophobic, and its purples and ochres engender a feeling of tension, almost of apprehension. Picabia himself said they should be seen together, and explained that they were 'memories of America ... which, subtly opposed like musical harmonies, become representative of an idea, of a nostalgia, of a fugitive impression'.[73]

The 'fugitive impression' is in some way embodied in the form of the paintings, for although they both have a strong physical presence, they seem to retreat as one looks at them, to become even more ambiguous and elusive, and this formal ambiguity reflects an equally strong emotional ambiguity in which depth of feeling is suggested but remains peculiarly inexplicit.

Udnie and *Edtaonisl* were the first works in which Picabia finally dispensed with compositions based on gravitational forces, for

247 Francis Picabia,
Udnie, jeune fille américaine
(danse), 1913 (300 × 300).

although he made the forms in his New York paintings immaterial, he tended to concentrate the heavier tones at the bottom of the paintings so as to suggest a ground plane (he seems to have tried to get away from this effect by turning upside down at least one painting, *Danseuse étoile sur un transatlantique*, Pl. 241). However, in his new paintings, he eliminated any tones which might suggest gravitational relationships, as well as any horizontal or vertical elements which might indicate spatial location or dimension. Picabia thus composed *Udnie* and *Edtaonisl* from forms which float freely in space. The change of structure can be seen more clearly if one compares *Udnie* with *Danses à la source I* (Pl. 224), which is composed of similar knots of small forms emerging from larger planes but which are frozen into specific positions because the ground and background planes are so strongly defined. Once Picabia had eliminated such spatial distinctions, it became more clear that he had reduced every element in his paintings to a single, unique, ambiguous substance, so that they fulfil Apollinaire's ideal of the artist's transformation of his material into a new form—a transformation symbolized by the flame which 'has the purity which will suffer nothing foreign to itself and which cruelly transforms that which it touches into itself'.[74]

Udnie and *Edtaonisl* are enigmatic, and Picabia clearly intended them to be so. Earlier in 1913 Apollinaire suggested that we look at Picabia's *Procession* 'the way we look at a machine whose function we do not know but whose movement and power astonish and worry us';[75] his words are even more relevant for Picabia's non-figurative paintings in which the artist has deliberately undermined any simple reading of the formal structure. For example, in *Udnie* he used contradictory clues to suggest that a plane could be seen as the facet of a volume or as a detached floating shape; as parallel to the picture surface or as receding into pictorial depth. He obtained these ambiguous effects by working directly on the canvas, improvising on linear structure as he had done in the New York paintings, but achieving richer complexities through the use of oil-paint. Examination of the surface of *Udnie* shows that Picabia drew in the contours of the large planes of the substructure and of most of the small detailed forms, and then 'filled in' these areas, but that he also did a considerable amount of overpainting—particularly with beautifully modulated 'shading' and with light-filled transparent planes—so that he made the structure even more dense and ambiguous, for as he painted he gave alternative readings to every successive illusion of depth, space, movement, or volume in such a way that one cannot look at a single element without its turning into something else before one's eyes. Thus the smaller, more evocative forms float out of the centre while simultaneously being drawn back into its blue depths; the plank-like forms on the lower left function like the pistons of a machine, but they are echoed by more organic forms in the upper part of the painting, and their flesh-like character is made even more ambiguous by the way in which they are assimilated into the fluid blues and greens on the left, creating with them a surface which is dense and heavy and which yet seems to drift upwards in floating transparencies; the tiny white rectangles and triangles on the light blue suggest a star-studded sky, but are so artificial that this suggestion is immediately undermined and the blue changes from sky-like airiness into a hard, shiny surface. These tiny

248 Francis Picabia, *Edtaonisl (ecclésiastique),* 1913 (302 × 300·5).

flickering shapes also appear in the rather curious *Le Poulailler* of 1912 (Pl. 223), where they create considerable ambiguity by countering the three-dimensional forms of the hens.

Edtaonisl is heavier and more sombre than the enigmatic and etherial *Udnie*; its movements are broken and chaotic, its composition cramped, its colours icy and dissonant. Picabia painted the upper third of the picture in heavy greys, blacks, and purples which he animated with a cold but intense blue. This upper section hangs over the lighter planes below, while dusky yellows and ochres form a plane underlying the whole painting so that light glows from within it (as in Kupka's study for *Amorpha, Chromatique chaude*, Pl. 14). The yellows pale to white, so that they appear to emerge from depth and to turn across the painting in a tense struggle with the black and grey spirals. There is something machine-like in the precision of the modelling of the steel-grey forms and in the way they enmesh others; however, other forms are bulgy and fleshy, like those in Duchamp's paintings on sexual themes of mid-1912. In fact the composition of *Edtaonisl*—with its diagonal flow of interlocked shapes between darker, stiller forms—may have been influenced by *Le Roi et la reine entourés de nus vites*, whose sinister character it also shares. Moreover, Duchamp may have shown Picabia how to use gentle shading to make forms bulge and float and to suggest the presence of beings whose existence is simultaneously denied by other visual information. In this way both painters created tightly woven structures which incorporate suggestive forms but which never coalesce into known forms. However, Duchamp's paintings were intimate in scale and more overtly sexual than Picabia's, which go beyond human scale and reference. One is immediately conscious of the potential implications of Duchamp's fusion of human and machine, but Picabia's forms only temporarily suggest such associations and remain much more elusive.

It is thus extremely difficult to interpret these paintings.[76] Picabia said that they were inspired by memories of America, and that they were based on several of the works he had painted in New York;[77] indeed, the angular, flat planes and the softly shaded bulging ones, the organic fleshy forms and the machine-like slabs and bars which characterize *Udnie* and *Edtaonisl* are all found in the New York paintings (these motifs also occur in earlier paintings—at least as far back as 1904—they are there obscured by the naturalistic structure). However, Picabia did not use the earlier works as *studies* for the larger paintings, for they were freely invented works which generated certain formal configurations which Picabia found meaningful and which evolved equally spontaneously when he improvised the larger works.

Gabrielle Buffet-Picabia stated that *Udnie, jeune fille américaine (danse)* was inspired by the exotic dancer whom Picabia met on board the liner which took them to the United States and that *Edtaonisl* represents a scene on board the transatlantic liner in which a Dominican priest watched the dancer perform her act (the word 'Edtaonisl' is a partial anagram of 'danseuse étoile' so that those in the secret would know that the title *Edtaonisl (ecclésiastique)* indicates the simultaneous presence of dancer and priest).[78] The painting thus unites the dance theme and the religious theme, both of which Picabia had painted in 1912 and both of which were inspired by scenes he had observed in 1909;[79] like *Udnie*, it therefore embodies remembered experience.

Both *Udnie and Edtaonisl* are composed from movements which develop in different directions at different speeds and on different layers in depth, and which must be experienced in time as distinct but interrelated elements which change as the focus of the eye changes: (the temporality of the experience becomes clearer if one compares Picabia's new pictorial structures with that of *Danses à la source I*, in which one is given sufficient information immediately to grasp the position of the figures in space). Such complex temporal structures were characteristic of Simultanist painting. Apollinaire referred to the 'poems painted by Picabia' in his article on Simultanism in 1914, and since he used the word 'poetry' and its derivatives to designate an art which was independent of the natural world and which had the power to impose its own emotional reality, he was probably referring to Picabia's non-figurative paintings.[80] Picabia had never been interested in literal Simultanism, that is, in the juxtaposition of heterogeneous images to indicate their simultaneous existence, but he was almost certainly aware of Bergson's concept of Simultanism as the consciousness of the continuity of an individual being whose past is kept alive by memory. Memory was also the creative principle of Apollinaire's poetry, and he himself found it significant in Duchamp's painting, writing in *Les Peintres cubistes*:

All the men, all the beings who have passed by us have left traces in our memory and these traces of life have a reality which one can scrutinize ... These traces acquire together a personality whose individual character one can indicate pictorially by a purely mental operation.
There are traces of these beings in the paintings of Marcel Duchamp.

Since Picabia's paintings of 1913 were in many ways the continuators of Duchamp's paintings of 1912, Apollinaire's comments on Duchamp's work can illuminate our understanding of Picabia's, particularly since his ideas were drawn from conversations with Duchamp in which Picabia would often have taken part.

Picabia had begun to attempt to express the workings of the mind in his New York paintings, but Duchamp had been imaging mental processes since mid-1911 in works like *Portrait (Dulcinée)*, *Yvonne et Magdeleine déchiquetées*, and *Portrait de joueurs d'échecs*, rather literal depictions of the fact that the mind contains multiple images of the real and the imagined, the past and the future, the defined and the insubstantial. However, in 1912 Duchamp seems to have discovered that he could embody deeply internalized experience through the processes of creating form, rather than project such experience into literal images which were, in a sense, external to him. The change that occurred in Duchamp's art was a recurrent theme of Apollinaire's poetry; indeed, he frequently used the image of the floating decapitated head—as when he cried, 'Où sont ces têtes que j'avais' as if he were contemplating externalized images of himself.[81]

He opposed such images of personal fragmentation (the 'morceaux de moi-même') to others which suggest internalization of all the experiences he had previously conceived as external. Duchamp used similar images of floating bodiless heads in *Yvonne et Magdeleine déchiquetées* (Pl. 219) to represent his sisters at different ages in a way that recalls Apollinaire's images of his fragmented past. However, in the *Passage de la vierge à la mariée* (Pl. 239) Duchamp was no longer simply the recorder of imagined experience, and he seems to have projected himself into a profoundly personal inner world in which sexual experience is suggested by haunting images of thrust and penetration and discharge but which is never stabilized in a finite descriptive structure. Between mid-1912 and mid-1913 Picabia made a comparable break from the imaging of mental experience as something external to the self (as in the memories of the *Danses à la source I*) to something internalized and less explicit. He ceased to depict the objects of memory and instead sought a way of embodying the most subtle movements of the mind.

This development in the art of Duchamp and Picabia correspond to Bergson's distinction between externalized and internalized awareness of the self:

When I direct my attention inward to contemplate my own self (supposed for the moment to be inactive), I perceive at first, as a crust solidified on the surface, all the perceptions which come to it from the material world. These perceptions are clear, distinct, juxtaposed ... they tend to group themselves into objects. Next, I notice the memories which more or less adhere to these perceptions and which serve to interpret them. These memories have been detached ... from the surface by the perceptions which resemble them; they rest on the surface of my mind without being absolutely myself.[82]

Bergson contrasted this viewing of the self as a collection of separate material states with the inner consciousness of the indivisible continuity of the self. This is not to say that Picabia and Duchamp were necessarily influenced by Bergson—for they probably attained such awareness through the specific processes of creation—yet because Bergson put into words a kind of thinking that was pervasive in Parisian artistic and intellectual circles, he may help one to understand the change that occurred in Picabia's Orphism.

Picabia seems to have sought this kind of consciousness in painting itself. All those who have described how Picabia worked emphasize his total absorption in the experience: Gabrielle Buffet-Picabia said that *Udnie* and *Edtaonisl* 'were painted with unimaginable speed and fever. He worked day and night without eating ...' Germaine Everling said that he painted in a half-hypnotized state; Arp stated that Picabia's '*need* to paint without interruption is explained by a fanatical, almost mad interest which counters his Dadaist irony. He gives himself body and soul to the act of creation'; and Picabia's own statements on improvization confirm that it was the act of painting itself that was meaningful to him.[83] It is in this context that Picabia's phrases a 'state of mind ... approaching abstraction' or 'the pure joy of the idea and consciousness' should be understood. On one level, these were paintings of memories whose origin was known to the painter, but during the process of painting Picabia gradually lost the specific reference and became conscious only of the developing needs of his forms, so that the work gradually became detached from its original source and grew into what Picabia later called 'an object living by itself and with its own expression'.

While Picabia was painting *Udnie* and *Edtaonisl* he wrote to Stieglitz: 'I'm thinking even more about a more pure painting, painting with one dimension no longer having a title, each work will have a name related to its pictorial expression, a proper name created solely for it.'[84] Such a name prevents the spectator from referring the painting to an external model, and emphasizes that it is 'an object living by itself'. Picabia probably got this idea from Duchamp who was the first to paint enigmatic titles on his works. Apollinaire commented on this practice in *Les Peintres cubistes:* 'In order to ward off all perceptions which might become conceptions from his art, Duchamp writes on the canvas the title which he confers upon it.'[85] His meaning is clarified by his assertion that Duchamp was not trying to 'disengage intellectual generalizations from nature', but that he was concerned with 'collective forms and colours perception of which has not become conception'; he thus suggested that Duchamp shared the widespread contemporary belief that conceptual knowledge prevents true consciousness of life, and above all of inner life. In fact Duchamp makes it impossible to give his work any straightforward conceptual meaning, for although the colours and forms of, for example, *Le Roi et la reine entourés de nus vites* are extremely suggestive, the non-sense title and the ambiguity of form and space prevent one from stabilizing them in any category of known experience.[86] The forms thus remain free and potent, and prey on the mind with the insistence of a withheld memory.

These ideas help one to understand Picabia's claim that the new art should express states of mind 'approaching abstraction'. He was not speaking of emotions like joy or grief which have definable causes and definable objects, and which may be classified in generalized categories, for definable emotions play the same role as recognizable forms: they concentrate attention on the act of recognition and turn consciousness away from its unknown depths.[87] Picabia intended that his paintings should communicate a sense of this inner life to others, and wrote: 'In my work the subjective expression is the title, the painting the object. But the object is nevertheless somewhat subjective, because it is the pantomime—the appearance of the title; it furnishes to a certain point the means of comprehending the potentiality—*the very heart of man.*'[88] His paintings are objects which arouse associations of so fleeting and tenuous a kind that they are impossible to define, and although the titles also draw the mind in pursuit of the association, it is impossible to resolve title and form. Thus, when one confronts these paintings, one is confronted by a conceptual void, and it is only in this void that one can attain full consciousness of the forms as the enigmatic creation of a complex, unknowable, but completely real individual, who was trying to find personal meaning at the very heart of mental experience.

By mid-1913 Picabia had developed compositions with forms which move ceaselessly in fluid non-gravitational space, and which are analogous to the contemporary works of Delaunay, Kupka, and Léger. Like them, he had created paintings which were independent of nature, and whose function was neither to describe external life nor to communicate specific meanings or emotions, but to awaken other levels of consciousness through one's absorption in their mobile, ambiguous structure. It made sense, therefore, to classify his works with those of the other Orphists, but within a very few months, Picabia was to reject non-figurative art.

Picabia was terrified by the prospect of boredom, and, as I have suggested, seems to have been compelled to destroy what he had discovered rather than to develop it. This was one of the reasons why he joined Duchamp and Apollinaire in their attack on established values and rational modes of thought. While he was painting *Udnie* and *Edtaonisl* Picabia had shown signs of mental disturbance, and by the end of the year this had become so severe that he had to take a long holiday.[89] His tendency towards mental instability was probably intensified by the strains and excitements of the year, perhaps by the fact that he and Apollinaire were smoking opium with surprising frequency, and undoubtedly also by his concentrated attempt to penetrate to the hidden depths of his being. Moreover, the almost contemptuous indifference of the critics (apparently including Apollinaire) to his most important paintings may have undermined his faith in what he was doing by implying that he had not found a means of embodying mental experience. It was not long before he began to reject the democratic views he had expressed in the United States, and to assert that his new art required intelligence, education, and a special training of the eye to understand it.[90] The delicate balance between allusion and abstraction which he had achieved in the *Udnie* and *Edtaonisl* painting was upset, and henceforth his paintings became either more abstract (as in *Culture physique*, Pl. 249) or more obviously expressive of private experience (as in *Je revois en souvenir ma chère Udnie*, Pl. 251).

249 Francis Picabia,
Culture physique, 1913
(89·5 × 117).

In *Culture physique*, one of the purest and most impressive of his non-figurative works, Picabia concentrated almost exclusively on the expression of movement: he made the 'ribbon' forms of the earlier works expand across the surface in overlapping chains, weave in and out of shallow space, and coil over one another without any focus, any point of rest, any clear distinction between form and space. The painting thus shares certain characteristics with the *Contrastes de formes* in which Léger abandoned the dense substantiality of his earlier works, fragmented his forms and scattered them across the surface in endless jostling movement (Pl. 204). Despite the precision of the forms, (which prefigure those of his machine style), Picabia's painting is disquieting—the retreating black depths are ambiguous, the shadows mysterious, and the warm red-browns, red-purples, and cosmetic pinks are made cold and dissonant by the blacks and greys. These disturbing qualities are even stronger in *Impetuosité française* (Pl. 250) where Picabia combined icy colours and machine-like handling with sexually suggestive forms, and made certain forms cast

250 Francis Picabia, *Impétuosité française*, 1913–14. Water-colour on composition board (54 × 64·8).

strange shadows into the void (Pl. 207). His use of disturbing shadows and suggestive shapes could have been influenced by De Chirico whom he knew and who exhibited *La Nostalgie de l'infini* and other works in the Indépendants of 1914.

Picabia obviously intended that *Je revois en souvenir ma chère Udnie* (Pl. 251) should suggest more explicit meanings than had the earlier *Udnie* paintings, for he followed Duchamp's precedent and began to suggest relationships between sexual and mechanical functions with greater clarity than before, and in this one can see his first move towards rejection of the non-conceptual meaning of Orphism.

Although there were machinist qualities in some of his earlier works, the first clear evidence of Picabia's interest in the machine occurred in New York where he did at least two drawings incorporating machine forms: *Fille née sans mère* (Pl. 254; the title may well have been added later), and *Mechanical Expression Seen Through Our Own Mechanical Expression* (Pl. 252) in which he depicted forms reminiscent of New York skyscrapers and a shape like an up-ended retort traversed by a bent rod labelled at one end, NEW YORK, and at the other, NPIERKOWSKA—presumably a light-hearted evocation of New York and his relationship with the dancer, and perhaps inspired by American parodies of his works as machines.[91] Gelett Burgess did a drawing called *Picabia Neurasthetic Transformer* which was particularly important since it suggested a

251 Francis Picabia, *Je revois en souvenir ma chère Udnie*, 1914 (250 × 198·8).

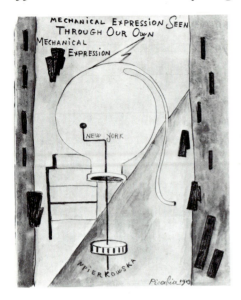

252 (*left*) Francis Picabia, *Mechanical Expression Seen Through Our Own Mechanical Expression*, 1913. Water-colour on paper (21 × 15·4).
253 (*right*) Marcel Duchamp, *La Mariée mise à nu par les célibataires*, 1912. Pencil and wash (23·8 × 32).

relationship between individual personality and machine. Picabia's paintings probably suggested machines to the Americans because their parts seem to be standardized and locked together in a mechanistic way. His French contemporaries may also have been sensitive to these characteristics, for Apollinaire had also mentally associated Picabia's *Procession* with a machine.[92] *Fille née sans mère* is more important, as it seems to contain the initial idea of *Je revois en souvenir ma chère Udnie*. The drawing is not very explicit but incorporates slightly curved forms, angular flat planes, and interlocking rods and bars which relate it to the *Danseuse étoile sur un transatlantique*; these forms are animated by the coiled springs which make its mechanistic operation clearer. Although it is far less accomplished, Picabia's drawing owed something to Duchamp's *La Mariée mise à nu par les celibataires* (Pl. 253) of 1912, in which there was the same ambiguous association of machine form and human activity, and the same contradictory shading which both suggests the presence of rounded forms and causes them to melt away.

Picabia did not use explicit machine forms in *Udnie* and *Edtaonisl*, but he painted the steely greys with great precision, giving them a metallic sheen, and in the centre of *Edtaonisl* he made the separate, standardized parts interlock to create a movement which is more like the movement of a machine than of an animate being, and which bears some relationship to the interlocking machinist forms of works like Léger's *Nu dans un atelier* (Pl. 196). However, Picabia did not make these mechanistic references clear until he painted *Je revois en souvenir ma chère Udnie* in 1914.[93]

The painting has a sinister power made more threatening by the tension between its apparently explicit forms and our inability to recognize them, for instead of distributing shapes evenly across the painting, Picabia centralized and isolated them so that they suggest the presence of specific forms but do not coalesce into recognizable ones. He increased the tension by cramping the expansive forms in shallow claustrophobic space and by his use of colour, composing the painting from sombre harmonies of closely related colours (purplish-browns, blacks, greys, and rusty-reds which turn to fleshy-pink as they curve), making them livid by the addition of ochres and of a small area of bright cold yellow like a gas-flame.

Picabia's forms not only suggest machine parts—screws, fans, and other sharp-edged metallic shapes—but simultaneously evoke the fleshy organs of the body, and they clearly owe much to the sinister suggestiveness of *Le Roi et la reine entourés de nus vites* and to the insidious fusion of flesh and machine in *Le Passage de la vierge à la mariée* and *La Mariée* (Pl. 16; Duchamp had given the latter to Picabia in 1912). The forms of the *Passage* suggest an imaginary dissection of the sexual organs (the expository character is implied by the transparent planes, cut-away opaque planes, and dotted lines) which could conceivably have been influenced by Leonardo's drawings of such dissections.[94] However, even if Duchamp was representing sexual penetration itself, it is not relevant to try to make a precise identification of any specific form in the painting, since Duchamp took care to render everything ambiguous, so that forms which at first sight seem clear, alter as one looks at them and melt

254 Francis Picabia, *La Fille née sans mère*, 1913–1915. Ink (26·7 × 21·6).

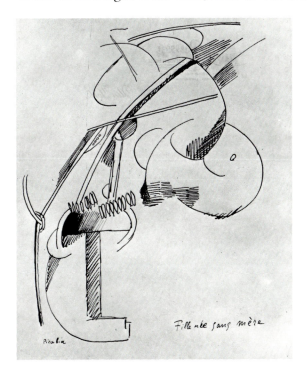

back into the mysterious shadowy recesses. The forms of *La Mariée* appear more explicit, for the bulbous shapes are more strongly realized and the warmer colours evoke flesh more directly, yet even here Duchamp created subtle formal and spatial ambiguities which undermine any over-precise identification of the forms (the scale of what is represented is particularly disorientating, for one is not certain whether one is looking at figures or at the internal organs of a figure).

Therefore, although these paintings invite psychological interpretation, their inner meaning was concealed by the artist and was perhaps inaccessible even to him. In fact, Duchamp did state that subconscious processes are 'mute', and that his conscious intention was to introduce humour into the 'sacrosant' world of the machine.[95] He was presumably trying to undermine the exaltation of the machine by the Futurists in Italy, and by the multitude of groups like the Paroxysts and Dynamists in France. They tended to give machines human characteristics, whereas Duchamp made the human mechanical, as in his 1912 drawing, *La Mariée mise à nu par les célibataires* (Pl. 253), which he inscribed as the 'mechanism of modesty', and in this he may have been influenced by Bergson who said that 'the attitudes, gestures, and movements of the human body are laughable in exact proportion as that body reminds us of a simple machine'.[96] The conscious implication of Duchamp's paintings of sexual themes in clear enough: they suggest that the act of love is analogous to the impersonal functioning of a machine, yet they contain something which makes them more threatening than any intellectual proposition and which is embodied in the formal structures in the way that what one thinks one sees, disintegrates before one's gaze. The profound ambiguity of these paintings suggests that Duchamp was not simply objectifying a conscious idea, but that he concentrated on the development of his pictorial structures in such a way that they could take on multiple aspects coloured by those emotions, associations, and memories which lay in the depths of his mind. This suggestion does, I think, help one to understand the haunting potency and resonance of his images.[97]

Je revois en souvenir ma chère Udnie also hints at deep personal experience (as do most of Picabia's paintings of 1913–14), and although one cannot know the nature of this experience, it clearly had something to do with Picabia's feelings for the enigmatic 'Udnie'. Picabia implied through his title that he was painting a memory, that is, trying to find forms with which to register extremely complex and subtle states of consciousness. Thus, like Duchamp, Picabia probably developed the associations between certain pictorial configurations, colours and textures, and machine or human forms during the painting process in response to the mood generated by past memories and by the forms themselves. Hence the 'meaning' of this painting, like Picabia's other Orphist paintings, remains impenetrable even when we are conscious of the emotional region in which it functions; it is precisely because it is ultimately unexplainable that the image haunts the mind like a partially remembered nightmare.[98]

This was Picabia's last Orphist painting, the last work in which he played on the complex associations aroused by non-representational forms, for after he had taken refuge in New York early in the war, he renounced the sensual forms of his Orphist works in order to depict the human machine with cold precision (just as Duchamp transformed human feeling into mechanical process in *La Mariée mise à nu par ses célibataires, même* by rejecting the deeply personal sensuousness of the earlier works). Picabia's new works were in the style of commercial art—dry, concise, expository—though in the earliest, like *Voilà le femme* of 1915 (Robert Lebel collection, Paris), he still used the pictorial ambiguities—the conflicting readings of solid and void, enigmatic shadows, indeterminate space—that he had evolved in his non-representational works, and it is these subleties of form rather than the prosaic metaphor which engage the imagination. However, when he depicted the *Young American Girl* simply as a sparkplug, Picabia abandoned such niceties, abandoned the 'state of mind approaching abstraction' for the straightforward proposition, and the 'pure joys of the idea and of consciousness' for the naked insult. The restlessness and destructiveness of his personality were aggravated by the dislocation of war in such a way that it was impossible for him to continue the exploration of the wordless depths of his inner being where his Orphism had taken him.

Conclusion

The Orphists moved away from figurative art because they believed that it kept the mind in the conceptual sphere which they wished to transcend. Changes in contemporary life had caused them to conceive the external world as composed of dynamic forces rather than of stable objects in static space. They believed that this conceptual change was accompanied by a change in consciousness, which they also conceived as dynamic—either as expansive and all-embracing, or as intensive and self-concentrating. This change of consciousness was central to the development of non-figurative art, for artists found that if they depicted the external world—even if they did so dynamically—they lost their sense of the continuity of their own consciousness. They sought more profound contact with this consciousness through the act of creation, developing modes of painting in which they could detach their minds from the external and so absorb themselves in the very process of creating form—a process which gave them a sense of their own inner being and of its relationship to the external world.

The Orphists' concern with the workings of consciousness led them away from the painting of the external manifestations of human life, to dispense with the human figure or absorb it in the dynamism of line and colour, and they replaced the specific human emotion with something much more tenuous. This rejection of humanist expression occurred in other contemporary arts: in his 'conversation poems' Apollinaire registered the sensations which beat in on his consciousness and the associations they aroused, without pausing to find meaning in them; Stravinsky sought to avoid the expression of 'human joy and grief' by eliminating chords 'too evocative of the human voice', in order to express the 'essential rhythms of nature'; the Futurists claimed that 'the new consciousness can no longer allow one to look on man as the centre of universal life'. Similarly, Léger asserted that the dynamism of modern life had destroyed the 'sentimental' and human-centred conception of life; Kupka said that one could not express mental experience with the human form; while Picabia wrote that 'the new forms of expression separate themselves from the sensorial pleasure which man may derive from man or nature ... to enter the domain of the pure joy of the idea and consciousness'. He added that this consciousness must be objectified if it is to be communicated, and he thus touched on the central paradox of the Orphists' aspirations: the fact that the desire of escaping human-centred consciousness demands the operation of that same consciousness if it is to be experienced. Romains expressed a similar paradox when he wrote in *La Vie unanime*:

> *Avec ce que me reste encore de conscience*
> *Je connais le bonheur de n'être presque pas*

The Orphists were confronted with the problem of representing the invisible movement of consciousness by means of the visible world of painting; the sense of the mind's totality by means of an opaque substance on a flat surface. The Symbolists, aware in particular of the problem of depicting light, had developed the theory of 'representation', according to which the painter should not attempt to imitate the external world, but should develop an independent pictorial structure which would enable the mind to realize experiences analogous to those of the external world. The theory confirmed what the Orphists had realized through pictorial experience, and made them confident that an abstract structure could stimulate the mental eye in such a way that it could interpret pigment as light and could move over the static surface of the painting in such a way that it would come aware of its own movement; or that the abstract structure could so absorb the mind in its still, concentrated form that it would feel its relation to the external world. However, while the Orphists inherited from the Symbolists the realization that it is the mind which interprets the world, and in this sense that the world exists through the mind, there is little in their paintings to suggest that they were preoccupied with the abstract idea as were the Symbolists. The Orphists were deeply involved in the materiality of creation, and found their sense of the reality of existence through their engagement with a material existence which seemed to develop a life that was separate from theirs even as they themselves formed it.

In the late nineteenth century, artists had become increasingly concerned with the creative experience itself, for with the breakdown of faith in external verities, it assumed significance as a means of acquiring a sense of personal meaning—of however temporary a kind—in an apparently chaotic world. This development was accompanied by an emphasis on improvisatory modes of creation which seemed to provide a means by which the self could be revealed to the self—either by embodying the mind's unknown depths (as with Redon), or by enabling him to escape generalized habits of seeing and to see how or what he saw (as with Monet and Cézanne). The Cubists were the first painters to use improvisatory techniques which were limited neither by the forms of the external world nor by generalized conceptions of such forms. Their painting did, of course, contain references to the external world, but they made these references internal to the painting by working serially on a very narrow range of themes, and developing their structures from painting to painting, and not from the external world. They were thus free to concentrate on 'the life of forms in the mind'—to use Metzinger's phrase—as they evolved on the canvas. Similarly, once the Orphists had stopped working from nature or from their memory images of nature, their attention shifted from the external world to their inner experience of it. Picabia, Delaunay, and Léger worked directly on to the canvas, developing dense ambiguous *unforeseen* structures from sketchy linear skeletons. They also worked in open-ended series in which their *personal* forms were gradually revealed. Kupka tended to prepare individual works in greater detail, but he too discovered personal form through the serial exploration of a limited number of themes, while Duchamp's densest, most ambiguous and personal paintings were those in which he developed closely related structures from one painting to another. For each painter, the structure seemed to develop its own momentum and to take over his self-consciousness as if he were being directed by the material as something separate from himself, and in this way he came to feel that his absorption in the dynamic evolution of form put him in touch with the dynamism of life itself.

It is necessary to understand the Orphists' processes of creation if one is to understand the meaning of their work. I have called attention to the parallels between Orphism and contemporary science, literature, and philosophy, and have in particular discussed the relationship between the circular imagery found in such sources and the pictorial development of non-gravitational structures based on centrifugal or centripetal movements. However, such structures existed in embryonic form in paintings which prefigured the Orphists' conscious modernism—in other words, their formal inclinations preceded specific external influences. They then went through a phase when they used their characteristic forms while illustrating specific ideas, but as these forms became stronger and clearer as a result of their improvisatory or serial approach, they came to regard them as the *content* of their art. It is therefore not meaningful to regard Delaunay's *Soleil, Lune. Simultané* or Léger's *Contrastes de formes* as representations of certain aspects of modern life; to interpret Kupka's *Fugue en deux couleurs* as illustrating any specific mystic belief, or Picabia's *Udnie* as a depiction of a particular subjective experience. They were, on the contrary, formal structures which had some internal meaning for their creators and which had attracted other meanings, other associations, which were internalized through the non-conceptual act of painting. Picabia spoke of 'a state of mind approaching abstraction' and this indicates the kind of consciousness operating during the process of creation. The deepening awareness of wordless levels of being is, of course, central to all creation, and non-figurative creation is distinct only in that the artist allows the work to remain at this level without making other levels of meaning explicit—for these meanings are implicit in consciousness itself. The intensity of the processes through which the painters achieved their personal forms explains their belief that their work had universal significance in embodying fundamental intuitions about the nature of being. While one may be aware of the relativity of this significance, it is also true that these paintings can have a more than individual meaning, which resides in their ability to absorb the spectator's attention so that he too may experience a suspension of conceptual consciousness through participation in formed matter.

The spectator's relationship to works of the literal modernist phase is different from his relationship to works of the non-figurative phase: for example, in *Danses à la source I* or *La Tour Eiffel*, Picabia and Delaunay tried to express the continuity of movement by creating a structure of variables which alter as the spectator's focus changes, so that the eye functions as a body and one identifies with the movement depicted. In this case, the spectator loses consciousness of the 'otherness' of the painting. Non-figurative Orphist paintings cannot be experienced in this way: one cannot 'identify' with Picabia's *Udnie*, with Kupka's *Amorpha, Fugue en deux couleurs*, Delaunay's *Soleil, Lune. Simultané*, or with Léger's *Contrastes de formes*, and although one may be deeply involved in the mobile structure of the painting, one remains outside it and thus aware of its otherness. This is because the paintings have no structural relationship to the external world: they have their own form of movement; they impose their own scale, and have their own internally coherent structure.

The Orphists attained Simultanist consciousness through the act of creating form when their consciousness opened on to the existence of something that was other than the self, and which was yet intimately connected with that self. The concentration of consciousness demanded by the act of creation gave awareness of the complex depths of the mind and of its power to absorb complex external experience. By seeking resolution of the ambiguities of the painting, the spectator too can become aware of its otherness, its impenetrability, and by this very separateness he may also become aware that it is his mind which experiences, which deals with the world.

In this sense, the Orphist painting is not a sign or symbol for other kinds of being, as it had been for the Symbolists. Recognizing this, Apollinaire—who took the idea from Picabia—spoke of an art 'without symbolic meaning'; while Delaunay quoted Leonardo's assertion that painting 'immediately satisfies the human mind like all things produced by nature'. Such an art rested on the assumption that the function of art is to awaken consciousness, and a realization that consciousness is to be found in involvement with the material. It was another early non-figurative painter, Piet Mondrian, who perhaps best expressed the nature of this consciousness: 'The life of the truly modern man is neither purely materialistic nor purely emotional. It manifests itself rather as a more autonomous life of the human mind becoming conscious of itself.'[1] The painters found this consciousness in painting, but their works, which (as Gleizes and Metzinger put it) 'nakedly present their reason for being', reveal enough of the processes by which they were created to enable the spectator to participate in the painter's experience.

Thus Orphism suggests that art has a function in a society whose tendency is to disperse consciousness. This function consists in creating a space, a silence, a place of concentration in which, as Delaunay said, 'l'homme s'identifie sur terre'—'man becomes conscious of himself on earth'.

Notes

Introduction

1 Robert Delaunay, *Du Cubisme à l'art abstrait*, ed. Pierre Francastel, 1957, 80. Translations are my own unless otherwise stated; however, in the footnotes I also refer to recent and more accessible translations which may differ from mine.

2 *Les Peintres cubistes: Méditations esthétiques*, 1913; ed. (1965) L. C. Breunig and J. Cl. Chevalier, 57; this edn. is the one referred to throughout. See Appendix A for a discussion of whether Apollinaire included Kupka in his definition of Orphism. Even if he did not, there are so many ways in which Kupka's art accorded with Apollinaire's definition and in which it related to the art of the other Orphists that I have discussed him as one of the 'group'. Apollinaire also included Picasso and Marie Laurencin: his reasons for naming Picasso are discussed on p. 73, while Marie Laurencin, his ex-mistress, was included for sentimental reasons.

3 Guillaume Apollinaire, 'La Peinture moderne', *Der Sturm* (Berlin), Feb. 1913, reprinted in Apollinaire, *Chroniques d'art*, ed. L. C. Breunig, 1960, 274; *Montjoie!* (Paris), 18 Mar. 1913, ibid. 297.

4 Marcel Duchamp in an interview with the author, Paris, Oct. 1966; G. Ribemont-Dessaignes, *Déjà jadis ou du mouvement Dada à l'espace abstrait*, 1958, 48; Delaunay, *Du Cubisme à l'art abstrait*, 169.

5 *L'Intransigeant* (Paris), 25 Mar. 1913, *Chroniques d'art*, 295; *Mercure de France*, 1 Mar. 1916, *Chroniques d'art*, 421.

6 Thus he mentioned Valensi only in a catch-all note at the end of his book (in which he also mentioned Pierre Dumont; *Les Peintres cubistes*, 96) and he did not include Jacques Villon who had painted works which approached abstraction but which lacked the formal density of fully developed abstract painting. Apollinaire did not mention Sonia Delaunay for, in late 1912, she was only just beginning to paint again after a gap of at least three years. Although she painted a few significant Orphist paintings, I have not discussed her work at length because her painting at this stage of her life was dependent on her husband's and because her really original contribution in these years was to the arts of design, whereas my study is concerned primarily with painting as an object of contemplation rather than painting as environment which demands a study in its own right.

For a discussion of decorative abstraction, see pp. 56–8.

7 Ludmilla Vachtovà, *Frank Kupka*, 1968, 13–17.

8 F. Gilles de la Tourette, *Robert Delaunay*, 1950, 9–10; Marc le Bot, *Francis Picabia et la crise des valeurs figuratives 1900–1925*, 1968, 20–2.

9 Preface to his exhibition, *Trente ans de peinture*, Galerie Léonce Rosenberg, Dec. 1930.

10 *Chroniques d'art*, 298.

Section I
Chapter 1
The history of Orphism

1 'Vendémiaire', *Œuvres poétiques*, 1962, 149; first published in *Les Soirées de Paris*, Nov. 1912.

2 Blaise Cendrars, 'La Tour Eiffel', a lecture given in 1924, *Œuvres complètes*, 1960, iv. 198–9; see also his poem, 'Crépitements' (1913), *Du monde entier: Poésies complètes*, 1967, 89; in the same year Delaunay wrote of 'the poetry of the Eiffel Tower which communicates mysteriously with the whole world', *Du Cubisme à l'art abstrait*, 111.

3 The best account of this situation is that given by Roger Shattuck in *The Banquet*

Years: the Arts in France 1885–1918, 1961.

4 ibid. 63–4.

5 *Montjoie!* (Jan.–Feb. 1914); see also *Figaro*, 9 Feb. 1914. Lists of those who attended the receptions were published in the journal in the Jan.–Feb. and Apr.–June numbers in 1914.

6 These lectures included Gleizes and Metzinger, 'Du Cubisme', *Poème et drame* Mar. 1913, 44–51; and Raymond Duchamp-Villon, 'L'Architecture et le fer', ibid., 1914, no. 7, 22–9. Lists of those who attended the dinners of the Artistes de Passy were published frequently.

7 *Œuvres poétiques*, 167, first published *Montjoie!*, 14 Apr. 1913.

8 Émile Bernard, 'Souvenirs sur Paul Cézanne et lettres inédites', *Mercure de France*, 1 and 16 Oct. 1907, 385–404, 606–27.

9 His occasional writings were published in 1912 as: *Théories (1890–1910): du symbolisme et de Gauguin vers un nouvel ordre classique*; many have been reprinted in Maurice Denis, *Du symbolisme au classicisme: Théories*, ed. Olivier Revault d'Allonnes, 1964, which is the edn. referred to throughout. See Gino Severini (*Tutta la vità di un pittore*, 1946, 80), on the survival of Symbolism.

10 Gauguin spoke of this relationship in his 'Notes synthétiques' published in *Vers et prose* (Paris), July–Sept. 1910, 5–55: trans. Herschel B. Chipp, *Theories of Modern Art*, 1968, 60–4.

11 The phrase occurred in an interview with Kupka (*New York Times*, 19 Oct. 1913); the reporter put it in quotation marks as if to indicate that it was Kupka's.

12 Wassily Kandinsky, *Ueber das Geistige in der Kunst*, 1912; reference is made throughout to M. Sadleir's translation, *Concerning the Spiritual in Art*, 1947, 24.

13 See Jules Romains, *La Vie unanime*, 3rd edn., 1913, 79, 219–20, etc.

14 Boccioni, Carrà, Russolo, Balla, Severini, 'Futurist Painting: Technical Manifesto' (1910), in U. Apollonio, *Futurist Manifestos*, 1973, 26.

15 *L'Hermitage*, 15 Dec. 1906; *Théories*, 172.

16 Delaunay, 'La Lumière' (1912), *Du Cubisme à l'art abstrait*, 146; Fernand Léger, 'Les Origines de la peinture et sa valeur représentative', *Montjoie!*, 29 May, 14–29 June 1913, trans. in Léger, *Functions of Painting*, 1973, 4 and 7; Severini, *Tutta la vità*, 82–3.

17 Apollinaire, *L'Intransigeant*, 18 Mar. 1910, 22 Apr., and 7 Aug. 1911, 19 Mar. 1912; *Chroniques d'art*, 73, 167, 192–3, 224.

18 'Cézanne', *L'Occident*, Sept. 1907; *Théories*, 165.

19 Henri Matisse, 'Notes d'un peintre', *La Grande Revue* (Paris), 25 Dec. 1908, trans. Alfred H. Barr, Jr. in *Matisse: his Art and Public*, 1951, 119–23.

20 Dora Vallier, 'La Vie fait l'œuvre de Fernand Léger: propos de l'artiste', *Cahiers d'art*, 1954, ii. 149; see also John Golding, *Cubism: a History and an Analysis, 1907–1914*, 1959, 23–4, 148–9.

21 See Gustav Vriesen and Max Imdahl, *Robert Delaunay: Light and Color*, 1969, 21–5. Delaunay's address in the catalogue of the Salon d'Automne of 1907 is 11 rue Legendre, Montmartre; in that of the Indépendants of 1909, it is 24 quai du Louvre; he moved to 3 rue des Grands-Augustins in 1910 and lived there until the war.

22 Albert Gleizes, *Souvenirs: le Cubisme 1908–1914*, 1957, 11–12. The distinction between the two kinds of Cubism was recognized at the time: Jacques de Gachons ('La Peinture d'après-demain', *Je sais tout* (Paris), 15 Apr. 1912, 356), called the two groups the 'cubistes' and the 'picassistes', since Kahnweiler denied that Braque and Picasso were Cubists.

23 Gleizes, *Souvenirs*, 14.

24 Daniel Robbins, 'From Symbolism to Cubism: the Abbaye de Creteil', *Art Journal*, xxiii/2 (winter 1963–4), 111–16. Apollinaire, 'La Phalange nouvelle' in *La Poésie symboliste* (with P.-N. Roinard and V.-E. Michelet), 1908, 136.

25 *Tutta la vità*, 138–9.

26 *Chroniques d'art*, 188; Gleizes, *Souvenirs*, 12–20.

27 *Pan* (Paris), Nov. 1911, trans. Edward F. Fry, *Cubism*, 1966, 60. Robbins ('From Symbolism to Cubism', 116), suggests that this 'was the first attempt to transform the Abbaye's synthetic literary concepts to visual forms', but it is likely that Metzinger's ideas were more directly influenced by the formal qualities of Braque's and Picasso's painting.

28 Roger Allard, 'Au Salon d'Automne de Paris', *L'Art libre* (Lyons), Nov. 1910; cited by Daniel Robbins, *Albert Gleizes*, catalogue to an exhibition, Solomon R. Guggenheim Museum, 1964, 16.

29 Pär Bergman, '*Modernolatria*' et '*simultaneità*': *Recherches sur deux tendances dans l'avant-garde littéraire en Italie et en France à la veille de la première guerre mondiale*, 1962.

Many other contemporary movements (such as Unanimism, Dramatism, Dynamism, Paroxym) had similar aspirations but I shall use Simultanism as the generic term.

30 'Enquête sur M. Henri Bergson et l'influence de sa pensée sur la sensibilité contemporaine', *La Grande Revue* (Paris), 10 and 25 Feb., 10 and 25 Mar., 10 Apr. 1914; René Gillouin, 'Bergsoniens et anti-bergsoniens', *Montjoie!*, 29 Mar. 1913; Tancrède de Visan, 'La Philosophie de M. Henri Bergson et l'esthétique contemporain', *La Vie de lettres* (Paris), Apr. 1913. Severini (*Tutta la vità*, 58) states that Bergson's ideas began to circulate in Parisian art-circles before 1910; Duchamp said that Bergson (together with mathematics and the fourth dimension) was studied at Puteaux: see William A. Camfield, 'La Section d'Or', unpublished M. A. thesis, Yale University, 1961, 141.

31 *La Grande Revue*, 10 Apr. 1914, 517.

32 Henri Bergson, *An Introduction to Metaphysics*, trans. T. E. Hulme, 1913, 8–10.

33 ibid. 15–16, 56–7.

34 Marianne W. Martin, 'Futurism, Unanimism and Apollinaire', *Art Journal*, xxviii/3 (spring 1969), 258–68.

35 He described his poem as a 'méditation sur la ville ... les hommes, les idées, le fleuve, le vapeur, le train, l'effort. Evocation des groupes au travail: l'usine, la terre, les fluides, les sciences, les forces... vision dramatique de la planète...' *Poème et drame*, Jan. 1913, 45.

36 Bergman, '*Modernolatria*' et '*simultaneità*', 158–84.

37 Reproduced (with Warnod's illustrations) in Marianne W. Martin, *Futurist Art and Theory 1909–1915*, 1968, facing 46.

38 Katherine Kuh, *The Artist's Voice*, 1962, 83.

39 Roger Allard ('Sur quelques peintres', *Les Marches du Sud-Ouest* (Paris), June 1911, 62) suggested that Delaunay's *Tour Eiffel* (Pl. 127) recalled the ideas expressed in the Futurist manifesto.

40 'Le Mouvement scientifique: le ciel et l'atmosphère', *Mercure de France*, 1 Sept. 1911, 161.

41 *La Vie unanime*, 163.

42 Gabrielle Buffet-Picabia, *Aires abstraites*, 1957, 30. However, Duchamp did not remember meeting Picabia before the Salon d'Automne of 1911 (Pierre Cabanne, *Dialogues with Marcel Duchamp*, 1971, 32). See also *Painters of the Section d'Or: the Alternatives to Cubism*, catalogue to an exhibition, Albright-Knox Gallery, 1967, 11.

43 André Warnod, *Comoedia* (Paris), 31 Oct. 1911.

44 Gleizes, *Souvenirs*, 28.

45 Letter to *Gil Blas* (Paris), 25 Oct. 1912.

46 Dora Vallier, *Jacques Villon: œuvres de 1897 à 1956*, n. d., 59.

47 Golding, *Cubism*, 164.

48 *Chroniques d'art*, 464, n. 2.

49 *Œuvres poétiques*, 74–6; Martin, *Futurist Art*, 99.

50 Alexandre Mercereau, 'Revue littéraire', *Revue indépendante*, Aug. 1911.

51 Michel Seuphor, *A Dictionary of Abstract Painting*, 1960, 203; see also Ribemont-Dessaignes, *Déjà jadis*, 32.

52 Umberto Boccioni, 'Il Dinamismo futurista e la pittura francese', *Lacerba* (Florence), 1 Aug. 1913; reprinted *Archivi del Futurismo*, ed. Maria Drudi Gambillo and Teresa Fiori, 1958, i. 166–9.

53 Draft letter to Kandinsky, *Du Cubisme à l'art abstrait*, 178–80.

54 ibid. 178.

55 Martin, *Futurist Art*, 205–6; Severini, *Tutta la vità*, 170–8.

56 *Le Petit Bleu* (Paris), 9 Feb. 1912, *Chroniques d'art*, 217; Severini (*Tutta la vità*, 131) praised the seriousness of this article.

57 Catalogue of the exhibition of 'Les Indépendants' (Brussels), June–July 1911, *Chroniques d'art*, 188.

58 Severini, *Tutta la vità*, 101; Martin, *Futurist Art*, 77–8.

59 Letter to Soffici, *Archivi*, i. 272; see also Boccioni, 'I Futuristi plagiati in Francia', *Lacerba*, 1 Apr. 1913, *Archivi*, i. 149.

60 *Chroniques d'art*, 216.

61 Apollinaire, 'Zone' and 'Vendémiaire', *Œuvres poétiques*, 39–44, 149–54; Blaise Cendrars, 'Pâques à New York' (1912), *Du monde entier: Poésies complètes*, 1967, 15–26.

62 *La Vie unanime*, 88.

63 Robert Lebel, *Marcel Duchamp*, 1959, 13.

64 I am grateful to William Rubin of the Museum of Modern Art, New York, who told me about the recent rediscovery of Picabia's *Danses à la source II* (my numeration), *La Source*, *Marriage comique*, and *C'est de moi qu'il s'agit*.

65 Delaunay, text of 1912 (see p. 355 n. 13); A. Cartault, 'Les Théories des peintres futuristes italiens', *Revue du mois* (Paris), 10 Mar. 1912, 363; Vallier, *Villon*, 53. The Futurists themselves soon came to similar conclusions; see Martin, *Futurist Art*, 169.

66 Albert Gleizes and Jean Metzinger, *Du Cubisme*, 1912, trans. Fry, *Cubism*, 106.

67 *Chroniques d'art*, 227, 274, and 287.

68 *Concerning the Spiritual in Art*, 44–5.

69 Paul Klee, 'Die Austellung des *Modernen Bundes* im Kunsthaus Zürich', *Die Alpen*, Aug. 1912, 699–700, trans. as 'Approches de l'art moderne' in Klee, *Théorie de l'art moderne*, 1964, 12–13.

70 *Du Cubisme à l'art abstrait*, 146–7 and 154–7.

71 Ribemont-Dessaignes, *Déjà jadis*, 37.

72 West, 'Painters of the Section d'Or', 10.

73 Christopher Green, *Léger and the Avant-Garde*, 1976, 48.

74 Vallier, *Villon*, 81. See pp. 110–3, 188–9, 337, for the interest of Kupka, Delaunay, and Duchamp in Leonardo.

75 Nicolas Beauduin, 'Les Temps héroïques: A propos du Salon de la Section d'Or', *Masques et visages*, June 1956, 6–7.

76 The lecture was not published, but Apollinaire incorporated his classification of Cubism in the proofs of *Les Peintres cubistes* (1965 edn. 23 and 57–8).

77 See Appendix A.

78 Denise Fédit, *L'Œuvre de Kupka*, Musée National d'Art Moderne, 1966, 112. She does not date the text, but Kupka's terminology and way of referring to past events suggests that it was written after the 1914–18 war.

79 Quoted by L. Arnould-Grémilly, *Frank Kupka*, 1922, 71.

80 *Les Peintres cubistes*, 88, n. 2 and 122–3, n. 7.

81 Beauduin, 'Les Temps héroïques', 7.

82 'Les Commencements du Cubisme', *Le Temps* (Paris), 14 Oct. 1912, *Chroniques d'art*, 265.

83 Some writers have dated this trip immediately before the exhibition (which opened on 8 October), but it probably occurred afterwards as there were comments in the press (*Gil Blas*, 24 Oct. 1912) that Apollinaire had missed a lecture he was to give there, and Picabia later described how he had tempted Apollinaire to Chartres when he was meant to lecture at the Section d'Or on Delaunay and the 'simultanist' curtains that Sonia Delaunay was making for him; the trip to the Jura occurred after this ('Guillaume Apollinaire'. *L'Esprit nouveau*, 1924, n. p.). Duchamp said that they went to the Jura after the opening of the Section d'Or, for he had returned from Germany only a few days before the opening; Camfield, 'La Section d'Or', 143. See Buffet-Picabia, *Aires abstraites*, 30, 48.

84 Nino Frank, ed., *Blaise Cendrars*, 1962, 163; *Blaise Cendrars vous parle*, ed. M. Manoll, 1962, 113–14.

85 *Du monde entier: Poésies complètes*, 97. Léger seems to have moved to the rue de l'Ancienne Comédie from his previous studio in 'La Ruche' in mid-1911 (addresses in Salon catalogues).

86 See his comments on Delaunay's 'Réalitè, peinture pure', *Du Cubisme à l'art abstrait*, 154 and 157.

87 *Chroniques d'art*, 271–5.

88 *Du Cubisme à l'art abstrait*, 188.

89 *Chroniques d'art*, 297.

90 *Gil Blas* 18 Mar. 1913.

91 *Comoedia*, 18 Mar. 1913.

92 *Chroniques d'art*, 295.

93 He listed this group of painters in his article in *L'Intransigeant*, *Chroniques d'art*, 292, but excluded Picabia in his article in *Montjoie!*, *Chroniques d'art*, 302. His writings for *Montjoie!* were generally more extreme than those for *L'Intransigeant* (compare this definition of Orphism with that for *Montjoie!*, *Chroniques d'art*, 297).

94 *Chroniques d'art*, 302–3. See Appendix B for a discussion of the *Plans Verticaux* shown in the Salon des Indépendants.

95 *Montjoie!*, 29 May and 14–29 June 1913; *Soirées de Paris*, 15 June 1914, trans. Léger, *Functions of Painting*, 3–10 and 11–19.

96 Boccioni, 'Il Dinamismo futurista …', *Lacerba*, 1 Aug. 1913, *Archivi*, i. 166.

97 F. Jean-Desthieux, 'Considérations sur la poétique de demain', *La Vie des lettres* (Paris), Oct. 1913, 514.

98 Georges Matisse, 'La Théorie moléculaire et la science contemporaine', *Mercure de France*, 1 June 1913, 520–5. He added that molecules were even more complex accumulations of 'stars and constellations' which were also charged with electricity.

99 Henri Bergson, *L'Évolution créatrice*, 1907, 210–11.

100 *La Vie unanime*, 143–4.

101 *Poème et drame*, Mar. 1913, 52–8.

102 'Contrastes' (Oct. 1913), *Du monde entier: Poésies complètes*, 75.

103 *Du Cubisme à l'art abstrait*, 186.

104 *L'Intransigeant*, 17 Apr. 1912.

105 Quoted by Henri Guilbeaux, 'La Poésie

dynamique', *La Revue* (Paris), 1 May 1914, 62–3.

[106] *La Vie unanime*, 137.

[107] *Functions of Painting*, 12.

[108] Cf. Maurice Raynal's comment that Cubists 'took from their own age a kind of mysticism of logic, of science and reason', 'Qu'est-ce que ... le "Cubisme"?'. *Comoedia illustré* (Paris), 20 Dec. 1913, trans. Fry, *Cubism*, 130.

[109] *Chroniques d'art*, 336–7.

[110] ibid. 344–6.

[111] Gertrude Stein, *The Autobiography of Alice B. Toklas*, 1961, 98.

[112] *Du Cubisme à l'art abstrait*, 155.

[113] Roger Bordier, 'Sonia Delaunay ou de la couleur avant toute chose', *Art d'aujourd'hui*, Sept. 1954, 12.

[114] *Montjoie!*, Mar. 1914, 22.

[115] *Les Synchromistes: Morgan Russell et S. MacDonald-Wright*, Galerie Bernheim-jeune (Paris), 27 Oct.–8 Nov. 1913. The quotations following are from this source.

[116] *Synchromism and Color Principles in American Painting 1910–1930*, 1965, 52. Agee states that both painters knew Delaunay.

[117] 'La Couleur et les formes' (extracts from a lecture given at his exhibition at the Galerie La Boëtie), *Montjoie!*, Nov.–Dec. 1913, 14.

[118] *Survage, Rythmes colorés 1912–13*, catalogue, Saint-Étienne, 1973. This also contains 'Le Rythme coloré' (extracts from a lecture), *Soirées de Paris*, July–Aug. 1914, 426–9, and other contemporary texts.

[119] Michel Hoog, 'Baranoff-Rossiné 1886–1942', *Cimaise*, Feb.–May, 1968; Jean Arp (*On my Way: Poetry and Essays 1912–1947*, 1948, 72) stated that Rossiné visited him in Switzerland in 1909 with unprecedented, completely abstract drawings.

[120] Another painter, Henry Ottman, was so insulted by Apollinaire's reference to his art that he wrote a letter to a newspaper, which Apollinaire felt had touched his honour to the extent that he challenged Ottman to a duel. Delaunay's feelings towards Apollinaire had so changed that he agreed to act as Ottman's second, while Léger acted for Apollinaire. In the end, Apollinaire accepted Ottman's apology and the duel was averted. *Chroniques d'art*, 348–52, 474–76.

[121] 'Orphisme, Orphéisme ou Orphéonisme', *Gil Blas*, 20 Mar. 1913.

[122] *Du Cubisme à l'art abstrait*, 114; quoted in a letter which Sonia Delaunay and Blaise Cendrars sent to the press to publicize the 'Transsibérien' (*Paris-Midi*, 11 Oct. 1913).

[123] The tradition of brightly coloured craft objects and interiors was stronger in Russia, the country of Sonia Delaunay's origin, than in Western Europe, and was currently being revived by avant-garde Russian artists and designers. The idea of a universal style may also have owed something to Chevreul as is indicated by the formidable title of his book which both the Delaunays studied: *De la loi du contraste simultané des couleurs; et de l'assortement des objets colorés, considéré d'après cette loi dans ses rapports avec la peinture, les tapisseries de Gobelins, les tapisseries de Beauvais pour meubles, les tapis, la mosaïque, les vitraux colorés, l'impression des étoffes, l'imprimerie, l'enluminure, la décoration des édifices, l'habillement et l'horticulture*', 1839. Sonia Delaunay experimented in many of these fields.

[124] Listed in Apollinaire's review, see *Chroniques d'art*, 344–6. Cendrars and Sonia Delaunay engaged in strong promotion of the book, sending a prospectus and letters to the press. Bergman, '*Modernolatria*' et '*simultaneità*', 314–26.

[125] V. Giannattasio, letter to Severini, Paris, 15 Nov. 1913, *Archivi*, i. 303.

[126] *Blaise Cendrars vous parle*, 141.

[127] *Du Cubisme à l'art abstrait*, 202. See also Apollinaire, *Mercure de France*, 1 Jan. 1914, Apollinaire, *Anecdotiques*, 1955, 137–8.

[128] *Du monde entier: Poésies complètes*, 83–4.

[129] Sebastien Voirol, 'A Propos du *Sacré du printemps*', *Poème et drame*, Sept.–Oct. 1913, 28–32; also 'Le Sacré du printemps' (a Simultanist poem), ibid. 15–16.

[130] *Montjoie!*, Apr.–May–June, 1914.

[131] *La Vie parisienne*, 22 Nov. 1913.

[132] Apollinaire, *Soirées de Paris*, 22 Mar. 1914, 186; Arthur Cravan, 'Exhibition at the Indépendants', *The Dada Painters and Poets*, ed. Robert Motherwell, 1951, 10–12 (Sonia Delaunay sued Cravan for his insulting references to her and was awarded a franc's damages, while Delaunay quarrelled with Cendrars who took Cravan's part). See also Buffet-Picabia, 'Some Memories of Pre-Dada: Picabia and Duchamp', ibid. 255–8.

[133] Salmon praised him as a predecessor of 'pure painting' in *La Jeune Peinture française*, 1912, 5; a whole issue of *La Vie* was devoted to him, Nov. 1912.

Chapter 2
Apollinaire's Orphism

[1] André Salmon, 'La Guerre des deux rives', *XXᵉ siècle*, June 1952, 20. Apollinaire himself noted in 1912 that 'Delaunay, Gleizes, Le Fauconnier, Metzinger, Léger, etc., c'est-à-dire la plupart des peintres cubistes, vivent dans la compagnie des poètes. Quant à Picasso ... il n'a vécu que parmi des poètes', *Mercure de France*, 16 Nov. 1912; *Anecdotiques*, 91–2.

[2] Letter to Soffici, 9 Jan. 1912 in '20 lettres de Guillaume Apollinaire à Ardengo Soffici', *Le Flâneur des deux rives*, Dec. 1954, 2.

[3] *Du Cubisme à l'art abstrait*, 67 (written *c.* 1939–40). The emphasis is his.

[4] Le Roy C. Breunig ('The Chronology of Apollinaire's *Alcools*', *Publications of the Modern Language Association*, Dec. 1952, 915–16) dates these poems to Apollinaire's Montmartre period (1905–8); 'Le Brasier' and 'Les Fiançailles' were published in 1908, and 'Cortège' in *Poème et drame*, Nov. 1912.

[5] Apollinaire, *La Poésie symboliste*.

[6] *Du Cubisme à l'art abstrait*, 169.

[7] Eva Kushner, *Le Mythe d'Orphée dans la littérature française contemporaine*, 1961, 77–135. Hermine B. Riffaterre, *L'Orphisme dans la poésie romantique. Thèmes et style surnaturalistes*, 1970. My account of Apollinaire's Orphism owes much to Margaret Davies's *Apollinaire*, 1964.

[8] Philippe Renaud ('La Structure d'*Alcools*: "un itinéraire magique"', *Les Critiques de notre temps et Apollinaire*, ed. Claude Tournadre, 1971, 64–71), gives a brilliant analysis of both *Alcools* and 'Zone' in terms of Orpheus' descent into Hell. One of Apollinaire's most striking images could derive from the story of the Bacchantes tearing Orpheus apart (a favourite nineteenth-century image for the destruction of the artist by philistines and his triumph over death). His lines 'il vit decapité sa tête est le soleil/Et la lune son cou tranché' ('Cortège') echo Virgil's 'sa tête arrachée de son cou marmoréen' (*Géorgiques*, iv. 523–7). Apollinaire transformed his still explicable image in the bizarre last line of 'Zone', 'Soleil cou coupé' (Orpheus was often identified with the sun). Redon's *Orphée* (1905) may also have influenced Apollinaire (see n. 21). As I will show, such fragmentation had deep meaning for Apollinaire.

[9] 'Cortège', *Œuvres poétiques*, 76; see n. 4.

[10] 'Poème lu au mariage d'André Salmon', *Œuvres poétiques*, 84; dated by Breunig ('The Chronology of Apollinaire's *Alcools*', 917), to 1909; published *Vers et prose*, Oct.–Dec. 1911.

[11] *Chroniques d'art*, 58.

[12] *Les Peintres cubistes*, 66.

[13] Charles Baudelaire, 'Victor Hugo', *Œuvres complètes*, 1964, 704.

[14] Marie-Jeanne Durry, *Guillaume Apollinaire: 'Alcools'*, 1956, iii, 191–212; Henri Meschonnic, 'Apollinaire illuminé au milieu d'ombres' (1966), in *Les Critiques de notre temps et Apollinaire*, 157–62; Jean-Pierre Richard, 'Étoiles chex Apollinaire' (1967), ibid. 125–9.

[15] 'Le Brasier', *Œuvres poétiques*, 108; see n. 4.

[16] 'Les Fiançailles', ibid. 132; see n. 4.

[17] *Chroniques d'art*, 60.

[18] He probably read Edouard Schuré's *Les Grands Initiés*, 1889 (with many subsequent editions), an immensely popular *summa* of such sources. In his chapter on Orpheus, Schuré evoked the revelation of the mysteries to an initiate, stating that there is a single god manifest in innumerable forms of light. His vivid imagery probably influenced Apollinaire's imagery of light, fire, and shadow.

[19] 'Matisse', *La Phalange* (Paris), 15 Dec. 1907; trans. Barr, *Matisse*, 101.

[20] *Œuvres poétiques*, 3 and 1037. It is often suggested that Apollinaire's use of the word, 'Orphism' derived from this poem, but he denied this in a letter in the *Paris Journal*, 29 June 1914.

[21] Durry (*Apollinaire: Alcools*, i. 154–6) states that his 'source' was Louis Ménard's translation of the hermetic texts, *Hermès Trismégiste* (Paris, 1867); the language of Book 1, ll. 1–16, is very close to his. Redon too may have influenced Apollinaire (who praised him in 1908, *Chroniques d'art*, 60) see his lithograph. *Le Profil de lumière* from the *Tentation de Saint-Antoine* suite, inspired by Flaubert's words, 'Sur les ténèbres le rayon du Verbe descendit et un cri violent s'échappa, qui semblait la voix de la lumière' (1967 edn., 115).

[22] Ballanche, 'Orphée', *Œuvres*, 1830, Book 2, 148–50.

[23] Stéphane Mallarmé. *Correspondance*, ed. Henri Mondor and Lloyd James Austin, 1965, ii. 266.

[24] ibid. ii. 301.

[25] William McC. Stewart, 'Peut-on parler d'un "Orphisme" de Valéry?', *Cahiers de l'Association internationale des études françaises* (*CAIEF*), 1970, 186–7.

[26] Letter to Madéline Pagès, 14 Oct. 1915, in

Tendre comme le souvenir, 1952, 209. He expressed a similar idea in less mystical terms in his article on Matisse (*La Phalange*, 1907), see Barr, *Matisse*, 102.

27 'L'Esprit nouveau et les poètes' (Paris, 1917), cited by Davies, *Apollinaire*, 154.

28 Letter to Louise de Coligny, 23 Apr. 1915, in *Lettres à Lou*, ed. Michel Décaudin, 1969, 315.

29 *La Vie unanime*, 30.

30 'Les Fiançailles', *Œuvres poétiques*, 135.

31 'Liens' (1913), ibid. 167.

32 *Chroniques d'art*, 188.

33 Cited by Marcel Raymond, *De Baudelaire au Surréalisme*, 1940, 26.

34 *Les Peintres cubistes*, 59 and frequently elsewhere.

35 Letter to Roger Allard, 17 Sept. 1918, in *La Nouvelle Revue française*, 1 Dec. 1962, 1146–51.

36 Letter to Roland Chavelon, cited by Noëmi Blumenkranz-Onimus, 'Apollinaire, critique d'art', *L'Information d'histoire de l'art*, 1961, no. 4, 106.

37 *Chroniques d'art*, 56.

38 'Notes of a Painter' in Barr, *Matisse*, 119–20. The warm tone of Apollinaire's interview with Matisse in 1907 (ibid. 101–2) suggests that they were on friendly terms.

39 *Chroniques d'art*, 56.

40 ibid. 60–1.

41 Apollinaire quoted him to this effect in his letter to Allard, *Nouvelle Revue française*, i Dec. 1962, 1148.

42 *Œuvres poétiques*, 84.

43 *Les Peintres cubistes*, 64–5.

44 ibid. 56.

45 *Chroniques d'art*, 125–6 and 188.

46 ibid. 165 and 199.

47 ibid.

48 *L'Intransigeant*, 19 Mar. 1912; cited by Blumenkranz-Onimus, 'Apollinaire, critique de l'art', 194.

49 'Simultanisme-librettisme', *Soirées de Paris*, 15 June 1914, 323. The Simultanism of *Les Peintres cubistes* is perceptively discussed by Breunig and Chevalier in the introduction to their edition of the book.

50 'Simultanisme-librettisme', loc. cit.

51 Apollinaire, letter to Soffici, 4 July 1913, *Le Flâneur des deux rives*, Dec. 1954, 4; Raynal, *Montjoie!*, Jan.–Feb. 1914, 20.

52 *Œuvres poétiques*, 39–44.

53 *Soirées de Paris*, Feb. 1912, and *Les Peintres cubistes*, 49.

54 *Les Peintres cubistes*, 57; 'Les Commencements du cubisme', *Le Temps* (Paris), 14 Oct. 1912, *Chroniques d'art*, 265; 'Le Salon des Indépendants', *L'Intrasigeant*, 25 Mar. 1913 in *Chroniques d'art*, 295.

55 *Les Peintres cubistes*, 49–50.

56 *Chroniques d'art*, 232. On the other hand, in the same review Apollinaire wrote that Léger's *Composition avec personnages* [*La Noce*] had 'no subject'.

57 *Les Peintres cubistes*, 90 and 120.

58 *Soirées de Paris*, May 1912, and *Les Peintres cubistes*, 66.

59 *Les Peintres cubistes*, 92.

60 Auguste Joly, 'Sur le futurisme', *La Belgique artistique et littéraire*, July 1912, 68–74. Apollinaire would probably have read the broadsheet, 'Le Futurisme et la philosophie'.

61 *Soirées de Paris*, Feb. 1912, and *Les Peintres cubistes*, 50.

62 *Chroniques d'art*, 217; cf. Kandinsky, *Concerning the Spiritual in Art*, 76.

63 *Du Cubisme à l'art abstrait*, 178 and 146–7. See pp. 188–9.

64 *Les Peintres cubistes*, 89.

65 Gabrielle Buffet-Picabia, 'Apollinaire', *Aires abstraites*, 56–8.

66 *Les Peintres cubistes*, 92.

67 See pp. 129–30, and ch. 1, nn. 75 and 78; also Appendix A.

68 'Le Salon d'Automne', *Soirées de Paris*, 15 Dec. 1913, 49. He goes on to say that the new painting may have the same relationship to imitative painting as music has to literature, but the former are experienced simultaneously, the latter successively.

69 'Les trois vertus plastiques', *Chroniques d'art*, 57.

70 'Simultanisme-librettisme', loc. cit.

71 'Les Fenêtres, *Œuvres poétiques*, 168–9; first published in Robert Delaunay's *Album* (Paris, n. d.); published in connection with his exhibition in Der Sturm gallery, Berlin, 27 Jan.–20 Feb. 1913.

72 See S. I. Lockerbie's 'Les Fenêtres: une esthétique toute neuve', *Les Critiques de notre temps et Apollinaire*, 88 ff. Lockerbie suggests elsewhere ('Qu'est-ce que l'Orphisme d'Apollinaire?', *Journées Apollinaire de Stavelot*, 1967, 81–7), that Apollinaire understood only the enumerative Simultanism of the *Ville de Paris* and not the abstract Simultanism of the *Fenêtres*. However, the impression that he was more sympathetic to enumerative Simultanism is partly due to the fact that he had more opportunity to write about it, since Delaunay did not exhibit abstract works in France.

73 *Chroniques d'art*, 274.

74 *Les Peintres cubistes*, 91.

75 *Œuvres poétiques*, 75–6; see n. 4.

76 *Soirées de Paris*, 15 Mar. 1914, 49. Some of

his literary polemics contribute to our understanding of his ideas on visual Orphism and Simultanism; see Bergman, '*Modernolatria*' *et* '*simultaneità*', 302–5; Roger Shattuck, 'Une Polémique d'Apollinaire', *Le Flâneur des deux rives*, Dec. 1954, 41–5.

Section II
Chapter 1 **Kupka**

1 See Appendix B for a discussion of the *Plans verticaux* shown in the Salon des Indépendants.

2 The book is generally known as *La Création dans les arts plastiques*, although it has not been published in French. Vachtovà (*Kupka*, 260) states that Kupka had determined its main theses by 1912. I have consulted one of the earliest drafts consisting of disjointed notes to which I shall refer as Kupka, *Notes* (irregular pagination).

3 Vachtovà, *Kupka*, 291–317 (catalogue raisonnée); Fédit, *L'Œuvre de Kupka*; Meda Mladék and Margit Rowell, *František Kupka 1871–1957. A Retrospective*, The Solomon R. Guggenheim Museum (New York, 1975).

4 Vachtovà, *Kupka*, 38.

5 References in this and the following paragraphs are to Kupka, *Notes*.

6 See Appendix A.

7 Reproduced, Vachtovà, *Kupka*, 299.

8 *Les Peintres cubistes*, 59.

9 *Notes*.

10 Vachtovà, *Kupka*, 23–4 and 253.

11 Dora Vallier, *Abstract Art*, 1970, 137–42.

12 *Notes*.

13 Kupka, 'Créer! Question de principe de la peinture', *La Vie des lettres et des arts*, July 1921, 569 and 574. The article is closely related to *La Création dans les arts plastiques*.

14 Vachtovà, *Kupka*, 253. The biographical information in the following paragraphs also come from this source (esp. 13–33).

15 Élisée Reclus, *L'Homme et la terre*, 1905–8, i, p. i.

16 Kupka (*Notes*) cited Blavatsky's assertion that, considered philosophically, man is an animal and that he requires 'soi-conscience' to rise above this state; he quoted from her *Doctrine secrète* 1888, 'La pierre devient plante; la plante devient animal; l'animal devient homme; l'homme devient esprit, et l'esprit devient dieu' (Stanza VII, § 5), and in the same context he referred to the theosophist theory of the cyclic evolution of consciousness.

17 Vachtovà, *Kupka*, 45.

18 ibid. 46.

19 'Lotus', *Encyclopaedia Britannica*, 1969, xiv. 329.

20 Fédit (*L'Œuvre de Kupka*, 39) states that the studies for this work go back to 1906, but the fresh colours, direct application of paint, and sensitivity to light suggest that it was painted slightly later.

21 Vachtova, *Kupka*, 24. Apparently he also rigged up a camera to take chronophotographs of himself running naked in his garden (information from Margit Rowell)—a curious example of the way he used contemporary science or technology to confirm his mystic beliefs!

22 See Appendix B.

23 Quoted by Yvonne Hagen in the catalogue to the exhibition, 'Kupka: Paintings, Pastels and Gouaches 1909–1923', 1960, as an 'excerpt from the unpublished journal . . . of 1911'. There is a similar passage in the *Notes*.

24 *The Dialogues of Plato*, trans. B. Jowett (1871), 1964 edn., vol. 2; *Republic*, vii. 532. Kupka studied Plato in Vienna (Vachtovà, *Kupka*, 18).

25 *The Upanishads*, trans. J. Mascaró, 1965, 70. Kupka had studied the *Vedas* (which included the *Upanishads* and the *Bhagavad Gita*) in Vienna (Vachtovà, *Kupka*, 18).

26 Vachtovà (*Kupka*, 23) suggests that Kupka was interested in the hidden symbolism in the work of the Czech painter, Hans Schwaiger (1854–1912).

27 Vachtovà, *Kupka*, 26; Fédit (in Jean Cassou and Denise Fédit, *Kupka: gouaches et pastels*, 1964, 19) also dates his 'crisis' to 1904, but states that it occurred after his move to Puteaux (generally dated 1905–6) as a result of his realizing the impossibility of capturing more than a 'moment' when he painted the living model or scenes in his garden.

28 Vachtovà, *Kupka*, 29; Fédit, 'Formation de l'art de Kupka', *Revue du Louvre*, 1964, no. 6, 337.

29 Illustrated: Vachtovà, *Kupka*, 276 and 291.

30 Reclus, *L'Homme et la terre*, i, p. iv.

31 *Upanishads*, 59 and 115.

32 *Notes*.

33 The *Bhagavad Gita*, trans. J. Mascarò, 1962, 9:6 and 9:8.

34 *Notes*.

35 *Bhagavad Gita*, 13:10.

36 *Notes*.

37 See Appendix B.

38 Kupka decided on (or, at least, agreed to)

the classification of his work into 'vertical', 'circular', and other forms, since the classification was used in the catalogue to his exhibition at the Jeu de Paume in 1936. Some of the drawings in the *Petite Fille au ballon* series contain elements which are also found in drawings related to the *Femme cueillant des fleurs* series; the small circles in the *Premier Pas* contain vertical planes.

[39] Vachtovà, *Kupka*, 265.

[40] Léonard de Vinci, *Textes choisis*, 1907, 93:175.

[41] Léonard de Vinci, *Traité de la peinture*, 1910, 136:364–5.

[42] *Textes choisis*, 106.

[43] *Traité de la peinture*, 155:429.

[44] *Évolution créatrice*, 99.

[45] *Notes*.

[46] The painting is inscribed 1909, a date generally accepted. However, since Kupka added this inscription many years later, it is possible that he had forgotten the exact year (although not the fact that it was a 'first step'). In 1909–10 he was still painting straightforward Fauvist works, and even his more experimental drawings were still close to nature. Its overlapping disks can faintly be seen in one of the *Petite Fille au ballon* drawings (Pl. 64), but they are still atmospheric. The composition with hard disks on a black ground is closer to the *Disques de Newton* of 1911–12 in the Musée National de l'Art Moderne (Pl. 80), so it would be reasonable to date it to *c*. 1910–11.

[47] Fédit (*L'Œuvre de Kupka*, 77) suggests that the painting was related to astronomical illustrations. It is also possible, in view of his interest in theosophy, that Kupka was inspired by Schuré's evocation (in his chapter on Orpheus) of the relation between the divine principle manifest in light, the individual deities manifest in stars, and the individual soul; 'each turning star', he wrote, 'draws into its etherial sphere hosts of demi-gods or radiant souls who were previously men and who, having descended the ladder of mortality, have gloriously re-ascended the cycle and have escaped the circles of the generations' (*Les Grands Initiés*, 247).

[48] Sven Sandström, *Le Monde imaginaire d'Odilon Redon*, 1955, ch. iii, 'Symbolisme évolutioniste', 62–92.

[49] The drawing is in the collection of the Museum of Modern Art. In view of the extreme importance of the theme of the generation of life to Kupka, it is worth

noting that he himself had no child.

[50] *Notes*.

[51] ibid.

[52] Annie Besant and C. W. Leadbeater, *Les Formes-pensées*, Paris 1905. Theosophist 'thought-forms' will be discussed later in this chapter.

[53] Vachtovà, *Kupka*, 304. Although the studies in the Museum of Modern Art and the Musée National d'Art Moderne (Fédit, *L'Œuvre de Kupka*, 69), are no more than rough scribbles, they show that Kupka had grasped the essential forms of the composition quite early.

[54] In his exhibition at the Galerie la Boëtie (16–31 Oct. 1924), Kupka exhibited no. 1: *La Création* (1911–20); nos. 2–3, *Printemps cosmique* (1911–20); no. 4: *Naissance* (1911–12); and nos. 24–7, *Conte de pistils et d'étamines* (1919–20). No *Ovale animé* is listed in this or any other exhibition at this time. However, the catalogue to the Kupka retrospective at the Musée National d'Art Moderne in 1958 states that the *Ovale animé* was shown at the Galerie la Boëtie exhibition of 1924.

[55] *Notes*.

[56] The depictions of intercourse, executed in a totally explicit academic-naturalistic style, probably date between 1895 and 1905 and are in the graphic collection of the Národní Galerie.

[57] Reclus, *L'Homme et la terre*, i. 353–4.

[58] *Les Peintres cubistes*, 52.

[59] *Évolution créatrice*, 288.

[60] *Notes*.

[61] *Évolution créatrice*, 11.

[62] Baudelaire, 'Victor Hugo', *Œuvres complètes*, 710.

[63] *Notes*.

[64] They are closely associated in many drawings in the Museum of Modern Art collection. The *Disques de Newton* are generally dated as 1911–12, but Kupka listed them as '*La fugue en deux couleurs (disques de Newton) 1912*', in the catalogue of his exhibition of the Galerie la Boëtie in 1924.

[65] Fédit, *L'Œuvre de Kupka*, 79; Lillian Lonngren, 'Kupka: Innovator of the Abstract International Style', *Art News*, Nov. 1957, 46 and 54–5. Margit Rowell has informed me that Kupka owned and annotated Signac's *D'Eugène Delacroix au néo-impressionisme*.

[66] *Upanishads*, 91; Sixten Ringbom (*The Sounding Cosmos. A Study in the Spiritualism of Kandinsky and the Genesis of Abstract Painting*, 1970, 57 points out that

Mme Blavatsky laid the foundations of theosophy in her books, *Isis Unveiled* (1877) and *The Secret Doctrine* (1888), which Kupka read in French. She claimed that there was one eternal truth given to man at creation, that this truth had been corrupted (especially by materialism) but that it was conserved in the esoteric traditions of the great initiates. She employed the image of white light diffracted into prismatic colours to symbolize the adulterated forms of truth conserved in different religions and philosophies, and claimed that it was the task of theosophy to reunite the colours in the white of revealed truth. Ringbom also discussed the use of such imagery by Steiner, Goethe, and the German Romantics (ibid. 78).

[67] *Notes*, 12.

[68] *Traité de la peinture*, 136:364–5 and 98:232.

[69] Riffaterre, *L'Orphisme dans la poésie romantique*, 262–6 (as an example, she quotes Lamennais, 'Ce que nos yeux voient . . . ne sont que les ombres . . . Car toute créature . . . s'efforce . . . de passer des ténèbres à la lumière . . . Le soleil si brillant . . . n'est que le vêtement, l'emblème obscur du vrai soleil qui éclaire et échauffe les âmes . . .' *Paroles d'un croyant*, xxvi. 1–3).

[70] *New York Times*, 19 Oct. 1913.

[71] His study of Newton may also have introduced him to Newton's ideas on the relationship between prismatic colours and the diatonic scale; light waves and sound waves.

[72] *Thought-Forms*, 75 and 82.

[73] Ringbom, *The Sounding Cosmos*, 80.

[74] Fernand Girod, 'Le Médiumisme et l'art', *La Vie mystérieuse* 10 Nov. 1911; Girod, 'Pour Photographier les rayons humains', ibid., 25 Mar. 1912.

[75] Ringbom, *The Sounding Cosmos*, 53–4; Besant and Leadbeater, *Formes-pensées*, 12–14.

[76] *Notes*, 43.

[77] *Notes*, 21, 25, 62–3.

[78] Vachtová, *Kupka*, 279–81. She suggests that the painting she illustrates on p. 94 (cat. no. 138) was a final study for *Amorpha, Fugue en deux couleurs*; this is unlikely, as few pre-war paintings were so flatly and drily painted (and it is closer to the work after it was altered between 1928–36 than to the work as it was exhibited in 1912). Kupka did several copies of his pre-war works late in his life, and this is probably one (as is the work which Fédit (*L'Œuvre de Kupka*, 72) de-

scribed as a final study for *Plans verticaux III*; she claims that it was exhibited in Kupka's exhibition in the Galerie Povolozsky in 1921, but there is nothing to identify it with this work). There is, however, a drawing in the Museum of Modern Art which is similar to the *Amorpha, Fugue en deux couleurs* which is numbered along two sides as if to prepare for enlargement to canvas-size.

[79] *Notes*.

[80] Since there are considerable variations in the dating of this series, a suggested chronology is given in Appendix B.

[81] *Textes choisis*, 163:343.

[82] Werner Hofmann (*Turning Points of Twentieth Century Art*, 1969, 126), reproduces an illustration of 1900 by Kupka for a poem, 'Nocturne', by René Paux in which there is the same dreamy romanticism as found in *Le Lac*. I have been unable to locate this work.

[83] Vachtová, *Kupka*, 75.

[84] *Notes*.

[85] Fédit, *L'Œuvre de Kupka*, 35. Seuphor (*L'Art abstrait*, 31–2) states that Kupka knew Picasso at this time.

[86] Some of the studies are more inventive than the finished work; in one (Museum of Modern Art), Kupka slid two diagonally intersecting grids of transparent planes over the body so, as they interpenetrate, they displace different parts of the body. Gris used similar devices in 1911.

[87] *Notes*.

[88] J. P. Hodin, Introduction to Vachtová, *Kupka*, 12.

[89] Ringbom (*The Sounding Cosmos*, 55) states that Besant and Leadbeater devoted the introduction of their *Thought-Forms* to a discussion of the work of Baraduc. 'It has long been known', they wrote, 'that impressions were produced by the reflection of ultra-violet rays from objects not visible by the rays of the ordinary spectrum. Clairvoyants were occasionally justified by the appearance on sensitive photographic plates of figures seen and described by them as present . . . though invisible to physical sight.' *Futurist Painting: Technical Manifesto* (1910), trans. by Martin in *Futurist Art and Theory, 1909–1915*, 53–4.

[90] The comments on the drawings which are cited in the following paragraphs occur on drawings in the collection of the Museum of Modern Art, New York. It was only in the early 1920s that Kupka entitled these works *Cathédrale*, etc.; orig-

inally he simply called them *Plans verticaux*.

91 For example Pl. 68, which has some similarities to Kupka's *Premier Pas* depicts two reactions to an accident: the sharp-edged form represents active assistance, the vaguer sphere, the thought-form of one who passively thinks 'Poor fellow, how sad!', Besant and Leadbeater, *Les Formes-pensées*, II. Kupka may at times have conceived his paintings in this literal way, for in 1913 he apparently said that his paintings were 'soul impressions' which conveyed 'sensations of comedy and tragedy', *New York Times*, 19 Oct. 1913.

92 Quotations in this and the following paragraphs are taken from Kupka's *Notes*.

Chapter 2 **Delaunay**

1 Michel Seuphor, *L'Art abstrait: ses origines, ses premiers maîtres* (Paris, 1950), 42.

2 Catalogue to Delaunay's exhibition at the Galerie Barbazanges, 28 Feb. 1912; quoted in Vriesen and Imdahl, *Robert Delauany: Light and Color*, 1969, 40.

3 Delaunay, letter to Auguste Macke, *Du Cubisme à l'art abstrait*, 186. Francastel dates the letter to 1912, but since Delaunay mentions seeing Macke among his paintings, it must have been written in 1913, after he had visited Macke in Bonn on the return from his trip to Berlin.

In this chapter, 'Habasque' followed by a number, refers to Habasque's catalogue of Delaunay's works in *Du Cubisme à l'art abstrait*. Despite this catalogue, Delaunay's dating remains problematic, since he frequently dated—and misdated—his works long after he had painted them. I have discussed these problems in Appendix C. Where possible, I have used the titles which Delaunay used in contemporary catalogues.

4 The *Paysage au disque* and the *Fiacre* (Habasque, nos. A. 29 and A. 31 are stylistically related to more securely dated works of 1906–7—for example, to *Portrait de Jean Metzinger* (Salon d'Automne 1906) (Habasque A. 27); their brushstrokes are looser and more abstract so they are probably slightly later. Delaunay was probably also concerned with effects of artificial light in the *Manège électrique* of 1907–8 (destroyed) which, Metzinger said, 'summed up the paroxysms of an explosive, chaotic age' (*Pan*, Oct.–Nov. 1910, 651).

5 *Du Cubisme à l'art abstrait*, 86–7 (possibly written in the late 1920s or early 1930s, since it is similar in tone and detail to the *Petit cahier* (ibid. 72–6) which may have been written slightly earlier since it contains no reference to any date after 1925.

6 The *Tour Eiffel. Première étude* (Habasque A. 69), which Delaunay gave to Sonia Delaunay as an engagement present, is inscribed 'Exposition Universelle 1889. La Tour à l'Univers s'Addresse' and 'mouvement profondeur 1909 France-Russie' which does suggest a modernist content (as does the association of the tower and a *dirigeable* in another work of 1909, Habasque A. 68). However, the inscription does not seem to be contemporary with the painting, and its content and phraseology seem more characteristic of Delaunay's development in 1912–14 (the phrase 'La Tour à la Roue s'Adresse' occurs in Apollinaire's poem of 1913, *Poésies complètes*, 200).

7 See Appendix C. §1. The *Tour* series.

8 *Du Cubisme à l'art abstrait*, 62 (written *c.* 1924).

9 See Appendix C. §1. The *Tour* series.

10 *Marches du Sud-Quest*, June 1911, 62.

11 Johannes Langner, 'Zu den Fenster-Bildern von Robert Delaunay', *Jahrbuch der Hamburger Kunstsammlungen*, 1962, no. 7, 69. For dating of the *Ville* series, see Appendix C. §2.

12 *Du Cubisme à l'art abstrait*, 62 (written *c.* 1924).

13 See Delaunay's comments on simultaneous contrasts in '*Réalité, peinture pure' (1912)*, *Du Cubisme à l'art abstrait*, 155; and in a text written after 1925, ibid. 113.

14 Draft of a letter to Franz Marc, probably written in late 1912, ibid. 182.

15 *Soirées de Paris*, Feb. 1912 and *Les Peintres cubistes*, 50.

16 Michel Hoog ('*La Ville de Paris* et Robert Delaunay: Sources et développement', *Revue du Louvre*, 1965, no. 1, 34) believes that the painting was begun in late 1911, was left in Paris in January 1912 while the Delaunays were at Laon, and was finished in February; Golding (*Cubism*, 156) states that it was painted on his return from Laon. Vriesen and Imdahl (*Delaunay*, 40) state that Delaunay executed the painting in fifteen days after having sent all his available paintings to his exhibition in late February. There are few preliminary studies; most are related to the group of women (an '*Esquisse de la Grace* pour un tableau, la Ville de Paris, 1912' was shown

in his February exhibition); there are only three studies of the whole composition (and one of these is a tracing); see Hoog, 'La Ville de Paris', 34, figs. 9–11.

[17] *Chroniques d'art*, 225.

[18] The major difference between the watercolour and the finished work is that the group of women has been moved to the centre. Hoog suggests that this was to arrange the main axes according to the 'Nombre d'Or', but this has no real effect on the structure of the work. Granié's comment in the *Revue d'Europe et d'Amérique* is cited by Hoog, 36, n. 17.

[19] Émile Zola, *L'Œuvre*, 1886, see esp. chs. viii and ix. Delaunay may also have been influenced by Le Fauconnier's *Abondance* of 1910–11; and the underlying traditionalism of his work is indicated by the fact that Kupka depicted a form of the Three Graces theme in his *Soleil d'automne* (Salon d'Automne, 1906), and by Kahn's comment that 'dans une allégorie de Paris', Delaunay 'cubise en somme l'ancien Besnard aux trois femmes symboliques', *Mercure de France*, 1 Apr. 1912.

[20] *Chroniques d'art*, 212 and 217. In his article, 'Symbolisme plastique et symbolisme littéraire' (*Mercure de France*, 1 Feb. 1916, 474), Severini stated that Dufy called his *Danse du Pan-pan a Monico* a 'Unanimist painting'.

[21] 'La Tour Eiffel', extract from a lecture of 1924, *Œuvres complètes*, 1960, iv, 195–200.

[22] Vriesen and Imdahl (*Delaunay*, 39) state that Delaunay met Romains in Laon in January. He could have met him before (see pp. 17–18), but a recent encounter may well have interested him in Unanimist themes.

[23] *Les Puissances de Paris*, 1911, 50. Sonia Delaunay did a binding for this book which was shown in the Herbstsalon in the autumn of 1913.

[24] *Du Cubisme à l'art abstrait*, 98 (written *c.* 1924) and 108 (probably written *c.* 1916 as it is a list with dates of Delaunay's series and contains a reference to an exhibition held in 1916, but to nothing after that year).

[25] ibid. 98.

[26] ibid. 62 (written *c.* 1924).

[27] ibid. 179: This is the draft of a letter probably written in late March or early April 1912, after the opening of the Indépendants (20 March) to which it refers. Klee visited Delaunay on the recommendation of Kandinsky on 11 April; since Delaunay made no reference to this,

the letter may have been written before then. It was certainly written before the summer for it contains none of the Leonardesque phrases which colour the texts he wrote in the summer.

[28] See Appendix C, § 3. The *Fenêtres*.

[29] *Du Cubisme à l'art abstrait*, 66 (written *c.* 1939–40).

[30] ibid. 171 (written, at least in part, by 1924; *Les Nouvelles littéraires*, 25 Oct. 1924). The emphasis is Delaunay's.

[31] *Du Cubisme à l'art abstrait*, 175. Delaunay took his notes from Léonard de Vinci, *Textes choisis*, trans. Péladan (Paris, 1907). He must also have read Péladan's translation (1910) of the *Traité de la peinture*, as he refers to matters contained in it. He probably made the notes in April or May after writing his letter to Kandinsky, when painting the first *Fenêtres* and before he wrote 'La Lumière' and 'Réalité, peinture pure' in the summer.

[32] *Du Cubisme à l'art abstrait*, 146–7. The emphasis is Delaunay's.

[33] ibid. 141–3. Francastel dates it to *c.* 1933, but Golding (*Cubism*, 43 n. 5) dates it to February 1912 and states that it was provoked by a lecture given by Marinetti at the time of the Futurist exhibition. It also contains phrases from Apollinaire's article 'La Peinture nouvelle' of May 1912 which Delaunay may have seen in draft.

[34] The phrase was frequently repeated by Apollinaire and Delaunay who may have been influenced by Leonardo's words, 'l'industrie des mortels a découvert le feu, par la vertu visuelle, qui d'abord perça les ténèbres', *Traité de la peinture*, 42:87.

[35] *Du Cubisme à l'art abstrait*, 156.

[36] *Traité de la peinture*, 41:86.

[37] 'La Tour Eiffel', *Œuvres complètes*, iv, 197–8 (Cendrars reversed the chronological development of Delaunay's paintings). Leonardo's experiment was not included in Péladan's translations of 1907 and 1910, but had appeared in Charles Revaisson-Mollien's translation, *Les Manuscrits de Léonard de Vinci*, ii, *les manuscrits B et D de la bibliothèque de l'Institut*, 1883.

[38] See p. 357, n. 61.

[39] Delaunay commented on these qualities in Cézanne's art in a text of the mid-1920s or early 1930s, *Du Cubisme à l'art abstrait*, 72.

[40] This painting was shown in the exhibition of Monet's *Venice* series at the Bernheim-jeune gallery in May 1912. Monet seems to have sent part of the series to the gallery in mid-April (Lionello

Venturi, *Les Archives de l'Impressionisme*, 1939, i, 430–1), so Delaunay may have seen them before May.

[41] *Concerning the Spiritual in Art*, 68–71. I am indebted to Dr. John Golding for this suggestion.

[42] 'La Lumière' (1912), *Du Cubisme à l'art abstrait*, 146.

[43] Draft letter to Marc, ibid. 188. The date is given as 11 January 1913, but since Delaunay refers to seeing Marc's works in Berlin which he visited late in January, and to the fact that he was painting the *Équipe du Cardiff F.C.*, it must have been written between early Frebruary and late March when it was exhibited. In 1918 Apollinaire wrote that Delaunay 'who didn't like either Picasso or Cubism, divided that school into Great Cubists (Picasso and Braque) and Little Cubists' (the others), *Nouvelle Revue française*, 1 Dec. 1962, 1148.

[44] *Du Cubisme à l'art abstrait*, 27; Fry, *Cubism*, 108.

[45] *Concerning the Spiritual in Art*, 66–7.

[46] *Du Cubisme à l'art abstrait*, 26; Fry, *Cubism*, 108–9.

[47] *Du Cubisme à l'art abstrait*, 155–6.

[48] *Du Cubisme à l'art abstrait*, 81 (written *c.* 1939–40).

[49] ibid. 141–2 and 146–7.

[50] Delaunay used the word 'simultané' in a grammatically invariable form to emphasize that it was a technical term (Hoog, preface to Damase, *Sonia Delaunay*, 14). In 1917 he said he did so in order to avoid the metaphysical connotations of the word 'simultanism', *Du Cubisme à l'art abstrait*, 130; see also 184 (1913). However, his articles of 1912 suggest that he conceived of Simultanism as a form of consciousness, not merely a technical device, so I have used the term 'Simultanism' when appropriate.

[51] Paul Klee, *Journal*, trans. Pierre Klossowski, 1959; entry for July 1917, 313–14. Klee was the first person to write about the *Fenêtres* which he described as 'the prototype of painting which is sufficient in itself, which borrows nothing from nature, and which has a completely abstract existence on the formal level', 'Die Austellung des *Modernen Bundes* im Kunsthaus Zürich', *Die Alpen*, Aug. 1912; trans. Klee, *Théories de l'art moderne*, 12–13.

[52] Léonard de Vinci, *Textes choisis* (1907), 198–205.

[53] See Martin, *Futurist Art*, 89–90.

[54] 'Collages de Sonia et de Robert Delaunay', *XXᵉ siècle*, Jan. 1956, 19. It is difficult to date Sonia Delaunay's first decorative objects, apart from an embroidery of 1909 and the coverlet of 1911. Hoog (*Robert et Sonia Delaunay*, 1967, 124) states that the cover for Cendrars's *Pâques*, executed in January 1913, was the first Simultanist object created by Sonia Delaunay. She had made some Simultanist curtains for Apollinaire before this, but her most sustained creation of such objects seems to have begun in 1913. She produced the first abstract *papier collé* in 1913–14 (Pl. 20), but it is hard to believe the date of 1912 given to the *Contrastes simultanés* (Hoog, *Robert et Sonia Delaunay*, 123; Pl. 163): theme and form suggest that it could not have been painted before mid-1913.

[55] Damase, *Sonia Delaunay. Rhythms and Colours*, 1972, 47; for Delaunay's comments on his wife's art, see *Du Cubisme à l'art abstrait*, 198–210.

[56] See Appendix C, §4: The *Formes circulaires* and *Disque*.

[57] *Du Cubisme à l'art abstrait*, 63 (written *c.* 1924).

[58] The sign with the names of the cities should probably be completed as 'Moscow', because the Delaunays had many connections—due, of course, to Sonia Delaunay—with Russian writers and artists. See *Du Cubisme à l'art abstrait*, 122, 125, and 140.

[59] Sonia Delaunay executed Simultanist posters from 1913 onwards (Pls. 21 and 153); she also executed a series of pastels 'inspired by electoral posters' (Roger Bordier, 'Sonia Delaunay ou de la couleur avant toute chose', *Art d'aujourd'hui*, Sept. 1954, 12); Apollinaire proposed to find inspiration in posters and incorporated poster images and techniques in 'Zone' and his 'calligrammes', as did Cendrars in his *Dix-neuf poèmes élastiques*; Léger too used the image of a poster contrasting vividly with a more passive landscape to embody the principle of contrast, the essence of modern life; see his lecture, 'Réalisations picturales actuelles' (1914), *Functions of Painting*, 12–13.

Bergman, '*Modernolatria*' et '*simultaneità*, 226, 230, 373–9.

[60] *Du Cubisme à l'art abstrait*, 98 (written *c.* 1924).

[61] Émile Szittya, 'Logique de la vie contradictoire de Blaise Cendrars', *Blaise Cendrars*, ed. Nino Frank, 1962, 70–1. I have not been able to find when the *Farbenlehre* was first translated into French.

However, even if it were not available to Delaunay in French, both Cendrars and Sonia Delaunay could read German and could have translated the short work for him.

[62] Charles Lock Eastlake, trans., *Goethe's Theory of Colours* (London, 1840), recently republished in *Goethe's Colour Theory*, ed. Rupprecht Matthaei, 1971. The page reference to this edition precedes the reference to the sections in Eastlake's translation; 211: Preface; 214: Introduction; 219: §60–1.

[63] Cited by Vriesen and Imdahl, *Delaunay*, 57.

[64] Cendrars, 'Le Contraste simultané', *Œuvres complètes*, iv, 192–3; *Du Cubisme à l'art abstrait*, 109 (Francastel dates this to 1913, but it was published in the *Bulletin de la vie artistique*, Oct. 1924, and besides containing Cendrars's passage of 1914, it contains phrases more characteristic of Delaunay's post-war writings).

[65] *Du Cubisme à l'art abstrait*, 113–14; see p. 349 nn. 122 and 124.

[66] Macke Archives, Bonn (the letter was translated into German by Sonia Delaunay); Vriesen and Imdahl, *Delaunay*, 61.

[67] Draft letter, 17 Apr. 1913, *Du Cubisme à l'art abstrait*, 161.

[68] ibid. 67 (written *c.* 1939–40).

[69] Delaunay himself wrote that the circular form 'which is very dear to me' first appeared in the *Saint-Séverin* series, ibid. 228 (written 1939).

[70] *La Vie unanime*, 139.

[71] *Du Cubisme à l'art abstrait*, 186; see n. 3.

[72] Bordier, 'Sonia Delaunay ou de la couleur avant toute chose', 12 (these are the interviewer's words).

[73] Illustrated, *Comoedia*, 2 June 1914, 2. The first version of the *Manège électrique* was painted in 1907–8 (see n. 4). The theme was also used by Romains: 'Pour railler la rotation des astres / Elle fait tourner ses manèges fous' (*La Vie unanime*, 115), and in the *Puissances de Paris* he evoked the rhythms 'à forme d'une onde' of a 'manège de cycles'. Cendrars took up the image of the circular movement of light: 'Il pleut les globes électriques ... Tout est halo...', 'Contrastes' (1913), *Du monde entier: Poésies complètes*, 75.

[74] *Goethe's Theory of Colour*, 221: §91, 95, and 98.

[75] ibid. 238: §383.

[76] ibid. 239: §398–408.

[77] *Du Cubisme à l'art abstrait*, 184.

[78] See Appendix C, §4. The *Formes circulaires* and the *Disque*.

[79] Sonia Delaunay said that the murder made 'a violent impression' on Robert ('Collages de Sonia et de Robert Delaunay', 19), but it is not clear why he should have chosen to paint it.

[80] *Du Cubisme à l'art abstrait*, 111 (written October 1913).

[81] ibid. 147. He asserted—like Bergson—that the object exists only in terms of our practical consciousness.

[82] *La Vie unanime*, 136.

[83] *Les Peintres cubistes*, 92.

[84] *Du Monde entier: Poésies complètes*, 75.

[85] 'Apothéose des forces', *Poème et drame*, Mar. 1913, 53–4.

[86] 'Le Salon', *Montjoie!*, Mar. 1914, 22.

[87] *Du Cubisme à l'art abstrait*, 63–4 (written *c.* 1924); my italics.

[88] ibid. 174–5; Léonard de Vinci, *Textes choisis*, 174: §357.

[89] *Du Cubisme à l'art abstrait*, 146.

[90] ibid. 76. The text was probably written between the mid-1920s and the early 1930s, but Delaunay expressed the same idea in 1913 (see pp. 211–12). His words so closely resemble Mallarmé's definition of poetry (see p. 64) as to suggest that they may have been influenced by it.

Chapter 2 **Léger**

[1] Vallier, 'La Vie fait l'œuvre de Fernand Léger', 140; Severini, *Tutta la vita*, 82–3; Gleizes, *Souvenirs*, 12–13.

[2] For some reason, Léger did not exhibit *Le Jardin* until the Salon d'Automne of 1909. The Corsican paintings are usually dated 1906–7 because Léger was then convalescing in Corsica; however, he also visited it several times in 1907–8.

[3] *Les Peintres cubistes*, 85; Léger denied that he was influenced by Fauvism (Vallier, 'La Vie fait l'œuvre de Fernand Léger', 149), but the term was no longer appropriate for Matisse.

[4] For Léger's contacts with Cubism, see pp. 231–2.

[5] Émile Bernard, 'Souvenirs sur Paul Cézanne et lettres inédites', *Mercure de France*, 16 Oct. 1907, 619.

[6] Vallier, 'La Vie fait l'œuvre de Fernand Léger', 149.

[7] Kahnweiler, 'Fernand Léger', *Burlington Magazine*, Mar. 1950, 63.

[8] Green, *Léger*, 12–19, suggests that the painting can best be understood against the

background of the writers of the Abbaye de Creteil and those who inspired them like Whitman and Verhaeren, and that their emphasis on dynamism and struggle helps one to understand Léger's aggressive anti-harmonious interpretation of the old theme of nudes in a landscape. His interpretation should more probably be seen in the context of the pictorial tension and disharmony of Cézanne's bathers and Picasso's nudes of 1907–9, for he had not come into contact with the Abbaye group until after he had begun the painting.

[9] Golding, *Cubism*, pl. 64A.

[10] *Les Peintres cubistes*, 85.

[11] 'Les Origines de la peinture et sa valeur représentative' (1913), trans. in *Functions of Painting*, 4.

[12] Bernard, 'Souvenirs de Paul Cézanne et lettres inédites', 617.

[13] *Du Cubisme*, 9.

[14] 'Réalisations picturales actuelles' (1914), trans. in *Functions of Painting*, 17.

[15] See, for example, Henri Guilbeaux, 'La Poésie dynamique', *La Revue* (Paris), 1 May 1914, 55: 'our sense of rhythm is clearly different from that of our ancestors... Our hearts beat in unison with motors. We have the hot, jerky pulsation of machines within us.' That Léger may have read such sources is suggested by the similarity between a passage from Paul Adam's *Morale des sports* (1907; quoted by Émile Magne in 'Le Machinisme dans la littérature contemporaine', *Mercure de France*, 16 Jan. 1910, 214), and Léger's account of how the strident contrast between cars and posters and a passive landscape expresses the essence of modern life: contrast. Adam described how the car 'adds the joys of its colours to the landscapes it crosses ... scarlet, blue, beige, white, the high-speed vehicles fly and hum across space ... a strident, speedy jewel suddenly illuminates the road enclosed by green and rusty fields...'

[16] *Chroniques d'art*, 165.

[17] *Les Bandeaux d'or* (Paris), Nov. 1911, 27; *Souvenirs*, 23.

[18] See Appendix D: The Dating of Léger's *Fumées sur les toits*, *Le Compotier*, *Le Fumeur*, and *La Noce*.

[19] Cf. Green (*Léger*, 28–30), who suggests that both Léger and Delaunay were interested in the durational significance of the city image, and that, in contrasting Notre-Dame and the old Quartier Latin with abstract shapes, Léger was opposing 'a self-conscious new energy with the fixed

forms of the past'. On the other hand this was simply the view from his studio.

[20] 'Les Origines de la peinture...' (1913), *Functions of Painting*, 7.

[21] See Green (*Léger*, 22–7) who discusses Léger's relationship with Unanimism and his expression of durational experience through the use of mobile perspective. Léger's use of mobile perspective was, however, rather limited.

[22] Bergson's philosophy was studied by the Puteaux group; Camfield, 'La Section d'Or', 141.

[23] Daniel Robbins (*Albert Gleizes*, catalogue of an exhibition at The Solomon R. Guggenheim Museum, 1964, 29), suggests that in *La Chasse*, Gleizes created a synthesis of social experience, showing two distinct types of human use of the land.

[24] See Appendix D, for a discussion of this dating and of the title of *Le Fumeur*.

[25] Léger seems to have been only once tempted by allegory, in his *Dessin pour un abondance* of 1911 (Pl. 189), but he was so averse to the universalizing qualities of true allegory that he merely depicted a nude woman behind a table covered with fruit.

[26] Green, *Léger*, 44.

[27] *Revue des beaux-arts* (Paris), 24 Mar. 1914, 4.

[28] 'The Exhibitors to the Public' (1912); trans. in Apollonio, *Futurist Manifestos*, 48.

[29] See Appendix D.

[30] 'The Exhibitors to the Public', Apollonio, *Futurist Manifestos*, 47.

[31] 'Les Réalisations picturales actuelles' (1914), *Functions of Painting*, 11.

[32] Definition of Orphic Cubism, *Les Peintres cubistes*, 57. However, Apollinaire remained undecided about how to classify Léger (see p. 38) and, in fact, said in a letter to Soffici that Léger was a 'weak' painter, '20 lettres de Guillaume Apollinaire à Ardengo Soffici', 4. It is difficult to know what Léger exhibited in the Section d'Or, for the catalogue lists only studies and sketches and a 'Composition' exhibited at the Indépendants of 1911 (probably the *Nus dans un paysage*).

[33] In chapter 2 of his book on Léger, Green gives a detailed and convincing account of the chronology of the *Contrastes* series.

[34] *La Femme en bleu* illustrated here is generally said to have been exhibited in the Salon, but a different version was illustrated in a review of the Salon (*Comoedia*, 30 Sept.); since the latter seems to have been lost, and since there were only minor

differences between the two, I have used the Basle version as a substitute.

[35] On the other hand, in his 1913 article (*Functions of Painting*, 7), he spoke of the general avant-garde tendency towards large dimensions. In terms of the contract with Kahnweiler, Léger agreed to sell all his production to him at prices ranging from 15 fr. for a drawing, to 500 fr. for a canvas above 120 cm. Kahnweiler was to take all Léger's oils, plus at least 50 drawings; the contract was to run from 1 October 1913 for three years. It is printed in *Fernand Léger: sa vie, son œuvre, son rêve*, ed. Guido Le Noci, 1971, no pagination.

[36] Vallier, 'La Vie fait l'œuvre de Fernand Léger', 150.

[37] 'Réalisations picturales actuelles', *Functions of Painting*, 11–13.

[38] Fernand Léger, *Textes choisis*, 1959, 29.

[39] 'Réalisations picturales actuelles', *Functions of Painting*, 16–17.

[40] Letter to Soffici, 12 June 1913, *Archivi del futurismo*, i, 272; Boccioni 'La dinamismo futurista e la pittura francese', *Lacerba*, Aug. 1913. ibid. i. 166.

[41] Second part of 'Les Origines de la peinture' *Montjoie!*, 14–29 June, *Functions of Painting*, 7. Severini stated that Léger even wanted to join the Futurists (*Tutta la vità*, 73).

[42] Vallier, 'La Vie fait l'œuvre de Fernand Léger,' 140; Léger, 'L'Esthétique de la machine' (1924), *Functions of Painting*, 60. This may have been in 1912, for Duchamp's response was to assert that 'painting is finished' and it was in the autumn of 1912 that he gave up painting and began his machine-work, *La Mariée mise à nu par ses célibataires, même*.

[43] The quotations in this and the following paragraph come from Léger's lectures of 1913 and 1914.

[44] Green (*Léger*, 64–9) gives a detailed analysis of the origin of the forms in the *Contrastes*, claiming that the pure *Contrastes* (as opposed to the figurative ones) derive from his landscapes. Although his argument is convincing in the case of certain configurations, I am not persuaded that such *Contrastes* derive exclusively from landscape: many of the forms in the abstract *Contrastes* can be found in earlier figurative works (for example, the important motif of the split cylinders can be seen in a less developed form in *Nus dans un paysage*).

[45] One gets a sense of this structural imperative in all Léger's comments on his paintings, and in particular on the development of the *Contrastes*. He once described how, when he had formed volumes 'as I wished', he then began to 'place' the colours. 'But how hard it was! How many canvasses did I destroy!...', Vallier, 'La Vie fait l'œuvre de Fernand Léger', 151.

[46] Bergson, *Le Rire*, 1900, 153–61.

[47] *Functions of Painting*, 16–17.

[48] 'Ma danse', *Du monde entier: poésies complètes*, 82.

[49] 'Déjà jadis', 34. He described Léger as 'at once cunning and powerful, a true Norman who ... forged quite simple and well-founded truths to which he held fast...'; Apollinaire described him in very similar terms in his account of Léger's 1914 lecture, *Chroniques d'art*, 374.

[50] 'Les Origines de la peinture...' *Functions of Painting*, 10.

[51] Quoted by Douglas Cooper, *Fernand Léger: Contrastes de formes 1912–15*, 1962, no pagination. His phrase recalls Delaunay's claim that he had discovered absolute pictorial equivalents for light which he called the 'eternal subject'; see p. 190.

[52] Vallier, 'La Vie fait l'œuvre de Fernand Léger', 149.

[53] *Du monde entier: poésies complètes*, 74.

[54] In 'A propos du corps humain considéré comme un object' (1945), *Functions of Painting*, 132, he commented that as long as the human body was given sentimental or expressive value 'no new evolution is possible in figure-painting.'

[55] *Fernand Léger; sa vie, son œuvre, sa rêve*, no pagination. See also 'L'Art et le peuple' (1946), *Functions of Painting*, 143, 146–7.

[56] *Les Peintres cubistes*, 86.

Chapter 3
Picabia and Duchamp

[1] *Les Peintres cubistes*, 116 n. 7 and 121.

[2] 'Propos recueillis par James Johnson Sweeney' (1946), Marcel Duchamp, *Le Marchand du sel*, ed. Michel Sanouillet, 1958, 111.

[3] Walter Pach, *Queer Thing, Painting*, 1938, 155.

[4] *Les Peintres cubistes*, 92.

[5] Jacques Nayral, preface to an exhibition of Cubist painting, Galerie J. Dalmau (Barcelona), Apr.–May 1912; cited in *Les Peintres cubistes*, 181.

[6] 'French Artists Spur on American Art', *New York Tribune*, 24 Oct. 1915, iv, 2.

7 Gabrielle Buffet-Picabia gives several versions of this incident, see le Bot, *Francis Picabia*, 1968, 75. Picabia used the same argument in 1913 when he was reported to have said 'The camera cannot reproduce a mental fact. Logically, pure art cannot reproduce a material fact', Hutchins Hapgood, 'A Paris Painter', *Globe and Commercial Advertiser*, 20 Feb. 1913, 8; reprinted *Camera Work*, Apr.–July 1913, 50. The reporter interviewed Picabia in French, but said that he was giving the spirit of what he said rather than his exact words.

8 Salmon, *La Jeune Peinture française*, 82; Apollinaire, *Les Peintres cubistes*, 53.

9 See his defence of his evolution in the preface to his exhibition, *Trente ans de peinture*, 1930. See p. 362 n. 50.

10 Picabia himself said that 'my morbid anxiety has always pushed me towards the unknown', *Trente ans de peinture*; Ribemont-Dessaignes (*Déjà jadis*, 44), gives a striking description of Picabia who, he said, 'has always been obsessive and anguished'. For his childhood experiences, see Buffet-Picabia, *Aires abstraites*, 17–19; and Germaine Everling (Picabia's second wife), *L'Anneau de Saturne*, 1970, 25–7.

11 Picabia 'How New York Looks to Me', *New York American*, 30 Mar. 1913, magazine section, 11.

12 William A. Camfield, *Francis Picabia*, catalogue of a retrospective exhibition, Solomon R. Guggenheim Museum, 1970, 15–17. I am indebted to Camfield's more detailed investigation, 'Francis Picabia (1879–1953); A Study of his Career from 1895 to 1918'.

13 Le Bot, *Picabia*, 27–36.

14 L. Roger-Milès, *Picabia*, preface to his exhibition, Galerie Haussman, 1907.

15 I have used the distinction between allegorical Symbolism and pictorial Synthetism established by Hendrik Rookmaakers, *Synthetist Art Theories*, 1959, 68–9.

16 *Aires abstraites*, 26.

17 ibid. 22. Picabia himself said that 'Impressionism was the umbilical cord which allowed me to develop my lungs' (*Trente ans de peinture*): the phrase is suggestive of Picabia's emotional attachment to the style—and of his difficulty of becoming independent of it.

18 Le Bot, *Picabia*, 39.

19 Le Bot (*Picabia*, 41–6) states that Picabia 'often testified that he never had any richer intellectual exchanges than he had with his first wife' and deals with her influence at some length.

20 *Aires abstraites*, 24–5.

21 Roger-Milès, preface to catalogue of Picabia's exhibition, Galerie Georges Petit, Mar. 1909, cited by Camfield, 'Picabia', 55 (in fact the works shown (Pl. 215) seem to have been less radical than Roger-Milès suggested). Picabia could not escape his commitment to hold this exhibition.

22 Buffet-Picabia ('Qui est Francis Picabia', unpublished essay cited by Le Bot, *Picabia*, 97) states that *Caoutchouc* 'is considered as the first known abstract painting whereas it clearly is inspired by a still-life.' Le Bot (ibid. 95–6) illustrates and discusses the two abstract drawings.

23 This was also a very productive year. Picabia's exhibited works included *Paris, Tarantella, Port de Naples* (apparently the first canvases on which Picabia painted the title); the second two works were exhibited by the Société normande de peinture moderne, Rouen, June–July; *Procession, Séville; Procession* (see n. 44); *Figure triste*; several unidentified landscapes, including *L'Arbre rouge* (see n. 25); the *Danses à la source* in the Arensberg collection, and the recently rediscovered *Danses à la source* and *La Source*, now in the Museum of Modern Art, New York (see p. 347 n. 64). Of the three, I think the Arensberg painting (which I have numbered I) is probably the earliest as it is the closest to nature; *La Source*, the second; and *Danses à la source II*, the third. Picabia exhibited one *Danses* in the Section d'Or, one in the Salon d'Automne. The latter was probably the second version as it is almost the same size as *La Source* (while the Arensberg painting is almost half its size); in the Salon d'Automne of 1913, Picabia also exhibited a pair of very large works of the same size—*Udnie* and *Edtaonisl*.

24 Hapgood ('A Paris Painter', 1913) said that Picabia claimed that 'Art can express the fourth dimension of the soul, but not the third dimension of actuality'; Cabanne, *Dialogues with Marcel Duchamp*, 39–40. Ribemont-Dessaignes (*Déjà jadis*, 36–7) gives a suggestive account of Duchamp's and Picabia's subversive influence at Puteaux.

25 Reproduced (upside down) in *Les Peintres cubistes* as *Paysage 1911*. A closely related work, *The Port of Naples from a Height* was reproduced in an interview with Picabia and said to have been painted in 1912 (*New York Times*, 16 Feb. 1913, arts section, 9;

Pl. 237). Since it had a more clearly defined foreground, middle ground, and 'sky' planes, it could have been painted before *L'Arbre rouge*. The *Canyon* (probably the *Ravin* shown in the Section d'Or) illustrated in the same article, was probably painted in late 1911 or early 1912 since it is closer to Picabia's earlier decorative Fauvism.

[26] 'Picabia, Art Rebel...' *New York Times*, 16 Feb. 1913.

[27] *Les Peintres cubistes*, 88 and 90.

[28] There is no specific evidence that Picabia visited the exhibition, but, in view of the excitement it generated, it seems likely that he would have done so. Even if he did not, he almost certainly knew Severini as they had many mutual friends.

[29] *La Vie unanime*, 101–11; *Puissances de Paris*, 111–13.

[30] 'Propos de Marcel Duchamp...' (1946), *Marchand du sel*, 110.

[31] *Les Peintres cubistes*, 116. He had second thoughts about this and crossed it out.

[32] *Aires abstraites*, 54–5.

[33] *Les Peintres cubistes*, 88 and 91.

[34] He added 'the... instinctive art of Picabia remains well on this side of... purity', but crossed this out (ibid. 123).

[35] Delaunay's articles, 'La Lumière' and 'Réalité, peinture pure' (mid–1912), give some idea of the kind of criticism Delaunay might have made of the presence of objective elements in Picabia's painting, *Du Cubisme à l'art abstrait*, 147 and 155–6.

[36] *Les Peintres cubistes*, 89.

[37] 'Francis Picabia and his Puzzling Art: An Extremely Modernized Academician', *Vanity Fair* (New York), Nov. 1915, 42.

[38] 'Notes synthétiques', *Vers et prose*, July–Sept. 1910, trans. Chipp, Theories of Modern Art, 61.

[39] *The World* (New York), 9 Feb. 1915, magazine section.

[40] *Dialogues with Marcel Duchamp*, 35.

[41] John Golding, *Duchamp: The Bride Stripped Bare by her Bachelors, Even*, 1973, 15–17. Duchamp dated the work to 1912, but it was, in fact, executed in 1911.

[42] 'A Post-Cubist's Impressions of New York', *New York Tribune*, 9 Mar. 1913, part ii, 1. The words are the reporter's.

[43] This hidden content is also suggested by the inscription on the reverse of *Jeune Homme triste*: 'Marcel Duchamp nu (esquisse), Jeune homme triste sur un train'. Duchamp said that this was a painting of himself on the train to Rouen, but the train may also have been a train of thought in which the idea of himself nude may have been stimulated by the idea of the nude descending a staircase, as the two paintings are very closely related.

[44] Picabia painted at least three versions of the *Procession*: *Procession*, *Séville* (Section d'Or and Armory Show); *Musique de Procession* (Section d'Or; lost); *Procession* (Salon des Indépendants and Herbstsalon, 1913). The latter is also lost, but was illustrated in the *New York Times* (16 Feb. 1913) and in the Herbstsalon catalogue where it is clearly inscribed *Procession* which makes it unlikely that it was the *Musique de Procession* shown in the Section d'Or. Picabia probably took a photograph of it to New York as an example of his most recent work. The date of the trip to the Jura is discussed p. 348 n. 83.

[45] 'Picabia, Art Rebel...', *New York Times*, 16 Feb. 1913. They had returned by early May, *La Vie parisienne*, 3 May 1913.

[46] Draft letter, 17 Apr. 1913, *Du Cubisme à l'art sbstrait*, 161.

[47] Francis Picabia, preface to the catalogue of his exhibition *Studies of New York*, Photo-Secession Gallery [291], Mar. 1913 (trans. Frank Haviland); reprinted *Camera Work*, Apr.–July 1913, 19–20.

[48] 'Picabia, Art Rebel...', *New York Times*, 16 Feb. 1913; a month later he praised the seriousness of the interest which many Americans took in modern art, 'A Post-Cubist's Impressions of New York', *New York Tribune*, 9 Mar.

[49] Maurice de Zayas, 'The Evolution of Form', *Camera Work*, Jan. 1913, 46; quoted by Camfield, 'Picabia', 179.

[50] Preface to *Studies of New York*, Photo-Secession Gallery.

[51] Samuel Swift, 'Art Photographs and Cubist Painting', *New York Sun*, Mar. 1913; reprinted *Camera Work* Apr.–July 1913, 46–7. (He was referring to the *Danses à la source I*.)

[52] 'A Post-Cubist's Impressions of New York', *New York Tribune*, 9 Mar. 1913.

[53] 'How New York Looks to Me', *New York American*, 30 Mar. 1913.

[54] Hapgood, 'A Paris Painter', *Camera Work*, Apr.–July, 50 (Hapgood gave the 'spirit' of Picabia's words, not exact quotations).

[55] 'Picabia, Art Rebel...' *New York Times*, 16 Feb. 1913.

[56] Review of the Armory show, ibid., 23 Feb. 1913, magazine section, 15.

57 'Extracts from *The Spiritual in Art*', *Camera Work*, July 1913, 34.

58 'How New York Looks to Me', *New York American*, 30 Mar. 1913.

59 'A Post-Cubist's Impressions of New York', *New York Tribune*, 9 Mar. 1913.

60 Ringbom, *The Sounding Cosmos*, 120–9 and *passim*.

61 Kandinsky, *Reminiscences* (1913), trans. Herbert, *Modern Artists on Art*, 1964, 24; *Samuel Swift*, review of Picabia's exhibition, *Studies of New York New York Sun*, reprinted *Camera Work*, Apr.–July 48. There are two versions of *Chanson nègre*: one in the Metropolitan Museum; the other in a private collection in New York, shown in the Picabia retrospective exhibition, Grand Palais, Paris, 1976 (no. 34). The second painting is the purple one.

62 Vivian du Mas, a theosophist (who was present at at least one *Montjoie!* reception in 1913–14) gave a lecture in 1932 on 'L'Occultisme dans l'art de Francis Picabia' (*Orbes* (Paris), 1932, 113–28). Picabia was present at the lecture and was astonished, for although he had not met du Mas, he felt that he had expressed 'the mental and physical states which I go through when I am expressing myself in painting' ('Monstres délicieux', *Orbes*, 1932, 129–31).

63 Quoted by Maurice Aisen, 'The Latest Evolution in Art and Picabia', *Camera Work*, June 1913, 18.

64 This interpretation is confirmed by Aisen (ibid. 16–17) whose article was partly based on conversations with Picabia. He spoke of the development of the 'psychical sense' in the twentieth century and related it to the increasing refinement of synaesthetic experience. He stated that 'Picabia has left the plane of the five senses in art which he calls "matière pensée" [the artist's interpretation of his model]. He concerns himself solely with psychic perception, or as he names it, "pensée pure".' See also Kupka, pp. 87 and 131.

65 *Autobiography of Alice B. Toklas*, 210. She adds that 'It was this idea that conceived mathematically influenced Marcel Duchamp and produced his *The Nude Descending the Staircase*.'

66 Swift, 'Art Photographs and Cubist Painting', *Camera Work*, Apr.–July 1913, 47.

67 See Appendix E: The Identity of Picabia's *Udnie*.

68 *Concerning the Spiritual in Art*, 76; 'A Post-Cubist's Impressions of New York', *New York Tribune*, 9 Mar. 1913. In his review of Picabia's exhibition, Swift refers to three different kinds of work: 'There are three drawings ... each called "Study for a Study of New York" [in which specific objects can be "divined"] ... But these are only the preliminaries. The studies which cover the wall in watercolor are the second state, and perhaps Picabia, after he has returned to Paris, will summarize these multitudinous impressions and expressions in a few large canvases ...'.

69 'How New York Looks to Me', *New York American*, 30 Mar. 1913.

70 Camfield, 'Picabia' 133 and n. 11, 177–8.

71 'A Paris Painter' *Camera Work*, Apr.–July 1913, 50–1.

72 Preface to *Studies of New York*, *Camera Work*, Apr.–July 1913, 20. Gabrielle Buffet-Picabia and Stieglitz helped Picabia write his preface and may have influenced its tone. Maybe it was Stieglitz who introduced a reference to Plato's *Philebus* and to the beauty of geometric forms, for it does not seem to be relevant to Picabia's painting. Gabrielle Buffet-Picabia amplified Picabia's statement in 'Modern Art and the Public', *Camera Work*, June 1913, 11: 'Out of the ever deepening consciousness of life which we derive from every new scientific discovery there arises a new and complex state of mind to which the external world appears *more clearly* in the abstract form of the qualities and properties of its elements than under the concrete form of our sense perceptions. Or more broadly speaking, we can say that at the same time that we have our perception of the external, we have the consciousness of all that exists above and beyond it.'

73 *Le Matin* (Paris), 1 Dec. 1913.

74 *Chroniques d'art*, 56.

75 ibid. 302.

76 In fact le Bot (*Picabia*, 107–13) goes so far as to deny any meaning to these works, claiming that they are dissociated one from the other and from his inner 'spiritual life'. Camfield ('Picabia' 202–5) takes a more positive view of Picabia's ability to communicate subjective experience, although I think he goes too far in attributing specific sexual meanings to the paintings of 1913–14, by identifying recurrent shapes and colours with specific sexual themes. This approach must be used cautiously because one can find such shapes and colours in contexts whose relevance is very ambiguous (for example, the irregular, inter-

twining, rounded forms scattered with tiny rectangles which characterize *Udnie* are also found in *Le Poulailler* of 1912; Pl. 223).

[77] Letter to Stieglitz, 16 June 1913, Alfred Stieglitz Archive, the collection of American Literature, Beinecke Rare Book and Manuscript Library, Yale University.

[78] *Aires abstraites*, 33. Philip Pearlstein decoded 'Edtaonisl' in his unpublished M.A. thesis, 'The Paintings of Francis Picabia, New York University, 1955, 109. The anagram was characteristic of the word-games played by Picabia, Duchamp, and Apollinaire. See also Appendix E.

[79] Picabia was in no sense a believer and his use of religious subjects is puzzling. In 1912 he even painted a *Crucifixion*: its subject is almost indecipherable and one can only speculate on what drove him to chose such a subject and to destroy its figurative content (Picabia retrospective exhibition, Grand Palais, Paris, no. 27).

[80] 'Simultanisme-librettisme', *Soirées de Paris*, June 1914, 325.

[81] 'Le Brasier', *Œuvres poétiques*, 108. The next stanza ends: '*Les têtes coupées qui m'acclament Et les astres qui ont saigné Ne sont que des têtes de femmes*'.

Perhaps these images influenced Duchamp. Redon—whom he acknowledged had deeply influenced him (Pach, *Queer Thing, Painting*, 163)—also represented floating heads.

[82] *Introduction to Metaphysics*, 8–9.

[83] *Aires abstraites*, 32 (Gabrielle Buffet-Picabia added that Picabia forgot the birth of his daughter after he had been telephoned the news); Germaine Everling, *Anneau de Saturne*, 169; Jean Arp, 'Picabia' *Art d'aujourd'hui*, Jan. 1950 (no pagination).

[84] Letter to Stieglitz, 16 June 1913, Alfred Stieglitz Archive, the collection of American Literature, Beinecke Rare Book and Manuscript Library, Yale University; cited by Camfield, 'Picabia', 184.

[85] *Les Peintres cubistes*, 91. In an article published in late 1912 Redon wrote 'The title is justified only when it is vague, indeterminate and even tending to create confusion and ambiguity…' *La Vie* (Paris), 30 Nov. 1912, Duchamp had used ambiguous titles for some time, but Picabia's were straightforward until mid-1913.

[86] The dual nature of the work is indicated in Duchamp's comment, 'there are no human forms or indications of anatomy. But in it one can see where the forms are placed; and … I would never call it an "abstract" painting' (1946), *Marchand du sel*, 111.

[87] Bergson (*Le Rire*, 157), asked 'When we experience love or hate… is it really our sentiment itself which comes to our consciousness with the thousand fugitive nuances and the thousand profound resonances which makes it something absolutely our own? … for the most part we perceive only the external disposition of our state of mind. We capture only the impersonal aspects of our sentiments—that which language can register once and for all, since it is more or less the same … for all men.'

[88] *291* (New York), Feb. 1916.

[89] Camfield, 'Picabia', 199.

[90] *Le Matin*, 1 Dec. 1913.

[91] William A. Camfield, 'The Machinist Style of Francis Picabia', *Art Bulletin*, Sept.–Dec. 1966, 309–22. He believes that *Fille née sans mère* was not executed until Picabia went to New York in 1915, since it was not shown in his New York exhibition of 1913 and was not reproduced until 1915 (*291*, June 1915), and also since Picabia said that he began his machinist style in New York in 1915. However, *Je Revois en souvenir ma chère Udnie* also preceded Picabia's machinist style proper and is implicitly rather than explicitly machinist. Moreover, the *Fille née sans mère* is stylistically utterly unlike the machinist works of 1915 and has the ambiguous shading, combination of angular and curved shapes, and narrow 'rods' that are found in the 1913 gouaches—in fact, it is very like the preliminary drawing which is clearly visible under the transparent paint in works like *Chanson nègre*.

[92] *Chroniques d'art*, 302.

[93] For its date see Camfield, 'The Machinist Style of Francis Picabia', 313, n. 25.

[94] See Léonard de Vinci, *La Génération, le mécanisme des fonctions intimes. Feuillets inédits reproduits d'après les originaux conservés à la bibliotèque du Château de Windsor*, Paris, 1901.

[95] From a letter of 1954, *Marchand du sel*, 163. Katharine Kuh, *The Artist's Voice*, 1962, 88.

[96] *Le Rire*, 30.

[97] It might also explain the seeming contradiction between the alchemical imagery in the *Mariée* series and Duchamp's denial

that he 'used' alchemy in any conscious way (Golding, *The Bride Stripped Bare by her Bachelors, Even*, 92).

98 In this painting, the firm structure contains—and makes powerful—the expression of inner emotion, but in two contemporary works, *Mariage comique* and *C'est de moi qu'il s'agit* (Museum of Modern Art, New York), the relationship between form and expression begins to disintegrate.

Conclusion

1 'Neo-Plasticism in Painting', *De Stijl*, 1917, i, no. 1; trans. Michel Seuphor, *Piet Mondrian: Life and Work*, 1957, 142.

Appendix A The problem of whether Kupka exhibited in the Salon de la Section d'Or, and whether Apollinaire included him in his category of Orphic Cubism

It seems impossible to be certain that Kupka did exhibit at the Section d'Or, or, more important, that Apollinaire described his work as Orphist in his lecture at the exhibition (as he could have done even if Kupka had not exhibited).

There is no contemporary reference to Kupka's appearance at the Section d'Or; his work was not listed in the catalogue, and his name was not mentioned in Apollinaire's definition of Orphic Cubism when it was inserted in the proofs of *Les Peintres cubistes* in October 1912. The catalogue may not have been wholly accurate, but in an interview in 1961, Duchamp said that he did not think that it needed correcting, and that he could not think of any artist who had been omitted, although he could not remember all the artists who did exhibit (Camfield, 'La Section d'Or', 140). His evidence is important, but a fifty-year-old negative memory is not conclusive (particularly since Duchamp did not explicitly deny Kupka's presence), and could be countered by Gabrielle Buffet-Picabia's slightly earlier memory that Kupka did exhibit, although she also named Delaunay who did not exhibit ('La Section d'Or', *Art d'aujourd'hui*, 1953, 74).

The only contemporary reference to Kupka's possible presence occurred in Kahn's review of the Salon d'Automne (*Mercure de France*, 16 Oct. 1912, 883–4) in which he said he would not talk at length about the works of Léger, Gleizes, Metzinger, and Kupka because he would soon see them in a general exhibition arranged by the Cubists, that is, the Section d'Or; however, when he did review the exhibition (ibid., 1 Nov. 1912, 181), he mentioned the works of Léger, Gleizes, and Metzinger (as well as Picabia and Valensi), but when he referred to Kupka, he mentioned only the works he had shown in the Salon d'Automne. No other critic named him, although they listed other exhibitors. On the other hand, there was no contemporary account of the content of Apollinaire's lecture, despite the great amount of critical attention it has received since that time.

This lack of evidence has led some writers to conclude that Kupka did not exhibit at the Section d'Or (Habasque, *Connaissance des arts*, 1960, 34; Camfield, 'La Section d'Or', 6). However, there has been a tradition that Kupka did exhibit and that he was mentioned by Apollinaire, which requires serious examination.

The first hints of Kupka's participation in the exhibition and inclusion in the definition occur in comments which derived from Kupka or his immediate friends in 1921. It could be suggested that these formed part of the process of 'improving' history in which so many artists indulged in the 1920s. However, Kupka was at pains to clarify his differences from Orphism as it was apparently defined by Apollinaire. Grémilly—who was the first to refer to Kupka's participation—said that in a lecture given at the Section d'Or, Apollinaire foretold the coming of a new form of painting 'where there would be colour, rhythm, and analogies with music' (*Kupka*, 14); he also said that when Kupka exhibited his two *Amorpha* paintings at the Salon d'Automne, Apollinaire 'greeted in him the appearance of Orphic painting . . . whose coming he had already announced . . .' (ibid., 18). Grémilly clearly confused the situation, for the Salon d'Automne preceded the Section d'Or, so perhaps he had misread Alexandre Mercereau's comment that it was in the Salon d'Automne that Kupka exhibited the *Amorpha* paintings 'in which the complete elimination of *trompe-l'œil* was noted and which Apollinaire *then* greeted as the appearance of Orphic painting' (*Les Hommes du jour*, June 1921, cited by Grémilly, *Kupka*, 78).

Kupka also told Grémilly that people had 'wished to see the birth of Orphism' in his work; but that in reality there had been a 'screen of silence' about his 'researches' and that this was just as well since 'the title of Orphist did not suit me at all' (*Kupka*, 40). Since he said this immediately after the war (during which he had not painted), he must have been referring to the pre-war period, and it is certainly true that no critic of that time tried to understand his 'researches'. Then, in a text which was probably written in this post-war period (see page 348, n. 78), Kupka wrote:

Already in the autumn, G. Apollinaire, still full of his Orpheus, spoke of this painting at the Section d'Or and called it 'Orphist'. The canvases of Kupka were rhythmic and, as a result, the analogy between the two arts, music and painting, seemed even more evident because they were labelled in musical terms. Kupka chose them because he did not, for the moment, know what to call them . . . But, in any case, [this painting] is not an illustration of music. (Fédit, *L'Œuvre de Kupka*, 112)

This brings one to a puzzling aspect of Apollinaire's definition of Orphism as it was published: the term Orphism obviously has musical connotations, and every contemporary who used it referred to its musical aspect. Gabrielle Buffet-Picabia (*Aires abstraites*, 56–8) stressed that Apollinaire mentioned the relationship between music and painting in his lecture (as did practically everyone who discussed it), and yet when the definition was published, there was no mention of music at all.

The next serious reference to Kupka and Orphism occurred in Turpin's article on Kupka in the *Dictionnaire biographique des artistes contemporains*, 1931 (ii, 286) which was apparently drafted by Kupka himself (Fédit, *L'Œuvre de Kupka*, 18). Turpin was a 'Paroxyst' poet who was apparently present at Apollinaire's lecture, so he would have been able to check on the truth of Kupka's statement:

Guillaume Apollinaire was one of the first to understand the immense contribution of Frank Kupka, and to designate this abstract art, guided only by the titles of the painter, he baptised it Orphism. Speaking at the Section d'Or, he drew the attention of the audience to the relationship of this painting which draws its dynamism from itself as music does. Frank Kupka has always denied that he wished to express music pictorially …

The claim that Apollinaire was guided by Kupka's titles suggests a connection between *Amorpha* and *Orphism*.

Finally there is the testimony of Nicolas Beauduin, the 'Dynamist' poet and friend of Kupka's, who was also present at Apollinaire's lecture and who described how Apollinaire paused in front of Kupka's works to give his definition of the new painting, stressing the relationship between painting and music. Beauduin's account is very late—over forty years after the event—but he gives so much lively circumstantial detail (see pp. 37–8) as to persuade one of its truth. One can dismiss his account only if one considers it a fabrication, and this would seem unlikely—if only because so many of those present at the Section d'Or were still alive. Fédit (*L'Œuvre de Kupka*, 98) states that he must be wrong in claiming that Kupka exhibited paintings called *Contrastes* and *Compliments*, because the work she reproduces as *Compliments* (Musée National d'Art Moderne) was being painted in 1919–22. However, the *Compliments* in the Musée National had been in Kupka's possession until his death, and seems to have been a reprise of earlier works related to the *Femme cueillant des fleurs*; whereas the work Beauduin mentioned was in his own collection.

We are, however, still left with the fact that Apollinaire *did not* mention Kupka in his definition. Even without the problem of Orphism, it is strange that not once in all his voluminous writings on art did Apollinaire refer to Kupka, for he must have mentioned nearly every other artist of the time. He was alert to any novelty, and whatever he may have thought of Kupka's art, it was in 1912–13 absolutely unique in its uncompromising purity. The strangeness of Apollinaire's silence about Kupka is intensified when one considers that there were many ideas which they shared, and many ways in which Kupka's art accorded with Apollinaire's pronouncements on the new art. All this suggests that there was a specific reason for Apollinaire's omission of Kupka. Beauduin stated that Kupka dissociated himself from Apollinaire's classification on the grounds that the music-painting analogy was inappropriate. Kupka was, of course, interested in the relationship between the two arts, but in all his comments (direct or indirect) on Orphism, he emphasized that he was not creating a visual equivalent of music, and he probably wished it to be quite clear that his painting could not be explained away by regarding it as music. Beauduin also claimed that Apollinaire was 'somewhat embarrassed' by Kupka's position, and since it took a great deal to embarrass Apollinaire, one would imagine that Kupka had been very upset or very angry. Apollinaire may have hoped to rectify his position, for Beauduin suggested that he planned to discuss Kupka with Delaunay (who was not discussed in *Les Peintres cubistes*) in another volume of 'meditations' on Orphism. If this was so, it is probable that Delaunay scotched the project, for he was anxious to appropriate Orphism to himself and would have felt that Kupka could not create pure Orphist colour structures since he still used line.

Thus, the evidence as to whether Kupka was included in Apollinaire's lecture at the Section d'Or is not sufficient to prove the case one way or the other, although, on balance, I believe that he was.

Appendix B   The dating of Kupka's *Plans verticaux*
and related works

1. *Les Cavaliers* and *Bois de Boulogne* group (Pls. 90 and 56–7). Fédit
(*L'Œuvre de Kupka*, 54), dates the *Cavaliers* to 1900–2 on the grounds that it
is like his journalistic illustrations of that date, and that Mme Kupka
remembers it as having always been in the studio. However, none of
Kupka's works of that date were so stylized, and were curvilinear rather
than rigidly vertical. Vachtovà (*Kupka*, 54–5) dates the drawing and
etching in the *Bois de Boulogne* group to 1904 and 1905, and the final oil to
1906–8 (it was post-dated '1907'), Although she gives no reason why these
lively studies should have been spread over four years. Kupka painted no
other unpretentious studies of everyday life before the middle of the
decade, and the fresh execution suggests that they were painted fairly close
to the Montmartre series of *c.* 1909–10 (Pl. 59) and to the *Portrait de famille*
(Pl. 58) of the same date. They could thus be dated *c.* 1907–8, with the
Cavaliers coming relatively late in the group because of its increased
stylization. In his article—drafted by Kupka himself—Turpin dated his
period of 'technical researches' to '1908–1911', and this suggests a useful
starting date for his studies of movement. These studies were at first
developed only in drawings, while in his paintings of *c.* 1906–10 Kupka was
working on relatively conventional Fauvist paintings of daily life.

2. The *Plans par couleurs. Le Grand Nu* (Pl. 102). This painting is dated 1909,
but was first exhibited at the Salon d'Automne of 1911, and since it is
essentially a geometrization of Kupka's Fauvism it should probably be
dated 1910–1911. (Kupka painted another version as early as 1905, to which
many studies of an academic kind are related.) I am indebted for this
information to Angelica Rudenstine, Research Curator at The Solomon
R. Guggenheim Museum.

3. The *Nocturne* (Pl. 101) is frequently dated 1910, but since it is so closely
related in palette and conception to the *Plans verticaux I* (Pl. 107) of 1912–
13, it is more probable that it was executed in 1911 (as was stated in the
article in the *Dictionnaire biographique*, 286).

4. The *Femme cueillant des fleurs* pastels (Pls. 91–4 and 105) and transparent
Plans par couleurs (Pls. 103–4). Fédit dates the pastels to 1910 'at the latest'
(*L'Œuvre de Kupka*, 56) on the grounds that they are closely related to the
Plans par couleurs (Musée National d'Art Moderne, Pl. 103), whose
inscribed date, '1910–11', she finds sound because it was exhibited in the
Indépendants of March 1912. However, the work was post-dated, and

since it is an advanced study in the use of transparent colour, with which Kupka began to experiment in 1910–11, it should probably be dated to 1911–2. The *Femme cueillant des fleurs* group would have been painted slightly earlier, in 1910–11.

5. The *Ordonnance sur verticales* series. The pastel (Pl. 95) is probably transitional between the *Femme cueillant des fleurs* and the red and blue *Ordonnances sur verticales* and *Ordonnances sur verticales en jaune* (Pl. 96). The latter is inscribed 1913, and the former generally dated to 1911–12. A sheet in the collection of the Museum of Modern Art, New York, contains sketches related to the red and blue *Ordonnance sur verticales* and to *Amorpha, Fugue en deux couleurs*—the latter being probably at quite an advanced stage in the evolution of the work which was completed by the autumn of 1912—which suggests that the group should be dated 1911–13.

6. The *Plans verticaux*. Although the *Plans verticaux I* (Pl. 107) is dated 1912 on the canvas, it is dated 1912–13 in the generally reliable catalogue of Kupka's exhibition at the Galerie la Boëtie in 1924, and in most other early sources. The same date is inscribed on the *Plans verticaux* in the Národní Galerie, Prague (Pl. 108), and this is quite reasonable. This work is generally called *Plans verticaux III* and is generally assumed to have been exhibited in the Salon des Indépendants of 1913, but it is not absolutely certain that this was so, for the work exhibited was simply called *Plans verticaux* (no. 1720), and Grémilly (*Kupka*, 73) quotes a contemporary description of it as 'several brown stripes on a grey ground'. However, since all published accounts—several of them directly informed by Kupka—agree that the work now called *Plans verticaux III* was the one shown at the Indépendants, it seems reasonable to accept this identification. It may, indeed, be possible that the description (which I have not been able to locate) referred to the *Solo d'un trait brun* which was shown in the same Salon, for this does contain brown stripes on a greyish ground.

Vachtovà (*Kupka*, 279) suggests that the 'much calmer handwriting' of *Plans verticaux III* indicates 'revision after 1930'. However, the same flat painting can be seen in the *Plans verticaux* (*Architecture philosophique*), and drawings for the painting suggest that he was deliberately avoiding the evocative either in shape or handling. He did some repainting to the *Plans verticaux III*, but made no major change to the position of the planes (he appears to have considered making the slight diagonal into a horizontal for he overpainted it to this effect, but then painted out the overpainting). He seems to have altered some of the colours, too, by overpainting, but it is impossible to decide when he did this (it was certainly not substantial enough to transform it from the 'brown stripes on a grey ground' described in 1913).

See n. 78 for a discussion of the so-called 'final study' for *Plans verticaux III*.

In summary, I would suggest that the *Femme cueillant des fleurs* pastels—a compact and quickly executed group—were produced in late 1910 or 1911, and that they were fairly soon succeeded by *Nocturne* in 1911, the *Ordonnance sur verticales* of 1911–13, and by the three *Plans par couleurs* (of the 1912 Indépendants) in 1911–2.

Appendix C   The dating of Delaunay's *Tour, Ville, Fenêtres,*
and *Formes circulaires* series

The dates given to many of Delaunay's pre-war works are contradictory.
Some can be checked against contemporary sources: the catalogues of the
Salon des Indépendants and of his one-man show at the Galerie
Barbazanges in late February to March 1912 (although the former tend to
be vague and the latter contains contradictions); the *Album* produced in
association with his exhibition at Der Sturm in late January 1913; and the
catalogue of his works at the Berlin Herbstsalon, 1913 (see the list of
Delaunay's exhibitions, *Du Cubisme à l'art abstrait*, 361–4). Delaunay gave
other dates in his many attempts to straighten out the history of twentieth
century art (published in *Du Cubisme à l'art abstrait*), and although they too
are frequently contradictory, certain probabilities do emerge from a
comparison of these sources. I have discussed these problems with Angelica
Rudenstine, Research Curator, The Solomon R. Guggenheim Museum,
whose catalogue of that collection contains a detailed account of the
chronology of Delaunay's paintings.

1. The *Tour* series. The earliest works in this series are clearly those with
closed silhouettes with the Eiffel Tower seen in the distance; the first is said
to be *La Tour, Première étude* (Habasque A. 69; Pl. 121) which Delaunay
gave to Sonia Terk as an engagement present and whose date of 1909 is
acceptable (although the inscription may not be contemporary; see page
127, n. 6). *La Tour Eiffel* (reverse of *Saint-Séverin nº 4*, Habasque A. 46;
Philadelphia Museum of Art, Pl. 122) may also be dated to 1909, since its
palette of rich greens, blues, and purples is close to the *Saint-Séverin* series,
and to the *Autoportrait* (Habasque A. 42; Pl. 6) of that year. Its planar
structure is also close to the portrait. Since the Philadelphia painting is the
most developed of the earlier *Tour Eiffel* pictures, it was probably the one
exhibited at the Salon des Indépendants of 1910. It has generally been
assumed that the version shown was one of the dynamic, fractured ones
(largely because Apollinaire said that Delaunay's paintings seemed to
'commemorate an earthquake', *Chroniques d'art*, 75); however, since most
evidence suggests that the more dynamic pictures of the Eiffel Tower were
not painted until after the Salon, it is more likely that his remark was
inspired by *Saint-Séverin nº 2* (Habasque, A. 44) which was shown in the
Salon.
    La Tour Eiffel aux arbres (Habasque A. 70; Pl. 124) is dated 1909, but
stylistically this is unlikely; moreover, several accounts state that Delaunay

began the mature *Tour Eiffel* series at La Cluse near Nantua where he and Sonia Terk spent the months April to September before they moved into their flat in the rue des Grands Augustins in November (Philippe Soupault, 'Robert Delaunay, peintre', *Les Feuilles libres*, Sept.–Oct. 1923, 176; Vriesen, *Delaunay*, 29). Rudenstine suggests that *La Tour Eiffel aux arbres* and *La Tour Eiffel* in a private collection at Krefeld (Habasque A. 83; Barbazanges catalogue, no 18, *Étude pour la Tour, 1910*; Pl. 126) were probably painted at La Cluse, and that the latter may have been a study for the *Tour Eiffel* (Habasque A. 77; Pl. 127) shown in the Indépendants of 1911 (listed as one of three works called *Paysage Paris*). This identification must be correct since this work was reproduced in Allard's article on the Salon (*Marches du Sud-Ouest*, June 1911). It was also exhibited in the Blaue Reiter exhibition of December 1911–January 1912 where it was purchased by Bernard Köhler, in whose collection it remained until destroyed in 1945. Rudenstine further suggests that *La Tour Eiffel* in The Solomon R. Guggenheim Museum (Habasque A. 78; Pl. 128) was painted after the Köhler picture (Delaunay dated it 1911 in a text of *c.* 1939–40, *Du Cubisme à l'art abstrait*, 79), and that the Basle *Tour Eiffel* (Pl. 4; Habasque A. 84) was painted shortly after that.

Rudenstine suggests that another group of more stylized Tour Eiffel paintings may have been started as late as the autumn of 1911, after the Futurists' visit to Paris: these were *La Tour rouge* of The Solomon R. Guggenheim Museum (Habasque, A. 89; dated 1911 in the Barbazanges catalogue, no. 24); the unfinished *Tour Eiffel* given to Apollinaire and now in the Museum Folkwang, Essen (Habasque A. 85); *La Tour Eiffel* (*Champs de Mars*) of the Chicago Art Institute (Habasque A. 88; Pl. 129) which, she points out, was reproduced in a less finished state in the Barbazanges catalogue and the Delaunay *Album*, and which is closely related to the Eiffel Tower in *La Ville de Paris*. Rudenstine is right in grouping these works and relating them to *La Ville de Paris*, but there is little to suggest that they were painted after the Futurists' visit, and one can state only that they were painted after the group executed between the autumn of 1910 and the early summer of 1911.

To summarize:

1. Habasque A. 69 and reverse of A. 46 (Sonia Delaunay collection and Philadelphia Museum of Art): 1909 to early 1910.

2. Habasque A. 70 and A. 83 (Solomon R. Guggenheim Museum and Krefeld private collection): spring–early autumn 1910.

3. Habasque A. 77, A. 78, A. 84 (ex-Köhler collection; Solomon R. Guggenheim Museum; Basle, Kunstmuseum): late autumn 1910–early summer 1911.

4. Habasque A. 89, A. 85, and A. 88 (Solomon R. Guggenheim Museum; Folkwang Museum, Essen; Chicago Institute of Art), as well as a drawing in the Gabrielle Münter Stiftung, Munich: summer–winter 1911–2.

There is also a group of highly developed pen and ink drawings of *La Tour et la Roue* most of which are inscribed 1910 (e.g. Habasque C. 510, Musée National d'Art Moderne, Paris) or even 1909–10 (Habasque C. 514, Museum of Modern Art, New York). Since they are far more closely related to the dynamic structure of the painting *Soleil, Tour, Aeroplane* (Habasque A. 123 (Albright-Knox Art Gallery, Buffalo) than to the works of 1910–11, and since two of them were first published in 1913—*Montjoie!*, 18 Mar. 1913 (Habasque C. 514); *Der Sturm*, Aug. 1913, nos. 173–4 (Habasque C. 513)—it is more likely that they were executed in 1913.

2. The *Ville* series. One can accept that the straightforward geometrizations of the view from the Arc de Triomphe across roof-tops to the distant Eiffel Tower were painted in 1909, as is generally stated. Langner ('Zu den Fensterbildern von Robert Delaunay', *Jahrbuch der Hamburger Kunstsammlungen* (Hamburg), 1962, vii) states that *La Ville* in the Winterthur Kunstmuseum (Pl. 119; Habasque A. 73) was the earliest of the series, and that it and *La Ville n° 1* (once in the Jawlensky collection; lost; Habasque A. 72) were painted in 1909. Rudenstine suggests that the one now in the Minneapolis Institute of Arts (reverse of *Saint-Séverin. n° 2*, Habasque A. 44) was the earliest, that the Winterthur one was next, and that both were painted in early 1910 with *La Ville. n° 1* and the *Ville* in the Tate Gallery (Habasque A. 71) which she suggests may have been a study for *Ville. n° 1*. Langner, Habasque, and Rudenstine all suggest that *Ville. n° 1* was shown in the Indépendants of 1910; Rudenstine states that it was then exhibited in the first Blaue Reiter exhibition which opened in December 1911, where it was dated 1910 and was purchased by Jawlensky. It was then shown in the Barbazanges exhibition with the date of 1909. Since this group of paintings is stylistically compatible with the geometric simplifications of other works of 1908–9, the confusion of the dates for *La Ville n° 1* suggests that it was begun in 1909 and finished in early 1910.

As with the *Tour* series, there was a second group of more complex works painted after the early simple geometric ones: *La Ville. n° 2 (étude)* (Habasque A. 82; Musée National d'Art Moderne; Pl. 130); *La Ville n° 2* (Habasque A. 87; Solomon R. Guggenheim Museum; Pl. 131); and *La Fenêtre sur la Ville. n° 3* (Habasque A. 86 as *La Fenêtre sur la Ville. n° 4*; Solomon R. Guggenheim Museum; Pl. 132). Delaunay was not entirely consistent in these titles: for example, *La Ville. n° 2 étude)* was illustrated as *Ville. n° 2* in the *Album*, but this may have been a simple mistake. However, when he post-dated many of his works after the war, he seems to have become confused about the rationale behind his thematic numbering and wrote *Fenêtre sur la Ville. n° 4* on the reverse of the work which is clearly identified as *n° 3* in contemporary texts. *La Ville. n° 2 (étude)* is dated 1910 on the canvas, 1910 in the list of works in the Barbazanges catalogue, but 1909–11 in the caption to the illustration in the same catalogue. *La Ville. n° 2* is dated 1911 both on the canvas and in the Blaue Reiter and Barbazanges catalogues. This seems quite probable, since it is directly related to *La Fenêtre sur la Ville. n° 3* which, despite post-dating to 1910–11, can be securely dated to December 1911—January 1912 (it is dated 1912 in the Barbazanges catalogue of February 1912, and December 1911 in the *Album* of early 1913; moreover, Delaunay regarded it as crucial to his development, and in an important text of October 1913 (*Du Cubisme à l'art abstrait*, 110) he dated it December 1911–January 1912). In the same text, Delaunay dated *La Ville. n° 2* to 1910–11. Delaunay was trying to evolve a means of dating his paintings thematically (for example, *La Ville de Paris* was inscribed 1910–11–12 to indicate the dates of its different motifs), so this may be why he dated *La Ville. n° 2 (étude)* 1910 and 1909–11 in the same catalogue.

Rudenstine suggests that the three works were painted in the last six to nine months of 1911, because of their close stylistic relationship and because the Paris *Ville. n° 2 (étude)* seems to have been a study for the New York *Ville. n° 2*. Therefore, she does not believe that either version of *La Ville. n° 2* was shown at the Indépendants of 1911 (although an inscription on the back of *Ville. n° 2 (étude)* says that it was). She is right to stress the close stylistic relationship between the three works, but I think it probable that the group could have occupied Delaunay between late 1910 and late 1911, for he was also working hard on a number of paintings in the *Tour Eiffel* series and other individual works. The Paris *Ville. n° 2 (étude)* cannot be regarded as a study in the normal sense since Delaunay did not use highly developed studies. He probably titled it in this way because he was trying to find a terminology to indicate his serial approach (as he did throughout this period).

To summarize:

1. The *Ville. n° 1* theme: a group of geometrically simplified architectural studies, begun in 1909, culminating in *La Ville. n° 1* (Habasque A. 72) which was probably finished in early 1910.

2. The *Ville. n° 2* theme (Habasque A. 82 and A. 87), in which the geometric forms on a vertical canvas were retained but were broken down into smaller forms by the use of a layer of small rectangular strokes: the first perhaps begun in late 1910, the second in the middle months of 1911.

3. The third theme, *La Fenêtre sur la Ville. n° 3* (Habasque A. 86), in which the vertical format of *n° 1* and *n° 2* is made horizontal: securely dated December 1911–January 1912.

3. The *Fenêtres* series. Most of the series may have been painted at La Chevreuse where the Delaunays spent the spring and summer of 1912 (Delaunay was still in Paris on 11 April when he was visited by Klee, and was back by 2 October when Marc and Macke came to see him). Habasque lists seventeen works in the series, the majority of which were painted by early 1913 when twelve were listed in Delaunay's *Album*. There is nothing to suggest that any were begun after this time (Habasque A. 146 was completed in 1914; but it is unlikely that it was begun in 1910 as suggested on the reverse). The first reference to the series occurs in Delaunay's draft of a letter to Kandinsky (*Du Cubisme à l'art abstrait*, 178–9; probably written late March–April, see p. 356, n. 27). Delaunay stated in many different contexts that the first *Fenêtres* were executed in April 1912 and there is no reason to doubt this, but it is very difficult to establish a firm chronology for the series, particularly since Delaunay clearly experimented with different ways of representing movement and space simultaneously through colour.

At least three paintings (Habasque A. 90, A. 104, A. 105) can probably be dated to April: *Les Fenêtres sur la Ville 1er partie 2ème motif n° 1*—I find no rationale for this numbering—(Pl. 141; Habasque A. 104; Jucker collection, Milan) is dated April on the reverse, and its pale pinks, blues, and greens are so close to the palette of *La Fenêtre sur la Ville. n° 3* and *La Ville to Paris* as to suggest that it was one of the earliest of the series. The same may be said of *Les Fenêtres simultanées* in the Kunstsammlung Nordrhein-Westfalen, Dusseldorf (Pl. 143). *Les Fenêtres simultanées* (Habasque A. 106) in The Solomon R. Guggenheim Museum, may also have been fairly early in the series, since it has similarities to the Düsseldorf painting and retains a clear division between warm and cool areas which suggests the recession of the cityscape in the *Ville* series. Delaunay created an analogous effect by emphasizing the diagonals of the frame of the painting in the Hamburg Kunsthalle (Pl. 144; Habasque A. 90). The work is dated 1911 on the reverse and Habasque accepts this, but such a date is quite improbable; it was illustrated with the title *1er Représentation. Les Fenêtres simultanées. Ville. 2e motif 1re partie* in the Delaunay *Album*, where it was dated April 1912. This seems to have been the first work in which Delaunay interwove really intense transparent oranges, violets, yellows, blues, and greens. The painting in the Musée de Grenoble (Habasque A. 108) is a more intensely worked abstract structure, The richness of the densely painted yet brilliant, unsullied colour was clearly the product of intensive experimentation, and the use of relatively opaque colours suggests that Delaunay was moving towards the greater materiality of *Les Trois Fenêtres, la Tour et la Roue* (Habasque A. 117; Mr. and Mrs. A. M. Burden collection; Pl. 148), and to *Une Fenêtre (Étude pour les 3 Fenêtres)* (Musée National d'Art Moderne, Habasque A. 116), dated 1912–13 in Delaunay's *Album*. *Les Trios Fenêtres, la Tour et la Roue* must have been finished in January 1913 before being exhibited in the *Sturm* exhibition later that month.

However, one cannot suggest a simple development from relatively cool transparent colours to more strongly contrasted warm and cool colours and more densely worked opaque structures, since the *2e Représentation. Les Fenêtres. Simultanéité. Ville. 1re partie 3 Motifs* (Habasque A. 112; Philadelphia Museum of Art; Pl. 145), which is dated June 1912 in the *Album*, is painted in cool transparent colours. However, despite the rather tentative use of colour, Delaunay no longer used it to create recessive perspective effects as in the earlier works in the series. *Les Fenêtres simultanées* (Peggy Guggenheim collection, Habasque A. 111; Pl. I) is stylistically close to the tripartite one, whereas *2e Représentation. Les Fenêtres. Simultanéité. Ville. 2e partie 5 motifs* (Habasque A. 118; Museum Folkwang, Essen; Pl. 147) was probably painted later in 1912, for Delaunay reintroduced strongly defined descriptive elements like those he used in *Les Trois Fenêtres, la Tour et la Roue*—after condemning the use of objective elements in the articles he wrote during the summer.

4. The *Formes circulaires*: the *Soleil, Lune. Simultané* series and the *Disque*. It is unlikely that this series was begun in 1912, although Delaunay frequently asserted that it was. Stylistically, it is improbable that any of the *Soleil, Lune* paintings preceded *Les Trois Fenêtres, la Tour et la Roue*, the *Équipe de Cardiff F.C. Esquisse*, or the *Troisième Représentation L'Équipe de Cardiff F.C.* (Habasque A. 124 and 125; Pls. 151–2) the first two of which were completed by late January 1913 (when they were exhibited), and the last work by late March when it was shown in the Indépendants. However,

Soleil 1 (Habasque A. 120; private collection, Germany; Pl. 160) was post-dated '1912' (although a label on the back dates it to 1913); *Soleil, Lune. Simultané 1* and *Soleil, Lune. Simultané 2* (Habasque A. 119 and A. 114; Stedlyk Museum and Museum of Modern Art; Pls. IV, 164, and 166) were post-dated '1912–13' and '1912' respectively. The first mention of the series occurred in a draft of a letter which Delaunay wrote on 17 April 1913 (*Du Cubisme à l'art abstrait*, 161) in which he referred to 'painting the sun which is nothing but painting'; the second in a letter written on 2 June 1913, saying 'my *last* picture is the sun . . .' (Vriesen, *Delaunay*, 61). There was no hint of their existence in Delaunay's exhibition at Der Sturm in January, in the Armory Show in February, or in the Indépendants in March, and they were first exhibited as a group of about thirteen works in the Berlin Herbstsalon which opened on 20 September 1913. It therefore seems likely that they were painted in the spring and summer of 1913, and this is confirmed by Vriesen (*Delaunay*, 61) who states that they were painted at Louveciennes where the Delaunays spent the spring and summer.

The *Disque* (Habasque A. 113; Pl. 168) was first mentioned as *Le Premier Disque* (1912) in the catalogue of Delaunay's exhibition at the Galerie Paul Guillaume in 1922. There is no doubt that it was painted before the war, but it is extremely unlikely that it was executed in 1912, for Delaunay *never* painted in flat, unmodulated colours before the second half of 1913. A work very like it may have been exhibited in the Herbstsalon (which opened in late September): it can be seen in an early photograph of *Première présentation des prismes, Sculpture simultanée: Cheval prisme, Soleil, Lune* (Habasque A. 136; Pl. 169), although it is hard to see whether it was part of the piece or coincidental background. I have not been able to find out when the *Disque* was mounted on a circular frame (Seuphor, *L'Art abstrait*, 208, illustrates it as an unstretched canvas, whereas the one shown with the *Cheval* seems to be mounted). Delaunay referred to it in a text of the early 1930s as having been painted in 1913 (*Du Cubisme à l'art abstrait*, 76) and this seems likely in view of its relationship to the *Cheval* and its similarity in colour and handling to the flat opaque disks and concentric rings in *Hommage à Bleriot* and *Drame politique* (Habasque, A. 140 and A. 149; Pls. 172–3). The *Blériot* was completed by late February, for it was shown in the Indépendants which opened on 1 March 1914.

Appendix D   The Dating of Léger's *Fumées sur les toits*,
Le Compotier, Le Fumeur, and *La Noce*

1. *Les Fumeés sur les toites*. Golding (*Cubism*, 152) states that the series was begun in September 1910 when Léger moved to the rue de l'Ancienne Comédie, since the view over roofs to the towers of Notre Dame was that from his studio window. However, Léger does not seem to have moved there until after the Salon des Indépendants of April 1911, for his address in the supplement to that catalogue was still given as 14 avenue du Maine. *Les Fumées sur les toits* (Pl. 186) was dated to 1910 in the catalogue, *Fernand Léger*, Musée des Arts Decoratifs, 1956, no. 6, on the grounds that it was a wedding present to the wife of his friend André Mare (although the catalogue is full of inaccuracies). However, even if Léger had been able to paint this particular view in late 1910, it is stylistically improbable, and the *Fumées sur les toits* series was almost undoubtedly begun in mid-1911 at the time when Léger began to compose his paintings from contrasting abstract and representational forms (see *Essai pour trois portraits*, Pl. 183). *Maisons et fumées* (Pl. 184; illustrated in Gleizes and Metzinger, *Du Cubisme*) must have been one of the earliest of the series, for although it has the contrasting flat planes and curvilinear bulging forms which characterize the series, these forms were fairly directly derived from the roofs, walls, and smoke of the cityscape, just as the forms of the *Essai* were all derived from observed forms. The balance between representation and abstraction in the *Maisons et fumées* is similar to that of the *Essai*, and although both works contain contrasts, these do not break up the surface of the painting, but are woven together by *passage* to create a continuous surface. The painting in the Minneapolis Institute of Arts and the closely related painting in the Weil collection (Pls. 185 and 186) were probably painted slightly later, for although their planes are arranged in a similar way, they are flatter, more abstract, and more geometric. The smoke forms are still clearly derived from smoke, but one no longer feels that they were observed in nature. Nevertheless, they are softer and more evanescent than those in *Le Fumeur* (Pl. 192), or *Les Fumées*—reproduced in Apollinaire's *Les Peintres cubistes* (Pl. 187) and there dated 1912. In *Les Fumées* the sources of the abstract forms are not longer apparent and the contrast between abstract and representational has been made more extreme. There is also a change in the distribution of the planes: in the works which I have attributed to mid-1911, the planes were arranged on the periphery of the composition and the centre was composed mainly of the representational building and cloud forms; however, in the works painted later that year and in 1912 the

abstract forms invade the centre (partly by means of the increasing abstraction of the smoke; partly by means of invented forms). Thus the Minneapolis *Fumées sur les toits* has a predominantly descriptive centre, whereas the centre of *Les Fumées* is dominated by a richly modelled geometric configuration. This development is also seen in the major figure-paintings: the abstract forms of the *Essai* have their basis in observed fact and tend to be subordinate to the descriptive forms; in *La Noce* (Pl. 190), abstract forms invade the centre of the composition, and the abstract and the representational are woven together; but in the centre of *La Femme en bleu* (Pl. 195), the representational forms have been overwhelmed by the large abstract planes. I would therefore suggest that *Les Fumées* was painted shortly after *La Noce*, for its angular scraps of the cityscape resemble those in *La Noce* but are no longer woven together atmospherically.

2. *Le Compotier* (Pl. 188). This work is frequently dated 1909, but this is stylistically improbable, for it is closely related to the *Fumées sur les toits* series in its contrast between abstract and representational forms. Its over-all greenish tonality relates it to the *Essai pour trois portraits*, but the fact that its angular and curved planes do not have a basis in observed reality suggest that it was painted slightly later. Léger 'modelled' these planes in the same way that he modelled the abstract planes in *La Noce* which he was probably painting in the winter of 1911–12. *Le Compotier* is also related to *La Noce* in the way dynamic movements swing down the right side of the painting. Léger arranged the abstract planes around the representational centre of the canvas as he had done in the Minneapolis *Fumées sur les toits*, but he also separated the compositional parts more sharply than in many works of 1911 (although he still bound them together atmospherically). All these factors suggest that *Le Compotier* was a transitional work painted in late 1911 or early 1912.

Le Compotier as reproduced in Gleizes' and Metzinger's *Du Cubisme* is slightly different from the work as it is today. They also reproduced *Dessin pour une abondance* (Pl. 189) which is so closely related to *Le Compotier* that it is worth considering whether the latter was once part of a larger work about the size of *Le Fumeur*.

3. *Le Fumeur, La Noce*, and the 'Composition avec personnages'. In the Salon des Indépendants of 1912, Léger exhibited a 'Composition avec personnages' which has usually been identified with the painting called *Les Fumeurs* (Pl. 192). This work should probably be called *Le Fumeur*, for the two heads are made to interpenetrate as if Léger were not depicting two heads but trying to represent continuous movement by repeating an image as he had done in details of the *Essai* (Pl. 183). This interpretation is supported by Apollinaire who referred to a single 'fumeur' (*Les Peintres cubistes*, 85). It is therefore not a painting of 'personnages' and would not have been the painting shown in the Indépendants. In that year the Cubists made a bid for recognition in large programmatic subject pictures (cf. Gleizes's *Les Baigneuses*, and Delaunay's *La Ville de Paris*). Léger's *La Noce* would have been appropriate in this context, but *Le Fumeur*, a small informal work, would not.

There is some uncertainty as to their dates. *La Noce* (Pl. 190) has even been dated to 1910–11, though it would clearly have been painted after the *Essai pour trois portraits* as its abstract elements have been strengthened and brought into sharper contrast with the representational ones, as was the general tendency of Léger's style in 1911–12. It would thus have been painted between the autumn of 1911 and March 1912 when it was first exhibited.

Le Fumeur has been variously dated 1911 or 1912, but I think that its composition, its colour, and its relationship between abstract and representational all suggest that it was painted between *La Noce* and *La Femme en bleu*. It reflects the tendency towards formal and thematic simplicity, discontinuity, and physical intensity which became increasingly strong in Léger's work in 1912 and which led directly to the *Contrastes de formes*.

The structure of *Le Fumeur*—with its extraordinary tug between the cityscape and the more specific focus demanded by the head—is more discontinuous than *La Noce*. The latter is composed of disparate elements which Léger wove together by means of atmospheric veils, whereas he tended to reduce such binding elements in *Le Fumeur*. In *La Noce*, the strongest colours are the local colours of the clothes and faces, while the non-representational forms are almost without colour as if they were made of some immaterial substance. Léger had used colour in a similar way in the *Essai* of the summer and autumn of 1911, but in *La Femme en bleu* of twelve months later the strongest colours are in the non-representational planes, while local colours are almost non-existent. *Le Fumeur* lies between these extremes, for its colours are concentrated in the non-representational shapes at the expense of the local colours. Apollinaire's poetic account of Léger's development seems to confirm this chronology, for he evoked the soft vaporous colours of the paintings succeeding the *Nus dans un paysage*, and intimated that more definite colours appeared when this vapour 'dissipated' in *Le Fumeur* (Les Peintres cubistes, 85). His comment is too vague to be taken as evidence on its own, but is suggestive in relation to the other evidence.

The *Étude pour la Noce* (Pl. 191) also supports this chronology, for it is closer to the *Essai* than is *Le Fumeur*. Its closely woven surface, in which the cloudy abstract forms are fused with the detailed representational shapes, is characteristic of the works of 1911 and very different from the way different elements are sharply separated in the works of 1912. Its composition—with abstract forms at the edge of the canvas like a frame to the representational centre—is also closer to the works of 1911 than to *Le Fumeur* and *La Femme en bleu*.

Appendix E   The identity of Picabia's *Udnie*

The title *Udnie, jeune fille américaine (danse)* has never been satisfactorily explained. Most writers have accepted Gabrielle Buffet-Picabia's claim that the 'dancer' was Napierkowska, whom Picabia met on board the liner taking them to New York, but this does not clarify the meaning of the word 'Udnie'. Pearlstein ('The Paintings of Francis Picabia', 109), referring to another of Picabia's titles, *Portrait d'une jeune fille américaine dans l'état de nudité* (1915), suggests that 'Udnie' is an anagram of 'nudité', and indeed, 'Dans l'état de nudité' is a near anagram of 'danseuse étoile Udnie', that is, of 'Udnie Edtaonisl' ($E^DT^AO^NI^SL$). There is also some ambiguity as to the identity of the dancer: Picabia did refer to Napierkowska in a New York drawing, *Mechanical Expression Seen Through Our Own Mechanical Expression* (Pl. 252); she was presumably the dancer in the *Danseuse étoile sur un transatlantique*, and she created something of a sensation in New York during Picabia's visit when she was summonsed for the alleged indecency of her 'Dance of the Bee' (*New York Times*, 28 and 29 March 1913). However, other works in the series suggest that this identification does not contain the whole of the story: *Udnie* was a 'jeune fille américaine', and Napierkowska was Polish; another work was called *Danseuse étoile et son école de danse*, but Napierkowska did not have a dancing school. The one notorious contemporary dancer to be American and to have a school of dancing was, of course, Isadora Duncan who lived in Paris at this time and who was well known in both the social and artistic worlds which Picabia frequented (she bought one of Duchamp's paintings from the Salon d'Automne (probably in 1910, although he did not know her at the time, Cabanne, *Dialogues with Duchamp*, 25). At some time she and Picabia must have had a liaison, for she later said to Germaine Everling, Picabia's second wife, that she would very much like to become Mme Picabia again 'and this time ... legitimately' (Everling, *L'Anneau de Saturne*, 140). Everling states that they met in New York, but they were not there at the same time and would probably have known one another in Paris. It is then possible that 'Udnie' was *Isadora Duncan nue*', the 'jeune fille américaine dans l'état de nudité'. Picabia may have begun the series with Napierkowska in mind, and then, by association, have gone on to Isadora in the 'école du danse' gouache. He may still have been in New York when the news of the tragic death of her two children by drowning was received on 20 April; for several days the newspapers carried stories of the drowning which, according to the *New York Times*, 'cast gloom over all classes in Paris', of the prominent artistic

and literary figures who went to pay their condolences, of the service—
attended by thirty children from the dancing school, and pathetic accounts
of the overwhelming grief of the mother. Raymond Duncan accompanied
his sister to the crematorium, wearing 'flowing purple robes' (*New York
Times*, 22 and 23 April). Pushing speculation further, one wonders if this
association could have suggested the sombre purples and mournful tension
of *Edtaonisl (ecclésiastique)*—dance-star/churchman. This suggestion does
not invalidate Gabrielle Buffet-Picabia's interpretation, but indicates that
Picabia was trying to embody a whole complex of conflicting emotions,
memories, and associations going back to experiences witnessed in 1909
and perhaps having even deeper roots. This complexity may have received
an added dimension when, two days after Duncan had asked for the release
of the chauffeur who was said to have been responsible for the accident,
Napierkowska, back in Paris, was complaining about the Americans as 'a
narrow-minded people ... utterly impervious to any beautiful impression
[and] ... hardly civilized' (*New York Times*, 24 and 26 April 1913). Picabia's
experience had been quite different, and the 'memories of America' which
he sought to embody would have been complex indeed. Shortly after the
Picabias' return to Paris, Isadora was reported dangerously ill: this was the
time at which Picabia began painting *Udnie* and *Edtaonisl*, and while he was
painting them, Gabrielle gave birth to their third child; this too may have
contributed to the intense but mysterious emotion that one senses in these
paintings.

Bibliography

Works with extensive bibliographies are marked with an asterisk.

The bibliography is divided as follows:
1. General works
2. Apollinaire
3. Kupka
4. The Delaunays   A. Robert Delaunay   B. Sonia Delaunay-Terk
5. Léger
6. Picabia
7. Duchamp

1 GENERAL WORKS

The following contemporary periodicals were consulted for references to exhibitions and for evidence about the diffusion and availability of ideas:
Comoedia (Paris), 1911–14.
Gil Blas (Paris), 1911–14.
L'Intransigeant (Paris), 1911–14.
Mercure de France (Paris), 1908–14.
Montjoie! (Paris), 1913–14.
Paris-Journal (Paris), 1911–14.
Poème et Drame (Paris), 1912–14.
Les Soirées de Paris (Paris), 1912–14.
Specific references to exhibitions are given in the footnotes.

Abstraction, création, art non-figuratif (Paris), 1932–6.
Allard, Roger, 'Au Salon d'Automne de Paris', *L'Art libre* (Lyons), Nov. 1910.
— 'Sur quelques peintres', *Les Marches du Sud-Ouest* (Paris), June 1911, 57–64.
— 'Orphisme et Futurisme', *Écrits français* (Paris), Feb. and May 1914.
⋆Archivi del futurismo, ed. Maria Druidi Gambillo and Teresa Fiori (Rome, vol. i, 1958; vol. ii, 1962).
Armory Show, catalogue to the International Exhibition of Modern Art (New York), 15 Feb. to 15 Mar. 1913.
Arp, Hans (Jean), *On My Way: Poetry and Essays 1912–1947* (New York, 1948).
Avantgarde Osteuropa, 1910–1930, catalogue to an exhibition at the Kunstverein and the Akademie der Kunst (Berlin) Oct.–Nov. 1957.
Banet-Rivet, P., 'La Représentation du mouvement et de la vie', *Revue des deux mondes* (Paris), 1 Aug. 1907, 591–621.
Barr, Alfred H., Jr., *Cubism and Abstract Art* (New York, 1936).
Barzun, Henri-Martin, 'Apothéose des forces', *Poème et drame* (Paris), Mar. 1913.

— 'Après le symbolisme', *Poème et drame* (Paris), May 1913.
— *L'Ère du drame* (Paris, 1912).
— 'Manifeste sur le simultanisme poétique', *Paris-Journal* (Paris), 27 June 1913.
— 'La Révolution de Berlioz', *Poème et drame* (Paris), Mar. 1913.
— 'Du symbole au drame', *Poème et drame* (Paris), Jan. 1913.
— *Orpheus, Modern Culture and the 1913 Renaissance 1900–56* (privately published, New York, 1956).
Bazin, Germain, 'L'Orphisme', *Histoire de l'art contemporain. La Peinture*, ed. René Huyghe and Germain Bazin (Paris, 1935).
Beauduin, Nicolas 'L'Homme cosmogonique: poème paroxyste en trois chants', *La Vie des lettres* (Paris), Oct. 1913, 369–406.
— 'Les Temps héroïques: à propos du Salon de la Section d'Or', *Masques et visages* (Paris), June 1956, 6–7.
Berger, John, *The Moment of Cubism and other Essays* (London, 1969).
★Bergman, Pär, '*Modernolatria*' et '*simultaneità*'. *Recherches sur deux tendances dans l'avant-garde littéraire en Italie et en France à la veille de la première guerre mondiale* (Uppsala, 1962).
Bergson, Henri, *Évolution créatrice* (Paris, 1907).
— *Le Rire* (Paris, 1900).
— *An Introduction to Metaphysics*, trans. T. E. Hulme (London, 1913).
Bernard, Émile, 'Souvenirs de Paul Cézanne et lettres inédites', *Mercure de France* (Paris), 1 Oct. 1907, 385–404; 16 Oct. 1907, 606–27.
Besant, Annie and Leadbeater, C. W., *Les Formes-pensées*, trans. from the English (Paris, 1905).
Blavatsky, Helena Petrowna, *La Doctrine secrète, synthèse de la science, de la religion et de la philosophie*, trans. from the English, 2nd edn. (Paris, 1906–10), 6 vols.
Boccioni, Umberto, 'Il Dinamismo futurista e la pittura francese', *Lacerba* (Florence), 1 Aug. 1913.
— 'I Futuristi plagiati in Francia', *Lacerba* (Florence), 1 Apr. 1913.
Braque, catalogue to an exhibition at the Tate Gallery, introduction by Douglas Cooper (London), 1961.
Brion, Marcel, *L'Art abstrait* (Paris, 1956).
Buffet (or Buffet-Picabia), Gabrielle, *Aires abstraites* (Geneva, 1957).
— 'Modern Art and the Public', *Camera Work* (New York), June 1913.
— 'Musique d'aujourd'hui', *Soirées de Paris* (Paris), 15 Mar. 1914.
— 'La Section d'Or', *Art d'aujourd'hui* (Paris), May–June 1953.
— 'Some Memories of Pre-Dada: Picabia and Duchamp', *The Dada Painters and Poets*, ed. Robert Motherwell (New York, 1951).
Calvesi, Maurice, 'Futurismo e Orfismo', *L'Arte moderna* (Milan, 1967), v, n. 43.
Camfield, William Arnett, 'La Section d'Or', unpublished M.A. thesis, Yale, 1961.
Canudo, Riciotto, 'Manifeste de l'art cérébriste', *Montjoie!* (Paris), Jan.–Feb. 1914.
— 'Notre esthétique: à propos du *Rossignol* de Igor Strawinsky', *Montjoie!* (Paris), Apr.–May–June 1914.
Cartault, A., 'Les Théories des peintres futuristes italiens', *Revue du mois* (Paris), 10 Mar. 1912.
Cattaui, Georges, *Orphisme et prophétie chez les poètes français, 1850–1950* (Paris, 1965).
Cendrars, Blaise, *Du monde entier: Poésies complètes, 1912–24* (Paris, 1967).
— *Œuvres complètes* (Lausanne, 1960), iv (incl. lecture on 'La Tour Eiffel' and Delaunay, 1924; essays on Léger and Delaunay).
— 'Lettre ouverte à Barzun', *Paris-Journal* (Paris), 24 June 1914.
— *Blaise Cendrars vous parle*, ed. Michel Manoll (entretiens de la radiodiffusion française; Paris, 1962).

— with Sonia Delaunay, 'Le Premier livre simultané', letter to the press, *Paris-Midi* (Paris), 11 Oct. 1913.

Blaise Cendrars (essays by various authors), ed. Nino Frank (Paris, 1962).

Chagall, Marc, *Ma vie* (Paris, 1931).

Chevreul, M.-E., *De la loi du contraste simultané des couleurs et de ses applications* (Paris, 1889 edn.).

Chipp, Herschell B., 'Orphism and Color Theory', *Art Bulletin* (New York), xl, 1958, 55–63.

— *Theories of Modern Art* ed. (Berkeley, 1968).

Cooper, Douglas, *The Cubist Epoch* (London, 1971).

Coquiot, Gustave, *Cubistes, Futuristes et Passéistes* (Paris, 1914).

— *Les Indépendants (1884–1920)* (Paris, 1920).

Color and Form 1909–14, catalogue to an exhibition, Fine Arts Gallery of San Diego, Nov. 1971–Jan. 1972 (essays by Henry G. Gardiner, Herschell B. Chipp, William C. Agee, Lillian Lonngren).

Cravan, Arthur, 'Exhibition at the Indépendants', trans. from *Maintenant* (Paris), in *The Dada Painters and Poets*, ed. Robert Motherwell (New York, 1951), 9–13.

da Vinci, Leonardo, *Textes choisis; pensées, théories, préceptes, fables et facéties*, trans. Péladan (Paris, 1907).

— *Traité de la peinture*, trans. Péladan (Paris, 1910).

Denis, Maurice, *Du symbolisme au classicisme: Théories*, ed. Olivier Revault d'Allones (Paris, 1964); contains many essays from his 1912 collection, *Théories (1890–1910)*.

Dorival, Bernard, *Les Peintres du XXe siècle* (Paris, 1957).

Dournic, René, 'L'Âge du cinéma', *Revue des deux mondes* (Paris), 15 Aug. 1913, 919 ff.

Eddy, Arthur Jerome, *Cubists and Post-Impressionism* (Chicago, 1914).

Favre, Louis, *La Musique des couleurs et les musiques de l'avenir* (Paris, 1900).

Fingelstein, Peter, 'Spirituality, Mysticism and Non-objective art', *Art Journal* (New York), fall 1961, xxi, no. 1, 2 ff.

Fry, Edward F., *Cubism* (London, 1966).

Futurist Manifestos, ed. Umberto Apollonio (London, 1973).

Gachons, Jacques de, 'La Peinture d'après-demain', *Je sais tout* (Paris), 15 Apr. 1912, 349–56.

Gillouin, René, 'Bergsoniens et anti-bergsoniens', *Montjoie!* (Paris), 29 Mar. 1913, 6–7.

Girod, Fernand, 'Le Médiumisme et l'art', *La Vie mystérieuse* (Paris), 10 Nov. 1911.

Gleizes, Albert, 'Jean Metzinger', *La Revue indépendante* (Paris), Sept. 1910.

— 'A propos du Salon d'Automne', *Les Bandeaux d'Or* (Paris), Nov. 1910.

— with Jean Metzinger, *Du Cubisme* (Paris, 1912).

— 'Le Cubisme et la tradition', *Montjoie!* (Paris), 10 and 25 Feb. 1913.

— 'Opinion', *Montjoie!* (Paris), Nov.–Dec. 1913.

— 'A propos de la Section d'Or de 1912', *Les Arts plastiques* (Paris), no. 1, 1925.

— *Souvenirs: Le Cubisme 1908–1911* (Audin, 1957).

★*Albert Gleizes 1881–1953*, catalogue to a retrospective exhibition, introduction by Daniel Robbins, Solomon R. Guggenheim Museum (New York), 1964.

Albert Gleizes and the Section d'Or, catalogue to an exhibition, prefaces by W. Camfield and D. Robbins, Leonard Hutton Galleries (New York), 1964.

Goethe, Johann Wolfgang von, *Farbenlehre*, trans. by Charles Locke Eastlake as *Goethe's Theory of Colours* (London, 1840); recently republished with extensive annotations by Rupprecht Matthaei, *Goethe's Colour Theory* (London, 1971).

★Golding, John, *Cubism: a History and an Analysis 1907–1914* (London, 1959).

Gray, Christopher, *Cubist Aesthetic Theories* (Baltimore, 1953).

Guilbeaux, Henri, 'Paul Signac et les Indépendants', *Les Hommes du jour* (Paris), 22 Apr. 1911.

— 'La Poésie dynamique', *La Revue* (Paris), 1 and 15 May 1914.

— 'Un Nouvel Art poétique', *Paris-Journal* (Paris), 25 June 1914.

Hamilton, George Heard and Agee, William C., *Duchamp-Villon* (New York, 1967).

Herbstsalon, catalogue of the *Erster Deutscher Herbstsalon*, Der Sturm galerie (Berlin), 20 Sept.–1 Nov. 1913.

Hofmann, Werner, *Turning Points in Twentieth-Century Art 1890–1917* (London, 1959).

Hoog, Michel, 'Baranoff-Rossiné 1886–1942', *Cimaise* (Paris), Feb.–May 1968.

Hourcade, Olivier, 'La Tendance de la peinture contemporaine', *La Revue de France et des pays français* (Paris), Feb. 1912, 35–41.

— 'Enquête sur le Cubisme', *L'Action* (Paris), 25 Feb., 17 Mar., 24 Mar. 1912.

Jean, Marcel, *Histoire de la peinture surréaliste* (Paris, 1959).

Jean-Desthieux, F., 'Considérations sur la poétique de demain', *La Vie des lettres* (Paris), Oct. 1913, 494–518.

Joly, Auguste, 'Sur le futurisme', *La Belgique artistique et littéraire* (Brussels), July 1912, 69–74; issued by the Futurists as a broad-sheet, 'La Futurisme et la philosophie'.

Kahnweiler, Daniel-Henry, *Confessions esthétiques* (Paris, 1963): includes a translation of *Der Weg zum Kubismus* (Munich, 1920), and articles on the influence of Seurat and Mallarmé on painting.

— *Mes galeries et mes peintres. Entretiens avec François-Crémieux* (Paris, 1961).

Kandinsky, Wassily, *Ueber das Geistige in der Kunst* (Munich, 1912); trans. *Concerning the Spiritual in Art*, by Michael Sadleir, revised edn., New York, 1947).

— *Reminiscences* (1913), trans. Robert. L. Herbert in *Modern Artists on Art* (Englewood Cliffs, New Jersey, 1964).

— and Franz Marc (eds.), *Der Blaue Reiter* (Munich, 1912, trans. London, 1974).

Klee, Paul, 'Die Ausstellung des *Modernen Bundes* im Kunsthaus Zürich', *Die Alpen* (Berne), Aug. 1912; trans. in Paul Klee, *Théories de l'art moderne* (Geneva, 1964), 9–14, as 'Approches de l'art moderne'.

— *Journal*, trans. Pierre Klossowski (Paris, 1959).

Kushner, Eva, *Le Mythe d'Orphée dans la littérature française contemporaine* (Paris, 1961).

Laporte, Paul M., 'Cubism and Science', *Journal of Aesthetics* (Cleveland), Mar. 1949, 243–56.

Larionov, Michel, 'Le Rayonisme picturale', *Montjoie!* (Paris), Apr.–June 1914.

MacDelmarle, Felix, 'Quelques notes sur la simultanéité en peinture', *Poème et drame* (Paris), Jan.–Mar. 1914, 17–21.

The Machine as seen at the end of the Mechanical Age, catalogue to an exhibition, written by K. G. Pontius Hulten, Museum of Modern Art (New York), 1968.

Magne, Émile, 'Le Machinisme dans la littérature contemporaine', *Mercure de France* (Paris), 16 Jan. 1910, 202–17.

Marey, Étienne Jules, *Le Mouvement* (Paris, 1894).

Marinetti, Filippo Tommaso, 'Fondation et manifeste du Futurisme', *Figaro* (Paris), 20 Feb. 1909.

— *Le Futurisme* (Paris, 1911).

— 'La Doctrine de F. T. Marinetti', *Excelsior* (Paris), 15 Feb. 1912.

Martin, Marianne, *Futurist Art and Theory 1909–1915* (Oxford, 1968).

— 'Futurism, Unanimism and Apollinaire', *Art Journal* (New York), spring 1969, xxviii, 3, 258–68.

Matisse, George, 'La Théorie moléculaire et la science contemporaine', *Mercure de France* (Paris), 1 June 1913.

Matisse, Henri, 'Notes d'un peintre', *La Grande Revue* (Paris), 1908; trans. Alfred H. Barr, Jr., *Matisse; his Art and Public* (New York, 1951).

Mercereau, Alexandre, review of spiritualist publications, *La Revue indépendante* (Paris), Aug. 1911.

Metzinger, Jean 'Note sur la peinture', *Pan* (Paris), Oct.–Nov. 1910, 649–52.

Orphism in nineteenth and twentieth century French literature, special number, *Cahiers de l'Association internationale des études françaises*, 1970.

Pach, Walter, *Queer Thing, Painting* (New York, 1938).

Painters of the Section d'Or: The Alternatives to Cubism, catalogue to an exhibition, written by Richard West, Albright-Knox Art Gallery (Buffalo), 1967.

Picard, Gaston and Tautain, Gustave-Louis, 'Enquête sur M. Henri Bergson et l'influence de sa pensée sur la sensibilité contemporaine', *La Grande Revue* (Paris), 10 Jan., 25 Feb., 10 and 25 Mar., 10 Apr. 1914.

Raymond, Marcel, *De Baudelaire au Surréalisme* (Paris, 1940).

Raynal, Maurice, 'Qu'est-ce que ... le Cubisme?', *Comoedia illustré* (Paris), 20 Dec. 1913; trans. Edward F. Fry, *Cubism* (London, 1966).

— 'Conception et vision', *Gil Blas* (Paris), 29 Aug. 1912, trans. Fry, *Cubism*.

— *Anthologie de la peinture en France de 1906 à nos jours* (Paris, 1927).

Redon, Odilon, *A soi-même: Journal, 1867–1951* (Paris 1961); includes 'Confidences d'artiste' (1909), *La Vie* (Paris), 30 Nov. 1912.

Reverdy, Pierre (ed.), *La Section d'Or* (Paris), 9 Oct. 1912 (one issue only).

Ribemont-Dessaignes, Georges, *Déjà jadis ou du mouvement Dada à l'espace abstrait* (Paris, 1958).

Riffaterre, Hermine B., *L'Orphisme dans la poésie romantique. Thèmes et styles surnaturalistes* (Paris, 1970).

★Ringbom, Sixten, *The Sounding Cosmos. A Study in the Spiritualism of Kandinsky and the Genesis of Abstract Painting* (Abo, 1970).

Robbins, Daniel, 'From Symbolism to Cubism: the Abbaye de Creteil', *Art Journal* (New York), winter 1963–4, xxiii, 111–16.

Romains, Jules *La Vie unanime* (Paris, 3rd edn. 1913).

— *Puissances de Paris* (Paris, 1911).

— *Souvenirs et confidences d'un écrivain* (Paris, 1938).

Rookmaakers, Hendrick, *Synthetist Art Theories* (Amsterdam, 1959).

Rosenblum, Robert, *Cubism and Twentieth Century Art* (New York and London, 1960).

Morgan Russell, catalogue to an exhibition, Dallas Museum for Contemporary Art, May–June 1960.

Saint-Point, Valentine de, review of G. de Pawlowski's *Voyage au pays du 4ème dimension*, *Montjoie!* (Paris), 14 Apr. 1913.

Salmon, André, *La Jeune Peinture française* (Paris, 1912).

— 'L'Orphéisme', *Action* (Paris), Nov. 1921.

— *L'Air de la Butte: Souvenirs sans fin*, Part I (Paris, 1945), Part II (Paris, 1956).

Sandström, Sven, *Le Monde imaginaire d'Odilon Redon* (Lund, 1955).

Schuré, Édouard, *Les Grands Initiés* (Paris, 1889).

La Section d'Or, catalogue to the exhibition, Galerie la Boëtie (Paris), 9 Oct. 1912.

Seuphor, Michel, (Paris, 1950). *A Dictionary of Abstract Painting* (London, 1960).

— 'L'Orphisme', *L'Art d'aujourd'hui* (Paris), Mar. 1950.

— *La Peinture abstraite, sa genèse, son expansion* (Paris, 1964).

— 'Synchromies', *L'Œil* (Paris), Jan. 1957, 56–61.

Severini, Gino, preface to an exhibition of his work at the Sackville Gallery (London), March 1912.

— 'Symbolisme plastique et symbolisme littéraire', *Mercure de France* (Paris), 1 Feb. 1916, 466–76.

— *Tutta la vità di un pittore* (Rome, 1946).

— 'Apollinaire et le futurisme', *XXᵉ siecle* (Paris), June 1952.

Shattuck, Roger, *The Banquet Years: the Arts in France 1885–1918* (New York, 1961).

Signac, Paul, *D'Eugène Delacroix au néo-impressionisme* (1899), ed. Françoise Cachin (Paris, 1964).

Soffici, Ardengo, 'Le Peintre Henri Rousseau', *Mercure de France* (Paris), 16 Oct. 1910, 748–55.

— *Cubismo e futurismo* (Florence, 1914).

Stein, Gertrude, *The Autobiography of Alice B. Toklas* (New York, 1961).

Strawinsky, Igor, 'Ce que j'ai voulu exprimer dans *La Sacré du printemps*' *Montjoie!* (Paris), 16 May 1913.

Survage, Rythmes colorés 1912–13, catalogue to an exhibition, Musée d'Art et d'Industrie (Saint-Étienne), 1973.

Synchromism and Color Principles in American Painting 1910–30, catalogue of an exhibition, written by William C. Agee, Knoedler and Co. Inc. (New York), Oct.–Nov. 1965.

Les Synchromistes: Morgan Russell and Stanton MacDonald-Wright, exhibition catalogue with statements by the artists, Bernheim-jeune Gallery (Paris), 27 Oct.–8 Nov. 1913.

Szathmary, Arthur, *The Aesthetic Theory of Bergson* (Cambridge, Mass., 1937).

Taylor, Joshua C., *Futurism* (New York, 1961).

Uhde, Wilhelm, *Rousseau* (Paris, 1913).

Valensi, Henri, 'La Couleur et les formes', *Montjoie!* (Paris), Nov.-Dec. 1913.

Valéry, Paul, *Introduction à la méthode de Léonard de Vinci*, first published 1894 (Paris, 1957).

— 'Méthodes: le temps', *Mercure de France* (Paris), 1 May 1899, 481–8.

Vallier, Dora, *Abstract Art* (New York, 1970).

— *Jacques Villon: œuvres de 1897 à 1956* (Paris, n.d.).

Vanderpyl, Fritz R. and Cros, Guy-Charles, 'Réflexions sur les dernières tendances picturales', *Mercure de France* (Paris), 1 Dec. 1912, 527–41.

La Vie mystérieuse (Paris), 1911–13 (a spiritualist journal).

Visan, Tancrède de, 'La Philosophie de M. Henri Bergson et l'esthétique contemporaine', *La Vie des lettres* (Paris), Apr. 1913, 124–37.

Vromant, Marc, 'A propos du Salon des Indépendants: Du cubisme et autres synthèses', *Comoedia* (Paris), 15 Apr. 1914.

— 'La Peinture simultaniste: à propos d'une étude de M. Smirnoff', *Comoedia* (Paris), 2 June 1914.

Wright, Willard H., *Modern Painting. Its Tendency and Meaning* (New York and London, 1915).

2 APOLLINAIRE

Works by Apollinaire

(with P.-N. Roinard and V.-E. Michelet), *La Poésie symboliste: Trois entretiens sur les temps héroïques*, lectures at the Salon des Indépendants, 1908 (Paris, 1908).

Le Bestiaire ou Cortège d'Orphée (Paris, 1911).

Les Peintres cubistes: Méditations esthétiques (Paris, 1913); references throughout are to the 1965 edition by L.-C. Breunig and J. Cl. Chevalier which contains much additional material and an analysis of the genesis of the work.

Alcools (Paris, 1913).

L'Esprit nouveau et les poètes (Paris, 1917).

Calligrammes (Paris, 1918).

Il y a (Paris, 1949); includes the articles on art published in the *Soirées de Paris*, 1912–1914.

Anecdotiques (Paris, 1955); material from his column, 'La Vie anecdotique', in the *Mercure de France*, 1911–18.

★*Œuvres poétiques*, ed. Marcel Adema and Michel Décaudin (Paris, 1959).

Chroniques d'art, ed. L.-C. Breunig (Paris, 1960).

'20 lettres de Guillaume Apollinaire à Ardengo Soffici', *Le Flâneur des deux rives* (Paris), Dec. 1954.

Tendre comme le souvenir (Paris, 1952).

Lettre à Roger Allard, *La Nouvelle Revue française*, (Paris), 1 Dec. 1962, 1146–51.

Lettres à Lou, ed. Michel Décaudin (Paris, 1969).

Works on Apollinaire

★Adema, Marcel, *Apollinaire le mal-aimé* (Paris, 1952).

Arboin, Gabriel, 'Devant l'idéogramme d'Apollinaire', *Soirées de Paris* (Paris), July–Aug. 1914.

Billy, André, 'Comment ju suis devenu poète', *Soirées de Paris* (Paris), Oct. 1912.

Blumenkranz-Onimus, Noëmi, 'Apollinaire, critique d'art', *L'Information d'histoire de l'art* (Paris), 1961, no. 4, 103–10.

Breunig, L.-C., 'The Chronology of Apollinaire's *Alcools*', *Publications of the Modern Language Association* (Baltimore), Dec. 1952, 907 ff.

Buffet-Picabia, Gabrielle, 'Apollinaire', *Aires abstraites* (Geneva, 1957).

Cameron, John Wesley, 'Apollinaire and the Painters: his Poetic Orphism', unpublished Ph.D. dissertation, Indiana University, 1956.

Carmody, Francis J., *Cubist Poetry: The School of Apollinaire* (n.p., 1954).

— 'The Evolution of Apollinaire's Poetics, 1901–1914', University of California, *Publications in Modern Philology*, x (Berkeley and Los Angeles), 1963.

— 'L'Esthétique de l'esprit nouveau', *Le Flâneur des deux rives* (Paris), Sept.– Dec. 1955, 11–20.

Champigny, Robert, 'Le Temps chez Apollinaire', *Publication of the Modern Language Association* (Baltimore), Mar. 1949, 3–14.

Davies, Margaret, *Apollinaire* (Edinburgh and London, 1964).

Décaudin, Michel, 'Le "changement de front" d'Apollinaire', *Revue des sciences humaines* (Paris), Nov.–Dec. 1956, 255–60.

— *Le Dossier d' 'Alcools'* (Geneva, 1960).

— 'Entretien avec ... Nicolas Beauduin', *Le Flâneur des deux rives* (Paris), Mar. 1956, 15–16.

Durry, Marie-Jeanne, *Guillaume Apollinaire: 'Alcools'* (Paris, 1956).

Golding, John, 'Guillaume Apollinaire and the Art of the Twentieth Century', *Baltimore Museum of Art News*, xxvi–xxvii, summer–autumn 1963.

Lockerbie, Ian, 'Qu'est-ce que l'Orphisme d'Apollinaire?', *Journées Apollinaire de Stavelot, Actes de colloque* (Stavelot, 1967), 81–7.

Mackworth, Cecily, *Guillaume Apollinaire and the Cubist Life* (London, 1961).

Moulin, Jeanine, *Guillaume Apollinaire: Textes inédites* (Geneva, 1952).

— 'Apollinaire, critique d'art', *Le Flâneur des deux rives* (Paris), June 1954, 12–13.

Picabia, Francis, 'Apollinaire', *L'Esprit nouveau* (Paris), Oct. 1924.

Shattuck, Roger, 'Une Polémique d'Apollinaire', *Le Flâneur des deux rives* (Paris), Dec. 1954, 41–5.

Tournadre, Claude (ed.), *Les Critiques de notre temps et Apollinaire* (Paris, 1971); contains important articles by Philippe Renaud, Henri Meschonnic, Jean-Pierre Richard, and S. I. Lockerbie.

3 FRANK KUPKA

Notes: Unpublished notes for Kupka's book, *Tvoření v umění výtvarném* (Prague, 1923) ('La Création dans les arts plastiques'). Kupka wrote several drafts in French for this book, beginning, apparently, in about 1911–12. I have consulted what is probably one of the earliest drafts, since it consists mainly of disjointed, scribbled notes.

Kupka Album (Prague, n.d., 1907?); collection of reproductions.

Theoretical statements by Kupka:

Letter written in response to an enquiry, 'Les Peintres et la lutte pour le pain', *Opinion* (Paris), 3 May 1913, 568.

'L'Origine du mot tachisme revient à Franck Kupka'; extract from one of Kupka's notebooks of 1913, *Art actuel international* (Paris), 1959, no. 8.

'Créer! Question de principe daus la peinture', *La Vie des lettres et des arts* (Paris), July 1921, 569–75.

'Raisons de l'évasion', preface to his exhibition at the Galerie la Boëtie (Paris), 16 to 31 Oct. 1924.

Quatres histoires de blanc et de noir (Paris), 1926.

Statements in *Abstraction, création, art non-figuratif* (Paris), 1932, i, 32; 1933, ii, 25.

Works on Kupka

Arnould-Grémilly, Louis, 'De l'Orphisme: à propos des tentatives de Kupka', *La Vie des lettres et des arts* (Paris), Oct. 1921, 670–86. Published separately as *Kupka* (Paris, 1922).

Beauduin, Nicolas, 'Les Temps héroïques: à propos du Salon de la Section d'Or', *Masques et visages* (Paris), June 1956.

Cassou, Jean, 'L'Œuvre de Kupka', *Revue des arts* (Paris), 1958, no. 6.

— with Denise Fédit, *Kupka* (Paris, 1964).

Fédit, Denise, 'Formation de l'art de Kupka', *Revue du Louvre* (Paris), 1964, xiv, no. 6, 333–42.

— *L'Œuvre de Kupka*, Inventaire des collections publiques françaises: no. 13, Musée National d'Art Moderne (Paris, 1966).

Habasque, Guy, 'Kupka, trois ans après sa mort, la célébrité', *Connaissance des arts* (Paris), July 1960, 30–7.

Lonngren, Lillian, 'Kupka: Innovator of the Abstract International Style', *Art News* (New York), Nov. 1957, 44–7 and 54–7.

Mercereau, Alexandre, 'Kupka', *Les Hommes du jour* (Paris), Nov. 1920.

*Mladek. M. and Rowell, M., *František Kupka. A Retrospective*, catalogue to an exhibition. The Solomon R. Guggenheim Museum (New York, 1975). This important book was published too late for me to make use of it.

Plée, Leon, 'Frank Kupka, idées, lumières', *Les Annales poétiques et littéraires* (Paris), 16 Nov. 1924.

Turpin, Georges, 'Kupka' in René Edouard-Joseph, *Dictionnaire biographique des artistes contemporains* (Paris, 1931), ii, 284–8 (drafted by Kupka).

*Vachtovà, Ludmilla, *Frank Kupka* (London, 1968).

Warshawsky, W., '"Orpheism", Latest of Painting Cults', *New York Times*, 19 Oct. 1913.

4 ROBERT DELAUNAY AND SONIA DELAUNAY-TERK

Apollinaire, Guillaume, 'Les Réformateurs du costume', *Mercure de France* (Paris), 1 Jan. 1914; reprinted, *Anecdotiques*, 137–8.

Hoog, Michel, *Robert and Sonia Delaunay*, Inventaire des collections publiques françaises: no. 15, Musée National d'Art Moderne (Paris, 1967).

Vromant, Marc, 'La Peinture simultaniste: à propos d'une étude de M. Smirnoff', *Comoedia* (Paris), 2 June 1914.

A ROBERT DELAUNAY

Texts published in the period up to 1914

'Réalité, peinture pure', *Soirées de Paris* (Paris), Dec. 1912 (ed. Apollinaire).

'La Lumière', trans. as 'Ueber das Licht', by Paul Klee for *Der Sturm* (Berlin), Jan. 1913, nos. 144–5 (both texts included in Robert Delaunay, *Du Cubisme a l'art abstrait*; see below).

Letter to *Gil Blas* (Paris), 25 Oct. 1912.

Letter to Herwarth Walden, 17 Dec. 1913, *Der Sturm* (Berlin), Jan. 1914, nos. 194–195.

Letter to *L'Intransigeant* (Paris), 10 Mar. 1914.

Robert Delaunay, *Album* (Paris, n.d., but contains 1913 dates; produced in connection with his one-man exhibition at Der Sturm, 27 Jan.–20 Feb. 1913). Apollinaire's 'Les Fenêtres' was used as preface.

Other published writings:

'Henri Rousseau, le douanier', *L'Amour de l'art* (Paris), Nov. 1920, 228–30.

'Réponse à une enquête: Chez les Cubistes', *Bulletin de la vie artistique* (Paris), Nov. 1924.

'Propos d'artistes: Robert Delaunay' (interview with Florent Fels), *Les Nouvelles littéraires* (Paris), Oct. 25, 1924.

'Le Peintre Robert Delaunay parle' (ed. Yvan Goll), *Surréalisme* (Paris), Oct. 1924.

'Témoignages pour ou contre l'art abstrait', *Cahiers des amis de l'art* (Paris), 1947, no. 11.

'Eléments pour l'histoire du cubisme' (letter to André Rouveyre), *Arts-documents* (Geneva), Jan. 1951.

'Un Texte inédite de Robert Delaunay', *Aujourd'hui* (Paris), Jan. 1957.

*Delaunay, Robert, *Du Cubisme à l'art abstrait* (Paris, 1957). A collection of Delaunay's writings on art, introduced and edited by Pierre Francastel. This essential reference also contains a catalogue of works and list of exhibitions by Guy Habasque.

Works on Delaunay

Busse, Erwin von, 'Die Kompositionsmittel bei Robert Delaunay', *Der Blaue Reiter* (Munich, 1912).

Cendrars, Blaise, 'Delaunay: le contraste simultané', *La Rose rouge* (Paris), 24 July 1919; reprinted in *Œuvres complètes* (Lausanne 1960), iv.

— 'La Tour Eiffel' (extract from a lecture of 1924), reprinted in *Œuvres complètes* (Lausanne 1960), iv.

Delteil, Joseph, 'Robert Delaunay, peintre de jour', *Les Arts plastiques* (Paris), 1 Mar. 1925.

Hoog, Michel, '*La Ville de Paris* de Robert Delaunay: Sources et développement',

Revue de Louvre (Paris), 1965, no. 1, 29–38.

Imdahl, Max, see Vriesen, Gustav, *Delaunay*.

Langner, Johannes, 'Zu den Fensterbildern von Robert Delaunay', *Jahrbuch der Hamburger Kunstsammlungen* (Hamburg), 1962, vii.

la Tourette, Gilles de, *Robert Delaunay* (Paris, 1950).

Princet, Maurice, preface to the catalogue of the exhibition of Delaunay's work, Galerie Barbazanges, 28 Feb.–13 Mar. 1912.

Rappaport, Ruthann, 'Robert Delaunay and Cubism, 1909–1913', unpublished M.A. dissertation, Institute of Fine Arts, New York University, 1963.

Robbins, Daniel, 'From Cubism to Abstract Art: The Evolution of the Work of Gleizes and Delaunay', *Baltimore Museum of Art News*, 1962, xxv, no. 3, 9–20.

Soupault, Philippe, 'Robert Delaunay, peintre', *Les Feuilles libres* (Paris), Sept.–Oct. 1923, 167–75.

★Vriesen, Gustav and Imdahl, Max, *Robert Delaunay: Light and Color* (New York, 1969).

Waldemar, Georges, 'Robert Delaunay et le triomphe de la couleur', *La Vie des lettres et des arts* (Paris), 1921, no. 11.

B SONIA DELAUNAY-TERK

Delaunay, Sonia (with Blaise Cendrars), 'Le Premier livre simultané', letter to the press, *Paris-Midi* (Paris), 11 Oct. 1913 (see *Du Cubisme à L'art abstrait*, 113–14).

Delaunay, Robert, 'Sonia Delaunay-Terk', *Du Cubisme à l'art abstrait*, 200–3.

— 'Les Tissues *simultanés* de Sonia Delaunay', *Du Cubisme à l'art abstrait*, 204–9.

Bordier, Robert, 'L'Art et la matière: une enquête sur la technique: Sonia Delaunay ou de la couleur avant toute chose', *Art d'aujourd'hui* (Paris), Sept. 1954.

Clay, Jean, 'The Golden Years of Visual Jazz: Sonia Delaunay's Life and Times', *Réalités* (Paris), Apr. 1968, 42–7.

Damase, Jacques, *Sonia Delaunay. Rhythms and Colours* (London, 1972).

Lhote, André, *Sonia Delaunay, ses peintures, ses objets, ses tissus simultanés, ses modes* (Paris, 1925).

Weelen, G., 'Robes simultanées', *L'Œil* (Paris), Dec. 1959, 78–85.

5 FERNAND LÉGER

Statements by Léger

Léger, Fernand, 'Les Origines de la peinture et de sa valeur représentative', *Montjoie!* (Paris), 29 May and 14–29 June 1913; reprinted in *Fonctions de la peinture* (see below).

— 'Les Réalisations picturales actuelles', *Soirées de Paris* (Paris), June 1914; reprinted in *Fonctions de la peinture*.

— *Entretien de Fernand Léger avec Blaise Cendrars et Louis Carré sur le paysage dans l'œuvre de Léger* (Paris, 1956).

— *Textes choisis* (Paris, 1959).

— ★*Fonctions de la peinture* (Paris, 1965); a collection of Léger's essays from 1913 to 1960 (trans. London, 1973).

Works on Léger

Cassou, Jean and Leymarie, Jean, *Fernand Léger. Drawings and Gouaches* (London, 1973).

Cooper, Douglas, preface to *Fernand Léger: Contrastes de formes, 1912–1915* (Collection Berggruen, no. 37; Paris, 1962).

★——*Fernand Léger et le nouvel espace* (Geneva, 1949).

Delevoy, D. L., *Léger* (Geneva, 1962).

Descargues, Pierre, *Fernand Léger* (Paris, 1955).

Garaudy, Roger, *Pour un réalisme du XXe siècle: Dialogue posthume avec Fernand Léger* (Paris, 1968).

★Green, Christopher, *Léger and the Avant-Garde* (Yale University Press, 1976).

Kahnweiler, Daniel-Henry, 'Fernand Léger', *Burlington Magazine* (London), Mar. 1950, 63–9.

Kuh, Katherine, *Léger* (University of Illinois Press, Urbana, 1953).

Fernand Léger, catalogue to a retrospective exhibition, Musée des Arts Décoratifs (Paris, 1956).

Fernand Léger, catalogue to a retrospective exhibition, Grand Palais (Paris, 1971).

le Noci, Guido (ed.), *Fernand Léger, sa vie, son œuvre, son rêve* (Milan, 1971).

Raynal, Maurice, 'Fernand Léger', *L'Esprit nouveau* (Paris) 1920, no. 4, 427–34.

Vallier, Dora, 'La Vie fait l'œuvre de Fernand Léger: propos de l'artiste recueillis par Dora Vallier', *Cahiers d'Art* (Paris) 1954, ii, 133–60.

Verdet, André, *Fernand Léger: Le Dynamisme pictural* (Geneva, 1955).

6 FRANCIS PICABIA

Statements by Picabia

Picabia, Francis, preface to his exhibition, *Studies of New York*, Photo-Secession Gallery [291], New York, Mar. 1913, trans. Frank Haviland and published in *Camera Work* (New York), Apr.–July 1913.

—— 'How New York Looks to Me', *New York American*, 30 Mar. 1913, magazine section, 11.

—— Interview in *Le Matin* (Paris), 1 Dec. 1913.

—— Statement in *Vanity Fair* (New York), Nov. 1915, 42.

—— Statement in *291* (New York), Feb. 1916.

—— Preface to his exhibition, *Trente ans de peinture*. Galerie Léonce Rosenberg (Paris), Dec. 1930.

—— 'Monstres délicieux', *Orbes* (Paris), 1932, no. 3, 129–32.

Works on Picabia

Aisen, Maurice, 'The Latest Evolution in Art and Francis Picabia', *Camera Work* (New York), June 1913.

André, Édouard, 'Francis Picabia. Exposition des tableaux et dessins', *L'Art décoratif* (Paris), Feb. 1907; reprinted as: *Francis Picabia: Le Peintre et l'aquafortiste* (Paris, 1908).

Arp, Jean, 'Francis Picabia'. *Art d'aujourd'hui* (Paris), Jan. 1950.

Buffet-Picabia, Gabrielle, 'Modern Art and the Public', *Camera Work* (New York), June 1913, 10–14.

—— 'Some Memories of Pre-Dada: Picabia and Duchamp', *The Dada Painters and Poets* (New York, 1951).

—— 'Picabia, l'inventeur', *L'Œil* (Paris), June 1956, 31–5, 47.

—— *Aires abstraites* (Geneva, 1957); a collection of earlier essays.

★Camfield, William Arnett, 'Francis Picabia (1879–1953); A Study of his Career from 1895 to 1918', Ph.D. dissertation, Graduate School, Yale University 1964; to be published by Princeton University Press.

★— *Francis Picabia*, catalogue to a retrospective exhibition, The Solomon R. Guggenheim Museum (New York), 1970.

— 'The Machinist Style of Francis Picabia', *Art Bulletin* (New York), Sept.– Dec. 1966, 309–22.

Duchamp, Marcel, 'Picabia', *Collection of the Société anonyme*, ed. George Heard Hamilton, Yale University Art Gallery, 1950.

du Mas, Vivian, 'L'Occultisme dans l'art de Francis Picabia', *Orbes* (Paris), 1932, no. 3, 113–28.

Everling, Germaine, *L'Anneau de Saturne* (Paris, 1970).

Hapgood, Hutchins, 'A Paris Painter', *Globe and Commercial Advertiser* (New York), 20 Feb. 1913, 8; reprinted in *Camera Work* (New York), Apr.–July 1913.

— *New York Times*, 16 Feb. 1913, 'Francis Picabia' (an article on Picabia's recent painting).

— *New York Tribune*, 9 Mar. 1913, part ii, 1; 'A Post-Cubist's Impressions of New York.

★le Bot, Marc, *Francis Picabia et la crise des valeurs figuratives* (Paris, 1968).

la Hire, Marie de, *Francis Picabia* (Paris, 1920).

Pearlstein, Philip, 'The Paintings of Francis Picabia', unpublished M.A. thesis, Institute of Fine Arts, New York University, 1955.

— 'The Symbolic Language of Francis Picabia', *Arts* (New York), Jan. 1958, 37– 43.

Roger-Milès, Louis, preface to the catalogue of Picabia's exhibition, Galerie Haussmann (Paris), Feb. 1905.

— preface to the catalogue of Picabia's exhibition, Galerie Haussman (Paris), Feb. 1907.

— preface to the catalogue of Picabia's exhibition, Galerie Georges Petit (Paris), Mar. 1909.

Sanouillet, Michel, *Picabia* (Paris, 1964).

Swift, Samuel, critique of Picabia's exhibition at the Photo-Secession Gallery [291], *New York Sun*, Mar.; reprinted *Camera Work*, Apr.–July 1913, 46–7.

7 MARCEL DUCHAMP

Statements by Duchamp

Marchand du sel, ed. Michel Sanouillet (Paris, 1958); a collection of texts by Duchamp including notes for the *Green Box* and interviews with J. J. Sweeney (1946 and 1955).

The Bride Stripped Bare by her Bachelors, Even: Towards a Typographical Rendering of the Green Box, ed. Richard Hamilton, trans. George H. Hamilton (London, n.d.).

Cabanne, Pierre, *Dialogues with Marcel Duchamp* (London, 1971).

Kuh, Katherine, *The Artist's Voice* (New York, 1962).

Works on Duchamp

Carrouges, Michel, *Les Machines célibataires* (Paris, 1954).

Golding, John, *Marcel Duchamp, The Bride Stripped Bare by her Bachelors, Even* (London, 1973).

★Hamilton, Richard, preface to the catalogue of the exhibition, *The Almost Complete Works of Marcel Duchamp*, Tate Gallery (London), June–July 1966.

★Harnoncourt, Anne and McShine, Kynaston (eds.), *Marcel Duchamp* (New York, 1973), issued in connection with a retrospective exhibition of Duchamp's works at the Philadelphia Museum of Art and the Museum of Modern Art, New York.

★Lebel, Robert, *Sur Marcel Duchamp* (Paris, 1959).

Paz, Octavio, *Marcel Duchamp or the Castle of Purity* (London and New York, 1970).

★Schwarz, Arturo, *The Complete Works of Marcel Duchamp* (London, 1969).

Tomkins, Calvin, *The Bride and the Bachelors* (New York, 1965).

Index